SOCIAL SECURITY MANUAL

2001

EDITED BY:

Joseph F. Stenken, J.D., CLU, ChFC

Assistant Editor

The National Underwriter Company

D1484175

The
NATIONAL
UNDERWRITER
Company

The National Underwriter Company · P.O. Box 14367 · Cincinnati, Ohio 45250-0367

ISBN 0-87218-276-2

Copyright © 2001

The National Underwriter Company
P.O. Box 14367, Cincinnati, Ohio 45250-0367

Printed in U.S.A.

The National Underwriter Company publishes the following Social Security/Medicare publications:

Social Security Manual
All About Medicare
Social Security Slide-O-Scope and Planner
Medicare Slide-O-Scope

TABLE OF CONTENTS

Q

iv

GENERAL INFORMATION

A-1. What is the Social Security Act?

The Social Security Act has established numerous programs which provide for the material needs of individuals and families, protect aged and disabled persons against the expenses of illnesses that could otherwise exhaust their savings, keep families together, and give children the opportunity to grow up in health and security.

Congress passed the Social Security Act in 1935 and the retirement benefits program went into effect on January 1, 1937. The law has been amended many times since its original enactment.

A-2. What programs are covered by the Social Security Act?

The following programs are covered by the Social Security Act:

- Social Security (retirement, survivors and disability insurance).

- Medicare (hospital and medical insurance for the aged, the disabled, and those with end-stage renal disease).

- Unemployment insurance.

- Black lung benefits.

- Supplemental Security Income (SSI).

- Public assistance and welfare services, including aid to needy families with children, medical assistance, maternal and child health services, child support enforcement, family and child welfare services, food stamps and energy assistance.

The *Social Security Manual* provides the reader with a description of Social Security, Medicare (Section I), benefits for federal government employees (Section L), benefits for servicemembers and veterans (Section M), and benefits for workers covered under the Railroad Retirement System (Section N).

Social Security is administered by the Social Security Administration and provides old age, survivors and disability benefits. Medicare provides hospi-

1

tal and medical insurance for the aged and disabled and is administered by the Health Care Financing Administration.

The original Social Security Act provided only retirement benefits for wage and salary earners. In 1939, benefits were added for family members after the worker's death or retirement. Most amendments have expanded the scope of the Social Security program — by extending coverage to more groups of persons, by increasing benefits, by creating new benefits (such as disability), by liberalizing requirements for benefits, or by increasing the wage base for taxes and benefits.

A-3. In general, who can receive Social Security benefits?

- A disabled insured worker under age 65.

- A retired insured worker at age 62 or over.

- The spouse of a retired or disabled worker entitled to benefits who: (1) is age 62 or over, or (2) has in care a child under age 16 or over age 16 and disabled, who is entitled to benefits on the worker's Social Security record.

- The divorced spouse of a retired or disabled worker entitled to benefits if age 62 or over and married to the worker for at least 10 years.

- The divorced spouse of a fully insured worker who has not yet filed a claim for benefits if both are age 62 or over, were married for at least 10 years, and have been finally divorced for at least two continuous years.

- The dependent, unmarried child of a retired or disabled worker entitled to benefits, or of a deceased insured worker if the child is: (1) under age 18, or (2) under age 19 and a full-time elementary or secondary school student, or (3) age 18 or over but under a disability which began before age 22.

- The surviving spouse (including a surviving divorced spouse) of a deceased insured worker if the widow(er) is age 60 or over.

- The disabled surviving spouse (including a surviving divorced spouse in some cases) of a deceased insured worker if the widow(er) is age 50-59 and becomes disabled within a specified period.

- The surviving spouse (including a surviving divorced spouse) of a deceased insured worker, regardless of age, if caring for an entitled child of the deceased who is either under age 16 or disabled before age 22.

2

- The dependent parents of a deceased insured worker at age 62 or over.

In addition to monthly survivor benefits, a lump-sum death payment is payable upon the death of an insured worker. For explanation of these benefits and eligibility requirements, see BENEFITS, SECTION E.

A-4. In general, what benefits are provided under the Hospital Insurance (Part A) Program for the aged and disabled?

The program provides the following benefits for persons age 65 or older and persons receiving Social Security disability benefits for 24 months or more:

- The cost of inpatient hospital services for up to 90 days in each benefit period (in 2001, the patient pays a deductible amount of $792 for the first 60 days plus $198 a day for each day in excess of 60). There are also 60 non-renewable lifetime reserve days with coinsurance of $396 a day.

- The cost of posthospital skilled nursing facility care for up to 100 days in each benefit period (the patient pays $99 a day in 2001 after the first 20 days).

- The cost of 100 post-hospital home health service visits made under a plan of treatment established by a physician, except that there is 20% cost-sharing payable by the patient for durable medical equipment (other than the purchase of certain used items).

- Hospice care for terminally ill patients.

For detailed explanation of these benefits, see MEDICARE, SECTION I.

A-5. In general, what benefits are provided under the Medical Insurance (Part B) program?

Medical Insurance is offered to almost all persons age 65 and over on a voluntary basis. In addition, the program is offered to all disabled Social Security and railroad retirement beneficiaries who have received disability benefits for at least 24 months. A person enrolled in the Medical Insurance program is required to pay a monthly premium of $50 per month (in 2001). There is also an annual deductible of $100. Medical Insurance pays 80% of the approved charges above the deductible. In general, covered services include medical services and certain outpatient hospital services. Medical services include doctors' services, inpatient and outpatient medical and surgical services and supplies, physical and speech therapy, diagnostic tests, durable medical equipment and other services. Dentists are considered doctors for certain dental surgeon functions.

For detailed explanation of Medical Insurance (Part B) benefits under Medicare, see MEDICARE, SECTION I.

A-6. How are the health insurance programs and the Old-Age Survivors and Disability Insurance (OASDI) program financed?

Retirement, survivors, and disability benefits and Hospital Insurance (Medicare Part A) are financed by taxes collected from employers, employees, and self-employed persons. (See SOCIAL SECURITY TAXES, SECTION J.)

Hospital Insurance (Part A) benefits for persons not on the Social Security or railroad retirement rolls are paid from premiums or, in the case of certain persons who were age 65 before 1975, from general revenues. (The Hospital Insurance premium rate is intended to meet all of the cost for persons who are covered only due to premium payment.)

The Hospital Insurance premium is reduced for certain individuals age 65 or over who are not automatically entitled to Hospital Insurance benefits. The Hospital Insurance premium is $300 a month in 2001. This premium is reduced, on a phased-in basis, for individuals and their spouses with credits for 30 or more quarters paid into the Social Security system to $165 a month. The reduction in premium payments will also apply to the surviving spouse or divorced spouse of an individual who had at least 30 quarters of coverage under Social Security.

Effective January 1, 1983, federal employees not fully covered by Social Security began contributing to the Hospital Insurance program only. Effective April 1, 1986, all newly hired state and local government employees not fully covered by Social Security began contributing to the Hospital Insurance program only.

To finance the voluntary Medical Insurance (Part B) program under Medicare, each person enrolled in the program pays a premium so that all Medical Insurance enrollees pay for about 25 percent of the program's cost. For 2001 the Medical Insurance premium is $50 per month. (See MEDICARE, SECTION K.)

A-7. What federal agency administers the OASDI program?

The Social Security Administration. The central office is located in Baltimore, Maryland. The administrative offices and the computer operations are housed at this location.

The Social Security Administration is an independent agency in the executive branch of the federal government. It is required to administer the retirement, survivors, and disability program under the Social Security and the

Supplemental Security Income (SSI) programs. The commissioner of the Social Security Administration is appointed by the President and approved by the Senate and serves a term of six years.

The local Social Security office is the place where a person can apply for a Social Security number, check on an earnings record, apply for Social Security benefits, black lung benefits, SSI, and Hospital Insurance (Medicare Part A) protection, enroll for Medical Insurance (Medicare Part B), receive assistance in applying for food stamps, and get full information about individual and family rights and obligations under the law. Also, a person can call the Social Security Administration's toll-free telephone number, 1-800-772-1213, to receive these services. This toll-free telephone number is available from 7 a.m. to 7 p.m. any business day.

Regular visits to outlying areas are made by the Social Security office staff to serve people who live at a distance from the city or town in which the office is located. The visits are made to locations called contact stations. A schedule of these visits may be obtained from the nearest Social Security office.

Social Security Administration regional offices are located in Atlanta, Boston, Chicago, Dallas, Denver, Kansas City, New York, Philadelphia, San Francisco, and Seattle. Approximately 1,300 Social Security offices throughout the United States, Puerto Rico, the Virgin Islands, Guam, and American Samoa deal directly with the public. Each region also has a number of teleservice centers located primarily in metropolitan areas. These offices handle telephone inquiries and refer callers appropriately.

Program service centers are located in Birmingham (Alabama), Chicago, Kansas City, New York, Philadelphia, and Richmond (California). These offices along with the Office of International Operations and the Office of Disability Operations in Baltimore house and service the records of individuals who are receiving Social Security benefits.

The Office of Hearings and Appeals administers the nationwide hearings and appeals program for the Social Security Administration. Administrative law judges, located in or traveling to major cities throughout the United States, hold hearings and issue decisions when a claimant or organization has appealed a determination affecting rights to benefits or participation in programs under the Social Security Act. The Appeals Council, located in Falls Church, Virginia, may review hearing decisions. (See FILING FOR BENEFITS, SECTION K.)

The Office of Central Records Operations maintains records of individuals' earnings and prepares benefit computations.

A-8. What federal agency administers Medicare programs for the aged and disabled?

The Health Care Financing Administration, whose central office is in Baltimore, Maryland, directs the Medicare and Medicaid programs. The Social Security Administration processes Medicare applications and claims, but it does not set Medicare policy. The Health Care Financing Administration sets the standards which hospitals, skilled nursing facilities, home health agencies, hospices, and other providers and suppliers of services must meet in order to receive payment for Medicare-covered services and items. The Health Care Financing Administration also sets the standards to be used by Utilization and Quality Peer Review Organizations, fiscal intermediaries, and carriers in making payment and coverage decisions for individuals covered by Medicare.

A-9. How and where are Social Security records maintained?

Every individual who is covered by Social Security (see COVERAGE, SECTION B) needs a Social Security number. The Office of Central Records Operations of the Social Security Administration in Baltimore, Maryland, maintains an earnings record for each individual who has a Social Security number.

The Social Security Administration receives reports of earnings of employees from employers and self-employed persons from the Internal Revenue Service. These amounts are then recorded in each person's earnings record and are identified by the individual's Social Security number.

The Internal Revenue Code requires an employer to file employment tax returns with the Internal Revenue Service each year. To help account for these returns and reports, the Internal Revenue Service assigns an employer identification number (EIN) to every employer.

If an employer reports an employee's wages to the Social Security Administration without the employee's Social Security number or with a different employee name or Social Security number than shown in the Social Security Administration's records, the Social Security Administration will write to the employee at the address shown on the wage report and request the missing or corrected information. If the wage report does not show the employee's address or shows an incomplete address, the Social Security Administration will write to the employer and request the missing or corrected employee information. The Social Security Administration notifies the Internal Revenue Service of all wage reports filed without employee Social Security numbers so that the Internal Revenue Service can decide whether to assess penalties for erroneous filing.

If an individual reports self-employment income to the Internal Revenue Service without a Social Security number or with a different name or Social Security number than shown in the Social Security Administration's records, the Social Security Administration will write to the individual and request the missing or corrected information. If the employer, employee, or self-employed individual does not provide the missing or corrected report information in response to the Social Security Administration's request, the wages or self-employment income cannot be identified and credited to the proper individual's earnings records. In such cases, the information is maintained in a Suspense File of uncredited earnings. Subsequently, if identifying information is provided to the Social Security Administration for an individual whose report is recorded in the Suspense File, the wages or self-employment income then may be credited to the individual's earnings record.

A-10. How does a person obtain a Social Security number?

By filling out Form SS-5 (Application for a Social Security Card) and submitting evidence of age, identity, and citizenship or alien status.

Parents applying for a Social Security number for their children under age seven will need to furnish only a birth record if no other record of age or identity has been established for the child.

Applicants 18 and older must apply in person at a Social Security office.

A Social Security number is needed not only for Social Security purposes, but also for income tax purposes. The Internal Revenue Service uses this number as a taxpayer identification number for processing tax returns and controlling the interest and dividend reports of banks and other financial institutions. Failure to put a valid Social Security number on a tax return may mean a delay or reduction in any refund claimed.

A Social Security number is also needed by persons age one or older who are claimed as dependents on someone's federal income tax return. All income tax returns claiming dependents (whether taxpayer's children or others) one year old or older must show the dependent's Social Security number. Failure to include a dependent's Social Security number on a tax return could result in the Internal Revenue Service disallowing related items such as the personal exemption, child tax credit, child care credit, or earned income credit.

A person must have a Social Security number in order to receive Social Security benefits. Those lacking a Social Security number are required to apply for one. Beneficiaries on the Social Security rolls prior to May 10, 1989 are not required to have a Social Security number.

If the Social Security card is lost, a person can apply for a duplicate card by filling out another Form SS-5 and showing a driver's license, voter registration card, school identification card, or other official proof of identity. The new card will have the same number as the one that was lost.

If a person wishes to correct or update the identifying information that was given on the original application for a number, a new Form SSA-5 (Request for Change in Social Security Records) must be submitted. A change in name (for example, upon marriage) should always be reported.

Foreign-born applicants of any age must submit evidence of United States citizenship or alien status.

Form SS-5 can be obtained from any local Social Security office.

A-11. What are the penalties for violation of the penal provisions of the Social Security Act?

The penalty upon conviction for violation of the penal provisions of the Social Security Act, or one of the related provisions of the Federal Criminal Code, may be a fine, or imprisonment, or both. Depending upon the provision of the law that is violated, the penalty ranges from a fine of not more than $500 or imprisonment of one year, or both, to a fine of not more than $10,000 or imprisonment of not more than 15 years, or both.

Criminal prosecutions for fraud may be instituted where a person knowingly:

- Furnishes false information as to someone's identity in connection with the establishment and maintenance of Social Security records.

- For the purpose of increasing a payment under Social Security or for the purpose of obtaining such payment: (1) uses a Social Security number obtained on the basis of false information, or (2) falsely represents a number to be his.

- Makes, or causes to be made, a false statement or misrepresentation of a material fact for use in determining eligibility rights to Social Security benefits.

- Makes, or causes to be made, any false statement or representation as to: (1) whether wages were paid, the period during which paid, the person to whom paid, or the amount of such wages, or (2) whether net earnings from self-employment were derived, the amount of such earnings, the period during which, or person by whom, derived.

- Conceals or fails to report any event affecting the initial or continued right to payment received or to be received by the individually personally or on behalf of another.

- Converts all or any part of a payment received on behalf of another to a use other than for the use and benefit of that person.

There are also civil monetary penalties for fraudulent claims. Any person or organization who makes, or causes to be made, a false or misleading statement for use in determining an initial or continuing right to a Social Security benefit is subject to a civil penalty of not more than $5,000 for each false statement or representation. Such person is also subject to an assessment of not more than twice the amount of benefits or payments paid by the Social Security Administration as a result of the statement or representation.

The civil monetary penalty and assessment may be imposed against any person who: (1) has made, or caused to be made, a statement or representation of material fact for use in determining any initial or continuing right to monthly benefits, and (2) knew, or should have known, that the statement or representation was false or misleading, omitted a material fact, or was made with knowing disregard for the truth. A material fact is defined as a fact which the Social Security Administration may consider in evaluating whether an applicant is entitled to Social Security benefits.

A person subject to the civil monetary penalty and assessment must be provided with written notice of the proposed penalty and assessment, and must be given the opportunity to request a hearing before an administrative law judge on the proposed penalty and assessment within 60 days.

Social security cards issued after October 31, 1983 are counterfeit-resistant and tamper-resistant.

A-12. How can a person check on his Social Security earnings record and receive an estimate of future Social Security benefits?

By filling out Form SSA-7004-SM (Request for Earnings and Benefit Estimate Statement). The form is available at any Social Security office or by calling the Social Security Administration's toll-free number, 1-800-772-1213. A statement of total wages and self-employment income credited to the earnings record and an estimate of current Social Security disability and survivor benefits and future Social Security retirement benefits will be mailed to the individual.

Also, persons with Internet access can request and receive an estimate of their future Social Security benefits. This version of the online benefit information request will include a benefit estimate and general information on eligibility. Other information, such as earnings and payroll tax information, normally included in the Request for Earnings and Benefit Estimate Statement, will be mailed to the Internet user upon request but will not be a part of the online statement. Delivery of information will be available only to those who have a registered electronic mail account, such as one with an employer or Internet service provider. Users will be required to provide five authenticating elements: name as it appears on their Social Security card, Social Security number, date of birth, state of birth, and mother's maiden name.

If all earnings have not been credited, the individual should contact a Social Security office and ask how to go about correcting the records. The time limit for correcting an earnings record is set by law. An earnings record can be corrected at any time up to 3 years, 3 months, and 15 days after the year in which the wages were paid or the self-employment income was derived. "Year" means calendar year for wages and taxable year for self-employment income. An individual's earnings record can be corrected after this time limit for a number of reasons, including to correct an entry established through fraud; to correct a mechanical, clerical, or other obvious error; or to correct errors in crediting earnings to the wrong person or to the wrong period.

The Social Security Administration must provide individuals, age 25 or older, who have a Social Security number and have wages or net self-employment income, with a Social Security account statement upon the request of the individual. These statements must show: (1) the individual's earnings, (2) an estimate of the individual's contributions to the Social Security program (including a separate estimate for Medicare Part A Hospital Insurance), and (3) an estimate of the individual's current disability and survivor benefits and also future benefits at retirement (including spouse and other family member benefits) and a description of Medicare benefits.

Earnings and benefit estimates statements are automatically mailed on an annual basis to all persons age 25 or over who are not yet receiving benefits.

This earnings and benefit estimates statements contain the following information:

(1) The individual's Social Security taxed earnings as shown by Social Security Administration records as of the date selected to receive a statement.

(2) An estimate of the Social Security and Medicare Part A Hospital Insurance taxes paid on the individual's earnings.

(3) The number of credits (i.e., quarters of coverage, not exceeding 40) that the individual has for both Social Security and Medicare Hospital Insurance purposes, and the number the individual needs to be eligible

for Social Security benefits and also for Medicare Hospital Insurance coverage.

(4) A statement as to whether the individual meets the credit (quarters of coverage) requirements for each type of Social Security benefit, and also whether the individual is eligible for Medicare Hospital Insurance coverage.

(5) Estimates of the monthly retirement, disability, dependents' and survivors' insurance benefits potentially payable on the individual's record if he meets the credits (quarters of coverage) requirements. If the individual is age 50 or older, the estimates will include the retirement insurance benefits he could receive at age 62 (or his current age if he is already over age 62), at full retirement age (currently age 65 to 67, depending on year of birth) or at the individual's current age if he is already over full retirement age, and at age 70. If the individual is under age 50, instead of estimates, the Social Security Administration may provide a general description of the benefits that are available upon retirement.

(6) A description of the coverage provided under the Medicare program.

(7) A reminder of the right to request a correction in an earnings record.

(8) A remark that an annually updated statement is available upon request.

A-13. What events must a beneficiary report to the Social Security Administration?

The following events, which affect the payment of benefits, should be reported immediately:

- A beneficiary (other than a disabled individual) is working and has, or expects to have, earnings in excess of the amount exempted under the earnings test explained in SECTION H.

- The marriage of a person who is entitled to child's, widow(er)'s, mother's, father's, parent's or divorced spouse's benefits.

- A beneficiary under age 62 entitled to spouse's, mother's or father's benefits no longer has in care a child entitled to benefits who is under age 16 or disabled.

- A person entitled to benefits because of disability has returned to work, or the condition has improved so that the person is able to work.

- The death of a beneficiary.

- A child beneficiary age 18 and not disabled is no longer attending elementary or secondary school full time.

- A beneficiary works outside the United States for more than 45 hours in a calendar month.

- A person under age 65 who is entitled because of disability becomes entitled to workers' compensation benefits or there is a change in the public disability payment rate.

- Imprisonment for a conviction of a criminal offense that carries a sentence for more than one year. In addition, individuals confined by court order to an institution at public expense in connection with a verdict or finding of guilty by reason of insanity or a similar verdict.

- A person begins to receive a governmental pension or annuity or there is a change in a present pension amount and the person receives a spouse's Social Security benefit.

The Social Security office should be notified of any event affecting the beneficiary's eligibility for payment. The office will make the change in the record or will forward the information to the program service center. The notice must show the beneficiary's Social Security claim number. The claim number is the nine-digit Social Security number followed by one or more letters such as A, B, C, HA, etc. The Social Security office or program service center will adjust benefit payments, as is necessitated by information coming to its attention, and will notify the beneficiary of the action.

A-14. Where does a person apply for Social Security benefits?

A person can apply for Social Security benefits via the mail, telephone or by visiting one of 1,300 field offices.

A Social Security Ruling (SSR 96-10p) issued in 1996 initiates the Social Security Administration's policy for allowing customers to communicate with the Social Security Administration electronically through access methods such as the Internet, video conferencing, and dial-up phone systems. The Social Security Administration will be able to use these access methods to accept reports, requests, applications, and other information.

A-15. Which government agency issues a beneficiary's Social Security check?

Social Security benefit checks are issued and mailed by the Treasury Department—not by program service centers. However, questions about checks or direct deposits should be directed to a Social Security office.

A-16. When does a Social Security beneficiary receive a monthly benefit check?

Social Security checks are usually dated and delivered on the third day of the month following the month for which the payment is due. For example, checks for January are delivered on February 3rd. Checks usually arrive about the same day each month.

If the third day of the month falls on a weekend or federal holiday, checks are dated and delivered on the first day preceding the third of the month which is not a Saturday, Sunday or federal holiday. For example, if the third is a Saturday or Sunday, checks are delivered on the preceding Friday.

Persons who begin receiving Social Security benefits after May 1, 1997, will be paid on a different monthly schedule than that described above. The payment day will be selected based on the day of the month on which the insured individual was born. Insured individuals born on the 1st through the 10th of the month will be paid on the second Wednesday of each month. Insured individuals born on the 11th through the 20th of the month will be paid on the third Wednesday of each month. Insured individuals born after the 20th of the month will be paid on the fourth Wednesday of each month. New beneficiaries living in foreign countries will have checks delivered on the third day of the month.

If a check mailed to a United States address is not received within three days after it is usually received or if the check has been stolen, lost, destroyed, or forged, the Social Security office should be notified promptly. The following information should be provided to the Social Security office: (1) the Social Security claim number on which the benefit is being paid, (2) the period of payment covered by the missing check, and (3) the name and address which should be shown on the check.

A change of address should be reported promptly to the Social Security office by telephone or in writing signed by the payee to avoid having the check mailed to the old address. The Social Security claim number and the person's old address should also be given.

A-17. To whom is a benefit check made payable?

Payment is made by check to the beneficiary, by direct deposit to a beneficiary's account with a financial institution, or to a representative payee if the beneficiary is incapable of managing finances.

All beneficiaries with accounts in financial institutions will have their benefit checks deposited directly into these accounts instead of mailed to their homes. A financial institution may be a bank, trust company, savings and loan association, or a federal or state chartered credit union. The beneficiary continues to be responsible for notifying the Social Security Administration of any changes which affect eligibility to receive benefits. Beneficiaries without accounts in financial institutions will continue to have their benefit checks mailed directly to their homes.

A minor child (a child under 18 years of age) is ordinarily considered incapable of managing benefit payments and a representative payee (usually a parent, close relative or legal guardian) will be selected to receive payments on the child's behalf.

However, payment will be made directly to a child over 18, or to a child under 18 if there is no indication that the child is immature or unstable and it appears to be in the minor's best interest to make direct payment.

Also, if alcoholism or drug addiction is a contributing factor in determining that an individual is entitled to disability benefits, the benefits must be paid through a representative payee.

A beneficiary outside the United States can have payments deposited directly into a United States bank or other financial institution. Direct deposit is also available to beneficiaries who wish to have their payments deposited into a bank or financial institution in the country where they live. Direct deposit is available in the United Kingdom, Canada, Germany, France, Ireland, Argentina, and Spain.

A-18. If a husband and wife are both receiving monthly benefits, do they receive one or two monthly checks?

Separate payments for Social Security benefits will be made to a husband and wife if only one elects direct deposit. However, monthly benefits payable to a husband and wife who are entitled on the same Social Security record and are living at the same address are usually combined in one check made out to them jointly. If it is a combined check, both persons must endorse it.

A-19. If several children are entitled to benefits, does each child receive a separate check?

No. Social Security benefit payments for minor children in one family unit are usually combined in one check. Where the children customarily reside in different households, separate checks will be issued to each family group.

A-20. Can a power of attorney be granted for the purpose of collecting and depositing checks?

Yes. If payments are to be deposited in an account at a United States financial institution, completion of Standard Form 1199 (Authorization for deposit of

Social Security Payments) is required. This form can be obtained at the financial institution to which payments are to be directed. If payments are to be directed to a foreign financial institution, Standard Form 233 or Treasury Form 6711 (Power of Attorney by Individual to a Bank for the collection of checks drawn on the Treasury of the United States) must be completed.

A-21. Can Social Security benefits be assigned?

No. The provision in the Social Security Act (section 207) prohibiting assignment of benefits or subjecting them to the operations of bankruptcy laws may not be superseded by another law unless the other law does so by express reference to section 207. Some bankruptcy courts have considered Social Security benefits listed by the debtor to be income for purposes of bankruptcy proceedings and have ordered the Social Security Administration to send all or part of a debtor's benefit check to the trustee in bankruptcy. Such orders are not appropriate.

A-22. Can Social Security benefits be attached for the beneficiary's debts?

Benefits are not subject to levy, garnishment, or attachment, except in very restricted circumstances, such as by court order for the collection of child support or alimony, or by the Internal Revenue Service for unpaid federal taxes.

A U.S. district court reaffirmed the right of the Internal Revenue Service to seize Social Security benefits to collect overdue taxes. The plaintiff owed the IRS over $100,000. The IRS sent a notice of levy to the Social Security Administration, garnishing the plaintiff's entire Social Security benefit for one month and approximately half of his benefit for each month thereafter. The plaintiff sought reimbursement of the benefit garnished by the IRS and a judgment declaring future benefits exempt from collection. The court ruled that Social Security benefits are subject to levy by the IRS, and that the IRS may garnish the plaintiff's Social Security benefits until his federal income taxes and assessed penalties are paid. *Leining v. U.S.*, 97-1 USTC ¶50,254 (D. Conn. 1996).

A-23. Are Social Security benefits subject to federal taxes?

Up to one-half of the Social Security benefits received by taxpayers whose incomes exceed certain base amounts is subject to income taxation. The base amounts are $32,000 for married taxpayers filing jointly, $25,000 for a single taxpayer, and zero for married taxpayers filing separately who did not live apart for the entire taxable year.

There is an additional tier of taxation based upon a base amount of $44,000 for married taxpayers filing jointly, $34,000 for unmarried taxpayers, and zero for married taxpayers filing separately who did not live apart for the entire taxable year. The maximum percentage of Social Security benefits subject to income tax increases to 85% under this second tier of taxation. (The rules listed in the paragraph above continue to apply to taxpayers not meeting these thresholds.)

After the end of the year, Form 1099 (Social Security Benefit Statement) is sent to each beneficiary showing the amount of benefits received. A worksheet (IRS Notice 703) is enclosed for figuring whether any portion of the Social Security benefits received is subject to income tax.

For a detailed explanation of taxation of benefits, see SECTION G.

A-24. What happens when a Social Security check is sent to a beneficiary by mistake?

A check sent to a beneficiary who is not entitled to the payment should be returned to the Regional Financial Center, Treasury Department, located in the city shown on the face of the check. If the holder of the check prefers, the check may be returned to a Social Security office. If a beneficiary is not entitled to payment and cashes the check, a refund is ordinarily required. Often the program service center will have later checks withheld to make up for the overpayment.

COVERAGE (OASDI)

B-1. What persons are covered by Social Security?

Generally speaking, most employees in private industry, most self-employed persons, and members of the U.S. Armed Forces are covered by Social Security. (See B-3 to B-24.)

Some groups of people are excluded from social security coverage. The main groups excluded are federal employees hired before 1984, and railroad employees, who come under the Railroad Retirement System. (See B-25 and B-26.)

Some people are subject to special coverage provisions. See: Family Employment (B-27); Employees of State and Local Governments (B-28); Ministers, Members of Religious Orders and Christian Science Practitioners (B-29); Employees of Non-Profit Organizations (B-30); Hospital Interns (B-31); Student Nurses (B-32); Domestics and Household Workers (B-33); Non-business Employment (B-34); Agricultural Laborers (B-35); Students Working for a College or College Club (B-36); Distributors and Vendors of Newspapers and Magazines (B-37, B-38); Americans Employed Outside the U.S. (B-39); Farmers (B-40); and Members of Certain Religious Sects (B-41).

Actually, it is not the person, but the employment or self-employment that is covered or excluded from coverage (See WAGES AND SELF-EMPLOYMENT INCOME, SECTION C.)

B-2. Is participation in the Social Security system compulsory?

Yes, participation is almost always compulsory unless the type of employment or self-employment is specifically excluded from coverage. This means that a person in covered employment or covered self-employment must pay Social Security taxes, and is entitled to benefits if he meets the insured status requirements.

However, ministers, members of religious orders and Christian Science practitioners may claim exemption on the basis of conscientious or religious objections (see B-29).

B-3. Are employees and self-employed persons treated differently under the Social Security program?

Yes. Although benefits and insured status requirements are the same for employees and self-employed individuals, differences in the tax rate, the effect of the retirement test (amount that can be earned without loss of benefits), and the computation of covered earnings make it necessary to determine whether a person is an employee or a self-employed person.

EMPLOYEES

B-4. Who are employees under the Social Security Act?

The Social Security Act defines three classes of workers as employees: (1) workers who are employees under the "common-law" test; (B-5); (2) officers of corporations (B-6 to B-9); and (3) persons who work in four specific occupations (B-10).

B-5. Who are employees under the common-law test?

Under the common-law test, workers are employees if the person for whom they work has the right to tell them what to do and how, when, and where to do it. The employer does not have to give these orders, but needs only the right to do so. In the next paragraph some factors are set forth that indicate control over details of work. These factors are to be weighed against or compared with those which point to an independent contractor status. (Independent contractors are covered as self-employed persons—unless they are included in the four occupational groups discussed in B-10 and B-11). Any single fact or small group of facts is not conclusive evidence of the presence or absence of control. All facts must be weighed and the conclusion must be based on a careful evaluation of all the facts and the presence or absence of factors which point to an employer-employee relationship, as well as those which point to an independent contractor status.

The following factors tend to indicate that a person is an employee:

- A person who is required to comply with instructions about when, where, and how to work is ordinarily an employee.

- Training of a person by an experienced employee is a factor of control because it is an indication that the employer wants the services performed in a particular method or manner.

- Integration of the person's services in the business operations generally shows that the person is subject to direction and control.

- If the services must be rendered personally, it indicates that the employer is interested in the methods as well as the results.

- Hiring, supervising, and paying assistants by the employer generally show control over all the workers on the job.

- The existence of a continuing relationship between an individual and the person for whom the individual performs services is a factor tending to indicate the existence of an employer-employee relationship.

- The establishment of set hours of work by the employer is a factor indicative of control.

- If the worker must devote full time to the business of the employer, the employer has control over the amount of time the worker spends working.

- Doing the work on the employer's premises is not control in itself; however, it does imply that the employer has control, especially where the work is of such a nature that it could be done elsewhere.

- If a person must perform services in the order or sequence set by the employer, it shows that the worker may be subject to control.

- If regular oral or written reports must be submitted to the employer, it indicates control in that the worker is compelled to account for actions.

- An employee is usually paid by the hour, week, or month.

- Payment by the employer of the worker's business and traveling expenses is a factor indicating control over the worker.

- The furnishing of tools, materials and facilities is indicative of control over the worker.

- The right to fire is an important factor, indicating that the person possessing the right is an employer.

- An employee has the right to end the relationship with the employer at any time without incurring liability.

The following factors, on the other hand, tend to indicate that the person is an independent contractor:

- Independent contractors ordinarily use their own methods and receive no training from the purchasers of their services.

- A significant investment by a person in facilities used in performing services for someone else tends to show an independent status.

- People who are in a position to realize a profit or suffer a loss as a result of their services are generally independent contractors.

- If a person works for a number of people or firms at the same time, it usually indicates an independent status.

- Workers who make their services available to the general public are usually independent contractors.

- Independent contractors cannot be fired as long as they produce results which measure up to their contract specifications.

- An independent contractor is paid on a commission or job basis.

- An independent contractor usually agrees to complete a specific job and is responsible for its satisfactory completion or is legally obligated to make good for failure to complete the job.

B-6. Is an officer of a corporation an employee for Social Security purposes?

Yes, an officer of a corporation is considered to be an employee, even though the officer does not meet the definition of an employee under the common-law test (see B-5) because no one actually controls the officer's work. A person in this position is an employee of the corporation.

A director of a corporation is not an employee with respect to services performed as a director. A director of a corporation is self-employed with respect to these services. However, any nondirectional services which the director may perform under the control of the board of directors would be performed as an employee of the corporation. For self-employment Social Security taxes and benefit purposes, the director fees are counted in the year when paid, except that, for the retirement earnings test, they are considered on a when-earned basis.

B-7. Is an officer of a Subchapter S corporation an employee?

Yes. Under Subchapter S of the Internal Revenue Code (IRC Secs. 1361-1379), certain corporations may elect to be taxed as pass through entities. Corporations that make the election are called "S corporations." Despite the election, however, officers of an S corporation are still employees. Their salaries are considered "wages" and they are treated generally as employees for Social Security purposes. (But for treatment of so-called "dividends" from Subchapter S corporations, see WAGES AND SELF-EMPLOYMENT INCOME, SECTION C.)

B-8. If an unincorporated association is taxable as a corporation, are the officers of the association treated as employees?

Yes. Under the federal income tax laws, certain unincorporated associations are taxable as corporations. Generally, an unincorporated association is taxable as a corporation only if it elects corporate taxation by filing an entity classification form under the "check-the-box" regulations. (However, certain entities will automatically be classified as corporations for federal tax purposes.) If an association is taxable as a corporation, members who perform duties similar to those of a corporate officer are treated as employees. (With respect to professional corporations and associations, see B-9.)

B-9. Are the stockholders of a professional corporation employees of the corporation?

Yes, if they perform services as employees for the corporation. Professional corporations and professional associations organized under state law are generally treated as corporations for federal tax purposes. Rev. Rul. 70-101, 1970-1 CB 278.

B-10. Persons in what four occupations are considered employees regardless of whether they meet the common-law test for classification as employees?

The following are usually considered employees for Social Security purposes even though they do not qualify as employees under the common-law test, and may report their income (for income tax purposes) as independent contractors.

1. Full-time life insurance agents who: (1) solicit life insurance or annuity contracts as their entire or principal business activity, and (2) work primarily for one life insurance company.

2. Agent-drivers and commission drivers who distribute the following items: meat or meat products, vegetables or vegetable products, fruit or fruit products, bakery products, beverages (other than milk), or laundry or dry cleaned clothing.

3. Full-time traveling or city salespersons who: (1) solicit orders for merchandise on behalf of another person or firm as their principal activity, (2) obtain their orders from wholesalers, retailers, contractors, or operators of hotels or restaurants, or businesses whose primary function is the furnishing of food and/or lodging, and (3) sell merchandise which is bought for resale or for use as supplies in their customers' business operations.

4. Home workers who: (1) work away from the employer's place of business, (2) work in accordance with the employer's specifications, (3) work on material or goods furnished by the employer, and (4) return the finished product to the employer or to someone whom the employer designates.

A person in one of the above occupational groups is considered an employee under Social Security if: (1) the contract of service intends that the person will personally perform substantially all of the work, (2) the person has no substantial investment in facilities used to do the work other than tools, equipment or clothing of the kind usually provided by employees, or transportation facilities such as a car or truck, and (3) there is a continuing work relationship with the person for whom the services are performed.

For additional conditions with respect to classifying a life insurance agent as an employee, see B-11.

B-11. Under what conditions is a life insurance agent classified as an employee?

Even if life insurance agents do not qualify as employees under the common-law test (B-5), and even if they file their income tax returns as independent contractors, life insurance agents will be considered employees for Social Security purposes if they are "full-time life insurance agents." To be a "full-time life insurance agent," they must: (1) solicit life insurance or annuity contracts as their *entire* or *principal* business activity; and (2) work primarily for *one* life insurance company. Generally the contract of employment reflects the intention of the agent and the company, or general agent, in regard to full-time activity. (The agent may be an employee of the company or of its general agent.)

Selling life insurance may be the agent's *entire* business activity even though the agent does not devote a normal workweek to it. In other words, an individual may work only a few hours a day, or a few days a week, and still qualify as a full-time life insurance agent. A *principal business activity* is one which takes the major part of the agent's working time and attention.

The agent's efforts must be devoted primarily to the sale of life insurance or annuity contracts. Occasional or incidental sales of other types of insurance for the employer or the occasional placing of surplus-line insurance will not affect this requirement. However, an agent who is required to devote substantial efforts to selling applications for insurance contracts other than life insurance and annuity contracts (for example, health and accident, fire, automobile, etc.) is not a full-time life insurance agent.

Regardless of whether selling life insurance is the agent's entire or principal activity, the life insurance agent will not be considered an employee unless, under the contract of employment, the agent is to perform substantially all the services personally. Nor will the agent be considered an employee if he has a substantial investment in the facilities he uses in connection with his work (other than transportation facilities). Life insurance agents are usually furnished office space, stenographic help, telephone facilities, forms, rate book, and advertising materials by the company or its general agent.

A life insurance agent who does not qualify as an employee under the common-law test, and who is not a "full-time life insurance agent," is covered under Social Security as a self-employed person. For example, a general agent or broker is ordinarily treated as a self-employed individual since a general agent or broker is not a "full-time life insurance agent" who sells contracts primarily for one life insurance company.

B-12. Is a manufacturer's representative an employee?

No, manufacturers' representatives who hold themselves out as independent businesspeople and serve the public through a connection with a number of firms are not employees. Multiple-line salespersons are generally not employees because they usually solicit orders for more than one principal. (See B-10.) However, the salespersons who solicit orders primarily for one principal can be employees of that principal even though they carry on incidental sideline activities on behalf of other persons or firms.

B-13. When did employees first come under Social Security?

The Social Security Act became effective January 1, 1937. The year 1937 was the first year of coverage for employees. (Self-employed persons were first covered in 1951—see B-15.)

SELF-EMPLOYED PERSONS

B-14. What self-employed persons are covered by Social Security?

Almost all self-employed persons are covered. In general, this includes everyone engaged in a trade, business or profession as a sole proprietor, partner, or independent contractor.

B-15. When did the various groups of self-employed persons come under Social Security?

• Most persons self-employed in a trade or business:

    First year of coverage: calendar year 1951; or, for fiscal-year taxpayers, taxable years beginning after 1950.

- Architects; professional engineers; accountants (including certified, registered, or licensed and full-time public accountants); funeral directors; farmers; and (on an elective basis) ministers, members of religious orders and Christian Science practitioners:

  First year of coverage: calendar year 1955; or, for fiscal-year taxpayers, taxable years ending after 1954.

- Lawyers; dentists; osteopaths; veterinarians; chiropractors; naturopaths; optometrists; and farm landlords who materially participate in the farming activities:

  First year of coverage: calendar year 1956; or, for fiscal-year taxpayers, taxable years ending after 1955.

- Persons self-employed in a trade or business in Guam or American Samoa:

  First year of coverage: calendar year 1961; or, for fiscal-year taxpayers, taxable years beginning after 1960.

- Physicians and Surgeons:

  First year of coverage: calendar year 1965; or, for fiscal-year taxpayers, taxable years ending after 1965.

- Ministers, Christian Science practitioners, and members of religious orders:

  First year of coverage: calendar year 1968; or, for fiscal year taxpayers, taxable years ending after 1967. Can opt out on grounds of religious principles or conscience.

B-16. Is it possible to be covered by Social Security without performing personal services in a trade, business, or profession?

Yes. Income received by an owner (or part-owner) of a trade or business will count as self-employment income even though the owner performs no personal services in the trade or business. For example, absentee owners or silent partners whose businesses are carried on by employees are covered as self-employed persons.

For taxable years beginning after 1977, limited partners are excluded from Social Security coverage. Previously, limited partners could be covered on the same basis as other partners.

B-17. Are partners generally covered as self-employed persons?

Yes, business partners are self-employed. A partnership is generally said to be created when two or more persons join together for the principal purpose of carrying on a trade or business. Each partner contributes in one or more ways with money, property, labor, or skill and shares in the profits and risks of loss in accordance with the partnership agreement or understanding.

The term "trade or business" for Social Security purposes has the same meaning as when used in section 162 of the Internal Revenue Code relating to income taxes.

In determining whether a partnership exists, it is necessary to determine whether the parties intended to join together to carry on a trade or business and share in the profits and losses. Intention of the parties is determined not merely from their statements, but to a large degree, from their conduct in carrying on the business, not only in regard to each other, but also in regard to third parties. Further light is cast on the true intent of the parties by such matters as the abilities and contributions of each and the control which each has over the operation of the business.

A partnership is the same for Social Security purposes as for income tax purposes except for the exclusion from Social Security coverage of a limited partner in a limited partnership. (See B-16.) Besides the ordinary partnership, the term "partnership" for federal income tax purposes includes a syndicate, group, pool, joint venture, or any other unincorporated organization which carries on a business. The term does not include corporations, trusts, estates, or associations taxable as corporations.

Two or more persons, including husbands and wives, may be self-employed as partners for income tax and Social Security purposes, even if they do not operate under a formal partnership agreement or even if they are not considered partners under state law because they have not complied with local statutory requirements.

For federal income tax purposes and for Social Security purposes, a partnership and a joint venture are essentially the same. The main distinction is that a partnership involves a continuing enterprise while a joint venture is usually for the accomplishment of a single project or transaction.

B-18. Are real estate agents and direct sellers covered as self-employed persons?

Certain qualified real estate agents and direct sellers, such as door-to-door salespersons, are treated as self-employed persons. The IRS has held that since these persons do not have taxes withheld as employees, they must be considered self-employed and are liable for tax on their self-employment income. Rev. Rul. 85-63, 1985-1 CB 292.

To be considered self-employed, a qualified real estate agent must: (1) be a licensed real estate salesperson, (2) derive substantially all remuneration received for services performed as a real estate salesperson directly from sales or other output, such as appraisal activities, rather than from the number of hours worked, and (3) perform these services under a written contract which stipulates that the person will not be treated as an employee with respect to the services for federal tax purposes.

To be considered self-employed, a direct seller must: (1) be engaged in a trade or business selling or soliciting the sale of consumer products directly to consumers or to anyone for resale to consumers in the home or in other than a permanent retail establishment, (2) derive substantially all remuneration received for services performed as a direct seller directly from the sales of the product or the performance of services such as motivation, training, and recruitment activities, rather than from the number of hours worked, and (3) perform these services under a written contract or agreement which stipulates that the person will not be treated as an employee with respect to the services for federal tax purposes.

B-19. If members of the same family conduct a business enterprise as partners, is each member covered by Social Security as a self-employed person?

Yes, if each family member is a true partner. For instance, a husband and wife or parents and children may conduct a business enterprise as a partnership. In such case, each partner is covered under Social Security as a self-employed person. In determining whether the legal relationship of partners exists, the same rules apply as for income tax purposes.

A family member may be a partner without performing services in the business, provided the family member actually owns a capital interest in the partnership. In this respect, a transfer of a capital interest in a family partnership to a member of the same family generally makes that member a partner if: (1) the partnership is one in which capital is a material income-producing factor; (2) there has been a bona fide gift or purchase of the capital interest; (3) the transferee actually owns the interest and is vested with dominion and control over it; and (4) a valid partnership was in existence before the transfer, or was created at the time of the transfer. Thus, even a minor child may be a partner, and the child's share of partnership income treated as self-employment income for tax and benefit purposes.

In deciding whether members of a family enterprise are partners in a business, the question is usually whether the parties entered into the arrangement with the intent to conduct a business as a partnership and in fact actually did so.

B-20. Is self-employment income considered as belonging one-half to the husband and one-half to the wife in a community property state?

No, community property laws are disregarded.

According to the Social Security Act, if income from a trade or business is considered community income, all the income is considered the husband's for Social Security purposes, and he is the only one covered (see also B-27). However, if the wife can show that she actually manages and controls the business, all the income is considered hers for Social Security purposes.

Note, however, that the community property provision of the Social Security Act described above has been held unconstitutional on the ground that it discriminates on the basis of sex in violation of the Fifth Amendment of the constitution. *Carrasco v. Secretary of Health, Education & Welfare*, 628 F.2d 624 (1st Cir. 1980); *Hester v. Harris*, 631 F.2d 53 (5th Cir. 1980); *Becker v. Harris*, 493 F.Supp. 991 (E.D. Cal. 1980). The courts found that, as a result of this provision, women responsible for a large part of the business's income were often credited with no quarters of coverage. (See D-4.) These women were either ineligible for retirement or disability benefits or entitled to a lower benefit because of the rule.

Because of the 1980 court decisions, the Internal Revenue Service determined that the rule in community property states should be the same as in non-community property states. That is, in the absence of a partnership, only the spouse carrying on the trade or business will be subject to self-employment tax. Rev. Rul. 82-39, 1982-1 CB 119.

Likewise, a husband's distributive share of partnership income is treated as entirely his. But if a husband and wife carry on a business as partners, each partner's distributive share will be treated as his or her earnings from self-employment, and each will be covered.

B-21. Are nonprofessional fiduciaries self-employed persons?

Generally, nonprofessional fiduciaries serve as executors or administrators only in isolated instances, and then as personal representatives for the estates of deceased friends or relatives. These individuals are not engaged in a trade or business (and their income as fiduciaries is therefore not covered by Social Security) unless all of the following conditions are met: (1) there is a trade or business among the assets of the estate, and (2) the fiduciary actively participates in the operation of this trade or business, and (3) the fees of the fiduciary are related to the operation of the trade or business.

B-22. Is the beneficiary of a trust, the beneficiary of an estate, or the ward of a guardianship, a self-employed person?

No.

B-23. Are writers who receive royalties engaged in a trade or business and consequently covered as self-employed persons?

Each case must be decided on the facts. A one-time venture of a short duration usually is not a trade or business, but a repetition of such ventures would constitute a trade or business. Thus, if an individual writes only one book as a sideline and never revises it, the writing activities would probably not constitute a trade or business. However, if the person prepares new editions from time to time or writes several books, the writing and editing activities would be a trade or business.

A person may engage in other related activities which, when considered together with the writing activities, may be a trade or business. For example, a college professor who writes a book on business administration and gives lectures and advice to business groups on the same subject probably would be considered in a trade or business as a self-employed person.

MEMBERS OF THE U.S. ARMED FORCES

B-24. Are members of the U.S. Armed Forces covered by Social Security?

Yes. Monthly retirement, disability, and survivors benefits under Social Security are payable to a veteran and dependents if the veteran has earned enough work credits under the program. In addition, the veteran may qualify at age 65 for Hospital Insurance (Part A) under Medicare. (A veteran can qualify for Medical Insurance (Part B) under Medicare without work credits by applying and paying premiums.)

Active duty (or active or inactive duty for training) in the United States uniformed services has counted toward Social Security since January 1957, when contributions were first withheld from a serviceman's basic pay. Since 1957, members of the uniformed services have received non-contributory wage credits for service of up to $300 per quarter during which they received active duty pay. Starting with 1978, the credit is $100 for each $300 of covered annual military wages, up to a maximum of $1,200 per year in free credits for $3,600 or more in covered military wages. This credit is in addition to credit for basic pay and is given in recognition of the fact that the covered basic pay is augmented by various allowances that are part of the actual reimbursement for services. These extra credits can result in increased benefits by increasing the average earnings on which benefits are figured. The cost of providing these wage credits comes from the general revenues.

The minimum active duty period for granting wage credits is 24 months of service or the full period called to active duty if the person served fewer than 24 months of active duty. This rule applies to: (1) persons enlisted in the Armed Forces for the first time on or after September 7, 1980, and (2) other members of the uniformed services whose active duty begins after October 13, 1982, provided they did not previously serve 24 months of active duty or were not discharged from prior service for the convenience of the government.

However, there are the following exceptions to these minimum service requirements: (1) discharge or release from active duty for the convenience of the government, (2) discharge or release from active duty for hardship, (3) discharge or release from active duty for disability incurred or aggravated in the line of duty, or (4) the establishment of entitlement to compensation for service-connected disability or death.

Active duty is: (1) full-time duty in the Armed Forces, (2) full-time duty (other than for training purposes) as a commissioned officer of the Regular or Reserve Corps of the Public Health Service, (3) full-time duty as a commissioned officer of the National Oceanic and Atmospheric Administration, and (4) full-time duty as a cadet or midshipman at the United States Military Academy, United States Naval Academy, United States Air Force Academy, or the United States Coast Guard Academy.

Active duty for training means: (1) full-time duty performed by a member of a Reserve component of a uniformed service in the active military or naval service of the United States for training purposes, (2) full-time duty as a commissioned officer of the Reserve Corps of the Public Health Service for training purposes, and (3) annual training duty performed for a period of 14 days or more as a member of the Reserve Officers' Training Corps, the Naval Reserve Officers' Training Corps, or the Air Force Reserve Officers' Training Corps.

Individuals with active duty between September 16, 1940, and December 31, 1956, and whose discharge was other than dishonorable, can qualify for gratuitous Social Security earnings credits of $160 for each month of service during this period. At least 90 days of active service is required, however, unless discharged because of disability or injury incurred or aggravated in the line of duty. The $160 a month noncontributory wage credits for military service are not actually posted on the veteran's Social Security record. When benefits are claimed on the veteran's Social Security record, the wage credits are then considered.

In determining their "average indexed monthly earnings," military personnel who have active service *after* 1956 may also utilize the gratuitous earnings credit of $160 for each month of military service after 1950 and before 1957, even though their armed forces retired pay is based in part on those years of service.

FEDERAL GOVERNMENT EMPLOYEES

B-25. Are civilian employees of the Federal Government who come under The Civil Service Retirement System covered by Social Security?
Work performed by the United States government by newly hired civilian employees and certain federal officials is covered by Social Security beginning January 1, 1984. Prior to 1984, most federal civilian employment was exempt from regular Social Security coverage, but subject to the Medicare Hospital Insurance (Part A) tax beginning January 1, 1983.

The following civilian employees and federal officials are covered under Social Security:

- Federal employees who on or after January 1, 1984: (1) are hired for the first time, or (2) are hired after a separation exceeding 365 days from previous federal employment.

- Legislative branch employees who were not participating in the Civil Service Retirement System (CSRS) or another federal civilian retirement system as of December 31, 1983.

- Legislative branch employees who were participating in the CSRS or another federal retirement system (other than one for members of the uniformed services) on December 31, 1983, and: (1) who receive lump-sum payments from the federal retirement system after December 31, 1983, or (2) who cease to be subject to CSRS after December 31, 1983.

- All members of Congress.

- The President, Vice President, and most executive-level political appointees.

- Federal judges, magistrates, bankruptcy judges, and referees in bankruptcy. This does not apply to remuneration paid to retired senior status federal justices and judges while actively performing judicial duties.

If a person returns to federal civilian employment after being transferred to an international organization, then the service performed for the organization is considered federal employment. If a person returns to federal civilian service after temporary military or reserve duty and has exercised restoration or reemployment rights, then no break-in-service is deemed to have occurred and service in the uniformed services will count as federal employment.

An individual who withdraws from the Civil Service Retirement System (CSRS) after June 14, 1984 and is refunded contributions will not be exempt from Social Security thereafter while employed in the legislative branch. Also, an individual will not be exempt from Social Security if employed in the legislative branch after June 14, 1984 and such employment is not covered by the CSRS. Legislative branch employees who take a leave of absence without taking a refund of their CSRS contributions may continue their coverage under the CSRS. If they are not automatically covered again under the CSRS, they will be covered under Social Security unless they rejoin the CSRS when they resume employment.

No exemption from Social Security coverage is available to a person who took a refund of CSRS contributions based on a separation or transfer from January 1, 1984 through June 14, 1984, or who has legislative branch employment which was not covered under the CSRS during that period. Exemption from Social Security can be reestablished, however, if the person was covered under the CSRS on December 31, 1983, and reentered the CSRS after the last withdrawal from it and before August 18, 1984. For a person who is not a federal employee on July 18, 1984, the 30-day period will run from the date on which the person again becomes a legislative branch employee. A person will be treated as having reentered the CSRS if an application is made within the appropriate time and coverage is subsequently made effective.

The Federal Employees' Retirement System (FERS) provides supplementary retirement protection for federal employees who begin work with the government after 1983.

RAILROAD EMPLOYEES

B-26. Are railroad employees covered by Social Security?

No, work covered by the Railroad Retirement Act is excluded from Social Security coverage. (Railroad employees have a special and separate retirement system administered by the Railroad Retirement Board.) However, earnings from railroad employment are counted for Social Security purposes at the death or retirement of a worker if the worker does not qualify under the railroad retirement program. For example, when a railroad worker retires with less than 120 months of railroad service, no railroad retirement annuity is payable. However, railroad earnings after 1936 would then be considered in determining the worker's rights to Social Security disability or retirement benefits.

FAMILY EMPLOYMENT

B-27. Is employment by a member of one's own family covered by Social Security?

The following "family employment" does not come under Social Security:

- A child, under age 18, in the employ of a parent.

- A child, age 18 to 21, in the employ of a parent, but not performing work in the course of the parent's trade or business.

- A man in the employ of his wife, but not performing work in the course of his wife's trade or business.

- A woman in the employ of her husband, but not in the course of her husband's trade or business.

- A parent in the employ of his or her son or daughter performing: (1) domestic service in or about the private home of the son or daughter, or (2) work not in the course of the son's or daughter's trade or business.

There is an exception to the domestic service rule. Domestic service by a parent for his or her son or daughter in or about the private home is covered by Social Security if: (1) there is a genuine employment relationship between parent and son or daughter, and (2) the son or daughter who employs the parent has a child or stepchild living in the private home who is under age 18, or, if the child is older, the child has a mental or physical condition that requires the personal care or supervision of an adult for at least four continuous weeks in the calendar quarter in which the domestic service is rendered, and (3) the employer is a widow or widower; or is divorced and has not remarried; or has a spouse living in the home and the spouse has a mental or physical condition and is incapable of caring for the child for at least four continuous weeks in the calendar quarter in which the parent performs the domestic service.

The term "child" includes an adopted child and a stepchild.

If a husband and wife work in the same business, and the business is a sole proprietorship, the spouse who is the owner of the business is covered. In addition, the spouse who is the employee is covered as an employee. This is usually true whether the couple lives in a community property state or in a common-law state—see B-20. If the husband and wife are partners, both are considered to be owners, and both are covered as self-employed persons.

If a woman works for a corporation, she will be covered as an employee of the corporation even though her husband is the sole stockholder.

Also, the rules excluding family employment do not apply to work performed as an employee of a partnership unless the relationship of minor child and parent exists between the employee and *each* of the partners. For example, if a minor is employed by a partnership composed of the minor's father and uncle as co-partners, the minor's work is covered. But if the partnership is composed of the minor's father and mother as sole co-partners, the minor's work is not covered. If the child is a bona fide partner, however, the child is covered as a self-employed person even though the child's parents are the only other partners (see B-19).

A person who is an employee of a partnership composed of his spouse and one or more other partners, is covered. If the person is a partner, he is covered as a self-employed person (see B-19).

EMPLOYEES OF STATE AND LOCAL GOVERNMENTS

B-28. Are employees of state and local governments covered by Social Security?

Before July 2, 1991, services of employees of state and local governments could be brought under full Social Security only by means of agreements entered into by the states with the Secretary of Health and Human Services. The Social Security Administration administers the coverage.

Services of most state and local government employees who were hired after March 31, 1986, were covered under the Hospital Insurance (Part A) portion of Medicare if the employees were not already covered under a state's Social Security agreement. In addition, a state can extend this Medicare-only coverage to employees hired before April 1, 1986, by a voluntary agreement with Health and Human Services.

Effective for services performed after July 1, 1991, services of most employees who are not members of the state or local government employer's retirement system are mandatorily covered for full Social Security. The Internal Revenue Service determines what constitutes a retirement system for purposes of mandatory coverage, and what constitutes membership in such a retirement system.

All states have entered into agreements. Some states have provided coverage for most employees while other states have provided coverage for only a few employees. Once an agreement has been entered into with a state, employees of the state and its political subdivisions are brought under the agreement in groups known as "coverage groups." There are two basic types of coverage groups: (1) groups composed of employees whose positions are not under a state or local retirement system, and (2) retirement system coverage groups, which are groups composed of employees whose positions are covered by a state or local retirement system.

The Social Security Act gives each state the right to decide which coverage groups are to be included under its agreement. A state may permit its political subdivisions to decide whether to include the subdivision's employees under the agreement. A state may include additional coverage groups. Note, however, that services of employees not under a retirement system who are not already covered for full Social Security under an agreement may be mandatorily covered. (See above.)

A coverage group composed of employees whose positions are not covered by a retirement group may consist of any of the following employees: (1) all state employees performing services in connection with governmental functions, (2) all state employees performing services in connection with one or more nongovernmental functions, (3) all employees of a political subdivision (e.g., city, county or township) performing services in connection with one or more governmental functions, (4) all employees of a political subdivision performing services in connection with one or more nongovernmental functions, (5) civilian employees of a state's National Guard units, and (6) inspectors of agricultural products employed by agreement between the state and the Department of Agriculture.

All, or only some, of the above groups in a specific state may be brought under Social Security by the state's agreement.

State and local government workers who are not covered by a retirement system in conjunction with their employment for a state or local government are automatically covered under Social Security and must pay Social Security taxes. An exception is provided for students employed in public schools, colleges, and universities, for whom coverage may be provided at the option of the state government. Other exceptions are hospital patients, "emergency" workers, and election officials or election workers if remuneration paid in a calendar year for their services is less than $1,100 in 2001 (this amount is adjusted for increases in wages).

A retirement system is defined as a pension, annuity, retirement, or similar fund or system established by a state or by a political subdivision of a state. A retirement system must provide a specified minimum benefit. This requirement can be satisfied under a defined contribution plan with a contribution equal to 7.5% of compensation. Under a defined benefit plan, the requirement can be met with a single life annuity beginning at age 65 equal to 1.5% of compensation for each year of service where compensation is based on the average of the highest three years of pay. If compensation is determined by using more than three years, the minimum benefit increases so that it would be 2% of compensation for each year of service for plans using compensation based on a period of more than 10 years.

Whether an employee is a member (i.e., a participant) of a retirement system is based upon whether that individual actually participates in the program. Thus, whether an employee participates is not determined by whether he holds a position that is included in a retirement system. Instead, the worker must actually be a member of the system. For example, an employee (whose job classification is of a type that ordinarily is entitled to coverage) is not a member of a retirement system if he is ineligible because of age or service conditions contained in the plan and, therefore, is required to be covered under Social Security. Similarly, if participation in the system is elective, and the employee elects not to participate, that employee does not participate in a retirement system and is to be covered under the Social Security system.

Other coverage groups are composed of employees who are under a state or local retirement system. A state coverage agreement cannot bring such groups under Social Security initially unless a referendum is held. Generally, if a majority of eligible employees vote in favor of being included, all will be covered (but see next paragraph below with respect to splitting a retirement system group). A retirement system coverage group for referendum and coverage purposes may, at the option of the state, consist of: (1) all employees under the system, (2) only state employees under the system, (3) all employees of one or more political subdivisions in positions under the system, (4) any combination of the foregoing groups, (5) employees of each institution of higher learning or of any hospital which is not a political subdivision in itself. This division may be made even though members of two or more of the groups are under the same state or local retirement system.

A retirement system of a state may be divided into two parts to obtain Social Security coverage for only the members who want it as of the time of the referendum. States may divide their retirement systems into two parts: one part consisting of members who desire coverage, and the other part consisting of members who do not desire coverage. Individuals who became members of the retirement system after the retirement system has been divided will be included in that part of the system which desires coverage.

A state may not terminate Social Security coverage of state and local government employees on or after April 20, 1983. Under prior law, a state could terminate coverage for groups of state and local employees by giving two years' advance written notice, providing the coverage had been in effect for at least five years. In addition, states and interstate instrumentalities, whose Social Security coverage terminated prior to April 20, 1983, are allowed to modify their agreements to cover groups whose coverage had been previously terminated. Prior law prohibited a terminated group from being covered again.

MINISTERS, MEMBERS OF RELIGIOUS ORDERS AND CHRISTIAN SCIENCE PRACTITIONERS

B-29. Is a minister, member of a religious order, or Christian Science practitioner covered by Social Security?

Yes, they are automatically covered for taxable years ending after 1967. This means that beginning in 1968, duly ordained, commissioned, or licensed ministers (including priests and rabbis), Christian Science practitioners, and members of religious orders who have not taken a vow of poverty, must pay Social Security taxes and are entitled to Social Security benefits under the rules applying to self-employed persons generally.

However, ministers, members and practitioners may claim exemption from Social Security on the ground of conscientious objection or religious principle. They must file application for an irrevocable exemption with the Internal Revenue Service (IRS Form 4029, Application for Exemption From Social Security Taxes and Waiver of Benefits) together with a statement that they are either conscientiously opposed, or opposed because of religious principle, to the acceptance of public insurance benefits. As a result of legislation in 1986 (Tax Reform Act), they must also submit proof that they informed their church body that they were taking this action, and the Internal Revenue Service has the responsibility of communicating with the applicant to be certain that the applicant is aware of the grounds for exemption and has sought exemption on such grounds.

Before a duly ordained, commissioned, or licensed minister of a church can request and be granted an exemption from Social Security coverage, the minister must be able to establish that the church qualifies as a religious organization exempt from income tax. Rev. Rul. 76-415, 1976-2 CB 255.

The time limit for filing an application for exemption with the Internal Revenue Service is on or before the due date of the tax return for the first taxable year in which the minister, member or practitioner had net earnings from self-employment of $400 or more, any part of which was derived from services as a minister, member of a religious order, or Christian Science practitioner.

A valid application for exemption is effective for the first taxable year ending after 1967 for which the applicant had net earnings of $400 or more, some part of which is derived from services as a minister, member, or practitioner.

The Tax Reform Act of 1986 gave clergy members who had elected to be excluded from Social Security coverage a one-time opportunity to obtain coverage. Generally, the election could have been made any time up to the filing due date for tax year 1997 (including extensions), and had to be made before the individual became entitled to benefits. Once the election was made, the individual had to pay self-employment tax.

The Ticket to Work and Work Incentives Improvement Act of 1999 provided another opportunity for members of the clergy to revoke their exemption from Social Security coverage. Clergy may revoke their exemption any time up to the filing due date for tax year 2001 (including extensions). Once this revocation is made, the clergy member may not apply for an exemption.

Individuals who perform services in the exercise of their ministry are treated as self-employed persons even though their income is derived from services as an employee. Thus, the income derived from the exercise of their ministry is treated as self-employment income and the individuals must pay the tax rate for self-employed persons. Coverage does not involve the church they serve.

Before 1968, a minister, Christian Science practitioner, or member of a religious order was exempt from Social Security coverage unless the person chose to be covered by filing a Form 2031 (Waiver Certificate To Elect Social Security Coverage for Use by Ministers, Certain Members of Religious Orders, and Christian Science Practitioners) with the Internal Revenue Service. The election to be covered was irrevocable; a person who chose to be covered may not elect to be exempt from coverage for services performed as a minister, practitioner, or member for taxable years ending after 1967.

Members of religious orders who have taken vows of poverty are not covered as self-employed individuals, but may be covered as employees if their orders elect Social Security coverage for their members.

EMPLOYEES OF NON-PROFIT ORGANIZATIONS

B-30. Are employees of non-profit religious, charitable or educational organizations covered by Social Security?

The Social Security Act provides:

- Mandatory coverage of all current and future employees of non-profit organizations, including employees of non-profit organizations that previously terminated coverage.

- Non-profit organizations may not terminate coverage of employees after 1982.

A non-profit religious, charitable or educational organization is defined in section 501(c)(3) of the Internal Revenue Code. A non-profit organization is exempt from income tax under section 501(a) of the Internal Revenue Code.

Non-profit employees age 55 or older on January 1, 1984 are fully insured for Social Security benefits after acquiring a given number of quarters of coverage, according to the following sliding scale, which is easier to meet than the regular requirements.

If on January 1, 1984 the person was	The number of quarters needed is
Age 60 or over	6
Age 59	8
Age 58	12
Age 57	16
Age 55-56	20

Exception: A church or qualified church-controlled organization, opposed for religious reasons to the payment of Social Security taxes, may elect to have services performed by their employees (beginning January 1, 1984) excluded from the definition of employment for Social Security purposes. Organizations in existence when the legislation was passed had to elect before October 31, 1984. Other organizations must elect before the date on which the first quarterly tax return is due. Services of employees of an electing church/ organization are treated as services performed in a trade or business and covered as self-employment.

The election is available to: (1) churches (including conventions or associations of churches), (2) elementary or secondary schools controlled, operated or principally supported by churches, and (3) certain church-controlled tax-exempt organizations. The election applies to services performed on or after January 1, 1984.

Employees of non-profit organizations who are covered on a mandatory basis by the Civil Service Retirement System (i.e., Legal Service Corporation employees) are considered federal employees for purposes of Social Security. They are covered by Social Security if newly hired after 1983, or if they had a break in federal service lasting more than 365 days. (See B-25.)

Participation in the Social Security system was optional for non-profit organizations prior to 1984. The non-profit organization had to file a certificate waiving its exemption from coverage. (In this way, the organization made itself subject to the Social Security tax on employers.)

HOSPITAL INTERNS

B-31. Are hospital interns covered by Social Security?

Work as an intern for a hospital is covered by Social Security as follows:

- If performed for a privately owned and operated hospital, coverage is compulsory.

- If performed for a federal hospital, determinations regarding work of interns and amounts of remuneration constituting covered wages are made by the head of the appropriate federal agency. The work is covered on the same basis as the work of other federal employees.

- If performed for a state or local hospital, coverage depends on whether the position is in a group covered under the federal-state agreement.

STUDENT NURSES

B-32. Are student nurses covered by Social Security?

No. Work by a student nurse for a hospital or nurses' training school is excluded from Social Security coverage if the student is enrolled and regularly attending classes in a nurses' training school which is chartered or approved under state law. This work is excluded from coverage even though the work of other employees of the hospital or nurses' training school is covered by Social Security.

The Internal Revenue Service, however, has held that a student nurse's services are not exempt from "employment" where they are performed on a full-time basis and the nurse performs the same duties and receives the same salary as the hospital's registered nurses. The Internal Revenue Service indicated that the services of a student nurse will be excepted from employment only where the work at the hospital or nurse's training school is substantially less than full time, the total amount of earnings is nominal, and the services are incidental parts of the training toward a qualifying degree as a nurse or in a specialized area of nursing. Rev. Rul. 85-74, 1985-1 CB 331.

DOMESTIC WORKERS

B-33. Is domestic work in a private home covered by Social Security?

Yes. Domestic service in the private home of the employer is covered by Social Security beginning with 1951. Only cash pay for this work is counted for Social Security purposes.

The threshold amount for Social Security coverage of a domestic worker is $1,300 per year in 2001. The $1,300 threshold will be indexed in future years for increases in average wages in the economy. Indexing will occur in $100 increments, rounded down to the nearest $100. Wages must be reported and both employer and employee Social Security taxes must be paid.

Exempt from Social Security taxes are any wages paid to a worker for domestic services performed in any year during which the worker is under age 18, except for workers under age 18 whose principal occupation is household employment. Being a student is considered to be an occupation for purposes of this test. Thus, for example, the wages of a student who is 16 years-old who also babysits will be exempt from the reporting and payment requirements, regardless of whether the amount of wages paid is above or below the threshold. On the other hand, the wages of a 17 year-old single mother who leaves school and goes to work as a domestic to support her family will be subject to the reporting and payment requirements.

Where a person performs domestic service for more than one employer, the cash pay test applies separately to the cash pay paid by each employer. The cash payments for a calendar quarter from various employers cannot be combined to meet the cash pay test. For example, if a domestic works for five employers and in one year receives only $750 from each employer (a total of $3,750), the pay does not come under Social Security.

Only cash payments are counted as Social Security wages. Room, board, and car tokens are not counted.

Domestic service means work ordinarily performed as an integral part of household duties that contributes to the maintenance of the employer's private home or administers to the personal wants and comforts of the employer, other members of the household, and guests. This includes work performed by cooks, waiters, waitresses, butlers, housekeepers, housemen, watchmen, governesses, maids, companions, nursemaids, valets, baby sitters, janitors, laundresses, furnacemen, caretakers, gardeners, footmen, grooms, seamstresses, handymen, and chauffeurs of family automobiles.

A private home is the fixed place of residence of one or more persons. Any shelter used as a dwelling may, depending on the circumstances, be considered a private home. Examples include a tent, boat, trailer, or a room or suite in a hospital, hotel, sanatorium, or nursing home.

In an apartment house, each apartment together with its private stairways, halls, and porches, etc. is a private home. If a house is used mainly as a commercial rooming or boarding house, only that part of the house which is used as the operator's living quarters is considered to be a private home.

Domestic workers employed by landlords or rental agencies to do work in or about property being rented as a private home are not performing work in the private home of the employer.

Domestic work performed by a child under age 21 for the child's parent, by a wife for her husband, by a husband for his wife, or by a parent for a son or daughter (except under some special circumstances) is not covered by Social Security (see B-27).

Domestic workers in rooming-houses, hotels, etc., are covered as regular employees regardless of their earnings. Also, different rules apply for household work on a farm (see B-35).

An employer who pays a domestic worker $1,300 or more in a year must report the wages for Social Security even though the employer has only the one employee. Payments may be rounded to the nearest dollar. (For method of reporting, see SOCIAL SECURITY TAXES, SECTION J.)

Domestic service does not include payment to a worker who is employed by a service company and hired out for a job (such as catering help or a painter), or payment to a self-employed person such as a gardener who brings special equipment.

NON-BUSINESS OR CASUAL EMPLOYMENT

B-34. Is an employee whose work is not connected with his employer's trade or business covered by Social Security?

Yes, but only "cash pay" for this type of work may be counted, and only if the employee is paid at least $100 in a calendar year.

Where the employee performs nonbusiness work for more than one employer, the cash-pay test is applied individually to the cash pay from each employer.

Non-business employment is any type of work that does not promote or advance the employer's business, such as work performed in connection with the employer's hobby or recreational activities or work as an employee in repairing the employer's private home. Employment for a corporation can never be considered "work not in the course of the employer's trade or business."

AGRICULTURAL LABOR

B-35. Under what conditions are agricultural laborers covered by Social Security?

Most types of agricultural labor have been covered by Social Security since 1951. However, only cash pay for farm work can be counted for Social Security purposes, and only if either:

- The cash was paid to an employee by an employer whose expenditures for agricultural labor are $2,500 or more, *or*

- the cash pay paid to an employee in a calendar year for agricultural labor by one employer amounts to $150 or more (the cash pay test) if the employer spends less than $2,500 in the year for agricultural labor.

However, wages paid to an employee who receives pay of less than $150 annually by an agricultural employer are not subject to social security tax even if the employer pays more than $2,500 in the year to all employees, if the employee (1) is employed as a hand harvest laborer and is paid on a piece rate basis in an operation which has been, and is customarily and generally recognized as having been, paid on a piece rate basis in the region of employment, (2) commutes daily from his or her permanent residence to the farm on which he or she is employed, and (3) has been employed in agriculture less than 13 weeks during the preceding calendar year.

If the employee receives cash pay from an employer for services which are agricultural labor and for services which are not agricultural labor, only the amounts paid for agricultural labor are counted in determining whether cash payments equal or exceed $150.

The Social Security Administration issued Social Security Ruling SSR 95-3p (July 27, 1995) to clarify its position on transactions involving noncash transfers for agricultural labor. The Internal Revenue Code provides that, for purposes of Social Security coverage and taxation, the term wages does not include any remuneration paid in any medium other than cash for agricultural labor. Any medium other than cash includes, for example, lodging, food, clothing, or agricultural commodities. Some farmers have attempted to use commodity payments as remuneration for agricultural purposes to avoid paying the Social Security tax. This practice can prevent farm workers from accumulating the quarters of coverage needed to qualify for Social Security benefits.

The Internal Revenue Service clarified in Revenue Ruling 79-207, 1979-2 CB 351, that a transfer of an in-kind item which is immediately converted to cash is, in economic reality, a payment in cash not subject to the wage exclusion. The effect of the ruling is that certain transactions involving in-kind transfers for agricultural labor have been considered cash payments and therefore wages subject to Social Security tax. The Social Security Administration policy has been not to treat such in-kind transfers as wages under the Social Security Act when evaluating them for Social Security coverage purposes. To achieve a consistent treatment between the Social Security Administration and the Internal Revenue Service, the Social Security Administration will consider the following:

1. Does an employer-employee relationship exist? Only noncash payments to an employee qualify for the exception. In-kind payments received by a self-employed individual engaged in farming are not subject to this exception and may be considered in determining self-employment income for Social Security coverage purposes. When a farmer's spouse performs agricultural labor for the farmer, the individual may be an employee. Generally, an employer-employee rela-

tionship exists when the person for whom the labor is performed has the right to control and direct the person who performs the services.

2. Is the in-kind transfer, in economic reality, equivalent to a payment in cash? If a bona fide transfer of the noncash medium from the employer to the employee has not occurred and the transaction is, in economic reality, equivalent to a payment in cash, the wage exclusion will not apply.

STUDENTS WORKING FOR A COLLEGE OR FOR A COLLEGE CLUB

B-36. Is a student working for a college or college club covered by Social Security?

No. Work by a student for a school, college or university at which the student is enrolled and regularly attending classes is excluded from Social Security coverage. Also excluded is domestic work by a student for a local college club, fraternity or sorority.

A local college club is one in which the membership is composed mainly of students enrolled in the college or of persons directly connected with the college. The membership of a local chapter of a college fraternity or sorority must be composed mostly of students enrolled in the college. However, the fact that a local college club or local chapter of a college fraternity or sorority has some alumni or faculty members is immaterial. An alumni club or alumni chapter of a fraternity or sorority, though, is not considered to be a college club or chapter.

Work performed by a student for a private, nonprofit auxiliary organization of the school, college, or university at which the student is enrolled and regularly attending classes is also excluded from coverage if the organization: (1) is organized and operated for the benefit of, to perform the functions of, or to carry out the purposes of the school, college, or university, and (2) is operated, supervised, or controlled by or in connection with the school, college, or university.

DISTRIBUTORS AND VENDORS OF NEWSPAPERS OR MAGAZINES

B-37. Is delivering or distributing newspapers or shopping news excluded from Social Security coverage?

Delivering or *distributing* newspapers or shopping news is excluded from Social Security coverage if:

- The work is performed as an employee and the person is under age 18, and

- The material is delivered or distributed to the ultimate consumer and not to a point from which later distribution or delivery is to be made.

Newspapers and shopping news also includes shopping guides, handbills and other types of advertising material. "Deliver or distribution" means retail sale, house-to-house delivery, or the passing out of handbills on the street. The exclusion does not apply to the delivery or distribution of magazines.

The *selling* of newspapers or magazines by an employee is excluded from Social Security coverage if:

- The magazines or newspapers are sold: (1) to the ultimate consumer, and (2) at an arranged fixed price, and

- The employee's pay is the difference between the fixed selling price and the amount at which they are charged to the employee whether or not: (1) the employee is guaranteed a minimum wage for services, or (2) the employee is entitled to be credited with any unsold newspapers or magazines which are turned back.

If a person under age 18 performs the work as an independent contractor, the work may be covered by Social Security as self-employment.

B-38. Are newspaper vendors who are 18 or over covered by Social Security?

Yes; but by special provision of the law, they are covered as self-employed persons even if they are employees.

AMERICANS EMPLOYED OUTSIDE THE U.S.

B-39. Is an American citizen who is employed by a foreign subsidiary of a U.S. Corporation covered by Social Security?

The Social Security Amendments of 1983 permit any American employer (a corporation, sole proprietorship, or partnership) to provide coverage for United States citizens and United States residents working outside the United States for a foreign affiliate when the American employer has not less than a 10% direct or indirect interest in the foreign employer. The employer must enter into an agreement with the Internal Revenue Service for the payment of Social Security taxes for such employees. All United States citizens and residents working for the subsidiary must be covered if any are to be covered. Prior to June 15, 1989, the agreement could have been terminated if it had been in effect for at least eight years and the employer had given two years advance notice. Currently, the employer may not terminate coverage for any workers in its foreign affiliates.

The President may enter into bilateral agreements with interested foreign countries to provide for limited coordination between the Social Security system of the United States and the equivalent system of the other country. These agreements, usually referred to as totalization agreements, have two main purposes: (1) to eliminate dual retirement, survivorship and disability coverage and taxation, the situation that occurs when a person from one country works in the other country and is required to pay Social Security and equivalent taxes to both countries for the same work, and (2) to eliminate situations in which workers lose benefit rights because they have divided their careers between two countries under an agreement. Such workers may qualify for partial United States or foreign benefits based on combined work credits from both countries. Each agreement must be transmitted to Congress with a report on the estimated cost and number of individuals affected. An agreement goes into effect if it is not rejected by either House of Congress within 90 days after both Houses have been in session.

FARMERS

B-40. Are self-employed farmers covered by Social Security?

Yes, but special rules apply for the reporting of farm income (see WAGES AND SELF-EMPLOYMENT INCOME, SECTION C).

RELIGIOUS SECTS

B-41. What persons can claim exclusion from Social Security because of their religious beliefs?

A person can claim exemption from the self-employment tax if he belongs to a religious sect (e.g., Old Order Amish), the teachings of which prevent him from accepting the benefits of any insurance, or social insurance, which makes payments in the event of death, disability, retirement, or for medical care. The sect must have been in existence at all times since 1950, and the exemption can be granted for all taxable years since 1950.

Prior to January 1, 1989, the exemption applied to self-employment income (e.g., farm income) only and not to earnings as an employee. Beginning on or after January 1, 1989, the exemption applies to the self-employed and their employees in cases where both the employee and the employer are members of a qualifying religious sect or division. This optional exemption applies to both the employer and employee portion of the Social Security tax.

45

Also, the exemption is available to employees of partnerships in which each partner holds a religious exemption from Social Security coverage. In addition, the exemption is available to workers in churches and church-controlled nonprofit organizations who are treated as self-employed because the employing church or organization exercised its option not to pay the employer portion of the Social Security tax.

Exemption is granted only if the individual files a waiver of all benefits under social security and only if he (or any person on his account) has never received any such benefits.

NONRESIDENT ALIENS

B-42. Is work done by nonresident aliens covered under Social Security?

Foreign students (nonimmigrant aliens) may be temporarily in the United States to attend a school or other recognized place of study approved by the Attorney General. On-campus work or work under permission granted by the Immigration and Naturalization Service which is done by these students is excluded from employment. Other work done by these foreign students is not excluded from employment.

Foreign students (nonimmigrant aliens) may be temporarily in the United States to pursue a vocational or nonacademic technical education approved by the Attorney General. Work done by these students to carry out the purpose for which they were admitted is excluded from employment. Other work done by these foreign students is not excluded from employment.

Exchange visitors (nonimmigrant aliens) may be temporarily in the United States to participate in exchange visitor programs designated by the Director of the United States Information Agency. Work done by these exchange visitors to carry out the purpose for which they were admitted and for which permission has been granted by the sponsor, is excluded from employment. Other work done by these exchange visitors is not excluded from employment.

Exchange visitors (nonimmigrant aliens) may be temporarily in the United States to participate in an international cultural exchange program approved by the Attorney General. Effective October 1, 1994, work done by these exchange students to carry out the purpose for which they were admitted is excluded from employment. Other work is not excluded from employment.

Work done by a foreign student's or exchange visitor's alien spouse or minor child who is also temporarily in the United States is usually not excluded from employment.

WAGES AND SELF-EMPLOYMENT INCOME

C-1. What earnings are subject to Social Security tax and are counted in computing Social Security benefits?

Earnings that are the *wages* of an employee or the *self-employment income* of a self-employed person. However, earnings are counted as "wages" or as "self-employment income" only if they are earned in employment or self-employment covered by the Social Security Act.

C-2. For Social Security purposes, what is meant by the term "wages"?

"Wages" mean pay received by an employee for employment covered by the Social Security Act. The maximum amount of wages subject to the Old-Age, Survivors and Disability Insurance tax (OASDI) and credited to a worker's Social Security record for any calendar year cannot exceed:

$3,000 received from each employer in any of the years	1937-1939
$3,000 paid in any of the years	1940-1950
$3,600 paid in any of the years	1951-1954
$4,200 paid in any of the years	1955-1958
$4,800 paid in any of the years	1959-1965
$6,600 paid in any of the years	1966-1967
$7,800 paid in any of the years	1968-1971
$9,000 paid in the year	1972
$10,800 paid in the year	1973
$13,200 paid in the year	1974
$14,100 paid in the year	1975
$15,300 paid in the year	1976
$16,500 paid in the year	1977
$17,700 paid in the year	1978
$22,900 paid in the year	1979
$25,900 paid in the year	1980
$29,700 paid in the year	1981
$32,400 paid in the year	1982
$35,700 paid in the year	1983
$37,800 paid in the year	1984
$39,600 paid in the year	1985
$42,000 paid in the year	1986
$43,800 paid in the year	1987
$45,000 paid in the year	1988
$48,000 paid in the year	1989
$51,300 paid in the year	1990
$53,400 paid in the year	1991
$55,500 paid in the year	1992
$57,600 paid in the year	1993
$60,600 paid in the year	1994
$61,200 paid in the year	1995
$62,700 paid in the year	1996
$65,400 paid in the year	1997
$68,400 paid in the year	1998
$72,600 paid in the year	1999
$76,200 paid in the year	2000
$80,400 paid in the year	2001

Employees pay the tax on wages up to the base amount from each employer, but receive a refund on their income tax returns for the excess of total taxes paid over the tax on the base amount. Each employer pays the tax on wages up to the base amount for all of its employees.

In addition to the regular Social Security tax on wages, all wages are subject to the Part A Medicare Hospital Insurance tax (HI). Formerly, the maximum taxable amount for HI was $135,000 in 1993 and was the same as for OASDI for years before 1991 (back to 1966, when the HI tax was first applicable).

The maximum earnings base is automatically adjusted each year by the Social Security Administration if average nationwide (covered and non-covered) total wages have increased.

Included in total wages is certain deferred compensation, including elective ("cash or deferred") contributions to 401(k) plans. Such compensation in the aggregate has been increasing more rapidly than other wages in recent years. For purposes of determining the maximum earnings base in 1990, an estimate of deferred compensation was included in the average wage for 1988, so that the maximum earnings base ($51,300) reflected what the result would have been if deferred compensation had been included in the average-wage computations in 1984-88. (It had not been included prior to 1990.) Actual deferred compensation amounts are used beginning with 1990 wages. For purposes of benefit computations and other program amounts, actual deferred compensation amounts are included in the average nationwide total wages beginning with 1990 wages, and the effect thereof is reflected in benefit computations and other program amounts beginning in 1993.

Benefits are automatically increased when the Consumer Price Index for All Urban Wage Earners and Clerical Workers from the third quarter of one year to the third quarter of the following year rises, and no general benefit increase has been enacted or become effective in the preceding year.

Benefits have been raised by the following percentages since 1977:

Month/Year	Increase in Benefits	Month/Year	Increase in Benefits
June 1977	5.9%	December 1989	4.7%
June 1978	6.5%	December 1990	5.4%
June 1979	9.9%	December 1991	3.7%
June 1980	14.3%	December 1992	3.0%
June 1981	11.2%	December 1993	2.6%
June 1982	7.4%	December 1994	2.8%
December 1983	3.5%	December 1995	2.6%
December 1984	3.5%	December 1996	2.9%
December 1985	3.1%	December 1997	2.1%
December 1986	1.3%	December 1998	1.3%
December 1987	4.2%	December 1999	2.4%
December 1988	4.0%	December 2000	3.5%

Note that the maximum amount of wages subject to the OASDI tax is also the maximum amount credited to a worker's record. For example, if an employee is paid $80,400 or less in 2001, the full amount of wages will be subject to OASDI tax and will be credited to the Social Security record for benefit purposes. But if an employee is paid $90,000 in 2001, only $80,400 will be subject to OASDI tax and credited to the Social Security record (but HI taxes will be paid on the entire $90,000).

In other words, earnings in excess of the maximum amount for a particular calendar year are not considered wages for Social Security coverage purposes.

A stabilizer provision protects the system from trust-fund depletions that could occur when price increases out-pace wage gains. This stabilizer provision goes into effect if reserves in the trust funds providing retirement, disability and survivor benefits fall below 20% of what is needed to meet outgo for a year. When the stabilizer takes effect, automatic cost-of-living benefit increases will be based on the lower of the annual percentage increase in the Consumer Price Index or the annual percentage rise in the nation's average wage.

Later, if the fund reserves exceed 32% of what is estimated to be needed for a year, recipients will be entitled to extra cost-of-living increases to compensate for losses in inflation protection resulting from having benefit increases tied to wage levels.

C-3. Are only payments in cash counted as wages?

No, amounts paid by check, promissory note, or in other media such as goods, clothing, board or lodging usually count as wages. In a few cases, however, only cash pay is counted (see C-14; Domestic and Household Workers, B-33; Non-business or Casual Employment, B-34; Agricultural Labor, B-35).

Any fringe benefit that is not specifically excluded from Social Security taxes is wages for Social Security purposes. The amount of wages is the difference between the discount price paid by the employee for the benefit and its fair market value.

The following five categories of fringe benefits are *not* wages:

(1) De minimus fringe (a property or service furnished by the employer which is so small in value that accounting for it would be administratively impractical).

(2) Gyms and other athletic facilities (the value of an employer-provided on-premises athletic facility).

(3) No additional cost service (any service provided by an employer to the employee for the employee's use).

(4) Qualified employee discount (employee discount with respect to property or services).

(5) Working condition fringe (any employer-provided service or property to the employee, such as a parking space).

Ordinarily only pay actually received by the employee in a calendar year is counted as wages for that year. However, pay that is "constructively received" during the year is also counted. Wages are constructively received when they have been credited or set apart for the employee without any substantial limitation or restriction on the time or manner of payment and are available to him so that he can get them at any time. A special provision applies to pay under a nonqualified deferred compensation plan which is generally based on payments made after 1983.

C-4. Are employer payments for group life insurance covered wages?

The cost of group term life insurance that is includable in the gross income of the employee is considered "wages" subject to Social Security tax. IRC Sec. 3121(a)(2). This provision applies generally to group term life insurance coverage in effect after December 31, 1987, but does not apply to coverage of former employees who separated from service before January 1, 1989, to the extent the cost is not for any period the employee was employed by the employer after separation.

The general rule is that the employee may exclude the cost of the first $50,000 of employer-provided group term life insurance from income. Therefore, generally, only the cost of coverage in excess of $50,000 will be subject to the Social Security tax.

The employer is required to report amounts includable in the wages of current employees for purposes of the Social Security tax on the employees' W-2. Generally, the employer may treat the wages as though paid on any basis so long as they are treated as paid at least once each year.

For group term life insurance coverage provided after December 31, 1990, the Social Security tax must be paid by the employee if the payment for the group term life insurance is considered wages and is for periods during which there is no longer an employment relationship between the employer and the employee. The employer is required to state the portion of an employee's wages which consist of payments for group term life insurance and the amount of the Social Security tax separately.

C-5. Are vacation pay and severance pay wages?

Yes, but the Internal Revenue Service ruled in 1996 that contributions of an employee's forfeitable vacation pay benefit to a qualified stock purchase plan with a cash or deferred arrangement are excludable from gross wages for Social Security purposes.

The company involved in the ruling had established a qualified stock purchase plan with profit sharing features and cash or deferred arrangements. Company employees were entitled to annual leave based on years of service and had to use it during the same year or forfeit it. Employees who did not use all of their paid vacation in excess of two weeks could elect to have the equivalent in pay contributed to the qualified plan. The employees could take the vacation time, forfeit the time, or contribute its value to the plan. They did not have the option to receive cash or any other taxable benefit in lieu of the contribution to the plan. Thus, the Internal Revenue Service considered the contribution of vacation pay to be a nonelective employer contribution and excluded from wages for Social Security purposes under IRC Sec. 3121(a)(5)(A). TAM 9635002.

C-6. Are payments on account of sickness or accident disability counted as wages for Social Security purposes?

Payments made to or on behalf of an employee or an employee's dependents for sickness or disability are generally considered wages. The following payments, however, are specifically excluded from the definition of wages:

(1) Any payment that an employer makes to an employee, or on the employee's behalf, on account of the employee's sickness or accident disability, or related medical or hospitalization expenses, if the payment is made more than six consecutive months following the last calendar month in which the employee worked for the employer. Payments made during the six consecutive months are included as wages.

(2) The exclusion listed in (1) above also applies to any payment made by a third party (such as an insurance company). In addition, if the employee contributed to the employer's sick pay plan, that portion of the third party payments attributable to the employee's contribution is not wages.

(3) Payments of medical or hospitalization expenses connected with sickness or accident disability are excluded from wages beginning with the first payment only if made under a plan or system of the employer for medical or hospitalization expenses connected with sickness or accident disability.

(4) Payments under workers' compensation law are not wages.

For payments to be excluded under a plan or system, the plan must provide for all employees generally or for a class or classes of employees. Some or all of the following features may also be a part of the plan:

- Set a definite basis for determining who is eligible, such as length of service, occupation or salary classification; and

- Set definite standards for determining the minimum duration of payments; and

- Provide a formula for determining the minimum amount to be paid an eligible employee.

Sick pay that is not paid under a plan or system by the employer is counted as wages for Social Security purposes if paid before the end of six calendar months after the last month in which the employee worked.

C-7. Are payments made under a deferred compensation plan counted as wages?

Generally, under a special timing rule, the "amount deferred" by an employee under a traditional nonqualified deferred compensation plan — whether a salary reduction or supplemental plan, whether a funded or unfunded plan, or whether a private or (eligible or ineligible) Section 457 plan — of an employer covered by the Social Security tax is considered "wages" for Social Security tax purposes at the *later of*: (1) when the services are performed, or (2) when the employee's rights to such amount are no longer subject to a substantial risk of forfeiture. IRC Sec. 3121(v)(2)(A). Once an amount is treated as wages, it, and any income attributable to it, will not be treated as wages for Social Security tax purposes in any later year. IRC Sec. 3121(v)(2)(B).

In general, many employees would prefer to have amounts deferred treated as wages for Social Security purposes at the time the services are performed. At such time, their salaries, in all likelihood, already exceed the Social Security taxable wage base (in 2001, $80,400 for OASDI), and the amounts deferred would thus escape Social Security taxes. (Remember, however, that the HI tax applies to all wages.)

Regulations expressly identify certain plans and benefits that do not provide for the deferral of compensation for Social Security tax purposes: stock options, stock appreciation rights, and other stock value rights; some restricted property received in connection with the performance of services; compensatory time, disability pay, severance pay, and death benefits; certain benefits provided in connection with impending termination, including window benefits; excess (golden) parachute payments; benefits established 12 months before an employee's termination if indication that benefits were provided in contemplation of termination; benefits established after termination of employment; and compensation paid for current services. Regs. §§31.3121(v)(2)-1(b)(4), 31.3306(r)(2)-1(a).

Under the regulations, the manner in which the amount deferred for a period is determined depends upon whether the nonqualified deferred compensation plan is an *account balance plan* or a *nonaccount balance plan*. If the plan is an *account balance plan*, the amount deferred for a period equals the principal amount credited to the employee's account for the period, increased or decreased by any income or loss attributable to the principal amount through the date the principal amount is required to be taken into account as wages for Social Security tax purposes. A plan is an *account balance plan* only if, under the terms of the plan, a principal amount is credited to an individual account for an employee, the income attributable to each principal account is credited or debited to the individual account, and the benefits payable to the employee are based solely on the balance credited to the individual account. Regs. §§31.3121(v)(2)-1(c)(1), 31.3306(r)(2)-1(a); see also Let. Rul. 9417013 (amounts deferred in defined-contribution-type plan with delayed vesting arc amounts attributable to employer contributions when such amounts vest).

If the plan is a *nonaccount balance plan*, the amount deferred for a period equals the present value of the additional future payment or payments to which the employee has obtained a legally binding right under the plan during that period.

C-8. Are payments made to or from a qualified pension or annuity plan counted as wages?

No, neither the employer's contribution to the plan nor payments to the employee from the plan are treated as wages. They are not subject to Social Security tax and are not creditable for benefit purposes.

The following payments made to or under a deferred compensation plan are *excludable* from the definition of wages:

(1) Payments made from or to qualified pension, profit-sharing, or stock bonus plans if, at the time of payment, the trust is exempt from tax under IRC Sec. 501(a), unless the payment is made to an employee of the trust as remuneration for services rendered as an employee and not as a beneficiary of the trust. IRC Sec. 3121(a)(5)(A).

(2) Payments made under or to an IRC Sec. 403(a) annuity plan. IRC Sec. 3121(a)(5)(B).

(3) Payments made under a simplified employee pension (SEP), other than any contributions made pursuant to a salary reduction agreement described in IRC Sec. 408(k)(6). IRC Sec. 3121(a)(5)(C).

(4) Payments under an annuity contract described in IRC Sec. 403(b), other than a payment for the purchase of the contract which is made by reason of a salary reduction agreement (whether evidenced by a written instrument or otherwise). IRC Sec. 3121(a)(5)(D).

(5) Payments under or to an exempt governmental deferred compensation plan. IRC Sec. 3121(a)(5)(E).

(6) Payments to supplement pension benefits under a plan or trust described above to take into account some or all of the increase in the cost of living since retirement. IRC Sec. 3121(a)(5)(F).

(7) Payments under a cafeteria plan (IRC Sec. 125) if the payment is not treated as wages without regard to the plan and it is reasonable to believe that IRC Sec. 125 would not treat any wages as constructively received. IRC Sec. 3121(a)(5)(G).

(8) Payments under a SIMPLE IRA plan arrangement, other than elective contributions under IRC Sec. 408(p)(2)(A)(i). IRC Sec. 3121(a)(5)(H).

(9) Amounts exempted from Section 457 requirements under Section 457(e)(11)(A)(ii) (plans paying solely length of service awards to bona fide volunteers (or their beneficiaries) on account of qualified services performed by such volunteers) and maintained by an eligible employer. IRC Sec. 3121(a)(5)(I).

C-9. If a teacher takes a reduction in salary to provide funds for a tax-sheltered annuity, how are his wages computed for Social Security purposes?

The salary before the reduction will be treated as wages. See IRC Sec. 3121(a)(5)(D); Rev. Rul. 65-208, 1965-2 CB 383. In other words, the amount of reduction, although paid to the insurer by the employer, is nevertheless not considered an employer contribution to a retirement fund. For example, suppose that a teacher, whose salary is $45,000, takes a $2,000 salary cut for 2000 so that this amount can be used to purchase a tax-sheltered annuity for his benefit. Social Security taxes will still be payable on the full $45,000, and this is the amount which will be credited to the teacher's Social Security account for benefit purposes.

Employer payments from employer funds into such plans are excluded from wages. Prior to 1984, employer payments were usually wages.

C-10. Are cash tips considered wages?

Tips received by an employee in the course of employment by any one employer are wages for Social Security purposes if the tips total $20 or more in a calendar month. This includes all tips received directly from customers, tips from charge customers that are paid by the employer to the employee, and any tips received under a tip-splitting arrangement. Noncash tips, such as passes, tickets or services, are not counted as wages. Tips are considered received when the employee reports the tips to the employer. If the employee fails to report the tips to the employer, the tips are treated as received when the employee actually received them.

For each calendar month during which an employee receives $20 or more in tips, the employee must give the employer a written statement of cash and charge tips by the 10th day of the month after the month in which the tips are received. IRS Form 4070 (Employee's Report of Tips to Employer) is available for this purpose.

A club, hotel, or restaurant may require customers to pay a service charge, which is given to the employees. The employee's share of this service charge is not a tip, but is part of wages paid to the employee by the employer.

(For method of reporting tips, see SOCIAL SECURITY TAXES, SECTION J.)

C-11. Do wages include the portion of an employee's Social Security taxes paid by an employer?

Yes, except for domestic service in the private home of the employer and agricultural labor. However, payments by a state or local employer are wages for Social Security tax purposes only if the payment is pursuant to a salary reduction agreement (whether evidenced by a written instrument or otherwise). The term salary reduction agreement includes any salary reduction arrangement, regardless of whether there is approval or choice of participation by individual employees or whether such approval or choice is mandated by state statute.

C-12. Are salesperson's commissions wages?

They are wages if the salesperson is an employee. (For rules to determine whether a commission salesperson is an employee, see B-10.) Where the commissions are the sole pay and no advances are given, the commissions are wages in the calendar year in which they are paid. However, where advances are made against future commissions, the year in which the advances are paid is the year to which the amount advanced is credited.

C-13. Under what circumstances are the first-year and renewal commissions of a life insurance agent treated as wages?

If the agent is an *employee* when the policy is sold, both first-year and renewal commissions are treated as wages when they are *paid* to him. (For rules to determine whether a life insurance agent is an employee, see B-11.) Thus, the commissions are subject to the employer-employee tax in each year as he receives them (see SOCIAL SECURITY TAXES, SECTION J). For retirement test purposes, however, if the agent is an employee when the policy is sold, both first-year and renewal commissions are treated as "earned" in the month and year in which the policy was sold (see LOSS OF BENEFITS BECAUSE OF EXCESS EARNINGS, SECTION H).

C-14. Is the value of meals and lodging furnished by an employer to an employee considered wages for Social Security taxation purposes?

The Supreme Court has held that the value of meals and lodging furnished to an employee for the convenience of the employer is not wages for Social Security coverage and tax purposes. *Rowan Companies, Inc. v. U.S.*, 452 U.S. 247 (1981).

Such meals must be provided at the employer's place of business. The employee must accept lodging at the employer's place of business in order for the value of the lodging to be excluded from wages.

The Social Security Amendments of 1983 state, however, that the exclusion of income from income tax withholding by the employer does not necessarily affect the treatment of the income for Social Security coverage and taxation purposes in other cases.

SELF-EMPLOYMENT INCOME

C-15. What is taxable and creditable self-employment income?

It is that part of an individual's net earnings from self-employment which is subject to Social Security tax and counted for Social Security benefits. In determining what part of a person's net earnings from self-employment is creditable for Social Security purposes, the following rules apply:

- 92.35% of all net earnings from self-employment is taxable and creditable self-employment income unless the trade, business or profession is not covered by the Social Security Act. The 92.35% factor has been used only in 1990 and after (when the self-employed first began paying the full employer-employee tax rate).

- If such amount for the taxable year is less than $400, the net earnings are not treated as self-employment income. That is, no Social Security tax is paid on the net earnings, and they are not credited to the person's Social Security account. (But see C-18.)

- The maximum amount of self-employment income for a taxable year that is subject to the Old-Age, Survivors and Disability Insurance tax (OASDI) and used to determine benefits cannot exceed:

$80,400	2001
$76,200	2000
$72,600	1999
$68,400	1998
$65,400	1997
$62,700	1996
$61,200	1995
$60,600	1994
$57,600	1993
$55,500	1992
$53,400	1991
$51,300	1990
$48,000	1989
$45,000	1988
$43,800	1987
$42,000	1986
$39,600	1985
$37,800	1984
$35,700	1983
$32,400	1982
$29,700	1981
$25,900	1980
$22,900	1979
$17,700	1978
$16,500	1977
$15,300	1976
$14,100	1975
$13,200	1974
$10,800	1973
$9,000	1972
$7,800	1968-1971
$6,600	1966-1967
$4,800	1959-1965
$4,200	1955-1958
$3,600	1951-1954

There is no limit to the amount of self-employment income subject to the (Part A) Medicare Hospital Insurance tax (HI). The HI tax applies to all self-employment income.

Net earnings in excess of the maximum amount for a particular taxable year are not considered self-employment income for Social Security purposes. No maximum amounts are given for years prior to 1951 since no self-employment was covered before 1951. (See B-15.)

C-16. How is the amount of self-employment income figured if a person has both wages and net earnings from self-employment in the same year?

If a person has both wages (as an employee) and net earnings from self-employment in a taxable year, then *self-employment income* is the difference,

57

if any, between wages and the maximum Social Security earnings base for that year (see C-15).

Example. Mr. Smith, an attorney, is employed as an instructor in a law school. In 2001, he draws a salary of $15,000 from the school and also earns $80,000 in private practice, which counts as $73,880 for Social Security purposes (i.e., 92.35% of $80,000). His self-employment income for OASDI purposes for 2001 is $65,400 ($80,400 maximum less $15,000 wages). Only $65,400 is subject to self-employment Social Security tax. $15,000 is subject to the employer-employee tax. Note, however, that $73,880 of the $80,000 earned in private practice is subject to the Part A Medicare Hospital Insurance tax for self-employed individuals. In addition, Mr. Smith must pay the Medicare Hospital Insurance tax for employees on the $15,000 he earned as a law school instructor.

C-17. In general, what constitutes net earnings from self-employment?

Net earnings from self-employment may be the net income from a trade, business or profession carried on by the individual alone, or it may be his distributive share of the ordinary net income of a partnership. In computing net earnings from self-employment, gross income and deductions are, for the most part, the same as for income tax purposes. However, the following differences must be taken into account:

• Rentals from real estate are excluded in determining net earnings from self-employment unless: (1) the rentals are received in the course of a trade or business by a real estate dealer, or (2) services are rendered primarily for the convenience of the occupants of the premises, as in the case of hotels, motels, etc. (but income from renting property for business or commercial use, such as a store, factory, office space, etc. is excluded regardless of the amount of services rendered to the tenant), or (3) in the case of farm rentals, the farm landlord materially participates in the management or in the production of farm commodities on land rented to someone else.

• Dividends on stock and interest on bonds do not count for Social Security unless they are received in the course of business by a dealer in stocks or securities. The term "bond" includes debentures, notes, certificates, and other evidence of indebtedness issued with interest coupons or in registered form by a corporation. Bonds also include government bonds. Other interest received in the course of a trade or business does count for Social Security. For example, interest received by a merchant on accounts or notes receivable are included in computing net earnings from self-employment.

• Partnerships are treated as individuals when it comes to the dividend and interest exclusion. Dividends and interest on securities held for investment are excluded from net earnings of the partners. However, if a partnership is in business as a securities dealer, income on the securities held for resale by the partnership is included as net earnings of the partners.

- Capital gains and losses, and gains and losses from the sale or exchange of property which is not inventory or stock in trade, are excluded in computing net earnings from self-employment.

- Retirement payments received by a retired partner from a partnership of which the individual is a member or a former member are excluded from net earnings from self-employment if the following conditions are met:

(1) The payments are made under a written plan of the partnership which provides for periodic payments because of retirement, to partners generally or to a class or classes of partners, to continue at least until the partner's death; and

(2) The partner rendered no services in any business conducted by the partnership (or its successors) during the taxable year of the partnership ending within or with the taxable year in which such payments were received; and

(3) At the end of the partnership's taxable year there is no obligation from the other partners to the retired partner other than for the retirement payments under the plan; and

(4) The partner's share in the capital of the partnership has been paid in full by the end of the partnership's taxable year.

- No deductions for net operating losses of other years are permitted in determining net earnings from self-employment.

- The following retirement benefits for ministers are not considered earnings from self-employment:

(1) Retirement benefits received from a church plan after retirement.

(2) The rental value or allowance of a parsonage, including utilities, furnished to the minister after retirement.

- Income taxable as "dividends" to shareholders of a Subchapter S corporation (a corporation electing not to be taxed as a corporation) is not considered "net earnings from self-employment." (But see B-7.)

C-18. If an individual's earnings from self-employment are quite low, is there a special provision available?

Yes. If the individual had at least $400 per year of earnings from nonfarm self-employment (after reduction by the 92.35% factor mentioned in C-15) in two of the preceding three years and gross income from self-employment for the taxable year is $2,400 or less, the individual can report either actual net income or two-thirds of gross income.

If the individual's gross income from nonfarm self-employment is over $2,400, and net income is over $1,600, the individual reports actual net income. But if gross income is over $2,400, and net income is less than $1,600, the individual may report either actual net income or $1,600. This provision also applies to partnerships.

Note that a non-farmer may use this method only if net earnings from self-employment are less than $1,600 *and* less than two-thirds of gross income from *all* trades and businesses carried on by the non-farmer. In addition, this option can only be used five times in nonfarm self-employment by one individual.

C-19. How does a self-employed life insurance agent report first-year and renewal commissions?

If the agent is self-employed *when the policy is sold*, commissions are treated as earnings from self-employment in the year they are paid to the agent. It is immaterial whether the agent is an employee or self-employed when the commissions are received. For retirement test purposes, renewal commissions paid to a self-employed agent after retirement are not included as earnings after the initial month of retirement if they were the result of services rendered prior to retirement. (For rules to determine whether a life insurance agent is an employee or self-employed, see B-11.) (For treatment of commissions as "earnings" for "retirement test" purposes, see LOSS OF BENEFITS BECAUSE OF EXCESS EARNINGS, SECTION H.)

INSURED STATUS

D-1. How does a person become qualified for retirement, survivor and disability benefits under Social Security?

By becoming "insured." Most types of benefits are payable if the person is *fully* insured. Some types of benefits are payable if the person is either *fully* or *currently* insured. A special insured status is required for disability benefits (see D-18).

A person becomes insured by acquiring a certain number of *quarters of coverage*.

QUARTERS OF COVERAGE

D-2. What is meant by a "calendar quarter"?

A "calendar quarter" means a period of three calendar months ending March 31, June 30, September 30, or December 31 of any year.

D-3. How are quarters of coverage determined for an employee?

1. For 2001, an employee receives one quarter of coverage for each $830 of earnings up to a maximum of four quarters.

    Example. Mrs. Hall works for two months in 2001 and earns $1,700. She is credited with two quarters of coverage for the year because she receives one quarter of coverage for each $830 of earnings, up to a maximum of four. In order to receive four quarters of coverage in 2001, Mrs. Hall would have needed earnings totaling $3,320 ($830 x 4 = $3,320).

    This method of determining quarters of coverage will be used for years after 2001 also, but the measure of earnings ($830 in 2001) will automatically increase each year to take account of increases in average wages.

    However, see D-6 for quarters that cannot be counted as quarters of coverage regardless of whether the earnings requirement has been met.

2. For years prior to 1978, an employee receives one quarter of coverage for each quarter in which wages paid were $50 or more in covered employment. In addition, each quarter of the year is counted as a quarter of

61

coverage if the employee's total wages (or wages and self-employment income) for any calendar year equal or exceed the maximum Social Security earnings base for that year. This is true even if the employee receives no wages in some of the quarters. (Maximum earnings creditable for calendar years before 1978 are shown in C-2.)

Example. Mr. Brown is unemployed from January 1, 1977 to May 1, 1977. During the last eight months of the year he worked in covered employment and was paid over $16,500 (the maximum Social Security earnings base for 1977). He is credited with four quarters of coverage for 1977 even though he received no wages in the first quarter.

3. For years after 1977 and before 2001, the amount of earnings needed for one quarter of coverage is as follows:

Year	Earnings for Quarter of Coverage
2000	$780
1999	740
1998	700
1997	670
1996	640
1995	630
1994	620
1993	590
1992	570
1991	540
1990	520
1989	500
1988	470
1987	460
1986	440
1985	410
1984	390
1983	370
1982	340
1981	310
1980	290
1979	260
1978	250

D-4. How are quarters of coverage determined for a self-employed person?

Quarters of coverage for self-employed persons are determined by using two different methods; one for years prior to 1978 and another for 1978 and after.

1. In 2001, a self-employed person receives one quarter of coverage for each $830 of earnings, up to a maximum of four.

2. The amount of earnings needed for one quarter of coverage between 1978 and 2000 is as follows:

Year	Earnings for Quarter of Coverage
2000	$780
1999	740
1998	700
1997	670
1996	640
1995	630
1994	620
1993	590
1992	570
1991	540
1990	520
1989	500
1988	470
1987	460
1986	440
1985	410
1984	390
1983	370
1982	340
1981	310
1980	290
1979	260
1978	250

3. For years prior to 1978, a self-employed person acquires four quarters of coverage for each calendar year in which the person has been credited with $400 or more of self-employment income. A self-employed person must have at least $400 in net earnings from covered self-employment in a taxable year before any of such net earnings can be counted as self-employment income. (For definition of the terms "net earnings from self-employment" and "self-employment income," see WAGES AND SELF-EMPLOYMENT INCOME, SECTION C.)

The method of determining quarters of coverage described in items 1 and 2 will be used for years after 2001 also, but the measure of earnings ($830 in 2001) will automatically increase each year to take account of increases in average wages.

(For calendar quarters that cannot be counted as quarters of coverage in any event, see D-6.)

D-5. How does a farm employee acquire quarters of coverage?

For years prior to 1978, a farm employee is credited with quarters of coverage based on total cash wages paid to the employee for farm work during a calendar year rather than on the amount of wages paid to the employee during a calendar quarter. A farm employee is credited with one quarter of coverage for each $100 in cash wages paid during the year as follows:

63

If the cash wages in a year prior to 1978 amount to:	The number of quarters of coverage credited is:
$400 or more	4
$300-$399.99	3
$200-$299.99	2
$100-$199.99	1
Under $100	0

In 2001, a farm employee receives one quarter of coverage for each $830 of earnings, up to a maximum of four.

The amount of earnings needed for one quarter of coverage prior to 2001 and after 1977 is as follows:

Year	Earnings for Quarter of Coverage
2000	$780
1999	740
1998	700
1997	670
1996	640
1995	630
1994	620
1993	590
1992	570
1991	540
1990	520
1989	500
1988	470
1987	460
1986	440
1985	410
1984	390
1983	370
1982	340
1981	310
1980	290
1979	260
1978	250

This method of determining quarters of coverage will be used for years after 2001 also, but the measure of earnings ($830 in 2001) will automatically increase each year to take account of increases in average wages.

D-6. What calendar quarters cannot be counted as quarters of coverage even though the earnings requirement has been met?

A calendar quarter cannot be a quarter of coverage if:

- It begins after the calendar quarter in which the person died.

- It has not started yet.

- It is within a period of disability that is excluded in figuring benefit rights (see COMPUTING BENEFITS, SECTION F). (However, the beginning and ending quarters of a prior disability period may be counted as quarters of coverage if the earnings requirement is met in these quarters.)

Example. Mr. Smith dies on June 24, 2001 after having earned $80,400 (the maximum earnings base for 2001). Normally he would be credited with four quarters of coverage for that year (see D-3). However, he is credited with only two because the quarters after his death cannot be counted.

D-7. Can quarters of coverage be acquired at any age?

Yes, quarters of coverage can be acquired even before age 21 or after retirement age.

D-8. Are quarters of coverage used in determining the size of a person's Social Security benefits?

No, quarters of coverage are used only to determine insured status. The law provides an exact method for computing benefits based on the person's average monthly earnings or average indexed monthly earnings. Calendar years are used in making the computation. (See COMPUTING BENEFITS, SECTION F.)

FULLY INSURED

D-9. How does a person become fully insured?

By acquiring a sufficient number of quarters of coverage to meet either of these two tests:

1. A person is fully insured if he has 40 quarters of coverage (a total of 10 years in covered work). Once a person has acquired 40 quarters of coverage he is fully insured for life, even if he spends no further time in covered employment or covered self-employment.

2. A person is fully insured if: (a) he has at least six quarters of coverage, and (b) he has acquired at least as many quarters of coverage as there are years elapsing *after* 1950 (or, if later, after the year in which he reaches age 21) and *before* the year in which he dies, becomes disabled, or reaches, or will reach age 62, whichever occurs first. (However, if a year, or any part of a year, fell within an established period of disability, that year need not be counted.) Note that prior to 1975, there is a transition period in effect for men. See D-11 and D-15.

The two tests above serve only to determine the *number* of quarters of coverage needed to be fully insured. It is immaterial when these quarters of coverage were acquired (but they can be acquired only after 1936). Also, in applying test No. 2, it is not necessary that the quarters of coverage be acquired during the elapsed period. All quarters of coverage, whether within or outside the elapsed period, are counted to determine whether the person has the required number.

(For method of determining fully insured status for retirement benefits, see D-10 to D-14. For method of determining fully insured status for survivors' benefits, see D-15. For method of determining fully insured status for disability benefits, see D-18.)

D-10. Must a person be fully insured to qualify for retirement benefits?

Yes, in addition to other requirements (see BENEFITS, SECTION E), a person must be fully insured.

D-11. How do you determine the number of quarters of coverage needed for a person to be fully insured for retirement benefits?

Count the number of years *after* 1950 (or, if later, after the year in which the person attained age 21), and *before* attaining age 62. (But do not count a year any part of which was in an established period of disability.) Generally, this is the minimum number of quarters of coverage a person will need to be fully insured. However, the person must have at least six quarters of coverage to be fully insured, and a person is fully insured in any event if the person has 40 or more quarters of coverage.

The 1972 amendments provided for a change in the retirement benefit computation point for men from age 65 to age 62 (the computation point in effect for women). The change became fully effective for men born in 1913 and reaching age 62 in 1975. For those born in 1911, the computation point is age 64 and for those born in 1912, it is age 63.

See TABLE 2, for minimum numbers of quarters of coverage needed to be fully insured for retirement benefits.

Example (1). Mr. Gray applies for retirement benefits in 2001; he attained age 62 in 1999. He needs 40 quarters of coverage to be fully insured (there are 40 years between 1958 and 1999, the year he attained age 62).

Example (2). Mr. Brown applied for retirement benefits in 1979, the year he attained age 65. He needed 25 quarters of coverage to be fully insured (there are 25 years between 1950 and 1976, the year he attained age 62).

Example (3). Miss Black applies for retirement benefits in 2001, the year she attains age 65. She needs 40 quarters of coverage to be fully insured (there are 40 years between 1957 and 1998, the year she attained age 62).

Example (4). Mr. Green was born in 1939 and will be 62 in 2001. Normally, he would need 40 quarters of coverage to be fully insured for retirement benefits. Suppose, however, that Mr. Green has a period of disability lasting from August 1968 to February 1970. He would need only 37 quarters of coverage to be fully insured for retirement benefits (the three years, 1968-1970, would not be counted in determining the number of quarters of coverage required.)

D-12. Does a woman need fewer quarters of coverage than a man to be fully insured for retirement benefits?

No, the determination for men and women is the same. However, women who reached age 62 before 1975 needed fewer quarters of coverage than men to be fully insured for retirement benefits. (See D-11.)

D-13. Can a person be fully insured for retirement benefits even though not working in covered employment for many years?

Yes. To be fully insured for retirement benefits a person needs at least as many quarters of coverage as there are years after 1950 (or, if later, the year of the person's 21st birthday) and before the year when the person reaches age 62. However, it is immaterial when these quarters of coverage were acquired.

Example. Mrs. Luck was born in 1936. In 2001 (at age 65) she applied for retirement benefits. She needs 40 quarters of coverage to be fully insured (1 quarter of coverage for each year between 1957 and 1998). Mrs. Luck worked in covered employment for 10 years (acquiring 40 quarters of coverage) prior to her 35th birthday in 1971. Mrs. Luck is fully insured — she has the required 40 quarters of coverage.

D-14. Can a person become fully insured after retirement age?

Yes. A person can acquire quarters of coverage after age 62.

D-15. How do you determine the number of quarters of coverage needed for a person to be fully insured at death?

Count the number of years *after* 1950 or, if later, after the year in which the person reached age 21, and *before* the year the person dies. (But do not count a year any part of which was in an established period of disability.) A person needs at least this many quarters of coverage to be fully insured at death. However, no person can be fully insured with less than six quarters of coverage; and a person is fully insured in any event with 40 quarters of coverage.

NOTE: A person born in 1929 reached age 21 in 1950. Consequently, for persons born in 1929 or before, count the years after 1950 and before the year of death. For persons born after 1929, see TABLE 3 for year of 21st birthday.

Example. Mr. Smith, who was born in 1938, dies in 2001. He is fully insured if he has 40 quarters of coverage (there are 40 years between 1959, the year he reached age 21, and 2001, the year in which he died, so that the maximum of 40 quarters of coverage applies).

Example. Mr. Jones, who was born in 1959, dies in 2001. He is fully insured if he has 20 quarters of coverage (there are 20 years between 1980, the year in which he reached age 21, and 2001, the year in which he died).

The above rule applies to persons who die before age 62. If a person dies after reaching age 62, count only the years between 1950 (or the year of attainment of age 21, if later) and age 62.

CURRENTLY INSURED

D-16. What benefits are payable if a person is only currently insured at death?

Child's benefits, mother's or father's benefits, and the lump sum death payment. Benefits for a widow(er) age 60 or over, and benefits for a dependent parent, are payable only if the worker was *fully insured* at death.

D-17. When is a person currently insured?

A person is currently insured if he has at least six quarters of coverage during the full 13-quarter period ending with the calendar quarter in which he: (1) died, or (2) most recently became entitled to disability benefits, or (3) became entitled to retirement benefits.

The six quarters of coverage need not be consecutive, but they must be acquired *during* the 13-quarter period. Since insured status is based on quarters of coverage, one can work for as little as two months in two different years and be currently insured. (Calendar quarters any part of which are in an established prior period of disability are not counted in figuring the 13 quarter period, except that the first and last quarters of the disability period are counted if they are quarters of coverage.)

Example. Mrs. Smith, who reached age 21 in 1996, dies in February, 2001. Mrs. Smith had started to work in covered employment on October 1, 1999 and worked until her death. During that period, she acquired nine quarters of coverage (four in 1999, because her earnings in October-December were at least $2,960; four in 2000, because her earnings in the year were at least $3,120; and one in 2001, because her earnings in January and February were at least $830). Mrs. Smith was currently insured at death because she had more than the required six quarters of coverage in the 13-calendar-quarter period.

INSURED STATUS FOR DISABILITY BENEFITS AND DISABILITY "FREEZE"

D-18. What insured status requirements must be met to qualify a person for disability benefits?

A person is insured for disability benefits if fully insured (see D-15) and:

1.   Has at least 20 of the quarters during a 40-quarter period ending with the quarter in which the person is determined to be disabled, that is the quarter the waiting period begins, and

2.   Is fully insured in that quarter by having at least one credit for each calendar year after 1950, or if later, after the year in which the person attained age 21, and prior to the year in which the person attains age 62 or dies or becomes disabled, whichever occurs earlier.

In order to meet the 20-out-of-40 quarters requirement, the 20 quarters of coverage need not be consecutive, but they must all be acquired during the 40-quarter period. (A quarter any part of which was included in a prior period of disability is not counted as one of the 40 quarters unless it was a quarter of coverage and was either the first or last quarter of the period.) Generally speaking, this requirement is met if the person has worked five years in covered employment or covered self-employment out of the last 10 years before disability.

Special insured status is needed by individuals who are disabled before age 31 to qualify for disability benefits or to establish a period of disability. The special insured status requirements are met if in the quarter that disability is determined to have begun or in a later quarter, a person:

1.   Is disabled before the quarter in which age 31 is attained, and

2.   Has credits in one-half of the quarters during the period beginning with the quarter after the quarter in which the person attained age 21 and ending with the quarter in which the person became disabled.

The credits must be earned in this period. If the number of elapsing quarters is an odd number, the next lower even number is used, and a minimum of six credits is required. If a person became disabled before the quarter in which age 24 is attained, the person must have six quarters of coverage in the 12-quarter period ending with the quarter in which the disability began.

A special insured status can apply to disabled individuals over age 31 who had a previous period of disability established prior to the attainment of age 31; had then met, and currently meet, the special insured requirements (as set out above); and who do not currently meet the 20/40 rule or fully insured status requirements.

To qualify for entitlement to disability benefits, fully insured status is required for a person who meets the statutory definition of blindness.

If a disability period is established for a person, his earnings record is frozen, and the period of disability may be excluded in determining his insured status when he becomes eligible for retirement benefits or dies. The disability period may also be excluded in figuring his Primary Insurance Amount for benefit purposes (see COMPUTING BENEFITS, SECTION F). The same insured status is required to qualify a person for a disability "freeze" as is required for disability benefits.

ALTERNATE METHOD FOR DETERMINING QUARTERS OF COVERAGE BEFORE 1951

D-19. What alternate method can be used in determining the number of quarters of coverage earned before 1951?

One quarter of coverage can be counted for each $400 of total wages earned before 1951. This alternate method cannot be used, however, unless: (1) the person will be fully insured on the basis of quarters of coverage before 1951 (derived by this method) plus quarters of coverage, if any, acquired after 1950, and (2) the individual's "elapsed years" are not less than seven (see D-9).

BENEFITS

RETIREMENT AND DISABILITY BENEFITS

E-1. What Social Security benefits are available for retired or disabled workers and their families?

- A monthly Retirement benefit for a retired worker, (see E-2 to E-11).

- A monthly Disability benefit for a disabled worker, (see E-12 to E-28).

- A monthly Spouse's benefit for a retired or disabled worker's spouse if: (1) at least 62 years old, or (2) caring for at least one child (under age 16, or over age 16 and disabled if disability began before age 22) of the retired or disabled worker (see E-29 to E-37).

- A monthly Child's benefit for a retired or disabled worker's child if the child is: (1) under age 18, or (2) age 18 and a full-time high school or elementary school student, or (3) age 18 or over and disabled if the disability began before age 22 (see E-38 to E-53).

RETIREMENT BENEFIT

E-2. In general, what requirements must be met to qualify a person for retirement benefits?

An individual is entitled to a retirement benefit if he or she: (1) is fully insured, (2) is at least age 62 throughout the first month of entitlement, and (3) has filed an application for retirement benefits.

E-3. Must a person be fully insured to qualify for retirement benefits?

Yes. (But a small monthly benefit is payable to some men who became age 72 before 1972 and some women who became age 72 before 1970).

E-4. What is the earliest age at which a person can start to receive retirement benefits?

Age 62. A retired worker who is fully insured can elect to start receiving a reduced benefit at any time between ages 62 and normal retirement age (which is gradually increasing from 65 to 67, see below), or wait until reaching normal retirement age and receive the full benefit rate. A person is not required to be

71

completely retired to receive retirement benefits. A person is considered "retired" if the retirement test is met. (See LOSS OF BENEFITS BECAUSE OF EXCESS EARNINGS, SECTION H). A fully insured person age 65 or over can receive retirement benefits even if not retired and regardless of the amount earned.

The retirement age when unreduced benefits are available (previously age 65) will increase by two months per year for workers reaching age 62 in 2000-2005. It will be age 66 for workers reaching age 62 in 2006-2016. It will increase again by two months per year for workers reaching age 62 in 2017-2022. Finally, the retirement age will be age 67 for workers reaching age 62 after 2022 (i.e., reaching age 67 in 2027). See F-28 for more detailed information about the increase in the normal retirement age.

The normal retirement age for spouse's benefits (also previously age 65) moves upward in exactly the same way as that for workers. The normal retirement age for widow(er)'s benefits also rises but in a slightly different manner (beginning for widow(er)s who attain age 60 in 2000 and reaching a normal retirement age of 67 in 2029).

Reduced benefits will continue to be available at age 62, but the reduction factors are revised so that there is a further reduction (up to a maximum of 30% for workers entitled at age 62 after the retirement age is increased to age 67, rather than only 20% for entitlement at age 62 under previous law). See Table, F-28.

E-5. Must a person file application for retirement benefits?

Yes. A person can file application within three months before the first month in which he becomes entitled to benefits. The earliest date for filing would be three months before the month of attaining age 62.

As evidence of age, a claimant must ordinarily submit one or more of the following: birth certificate; church record of birth or baptism; Census Bureau notification of registration of birth; hospital birth record; physician's birth record; family Bible; naturalization record; immigration record; military record; passport; school record; vaccination record; insurance policy; labor union or fraternal record; marriage record; other evidence of probative value.

If a person is receiving Social Security disability benefits for the month before the month he reaches normal retirement age (see E-4), no application is required; the disability benefit ends and the retirement benefit begins automatically. For an explanation of how to file for benefits, see FILING FOR BENEFITS, SECTION K.

E-6. What is the amount of a retirement benefit?

A retirement benefit which starts at normal retirement age (see E-4) equals the worker's primary insurance amount (PIA). But a worker who elects to have benefits start before normal retirement age will receive a monthly benefit equal to only a percentage of the PIA. The PIA will be reduced by 5/9 of 1% for each of the first 36 months the worker is under normal retirement age when payments commence and by 5/12 of 1% for each such month in excess of 36. (See Table 10 for reduced retirement benefits.)

As a general rule, a person taking reduced retirement benefits before normal retirement age will continue to receive a reduced rate after normal retirement age.

An individual can obtain higher retirement benefits by working past normal retirement age. See F-27.

The estimated average monthly benefit amount for all retired workers is $845 in 2001.

E-7. What is the first month for which a retired person receives a retirement benefit?

A monthly benefit is available to a retired worker when he reaches age 62, provided he is fully insured.

Workers and their spouses (including divorced spouses) do not receive retirement benefits for a month unless they meet the requirements for entitlement throughout the month. The major effect of this provision is to postpone, in the vast majority of cases, entitlement to retirement benefits for persons who claim benefits in the month in which they reach age 62 to the next month. Only in the case of a person who attains age 62 on the first or second day of a month can benefits be paid for the month of attainment of age 62. Note that a person attains his age on the day preceding the anniversary of his birth. For example, if an individual was born on May 2, 1939, he is considered 62 years old on May 1, 2001.

Most entitlement requirements (other than the entitlement of the worker) affecting young spouses or children of retired or disabled workers are deemed to have occurred as of the first of the month in which they occurred. However, in the case of a child who is born in or after the first month of entitlement of a retired or disabled worker, benefits are not payable for the month of birth (unless born on the first day of the month).

Retroactive benefits are usually prohibited if permanently reduced benefits (as compared with what would be payable for the month the application is filed) would occur in the initial month of eligibility. However, retroactive benefits may be applied for if: (1) with respect to widow(er)'s benefits, the application is for benefits for the month of death of the worker, if filed for in the next month, and (2) retroactive benefits for any month before attaining age 60 are applied for by a disabled widow(er) or disabled surviving divorced spouse.

E-8. Can a person receive retirement benefits regardless of the amount of his wealth or the amount of his retirement income?

Yes, a person is entitled to retirement benefits regardless of how wealthy he is. Also, the amount of retirement income a person receives (e.g. dividends, interest, rents, etc.) is immaterial. A person is subject to loss of benefits only because of excess earnings arising from his personal services (see E-9 and LOSS OF BENEFITS BECAUSE OF EXCESS EARNINGS, SECTION H).

E-9. Can a person lose retirement benefits by working?

Yes, a person can lose some or all monthly benefits if he is under the normal retirement age (see E-4) for all of 2001 and his earnings for the year exceed $10,680. A person may lose benefits in the year he reaches normal retirement age if he earns over $25,000 in that year, but only those earnings earned before the month he reaches normal retirement age count towards the $25,000 limit. The amount of loss depends on the amount of earnings in excess of these earnings limits. In no case will a person lose benefits for earnings earned after reaching normal retirement age. For the initial year of retirement of a person who is under the normal retirement age for all of 2001, the monthly earnings limit is $890. For purposes of this test, "earnings" include not only earnings in covered employment, but also earnings in noncovered employment in the United States. As to noncovered employment outside the United States, benefits are lost for any month before reaching normal retirement age when so employed for more than 45 hours, regardless of the amount of earnings.

The dollar exempt amount mentioned in the above paragraph for persons under normal retirement age will be increased automatically after 2001 as wage levels rise. (See LOSS OF BENEFITS BECAUSE OF EXCESS EARNINGS, SECTION H.) See F-28 for a discussion of the increase in the normal retirement age.

E-10. When do retirement benefits end?

At the worker's death. No retirement benefit is paid for the month of death.

E-11. Can a husband and wife both receive retirement benefits?

Yes. If each is entitled to receive benefits based on their own earnings record, each can receive retirement benefits independently of the other's benefits.

However, a woman or man who is entitled to a retirement benefit and a spouse's benefit cannot receive both in full. (For details of how benefits are determined, see E-32.)

DISABILITY BENEFITS

E-12. In general, what requirements must be met to qualify a person for disability benefits?

A worker is entitled to disability benefits if he: (1) is insured for disability benefits, (2) is under age 65, (3) has been disabled for 12 months, or is expected to be disabled for at least 12 months, or has a disability which is expected to result in death, (4) has filed application for disability benefits, and (5) has completed a 5-month waiting period or is exempted from this requirement.

Determinations of disability are generally made by Disability Determination Services (DDS) which are agencies of each individual state. The Social Security Administration makes disability insurance determinations for persons living outside the United States and for a few other applicants whose cases are specifically excluded from the federal-state regulations. Disability claims and supporting evidence are sent to the DDS located in the state where the claimant resides. The evaluation team makes every reasonable effort to obtain medical evidence from the claimant's treating sources. This team is composed of a medical consultant and a lay disability evaluation specialist and is responsible for making the disability determination.

The Social Security Administration's Office of Program and Integrity Reviews may reverse a DDS finding that no disability exists, or on the basis of evidence in the folder, reverse an allowance of disability.

The claimant may request a reconsideration of the claim and submit new evidence if available. A reconsideration determination as to disability is generally handled by the DDS who made the original determination, and is reviewed by a special group in the Office of Disability Operations. In a further appealed case, an administrative law judge or the Appeals Council of the Office of Hearings and Appeals may issue an independent decision.

The Social Security Administration uses a multi-step process to determine whether someone is eligible for disability benefits. These steps are as follows:

Step 1: Is the individual engaging in substantial gainful activity? If yes, deny. If no, continue to Step 2.

Step 2: Does the individual have a severe medically determinable physical or mental impairment? If no, deny. If yes, continue to Step 3.

Step 3: Does the individual have an impairment included in the Listing of Impairments? If yes, allow. If no, continue to Step 4.

Step 4: Does the impairment prevent the individual from doing past relevant work? If the individual is able to do work that was done in the past, then deny. If not, continue to Step 5.

Step 5: Does the impairment prevent the individual from doing any other work? If yes, allow. If no, deny.

See K-10 for additional information on disability claims.

E-13. What insured status is required for disability benefits?

Generally, a person is insured for disability benefits if he: (1) is fully insured, and (2) has worked under Social Security for at least five of the 10 years (20-out-of-40 quarters) just before becoming disabled, or if disability begins before age 31 but after age 24, for at least one-half of the quarters after reaching age 21 and before becoming disabled (but not less than six). If a person becomes disabled before the quarter in which he attains age 24, he must have six quarters of coverage in the 12 quarter period ending with the quarter in which the disability began.

However, a person who had a period of disability that began before age 31, who subsequently recovered, and then became disabled again at age 31 or later, is again insured for disability benefits if he has one quarter of coverage for every two calendar quarters elapsing after age 21 and through the quarter in which the later period of disability began (up to a maximum of 20 quarters of coverage out of the last "countable" 40 calendar quarters), but excluding from such elapsed quarters any quarters in the previous period of disability which were not quarters of coverage. Quarters acquired during the first period of disability are excluded in counting the "elapsed" quarters, however, and the quarters of coverage must be acquired during the measuring period. This provision provides relief to those workers who could otherwise not get disability benefits because they did not have time following recovery from an earlier disability to work long enough before a second disability to meet the 20-out-of-40 quarters insured status test.

E-14. How disabled must a person be to qualify for disability benefits?

Disability is defined as the inability to engage in any substantial gainful activity by reason of any medically determinable physical or mental impairment which can be expected to result in death or which has lasted or can be expected to last for a continuous period of not less than 12 months. A person must be not only unable to do his previous work but cannot, considering age, education, and work experience, engage in any other kind of substantial work which exists in the national economy. It is immaterial whether such work exists in the immediate area, or whether a specific job vacancy exists, or whether the worker would be hired if he applied for work.

The worker's impairment or impairments must be the primary reason for his inability to engage in substantial gainful activity, although age, education, and work experience are also taken into consideration in determining the worker's ability to do work other than previous work.

The term "substantial gainful activity" is used to describe a level of work activity that is both substantial and gainful. Substantial work activity involves the performance of significant physical or mental duties, or a combination of both, which are productive in nature. Gainful work activity is activity for remuneration or profit, whether or not a profit is realized. For work activity to be substantial, it need not necessarily be performed on a full-time basis; work activity performed on a part-time basis may also be substantial.

Illegal activities can constitute substantial gainful activity. For example, tax fraud is an illegal activity that can be both substantial and gainful because of the possibility of significant mental activity and potential gain involved.

Impairments related to the commission of a felony for which the individual is subsequently convicted, or related to confinement in a correctional facility for conviction of a felony, may not be used to establish a disability for Social Security benefits.

E-15. Does blindness qualify a person for disability benefits?

A special definition of "disability" is provided for an individual age 55 or over who is blind. Such an individual is disabled for the purpose of disability benefits if he is unable to engage in substantial gainful activity requiring skills or abilities comparable to those of any gainful activity in which he has previously engaged with some regularity and over a substantial period of time.

A person who is not statutorily blind and is earning more than $740 (in 2001) a month (net of impairment-related work expenses) is ordinarily considered to be engaging in substantial gainful activity.

The Social Security Act has established a higher substantial gainful activity amount for statutorily blind individuals. The monthly substantial gainful activity amount for blind individuals is $1,240 in 2001 ($1,170 in 2000).

Blindness, for Social Security purposes, means either central visual acuity of 20/200 or less in the better eye with the use of a correcting lens, or a limitation in the fields of vision such that the widest diameter of the visual field subtends an angle of 20 degrees or less. However, no benefits will be payable for any month in which the individual engages in substantial gainful activity.

E-16. At what age can a person receive disability benefits?

At any age under the normal retirement age (see E-4). If a person is receiving disability benefits when he reaches normal retirement age, the disability benefit automatically ends and a retirement benefit begins.

E-17. Is there a waiting period for disability benefits?

There is a full five month waiting period. Generally, benefits will start with the 6th full month of disability. However, if application is not made until later, benefits are payable retroactively for up to 12 months, beginning with the first month after the waiting period.

Ordinarily, no benefits are payable for the first five full months of disability. Under some circumstances, however, where the person has had a prior period of disability, benefits will begin with the first full month of disability. Benefits will begin with the first full month of disability if: (1) the new disability arises within five years after the previous one ended, and (2) the new disability is expected to last for at least 12 months, or to result in death.

E-18. When must an application for disability benefits be filed?

An application for disability benefits may be filed before the first month for which the person can be entitled to benefits. An application filed before the first month in which the applicant satisfies the requirements for disability benefits is valid only if the applicant satisfies the requirements at some time before a final decision on his application is made. If the applicant is found to satisfy the requirements, the application is deemed to have been filed in the first month in which he satisfied the requirements. An application for disability benefits may be made retroactively effective for as many as 12 months before the one which application is filed. For an explanation of how to file for benefits, see FILING FOR BENEFITS, SECTION K.

Social Security disability benefits may be reinstated without a new disability application if, during the 15-month period following a trial work period, a person who has not recovered medically no longer engages in substantially gainful activity. (See E-27.)

E-19. What is the amount of a disability benefit?

The amount of a disabled worker's benefit generally equals his primary insurance amount (PIA), determined as if the worker were at normal retirement age and eligible for retirement benefits in the first month of his waiting period.

However, the formula for determining a disabled worker's AIME (Average Indexed Monthly Earnings) and PIA differs from the formula used for a retiring worker. See Primary Insurance Amount, SECTION F. There are also different limits on the amount of family benefits that can be paid to a disabled worker and his family. See Maximum Family Benefits, SECTION F.

The average monthly benefit for a disabled worker in 2001 is $786.

Disability benefits may be reduced before the worker attains normal retirement age (see E-4) to fully or partially offset a workers' compensation benefit or disability benefit under a federal, state, or local public law. This reduction will be made only if the total benefits payable to the worker (and dependents) under both programs exceed the higher of 80% of his "average current earnings" before the onset of disability, or the family's total Social Security benefit.

"Average current earnings" is defined as the highest of: (1) the "average monthly wage" used for computing primary insurance amounts for some beneficiaries, even though not used for this particular one, or (2) the average monthly earnings from covered employment during the highest five consecutive years after 1950, or (3) the average monthly earnings based on the one calendar year of highest earnings from covered employment during a period consisting of the year in which disability began and the five preceding years. Note that the "highest earnings" in items (2) and (3) are determined *without* considering the maximum taxable earnings base.

Different factors are used in determining whether there is an offset and the amount of the offset. The factors used are determined by the date the worker first became disabled and the date the worker first became entitled to benefits. For workers who first became disabled after February 1981, and who first became entitled to disability benefits after August 1981, benefits paid as workers' compensation and received under a federal, state, or local public program will be considered in determining the amount of the offset.

Specifically excluded are all VA disability benefits, needs-based benefits, federal benefits based on employment covered for Social Security purposes, and state and local benefits based on covered state and local employment. Private pension or insurance benefits will also not be considered in determining the amount of the offset. The offset of benefits will continue until the worker reaches normal retirement age.

For a worker disabled and receiving benefits prior to the above dates, only benefits paid as workers' compensation are considered in determining the amount of the offset. The offset of benefits stops when the worker reaches age 62 (rather than normal retirement age).

The amount of the reduction is the amount by which Social Security benefits plus workers' compensation and, where applicable, public disability benefits exceeds 80% of the average current earnings. The combined payments after the reduction will never be less than the total Social Security benefits were before the reduction. However, the amount of Social Security benefits can fluctuate based on the decrease or increase in the amount of workers' compensation. In addition, the amount of the reduction is adjusted periodically to take into account increases in national earnings levels as applied to the initially-determined average current earnings, but this adjustment will never decrease the amount of benefits payable on the worker's earnings record.

When a state workers' compensation law and, where applicable, a federal, state, or local public disability benefit law or plan *generally* provides for periodic payments but permits a lump-sum settlement either in the form of a commutation or compromise agreement which discharges the liability of the insurer or the employer, such settlement is a substitute for periodic payments and is subject to the offset provisions. In this situation, the lump sum is prorated to reflect, as accurately as possible, the monthly rate that would have been paid had the lump-sum award not been made. Medical and legal expenses incurred by the worker in connection with the workers' compensation/public disability benefit claim may be excluded from computing the offset.

In Oregon, when prorating a lump-sum award or settlement made under Oregon workers' compensation law for a permanent disability, the Social Security Administration will treat the lump-sum as a substitute for periodic payments and will calculate the offset rate on a monthly basis by dividing the lump-sum by the number of months between the date of the award and the date the worker reaches age 65. However, if a workers' compensation award expressly establishes an offset rate under the Oregon statutory scheme, the Social Security Administration will prorate the lump-sum award according to that expressly stated offset rate. *Social Security Acquiescence Ruling 95-2(9).*

Workers' compensation payments for loss of bodily function, in addition to wage loss, can be used to offset Social Security disability insurance benefits. In a New Hampshire case, the claimant applied for and was found entitled to Social Security disability benefits. However, these benefits were offset because he also received New Hampshire workers' compensation payments, including a permanent impairment lump-sum award. After unsuccessfully appealing his case through administrative channels, the claimant appealed to the district court claiming that the portion of his lump-sum settlement representing compensation for permanent impairment was not subject to offset. The district court held that permanent impairment payments under workers' compensation were to compensate an individual for loss of bodily function, not loss of wages, and, thus, could not be used to offset Social Security disability benefits.

The U.S. Court of Appeals for the First Circuit reversed the decision of the district court, holding that, although permanent impairment awards may be paid regardless of any actual loss of wages, the awards were never intended to be a departure from, or an exception to, the wage-loss principle. Permanent impairment benefits under New Hampshire workers' compensation law are for compensable disability under a state workers' compensation law and, therefore, are subject to offset against Social Security disability benefits. *Davidson v. Sullivan*, 942 F.2d 90 (1st Cir. 1991).

E-20. Is a person entitled to disability benefits regardless of wealth?

Yes, benefits are not payable on a "needs" basis. If a person meets the requirements for entitlement, disability benefits are payable regardless of wealth.

E-21. Can a disabled person receive disability benefits even though his spouse is employed?

Yes, if the person is entitled to benefits based on his own earnings record. Entitlement to benefits as a worker is entirely independent of a spouse's employment.

E-22. What is the trial work period?

A trial work period is provided as an incentive for personal rehabilitation efforts for disabled workers, disabled widow(er)s and childhood disability beneficiaries who are still disabled but return to work. It allows them to perform services in as many as nine months (within a 60-consecutive-month period if nine months of services were not completed before January 1992) without affecting their right to benefits during the trial work period if their impairment does not improve during this period. (Since benefits will continue for the month the disability is determined to have ceased and the two months after that, benefits may be paid for at least 12 months during which the individual works.)

A person is generally entitled to a trial work period if receiving disability insurance benefits, child's benefits based on disability, or widow(er)'s or surviving divorced spouse's benefits based on disability.

The trial work period begins with the month in which the person becomes entitled to disability insurance benefits, to child's benefits based on disability, or to widow(er)'s or surviving divorced spouse's benefits based on disability. It cannot begin before the month in which the person files an application for benefits. It ends with the close of whichever of the following calendar months is the earlier:

1. The ninth month (whether or not the months have been consecutive) in which the person has performed services if that ninth month is prior to January 1992, or

2. The ninth month (whether or not the months have been consecutive and whether or not the previous eight months of services were prior to January 1992) in which the person has performed services within a rolling 60-month period if that ninth month is after December 1991, or

3. The month in which new evidence, other than evidence relating to any work the person did during the trial work period, shows that the person is not disabled, even though the person has not worked a full nine months. The Social Security Administration may find that the disability has ended at any time during the trial work period if the medical or other evidence shows that the person is no longer disabled.

A person is not entitled to a trial work period if:

1. The person is entitled to a period of disability but not to disability insurance benefits, child's benefits based on disability, or widow(er)'s or surviving divorced spouse's benefits based on disability, or

2. The person performs work demonstrating the ability to engage in substantial gainful activity during any required waiting period for benefits, or

3. The person performs work demonstrating the ability to engage in substantial gainful activity within 12 months of the onset of the impairment(s) which prevented him from performing substantial gainful activity and before the date of the decision awarding him disability benefits, or

4. The person performs work demonstrating the ability to engage in substantial gainful activity at any time after the onset of the impairment(s) which prevented him from engaging in substantial gainful activity but before the month he files his application for disability benefits.

E-23. What is the reentitlement period?

The reentitlement period is an additional period after nine months of trial work during which a person may continue to test his ability to work if he has a disabling impairment. A person will not be paid benefits for any month after the second month following the month disability ceased due to substantial gainful activity in this period in which he did substantial gainful activity. A person will be paid benefits for months in which he did not do substantial gainful activity.

If anyone else is receiving monthly benefits based on a disabled person's earnings record, that individual will not be paid benefits for any month for which the disabled person cannot be paid benefits during the reentitlement period. If a disabled person's benefits are stopped because he does substantial gainful activity, they may be started again without a new application and a new determination of disability if the person discontinues doing substantial gainful activity during this period. In determining, for reentitlement benefit purposes, whether a person does substantial gainful activity in a month, the Social Security Administration considers only work in or earnings for that month. It does not consider the average amount of work or earnings over a period of months. See E-27.

E-24. Can a person become entitled to disability benefits after becoming entitled to some other type of Social Security benefit?

Yes. For example, a person who is receiving a reduced retirement benefit before normal retirement age can become entitled to disability benefits. However, the disability benefit is actuarially reduced for the months that the person has already received retirement benefits.

E-25. Will a disabled person lose benefits by refusing to accept rehabilitation services?

A person will lose the disabled worker's benefit by refusing without good cause to accept vocational rehabilitation services.

Good cause for refusing vocational rehabilitation services exists if, for example, the person is a member of any recognized church or religious sect which teaches reliance solely upon prayer or spiritual means for the treatment of any impairment, and refusal to accept vocational rehabilitation services is based solely on adherence to these teachings.

E-26. What are the special rules for disability benefits when alcoholism or drug addiction is involved?

An individual is not considered disabled if alcoholism or drug addiction is a contributing factor material to the Social Security Administration's determination that the individual is disabled.

A beneficiary who qualifies for disability benefits on a basis other than alcoholism or drug addiction, but is determined by the Social Security Administration to have an alcohol or drug addiction and to be incapable of managing the disability benefits, must have the disability benefit paid to a representative payee. The Social Security Administration must notify the beneficiary that benefits are being mailed to a representative payee because of alcoholism or drug addiction. In addition, the Social Security Administration must refer such individuals to the appropriate state agency administering the state plan for substance abuse treatment services.

The Social Security Administration determines whether drug addiction or alcoholism is a contributing factor material to the determination of disability by evaluating which physical and mental limitations would remain if the disabled person stopped using drugs or alcohol. If the Social Security Administration determines that the disabled person's remaining limitations are not disabling, the Social Security Administration will find that drug addiction or alcoholism is a contributing factor material to the determination of disability and deny disability benefits.

E-27. When do a person's disability benefits end?

The last month of entitlement to a disabled worker's benefit generally is whichever of the following occurs earliest: (1) the second month after the month in which the disability ceases, (2) the month before the month the worker attains normal retirement age (at which time benefits are automatically converted to retirement benefits), or (3) the month before the month in which the worker dies.

However, there are certain conditions under which benefits may continue or reentitlement to benefits may be established after disability ceases:

1. *Benefits for persons in vocational rehabilitation programs.* Benefits for disabled and blind workers participating in a vocational rehabilitation program may continue until completion of the program or for a specified period of time in certain situations where disability ceases prior to completion of the program. This provision applies only to disabled individuals who have medically recovered, who began the vocational rehabilitation program before disability ceased, and for whom the Social Security Administration has determined that continued participation in the vocational rehabilitation program would increase the likelihood of permanent removal from the disability benefit rolls.

2. *Extended period of eligibility for reentitlement to benefits following trial work period.* Individuals who continue to have a disabling impairment receive an extended period of eligibility immediately following the completion of a 9-month trial work period. If disability ceased because of work activity and earnings subsequently fall below the level considered substantial gainful activity within a specified period, benefits may be reinstated without the need for a new application and disability determination. This reentitlement period to disability benefits is 36 months. Benefits for the family of the worker are suspended during this period if the worker's benefits are suspended.

Example. A disabled person completes the trial work period in December 1997. He is then working at the substantial gainful activity level and continues to do so throughout the 36 months following completion of his trial work period and thereafter. The disabled person's termination month is January 2001, which is the 37th month — that is, the first month in which the disabled person performed substantial gainful activity after the 36th month following his trial work period.

Example. A disabled person completes the trial work period in December 1997 but he is not able to work at the substantial gainful activity level until March 2001, three months after the last month of his reentitlement period. The disabled person's termination month is June 2001 — that is, the third month after the earliest month he performed substantial gainful activity.

The Social Security Administration may use a "medical improvement standard" to terminate disability benefits. Benefits can be terminated only if: (1) there is substantial evidence that there has been medical improvement in the individual's impairment or combination of impairments (other than medical improvement which is not related to the person's ability to work), *and* the individual is able to engage in substantial gainful activity (see E-14), (2) there is substantial evidence which demonstrates that although there is no medical improvement, the person has benefited from advances in medical or vocational therapy or technology related to the ability to work, *and* the person is now able to perform substantial gainful activity, (3) there is substantial evidence that although there is no medical improvement, the person has benefited from vocational therapy, *and* the beneficiary can now perform substantial gainful activity, (4) there is substantial evidence that, based on new or improved diagnostic techniques or evaluations, the person's impairment or combination of impairments is not as disabling as it was considered to be at the time of the prior determination, and, therefore, the individual is able to perform substantial gainful activity, (5) there is substantial evidence either in the file at the original determination or newly obtained showing that the prior determination was in error, (6) there is substantial evidence that the original decision was obtained by fraud, or (7) if the individual is engaging in substantial gainful activity and fails without good cause to cooperate in the review or follow prescribed treatment or cannot be located.

E-28. Are benefits payable to the family of a disabled worker?

Yes. (See SPOUSE'S BENEFIT and CHILD'S BENEFIT, immediately following.)

SPOUSE'S BENEFIT

E-29. Is the spouse of a retired or disabled worker entitled to benefits?

An individual is entitled to spouse's benefits on a worker's Social Security record if:

- The worker is entitled to retirement or disability benefits, and

- The individual has filed an application for spouse's benefits, and

- The spouse is not entitled to a retirement or disability benefit based on a primary insurance amount equal to or larger than one-half of the worker's primary insurance amount, and

- The spouse is either age 62 or over, or has in care a child under age 16, or disabled, who is entitled to benefits on the worker's Social Security record.

The spouse of a worker must also meet *one* of the following conditions: (1) the spouse must have been married to the worker for at least one year just before filing an application for benefits; (2) the spouse must be the natural mother or father of the worker's biological child; (3) the spouse was entitled or potentially entitled to spouse's, widow(er)'s, parent's, or childhood disability benefits in the month before the month of marriage to the worker; or (4) the spouse was entitled or potentially entitled to a widow(er)'s, parent's, or child's (over 18) annuity under the Railroad Retirement Act in the month before the month of marriage to the worker. A spouse is "potentially entitled" if he or she meets all the requirements for entitlement other than the filing of an application and attaining the required age.

E-30. What is meant by having a child "in care"?

Having a child in care is a basic requirement for spouse's benefits when the spouse is under age 62 and for mother's and father's benefits (see E-55 through E-68). "In care" means that the mother or father: (1) exercises parental control and responsibility for the welfare and care of a child under age 16 or mentally incompetent child age 16 or over, or (2) performs personal services for a disabled mentally competent child age 16 or over.

E-31. Is the divorced spouse of a retired or disabled worker entitled to a spouse's benefits?

The spouse is entitled to a divorced spouse's benefit on the worker's Social Security record if: (1) the worker is entitled to retirement or disability benefits, (2) the spouse has filed an application for divorced spouse's benefits, (3) the spouse is not entitled to a retirement or disability benefit based on a primary insurance amount which equals or exceeds one-half the worker's primary insurance amount, (4) the spouse is age 62 or over, (5) the spouse is not married, and (6) the spouse was married to the worker for at least 10 years before the date the divorce became final.

A divorced spouse who is age 62 or over and who has been divorced for at least two years is able to receive benefits based on the earnings of a former spouse who is eligible for retirement benefits, regardless of whether the former spouse has retired or applied for benefits. This two-year waiting period for independent entitlement to divorced spouse's benefits is waived if the worker was entitled to benefits prior to the divorce. A spouse whose divorce took place after the couple had begun to receive retirement benefits, and whose former spouse (the worker) returned to work after the divorce (thus causing a suspension of benefits), will not lose benefits (on which he or she had come to depend).

E-32. What is the amount of a spouse's benefit?

If the spouse of a retired or disabled worker is caring for the worker's child under age 16 or disabled child, the monthly benefit equals 1/2 of the worker's PIA regardless of his age. If the spouse is not caring for a child, monthly benefits starting at normal retirement age likewise equal 1/2 of the worker's PIA; but if the spouse chooses to start receiving benefits at or after age 62, but before normal retirement age, the benefit is reduced. (See Table 10 for spouse's reduced benefits.)

If the spouse chooses to receive, and is paid, a reduced spouse's benefit for months before normal retirement age, the spouse is not entitled to the full spouse's benefit rate upon reaching normal retirement age. A reduced benefit rate is payable for as long as the spouse remains entitled to spouse's benefits. (But see F-34, Recomputation of Benefits.)

A spouse will not always receive a spouse's full benefit; under the following circumstances a spouse will receive a smaller amount:

(1) If the total amount of monthly benefits payable on the worker's Social Security account exceeds the Maximum Family Benefit, all benefits (except the worker's benefit) will be reduced proportionately to bring the total within the family maximum limit. (See SECTION F, Maximum Family Benefits.)

(2) If a spouse who is not caring for a child elects to start receiving a spouse's benefit at age 62 (or at any time between the ages 62 and normal retirement age), the benefit will be reduced by 25/36 of 1% for each of the first 36 months that the spouse is under normal retirement age when benefits commence and by 5/12 of 1% for each such month in excess of 36.

(3) If the spouse is entitled to a retirement or disability benefit which is smaller than the spouse's benefit rate, the spouse will receive a spouse's benefit equal to only the difference between the retirement or disability benefit and the full spouse's benefit rate.

(4) The amount of a spouse's monthly benefit is usually reduced if the spouse receives a pension based on his or her own work for a federal, state, or local government that is not covered by Social Security on the last day of such employment. (See E-37.)

If a spouse is entitled to a retirement or disability benefit which is larger than the spouse's benefit rate, he or she will receive only the retirement or disability benefit.

E-33. What is the amount of a divorced spouse's benefit?

The amount of a divorced spouse's benefit is the same as a spouse's benefit amount. As a general rule, it will equal 1/2 of the beneficiary's former spouse's PIA and will be reduced if he or she elects to start receiving benefits before normal retirement age. However, a divorced spouse's benefit is paid independently of other family benefits. In other words, it will not be subject to reduction because of the family maximum limit, and will not be taken into account in figuring the maximum limit for the former spouse's family.

E-34. Must a spouse be dependent upon the worker for support to be eligible for a spouse's benefits?

No, a spouse is entitled to benefits if the worker is receiving benefits and the spouse is otherwise qualified. A spouse need not be dependent upon the worker, and may be independently wealthy.

E-35. May a spouse lose benefits if the worker works or if the spouse works?

Yes, a spouse can lose some or all of his or her monthly benefits if the worker is under the normal retirement age for all of 2001 and earnings exceed $10,680. A spouse may also lose benefits in the year the worker reaches normal retirement age if the worker earns over $25,000 in that year, but only earnings earned before the month the worker reaches normal retirement age count towards the $25,000 limit. Similarly, if the spouse is under normal retirement age for the entire year and has earnings of over $10,680 (or earnings of over $25,000 in the year that normal retirement age is attained), some or all benefits can be lost. (See LOSS OF BENEFITS BECAUSE OF EXCESS EARNINGS, SECTION H.) See F-28 for a discussion of the increase in the normal retirement age.

When both the worker and the spouse have earnings in excess of the earnings limitation: (1) 50% of the worker's "excess" earnings are charged against the total monthly family benefits if the worker is under the normal retirement age, and 33⅓% in the year the worker is to reach the normal retirement age, and then (2) the spouse's "excess" earnings are charged against his or her own benefits in the same manner depending upon the age of the spouse, but only to the extent that those benefits have not already been charged with the worker's excess earnings.

Example. Mr. Smith, age 62 on January 1, 2001, is entitled to a monthly retirement benefit of $346, and his wife, also age 62 on January 1, 2001, is entitled to a monthly spouse's benefit of $162. Mr. Smith had earnings that were $4,064 in excess of the earnings limitation. His wife had earnings which were $1,620 in excess of the earnings limitation. Mr. Smith's earnings are charged against the total monthly family benefit of $508 ($346 + $162), so neither Mr. Smith nor his wife receives payments for January through April (50% of $4,064 = $2,032, and 4 x $508 = $2,032). The wife's excess earnings are charged only against her own benefit of $162. Since her benefits for January through April were charged with the worker's excess earnings, the charging of her own earnings cannot begin until May; she thus receives no benefits for May through September (50% of $1,620 = $810, and 5 x $162 = $810).

Exception. The excess earnings of the worker do not cause deductions from the benefits of an entitled divorced spouse who has been divorced from the worker at least two years or whose former spouse was entitled to benefits before the divorce.

E-36. When does a spouse's benefit end?

A spouse's benefits end when: (1) the spouse dies; (2) the worker dies (in this case the spouse will be entitled to widow(er)'s, mother's, or father's benefits); (3) the worker's entitlement to disability benefits ends and he or she is not entitled to retirement benefits (unless the divorced spouse meets the requirements for an independently entitled divorced spouse); (4) the spouse is under age 62 and there is no longer a child of the worker under 16 or disabled who is entitled to child's benefits; (5) the spouse becomes entitled to retirement or disability benefits and his or her PIA is equal to or larger than one-half of the worker's PIA; (6) the spouse and the worker are divorced before the spouse reaches age 62 and before the spouse and worker had been married for 10 years; or (7) the divorced spouse marries someone other than the worker. However, the divorced spouse's benefit will not be terminated by marriage to an individual entitled to widow(er)'s, mother's, father's or parent's monthly benefits, or to an individual age 18 or over who is entitled to childhood disability benefits.

A spouse is not entitled to a spouse's benefit for the month in which any of the above events occurs. The last payment will be the payment for the preceding month.

E-37. Will a spouse's benefit be reduced if the spouse is receiving a government pension?

Social Security benefits payable to spouses—including surviving spouses and divorced spouses—are reduced (but not below zero) by two-thirds of the amount of any governmental (federal, state, or local) retirement benefit payable to the spouse based on *his own earnings* in employment not covered by Social Security on the last day of such employment. The reduction is two-thirds of the pension. Thus, for the affected group, the spouse's benefit is reduced $2 for every $3 of the government pension.

This offset against Social Security benefits did not apply prior to December 1977, or if the individual: (1) met all the requirements for entitlement to Social Security benefits that existed and were applied in January 1977, and (2) received or was eligible to receive a government pension between December 1977 and December 1982. In addition, it does not apply to those first eligible to receive a government pension prior to July 1983 if they also meet the one-half support test.

Generally, federal workers hired before 1984 are part of the Civil Service Retirement System (CSRS) and are not covered by Social Security. Most Federal workers hired after 1983 are covered by the Federal Employees' Retirement System Act of 1986 (FERS), which includes coverage by Social Security. The FERS law provided that employees covered by the CSRS could, from July 1, 1987 to December 31, 1987, make a one-time election to join FERS (and thereby obtain social security coverage). Thus, a CSRS employee who switched to FERS during this period immediately became exempt from the government pension offset. Also, an employee who elected FERS on or before December 31, 1987 is exempt from the government pension offset even if that person retired from government service before his FERS coverage became effective.

However, federal employees who elect to become covered under FERS during any election period which may occur on or after January 1, 1988, are exempt from the government pension offset only if they have five or more years of federal employment covered by Social Security after January 1, 1988. This rule also applies to certain legislative branch employees who first become covered under FERS on or after January 1, 1988.

Pensions based wholly on service performed as a member of a uniformed service, whether on active or inactive duty, are excluded from the offset.

CHILD'S BENEFITS (CHILD OF RETIRED OR DISABLED WORKER)

E-38. Is a child of a retired or disabled parent entitled to Social Security benefits?

Yes, if: (1) the parent is entitled to retirement or disability benefits, (2) the child is (or was) dependent upon the parent (but see E-40 to E-43), (3) the child is under age 18, or between the ages of 18 and 19 and a full-time elementary or high school student, or 18 or over and under a disability that began before age 22, (4) the child is unmarried (but see E-49), and (5) an application for the child's benefit has been filed.

A grandchild or stepgrandchild is considered the child of the worker in the following certain circumstances:

1. The grandchild's natural or adoptive parents are deceased or disabled: (1) at the time the worker became entitled to retirement or disability benefits or died, or (2) at the beginning of the worker's period of disability which continued until the worker became entitled to disability or retirement benefits, or

2. The grandchild was legally adopted by the worker's surviving spouse in an adoption decreed by a court, and the grandchild's natural or adopting parent or stepparent was not living in the same household and making regular contributions to the child's support at the time the insured worker died.

The grandchild or stepgrandchild also must be dependent on the insured. (See E-40.)

An illegitimate child is eligible for child's benefits if the worker: (1) has acknowledged in writing that the child is his or her son or daughter, (2) has been decreed by a court to be the father or mother of the child, (3) has been ordered by a court to contribute to the support of the child because the child is his or her son or daughter, or (4) has been shown to be the child's father or mother by other satisfactory evidence and was living with the child or contributing to the child's support when the child's application is filed (in life cases) or when the worker died (in survivor cases).

E-39. Who is considered a "child" of a retired or disabled worker for benefit purposes?

The term "child" includes the worker's: (1) legitimate child, or any child who would have the right under applicable state law to inherit intestate personal property from the worker as a child, (2) stepchild, under certain circumstances, (3) legally adopted child, (4) illegitimate child, under certain circumstances (see E-38), and (5) grandchild or stepgrandchild, under certain circumstances (see E-38).

A stepchild-stepparent relationship arises when the worker marries the child's natural parent or marries the child's adopting parent after the adoption.

91

Death of the stepparent does not end the relationship. If the stepparent and the child's natural parent are divorced, the stepparent-stepchild relationship ends. However, in either case, there is no termination of a stepchild's existing established entitlement to child's benefits as a child of a stepparent. A stepchild must have been a stepchild of the parent on whose Social Security record the claim for benefits is filed for at least one year before the day the child's application is filed if the parent is alive.

E-40. Must a child be dependent upon the worker to qualify for child's benefits?

A child must be dependent upon the worker to qualify for benefits on the worker's Social Security record. The factors that determine whether a child is dependent upon a worker vary, depending upon whether the worker is the natural parent (see E-41), the legally adopting parent, the stepparent (see E-42), or the grandparent (see below).

To be dependent on the worker, a grandchild or stepgrandchild must have: (1) begun living with the worker before the grandchild became 18 years old, and (2) lived with the worker in the United States and received at least one-half support for the worker. The support test is met if the worker provides one-half of the support: (1) for the year before the month the worker became entitled to retirement or disability benefits or died, or (2) if the worker had a period of disability that lasted until he or she became entitled to benefits or died, for the year immediately before the month in which the period of disability began.

E-41. Is a child considered to be dependent upon his father or mother regardless of actual dependency?

A child is deemed to be dependent upon his parent (father or mother). The fact that the parent and child are not living together, or the parent is not contributing to the child's support, is not a factor unless the child has been adopted by another person.

E-42. Under what circumstances is a child considered to be dependent upon a stepparent?

The child is considered dependent upon a stepparent if the stepparent is contributing at least one-half of the child's support, or if the child is living with the stepparent.

E-43. Can a child receive benefits based on one parent's Social Security account even though the other parent is working and furnishing his support?

Yes. A good example would be where the child is entitled to benefits due to the death of his mother who was a covered worker. The fact that the child's father was supporting him would not matter.

E-44. When is a child a full-time elementary or secondary school student?

A child may be eligible for child's benefits if he is a full-time elementary or secondary school student.

A child is a full-time elementary or secondary school student if he attends a school that provides elementary or secondary education as determined under the law of the state or other jurisdiction in which it is located. Participation in the following programs also meets the requirements:

(1) The child is instructed in elementary or secondary education at home in accordance with a home schooling law of the state or other jurisdiction in which the child resides. Students in these types of situations include a wide range of individuals. For example, home schooling students may be in that situation for religious reasons or because the parents do not agree with the local school curriculum.

(2) The child is in an independent study elementary or secondary education program in accordance with state law or other jurisdiction in which he resides which is administered by the local school or school district jurisdiction. Students in independent study programs may include those individuals who cannot take advantage of the traditional school setting, such as hard-to-keep-in-school students (unable to adjust or delinquents), single mothers, or expectant mothers.

A child must be in full-time attendance in a day or evening course of at least 13 weeks duration and must be carrying a subject load which is considered full-time for day students under the institution's standards and practices. If a child is in a home schooling program, the child must be carrying a subject load which is considered full-time for day students under standards and practices set by the state or other jurisdiction in which the child resides.

To be considered in full-time attendance, a child's scheduled attendance must be at the rate of at least 20 hours per week. If a child is in an independent study program, the number of hours spent in school attendance are determined by combining the number of hours of attendance at a school facility with the agreed upon number of hours spent in independent study.

A child may still be considered in full-time attendance if the scheduled rate of attendance is below 20 hours per week if the Social Security Administration finds that:

(1) The school attended does not schedule at least 20 hours per week and going to that particular school is the child's only reasonable alternative; or

(2) The child's medical condition prevents him from having scheduled attendance of at least 20 hours per week. To prove that a child's medical condition prevents scheduling 20 hours per week, the Social Security Administration may request that the child provide appropriate medical evidence or a statement from the school.

A child enrolled solely in correspondence courses is not a full-time elementary or secondary school student.

Benefits paid to students age 18 who attend elementary or secondary schools on a full-time basis end with the last month they are full-time students or, if earlier, the month before the month they become age 19.

E-45. Is the disabled child of a retired or disabled worker entitled to benefits past age 22?

Yes, if the disability began before the child reached age 22 and continued until the filing date of the application. The definition of "disability" is the same as for a worker applying for disability benefits (see E-14).

E-46. What is the amount of the benefit for a retired or disabled worker's child?

The child of a retired or disabled worker is entitled to a monthly benefit equal to 50% of his parent's PIA. Usually this is an amount equal to one-half of the worker's benefit, but if the worker has elected to receive a reduced retirement benefit before normal retirement age (see E-4), the child's benefit will be based on one-half of his parent's PIA, not on one-half of the reduced benefit. If the worker receives a larger benefit than the PIA, due to delayed retirement beyond normal retirement age, the child's benefit is still only 50% of the PIA.

Although a child's full benefit is equal to one-half his parent's PIA, in many cases the benefit actually paid to a child will be smaller because of the "family maximum" limit. Thus, if the total amount of benefits based on the parent's Social Security account exceeds the family maximum, all benefits (except the worker's benefit) will be reduced to bring the total within the family maximum. (See F-15, Maximum Family Benefits and Table 11.)

Notice that the benefit for a retired or disabled worker's child is less than the benefit for a deceased worker's child. The child of a deceased worker is entitled to a benefit equal to 75% of his deceased parent's PIA (see E-69, Child's Benefit, Child of Deceased Worker).

E-47. Can a child lose his benefits by working?

Yes, a child can lose some or all of his benefits if he works and earns over $10,680 in 2001. (See LOSS OF BENEFITS BECAUSE OF EXCESS EARNINGS, SECTION H.)

E-48. If the retired or disabled parent loses benefits, will the child lose benefits also?

Yes. For example, if a disabled worker loses his benefits because he refuses to accept rehabilitation services, his child's benefits will be stopped also. Or, if the disabled worker recovers and is no longer entitled to benefits, the child's benefits will end.

E-49. Will a child lose his benefits if he marries?

Yes, with one exception: a disabled child age 18 or over will not lose his benefits because of marriage to another disabled child age 18 or over who is receiving child's benefits, or because of marriage to a person entitled to retirement, widow(er)'s, mother's, father's, parent's, disability, or spouse's benefits.

E-50. When does a child's benefit end?

Child's benefits end when: (1) the child dies; (2) the child marries (but not if the child is a disabled child over 18 and the child marries another Social Security beneficiary), (3) the child's parent is no longer entitled to disability benefits, unless such entitlement ended because the insured parent became entitled to retirement benefits or died, or (4) the child reaches age 18 and is neither under a disability nor a full-time student. Benefits for full-time elementary or secondary school students end when the child reaches age 19. Entitlement to childhood disability benefits ends when the child over age 18 ceases to be under a disability, which began before age 22, unless the child is age 18-19 and a full-time elementary or secondary school student.

The beneficiary is not entitled to child's insurance benefits for the month in which any of the above events occur, except that a disabled child's benefits will end with the second month following the month in which the child ceases to be under a disability.

Also, if the benefits of a stepchild are based on the wages or self-employment income of a stepparent who is subsequently divorced from the child's natural parent, the stepchild's benefit ends the month after the month in which the divorce becomes final.

A child's benefit may also end if the child is missing. In 1993, the Social Security Administration suspended benefits for a child who disappeared mysteriously and was missing for five years. Further payment of benefits has been suspended until the beneficiary's whereabouts and continuing eligibility for benefits have been determined. *Social Security Ruling SSR 93-3.*

E-51. If a child is neither disabled nor a full-time elementary or secondary student, when does the benefit end?

When the child reaches age 18, unless the child marries before then. The last benefit is the benefit for the month preceding the month when the child reaches age 18.

E-52. Who files application for a child's benefits?

If the child is at least age 18 and physically and mentally competent, the child must file the application form. Otherwise, an application may be filed on the child's behalf by a legal guardian or by the person (e.g., parent or relative) who is caring for the child. (See FILING FOR BENEFITS, SECTION K.)

E-53. Who receives a child's benefits?

A representative payee, such as a parent or relative, will be appointed to receive the child's benefits. However, if the child is over age 18 and competent, payment will be made directly to the child. Also, if the child is under 18, away from home (e.g., in the Army), and is deemed mature enough to handle the benefit, payment may be made directly to the child.

SURVIVOR'S BENEFITS

E-54. What benefits are payable to the survivors of a deceased insured worker?

- Mother's or Father's benefit (monthly benefit for widow(er), regardless of age, who is caring for at least one child, under 16 or disabled before age 22, of the deceased worker)—see E-55 to E-68.

- Child's benefit (monthly benefit for each child who is: (1) under age 18, (2) over age 18 and disabled before age 22, or (3) under age 19 and attending a full-time elementary or high school)—see E-69 to E-82.

- Widow(er)'s benefit (monthly benefit for widow(er), or surviving divorced widow(er), age 60 or older)—see E-83 to E-93.

- Disabled Widow(er)'s benefit (monthly benefit for a disabled widow(er), age 50-60)—see E-94.

- Parent's benefit (monthly benefit for parent age 62 or older who was dependent upon deceased worker for support)—see E-95 to E-104.

- Lump-sum death payment—see E-105 to E-107.

MOTHER'S OR FATHER'S BENEFIT

E-55. Is the surviving spouse of an insured worker entitled to a monthly Mother's or Father's benefit at any age?

Yes, if caring for a child of the deceased worker under age 16 or disabled before age 22. Otherwise a surviving spouse is not eligible for benefits until age 60 (or age 50-59 if disabled).

The surviving spouse of a fully or currently insured worker is entitled to a mother's or father's benefit at any age if: (1) he or she is caring for a child of the deceased worker under age 16 or disabled before age 22 who is entitled to a child's benefit on the deceased worker's account, (2) he or she is not married, (3) he or she is not entitled to widow(er)'s benefits, (4) he or she is not entitled to a retirement benefit based on his or her own work record that is equal to or larger than the amount of the unadjusted mother's or father's benefit, and (5) he or she has filed an application for benefits.

One of the following requirements must also be met: (1) the surviving spouse was married to the deceased worker for at least nine months before the worker died (see exception below), (2) the surviving spouse is the biological mother or father of the worker's child, (3) the surviving spouse legally adopted the worker's child during their marriage and before the child reached age 18, (4) the surviving spouse was married to the worker when they both legally adopted a child under age 18, (5) the worker legally adopted the surviving spouse's child during their marriage and before the child reached age 18, or (6) the surviving spouse was entitled or potentially entitled to spouse's, widow(er)'s, father's, mother's, parent's, or childhood disability benefits in the month before the month the surviving spouse married the deceased worker.

A surviving spouse is "potentially entitled" if he or she meets all requirements for entitlement, other than the filing of an application and attainment of the required age.

There is an exception to the requirement that the surviving spouse be married to the deceased worker for at least nine months before the worker died. The rule is waived if the worker's death was accidental, or if it occurred in the line of duty while a member of a uniformed service serving on active duty, or if the surviving spouse who was married to the worker at the time of death, was previously married to and divorced from the worker and the previous marriage had lasted nine months. The worker's death is defined as accidental only if the worker received bodily injuries solely through violent, external, and accidental means and, as a direct result of the bodily injuries and independently of all other causes, died within three months after the day the injuries were received. The exception does not apply if, at the time of the marriage, the worker could not reasonably have been expected to live for nine months.

E-56. Can a divorced spouse qualify for a survivor's benefit?

Yes, a person is entitled to mother's or father's benefits as a surviving divorced spouse of a worker who died fully or currently insured if he or she: (1) is the father or mother of the worker's child, or was married to the worker when either of them adopted the other's child or when both of them adopted a child and the child was then under 18, (2) filed an application for these benefits, (3) is not married, (4) is not entitled to a widow(er)'s benefits, or to a retirement benefit that is equal to or larger than the mother's or father's full benefit, and (5) has in care the worker's child who is entitled to child's benefits based on the worker's earnings record. The child must be under age 16 or disabled.

E-57. Must a worker be fully insured at death to qualify for the mother's or father's benefit?

No; the mother's or father's benefit is payable if the worker was *either* fully or currently insured (See D-15 to D-17).

E-58. What is the amount of a mother's or father's benefit?

The amount of a mother's or father's benefit is equal to 75% of the deceased spouse's primary insurance amount (PIA). However, because of the "family maximum" limit, the monthly benefit actually received by the surviving spouse may be less. If the total benefits payable on one worker's Social Security account exceed the family maximum, all benefits are reduced proportionately to bring the total within the family maximum. See Maximum Family Benefits, F-15. A surviving divorced mother's or father's benefit is the same amount. However, benefits paid to a divorced mother or father will not be reduced because of the limit on total family benefits, and such benefits are not counted in figuring the total benefits payable to others on the basis of the deceased worker's account.

If the surviving spouse is entitled to a smaller retirement or disability benefit based on his own earnings record, he will receive the benefit based on his own account, and will receive as a mother's or father's benefit only the difference between the mother's or father's benefit rate and the other benefit rate.

E-59. What are the differences between a mother's or father's benefit and a widow(er)'s benefit?

A *mother's or father's* benefit is payable to a surviving spouse at any age, but he or she must be caring for at least one child under age 16 or a disabled child of the deceased spouse. A *widow(er)'s* benefit is not payable until the surviving spouse reaches age 60 unless disabled at age 50-59.

A surviving spouse will qualify for a *mother's or father's* benefit if the deceased spouse was either fully or currently insured at death. However, a surviving spouse will not qualify for a *widow(er)'s* benefit unless the deceased spouse was fully insured at death.

A full *mother's or father's* benefit is equal to only 75% of the deceased spouse's PIA. A full *widow(er)'s* benefit (at the normal retirement age, see E-4) is equal to 100% of the deceased spouse's PIA.

E-60. Is a mother's or father's benefit payable regardless of the surviving spouse's need?

Yes, if the surviving spouse qualifies (see E-55), he or she will receive benefits regardless of wealth.

E-61. Can a surviving spouse lose some or all of the benefits by working?

Yes, in 2001, by earning over $10,680 a year if under the normal retirement age (see E-4) for the entire year. In the year the surviving spouse reaches normal retirement age, benefits may be lost by earning over $25,000. However only earnings earned before the month the surviving spouse reaches normal retirement age count toward the $25,000 limit. (See LOSS OF BENEFITS BECAUSE OF EXCESS EARNINGS, SECTION H.) However, the loss of benefits by a surviving spouse will not cause the children to lose their benefits.

E-62. If the only child in a surviving spouse's care loses benefits by working, will this cause the child's mother or father to lose benefits?

No. (See LOSS OF BENEFITS BECAUSE OF EXCESS EARNINGS, SECTION H.)

E-63. Must a surviving spouse file application for a mother's or father's benefit?

Yes, unless receiving a spouse's benefit before the worker's death. The application should be filed within six months after the worker's death because no more than six month's benefit will be paid retroactively.

E-64. When do a mother's or father's benefits begin?

If a surviving spouse qualifies, benefits will begin with a payment for the month in which his or her spouse died (but see E-63).

E-65. When do a mother's or father's benefits end?

Mother's or father's benefits end when: (1) no child of the deceased worker under age 18 or disabled is entitled to a child's benefit, (2) in the case of a surviving divorced father or mother, no natural or legally adopted child of the surviving spouse under age 16 or disabled is entitled to a child's benefit on the deceased worker's earnings record, (3) the surviving spouse becomes entitled to a widow(er)'s benefit, (4) the surviving spouse dies, (5) the surviving spouse becomes entitled to retirement benefits in an amount equal to or greater than 3/4 of the deceased spouse's PIA, or (6) the surviving spouse marries. However, if the surviving spouse marries a person entitled to retirement, disability, divorced spouse's, widow(er)'s, father's, mother's, parent's, or childhood disability benefits, the marriage has no effect on entitlement (unless marriage is to a child under age 18 or a full-time student under the age 19, in which case both benefits terminate).

If the subsequent marriage ends, the surviving spouse may be reentitled to mother's or father's benefits on the prior deceased spouse's (or former spouse's) earnings record beginning with the month the subsequent marriage ends.

The surviving spouse can receive no further benefits until he or she becomes entitled to a widow(er)'s benefit at age 60 (or a disabled widow's or widower's benefits at age 50). The period during which the surviving spouse is entitled to no benefits is known as the *black-out period*. The fact that a child's benefits will continue after age 16 does not entitle the child's mother or father to a continuation of benefits.

E-66. Will a mother's or father's benefit be reduced if he or she is receiving a government pension?

Social Security benefits payable to spouses—including surviving spouses and divorced spouses—are reduced (but not below zero) by two-thirds of the amount of any governmental (federal, state, or local) retirement benefit payable to the spouse based on *his or her own earnings* in employment not covered by Social Security on the last day of such employment. The reduction is two-thirds of the pension. Thus, for the affected group, the spouse's benefit is reduced $2 for every $3 of the government pension.

This offset against Social Security benefits does not apply if the individual: (1) met all the requirements for entitlement to Social Security benefits that existed and were applied in January 1977, and (2) received or was eligible to receive a government pension between December 1977 and December 1982.

Pensions based wholly on service performed as a member of a uniformed service, whether on active or inactive duty, are excluded from the offset.

E-67. Will a mother's or father's benefits stop when the youngest child (or only child) reaches age 16?

Yes (unless the child is disabled and was disabled before age 22), and he or she will not become eligible for widow(er)'s benefits until age 60 (unless disabled at ages 50-59). The time in between when a surviving spouse is not entitled to any Social Security benefits is commonly called the *black-out period*. But if the surviving spouse is caring for a disabled child whose disability began before age 22, mother's or father's benefits will not stop so long as the child continues to be disabled and entitled to a child's benefits. If the surviving spouse is disabled, he or she may qualify for a disabled widow(er)'s benefit at age 50. (See E-93.)

E-68. Does a mother or father continue to receive benefits until the youngest child (or only child) is age 22 if the child is attending school?

No. A mother's or father's benefits are payable only so long as the child in his or her care is under age 16 or disabled. See E-44.

CHILD'S BENEFIT (Child of Deceased Worker)

E-69. Is a child of a deceased worker entitled to Social Security benefits?

If a worker dies either fully *or* currently insured, each child who meets the relationship requirements is entitled to a child's benefit if: (1) under age 18, or over age 18 and disabled by a disability that began before age 22, or under age 19 and a full-time elementary or secondary school student, (2) not married, (3) dependent upon the deceased parent, and (4) an application has been filed for benefits.

The Social Security Administration agreed to pay a survivor's benefit to a child who was conceived through artificial insemination after her father's death. An administrative law judge ruled in 1995 that the child was entitled to $700 a month in Social Security child's benefits.

E-70. Must a parent be fully insured at death to qualify the child for a child's benefits?

No, the child is eligible for benefits on the parent's Social Security account if the parent was either fully or currently insured at death. (See D-15 to D-17.)

E-71. Must a child have been dependent upon the deceased parent to be eligible for a child's benefit?

Yes, the child must have been dependent upon the deceased worker.

The factors that determine whether a child is dependent upon a worker vary, depending upon whether the worker is the natural parent, the legally adopting parent, the stepparent, or the grandparent.

A child is "deemed" dependent upon the worker if the child has not been legally adopted by someone other than the worker and: (1) is the legitimate child of the worker, (2) an illegitimate child who would have the right under applicable state law to inherit intestate property from the worker as a child, (3) the child of a void or voidable marriage, (4) the child of an invalid ceremonial marriage, or (5) the legally adopted child of the worker adopted prior to the worker's death.

E-72. Under what circumstances is a child considered dependent upon his grandparent, step-grandparent, great-grandparent, or step great-grandparent?

A child is dependent upon a grandparent, step-grandparent, great-grandparent, or step great-grandparent if the child: (1) began living with the worker before he or she reached age 18, and (2) lived with the worker in the United States and received at least one-half support from the worker. The support test is met if the worker provides one-half of the support: (1) for the year before the month the worker died, or (2) if the worker had a period of disability that lasted until he or she became entitled to benefits, for the year immediately before the month in which the period of disability began.

E-73. Under what circumstances is a child considered dependent upon a stepfather or stepmother?

The child is considered dependent upon a stepfather or stepmother if the stepfather or stepmother is contributing at least one-half of the child's support. The child does not have to be living with the stepfather or stepmother.

A stepchild must have been the stepchild of the insured worker for at least nine months immediately preceding the day the worker died, unless the worker and the child's natural or adopting parent were previously married, divorced, and then remarried at the time of the worker's death, and the 9-month-duration-of-relationship requirement was met at the time of the divorce. If the death of the worker was accidental or occurred in the line of duty while a member of a uniformed service serving on active duty, the 9-month requirement may be considered satisfied, unless at the time of the marriage, the worker could not have been expected to live for nine months. A child who was not legally adopted by the worker will nevertheless be treated as a legally adopted child if the child was living in the worker's home or receiving at least one-half of his support from the worker at the time of the worker's death, and the child is adopted by the worker's surviving spouse after the worker's death (but only if adoption proceedings were instituted by the worker before his death or adoption by the surviving spouse occurs within two years after the worker's death). However, such a child will not be treated as the worker's legally adopted child if at the time of the worker's death he was receiving regular contributions toward his support from someone other than the worker or the worker's spouse or a public or private welfare organization.

A child is eligible for benefits based on his parent's Social Security earnings record even if the child was supported by a stepparent when the parent died.

If a stepchild's benefits are based on the wages and self-employment income of a stepparent who is subsequently divorced from the child's natural parent, benefits to the stepchild terminate the month after the month in which the divorce becomes final.

E-74. Can a child receive benefits based on a deceased parent's Social Security account even though the other parent is still living and supporting the child?

Yes.

E-75. Is a child age 18 or over entitled to benefits if attending school?

A child may be eligible for child's benefits if he is under age 19 and a full-time elementary or secondary school student.

Benefits paid to a student age 18 who attends elementary or secondary schools on a full-time basis end with the last month that the student is a full-time student or, if earlier, the month before the month the student becomes age 19.

A child is a full-time elementary or secondary school student if he attends a school that provides elementary or secondary education as determined under the law of the state or other jurisdiction in which it is located. Participation in one of the following programs also meets the requirements:

(1) The child is instructed in elementary or secondary education at home in accordance with a home schooling law of the state or other jurisdiction in which the child resides. Students in these types of situations include a wide range of individuals. For example, home schooling students may be in that situation for religious reasons or because the parents do not agree with the local school curriculum.

103

(2) The child is in an independent study elementary or secondary education program in accordance with state law or other jurisdiction in which he resides which is administered by the local school or school district jurisdiction. Students in independent study programs may include those individuals who cannot take advantage of the traditional school setting, such as hard-to-keep-in-school students (unable to adjust or delinquents), single mothers, or expectant mothers.

A child must be in full-time attendance in a day or evening course of at least 13 weeks duration and must be carrying a subject load which is considered full-time for day students under the institution's standards and practices. If a child is in a home schooling program, the child must be carrying a subject load which is considered full-time for day students under standards and practices set by the state or other jurisdiction in which the child resides.

To be considered in full-time attendance, a child's scheduled attendance must be at the rate of at least 20 hours per week. If a child is in an independent study program, the number of hours spent in school attendance are determined by combining the number of hours of attendance at a school facility with the agreed upon number of hours spent in independent study.

A child may still be considered in full-time attendance if the scheduled rate of attendance is below 20 hours per week if the Social Security Administration finds that:

(1) The school attended does not schedule at least 20 hours per week and going to that particular school is the child's only reasonable alternative; or

(2) the child's medical condition prevents him from having scheduled attendance of at least 20 hours per week. To prove that a child's medical condition prevents scheduling 20 hours per week, the Social Security Administration may request that the child provide appropriate medical evidence or a statement from the school.

A child enrolled solely in correspondence courses is not a full-time elementary or secondary school student.

E-76. What is the amount of the monthly benefit for a child of a deceased worker?

The surviving child's benefit is equal to 75% of the deceased parent's primary insurance amount. However, because of the "family maximum" limit, the monthly benefit actually received by the child may be less. If the total amount payable in benefits based on one worker's Social Security account exceeds the "family maximum," all benefits are reduced proportionately to bring the total within the "family maximum." (See Maximum Family Benefits, F-15 to F-18.)

A child entitled to benefits based on more than one worker's record will get the benefit based on the record that provides the highest amount, if the payment does not reduce the benefits of any other individual who is entitled to benefits based on the same earnings record.

E-77. Will a child lose benefits if the child works or the child's parent works?

The child can lose part or all of his benefits if he earns over $10,680 in 2001. However, none of the child's benefits will be lost because his surviving parent works. Also, the child's work will not affect the parent's benefits. (See LOSS OF BENEFITS BECAUSE OF EXCESS EARNINGS, SECTION H.)

E-78. If a child is entitled to benefits on more than one person's Social Security account, will the child receive both benefits?

No, the child will receive only the higher benefit. (But see F-35.)

E-79. When does a child's benefit begin?

Ordinarily, the first benefit is payable for the month in which the parent died. However, unless the child was receiving benefits before the parent's death, an application should be filed within six months after death. Benefits will be paid retroactively for not more than six months.

E-80. When does a child's benefit end?

A child's benefit ends: (1) at death, (2) at age 18 (age 19 if full-time elementary or secondary school student), (3) when disability ceases if benefits are received only because the child was disabled before age 22 (but further benefits may be available if disability occurs again within seven years after childhood disability benefits terminate), or (4) when married. However, marriage of a disabled child age 18 or over to another Social Security beneficiary over age 18 (other than to a person receiving child's benefits under age 18 or age 18 as a full-time elementary or secondary school student) will ordinarily not terminate the child's benefits.

The benefits of a childhood disability beneficiary, regardless of sex, continue after the child's spouse is no longer eligible for benefits as a childhood disability beneficiary or disabled worker beneficiary.

The child is not entitled to a payment for the month in which any of the foregoing events occur, but benefits will be continued through the second month after the month that a disabled child's disability ceases.

A child's benefit may end if the child is missing. In 1993, the Social Security Administration suspended benefits for a child who disappeared mysteriously and was missing for five years. Further payment of benefits was suspended until the beneficiary's whereabouts and continuing eligibility for benefits could be determined. *Social Security Ruling SSR 93-3.*

E-81. Will a child's benefits end if the child marries?

Yes, as a general rule. However, marriage of a disabled child over age 18 to another Social Security beneficiary over age 18 will ordinarily not terminate the child's benefits (see E-80).

E-82. Who files application for a child's benefits and who receives the benefits?

See E-52 and E-53.

WIDOW(ER)'S BENEFIT

E-83. Is the widow(er) of an insured worker entitled to benefits if there are no children in his or her care?

A widow(er) is entitled to a widow(er)'s benefit based on the deceased spouse's earnings if: (1) the widow(er) is age 60 or over, or is at least age 50 but not age 60 and is disabled, (2) the worker died fully insured, (3) the widow(er) is not entitled to a retirement benefit that is equal to or larger than the worker's primary insurance amount, (4) the widow(er) has filed an application for widow(er)'s benefits, and (5) the widow(er) is not married except under special circumstances discussed below.

In addition, *one* of the following conditions must be met: (1) the widow(er) was married to the deceased worker for at least nine months immediately prior to the worker's death (see exceptions below), (2) the widow(er) is the biological mother or father of the worker's child (this requirement is met if a live child was born to the worker and the widow(er), although the child need not still survive), (3) the widow(er) legally adopted the worker's child during their marriage and before the child reached age 18, (4) the widow(er) was married to the worker when they both legally adopted a child under age 18, (5) the worker legally adopted the widow(er)'s child during their marriage and before the child reached age 18, or (6) the widow(er) was entitled or potentially entitled to spouse's, widow(er)'s, father's (based on the record of a fully insured individual), mother's (based on the record of a fully insured individual), parent's, or childhood disability benefits, or to a widow(er)'s, child's (age 18 or over) or parent's annuity under the Railroad Retirement Act, in the month before the month the widow(er) married the deceased worker.

A widow(er) is "potentially entitled" if he or she meets all requirements for entitlement, other than filing of an application and attainment of the required age.

The 9-month duration of marriage requirement is waived if the worker's death was accidental or it occurred in the line of duty while a member of a uniformed service serving on active duty, or if the widow(er) who was married to the worker at the time of death, was previously married to and divorced from the worker and the previous marriage had lasted nine months.

The worker's death is "accidental" if he or she received bodily injuries solely through violent, external, and accidental means and, as a direct result, died within three months after the day the injuries were received. The exception to the 9-month duration of marriage requirement does not apply if, at the time of marriage, the worker could not reasonably have been expected to live for nine months.

An application for widow(er)'s benefits is not required if the person was age 65 or over and entitled to spouse's benefits for the month immediately preceding the month in which the worker died, or if the person was entitled to mother's or father's benefits for the month immediately preceding the month in which age 65 was attained. If an entitled spouse is between ages 62 and 65 when the worker dies and the spouse is not also entitled to a disability or retirement benefit, the spouse's benefits will automatically be converted to widow(er)'s benefits.

E-84. Must the worker be fully insured at death to qualify the widow(er) for a widow(er)'s benefit?

Yes, the widow(er) will not be entitled to a widow(er)'s benefit at age 60 or over if the worker was only currently insured at death (see D-16, D-17, E-59).

E-85. Can the divorced spouse of a deceased worker qualify for a widow(er)'s benefit?

A widow(er) is entitled to surviving divorced spouse's benefits on the worker's Social Security record if: (1) the surviving divorced spouse was married to the worker for at least 10 years prior to the date the divorce became final, (2) the surviving divorced spouse is age 60 or over, or is at least age 50 but not age 60 and is disabled, (3) the deceased spouse died fully insured, (4) the surviving divorced spouse is not married (but see E-87 below), (5) the surviving divorced spouse is not entitled to a retirement benefit that is equal to or greater than the deceased worker's primary insurance amount (PIA), and (6) the surviving divorced spouse has filed an application for widow(er)'s benefits.

A surviving divorced spouse meets the 10-year marriage requirement, even if, within the 10-year period, they were divorced, provided they remarried each other no later than the calendar year after the year of the divorce.

E-86. What is the earliest age at which a widow(er) can receive a widow(er)'s benefit?

A widow(er) can elect to start receiving a reduced widow(er)'s benefit at age 60 (see E-87). A disabled widow(er) can start receiving benefits at age 50.

E-87. What is the monthly rate of a widow(er)'s benefit?

A widow(er) who is eligible for a widow(er)'s benefit may apply for a reduced benefit at any time between 60 and normal retirement age, or may wait until normal retirement age to receive a full widow(er)'s benefit. If the widow(er) is normal retirement age or older when benefits commence, the monthly benefit is equal to 100% of the deceased worker's PIA (the amount the worker would have been entitled to receive upon retirement at normal retirement age) plus any additional amount the deceased worker was entitled to because of delayed retirement credits (the delayed retirement credit is discussed at E-90 and F-27). If the worker was actually receiving benefits that began before normal retirement age, the widow(er) would be entitled to an amount equal to the reduced benefit the worker would have been receiving had he lived (but not less than 82.5% of the PIA).

If the widow(er) chooses to receive, and is paid, a reduced widow(er)'s benefit for months before normal retirement age, he or she is not entitled to the widow(er)'s full benefit rate upon reaching normal retirement age. A reduced benefit is payable for as long as he or she remains entitled to widow(er)'s benefits.

Currently, the widow(er)'s benefit is reduced by 19/40 of 1% for each month that the widow(er) is under age 65 when the benefits commence. A benefit beginning at age 60 will equal 71.5% of the deceased worker's PIA; one beginning at age 62 will equal 82.9% of the PIA. When normal retirement age is more than 65, the 71.5% at age 60 will remain unchanged, but the reduction factor will be different (based on 71.5% at age 60 and 100% at normal retirement age).

The monthly payment amount of a widow(er) who remarries after attaining age 60 is not reduced.

The average monthly benefit for a widow(er) in 2001 is $811.

If there are other survivors entitled to benefits based on the deceased worker's earnings record, the widow(er) could receive a smaller benefit because of the family maximum limit. (See Maximum Family Benefits, F-15 to F-18, and Table 11.)

If the widow(er) has in care the deceased spouse's child, under 16 or disabled, who is entitled to child's benefits, for some months while he or she is under 65, his or her widow(er)'s benefits are not reduced for those months below 75% of the deceased spouse's PIA.

The surviving divorced spouse's benefit is the same amount as a widow(er)'s benefit. However, it is paid independently of benefits for the former spouse's family. In other words, it is not subject to reduction because of the family maximum limit, and does not affect the family maximum for the former spouse's family.

A widow(er) who files an application for actuarially reduced widow(er)'s benefits in the calendar month following the month his or her spouse died is entitled to one month of retroactive benefit payments.

E-88. How does remarriage affect a widow(er)'s benefits?

The remarriage of a widow(er) or surviving divorced spouse after age 60, or the remarriage of a disabled widow(er) or disabled surviving divorced spouse after age 50 and after the date he or she became disabled, will not prevent that individual from becoming entitled to benefits on his or her prior deceased spouse's Social Security record.

A widow(er) or a surviving divorced spouse's remarriage before age 60 will prevent entitlement unless the subsequent marriage ends, whether by death, divorce or annulment. If the subsequent marriage ends, the widow(er) or surviving divorced spouse may become entitled or reentitled to benefits on the prior deceased spouse's earnings record beginning with the month the subsequent marriage ends.

A widower is entitled to benefits even when remarriage takes place prior to the death of the former spouse.

There is a distinct advantage in being able to receive the widow(er)'s benefit instead of the spouse's benefit. Part or all of a spouse's benefit could be lost if the new spouse is under normal retirement age and loses benefits by working and earning more than the Social Security earnings limit. The widow(er)'s benefit, on the other hand, will be unaffected by the new spouse's work.

E-89. If a widow(er) is entitled to a retirement benefit and a widow(er)'s benefit, will the widow(er) receive both benefits?

No, the widow(er) will receive the retirement benefit plus the difference if the widow(er)'s benefit is greater. In other words, the widow(er) will receive only the larger benefit. (See also Reduction in Benefits, F-29 to F-33.)

E-90. How does the delayed retirement credit affect a widow(er)'s benefit?

A widow(er) whose spouse reaches age 65 in 2000-01 receives an increase in benefits equal to 6% for each year (12/24 of 1% per month) in which his or her spouse deferred retirement benefits between normal retirement age and age 70. For spouse's reaching age 65 prior to 2000-01, the increases per year of deferring retirement were as follows: age 65 in 1998-99, 5.5%; age 65 in 1996-97, 5%; age 65 in 1994-95, 4.5%; age 65 in 1992-93, 4.0%; age 65 in 1990-91, 3.5%; age 65 in 1982-89, 3%; and age 65 before 1982, 1%.

This delayed retirement credit is being gradually increased until reaching 8% per year for workers reaching age 65 after 2008 (in 2009, the normal retirement age will be 66). The delayed retirement credit is based on the year of attainment of age 62, not the year of work, and it can be earned only after normal retirement age. (See F-27 for further information.)

A surviving divorced spouse is entitled to the same increase that had been applied to the benefit of the deceased worker or for which the deceased worker was eligible at the time of death.

E-91. Can a widow(er) lose benefits by working?

Yes. Although benefits are payable regardless of how wealthy the widow(er) is, the widow(er) will lose some or all benefits if she is under the normal retirement age (see E-4) for the entire year and her earnings exceed $10,680 in 2001. In the year the widow(er) reaches normal retirement age, the widow(er) will lose some or all benefits if her earnings exceed $25,000 in 2001. However, only earnings earned before the month that normal retirement age is reached count towards the $25,000 limit. See LOSS OF BENEFITS BECAUSE OF EXCESS EARNINGS, SECTION H.

E-92. Will a widow(er)'s benefits be reduced if the widow(er) is receiving a government pension?

Social Security benefits payable to spouses—including surviving spouses and divorced spouses—are reduced (but not below zero) by two-thirds of the amount of any governmental (federal, state, or local) retirement benefit payable to the spouse based on *his or her own earnings* in employment not covered by Social Security on the last day of such employment. The reduction is two-thirds of the pension for people eligible for a government pension. Thus, for the affected group, the spouse's benefit is reduced $2 for every $3 of the government pension.

This offset against Social Security benefits does not apply if the individual: (1) met all the requirements for entitlement to Social Security benefits that existed and applied in January 1977, and (2) received or was eligible to receive a government pension between December 1977 and December 1982.

Generally, federal workers hired before 1984 are part of the Civil Service Retirement System (CSRS) and are not covered by Social Security. Federal workers hired after 1983 are covered by the Federal Employees' Retirement System Act of 1986 (FERS), which includes Social Security coverage. Legislation provided an opportunity for federal employees covered by CSRS to join FERS in 1987 (and thereby obtain Social Security coverage). Thus, a CSRS employee who switched to FERS during this period immediately became exempt from the government pension offset.

Federal employees who switch from CSRS to FERS during any election period on or after January 1, 1988, are exempt from the government pension offset only if they have five or more years of federal employment covered by Social Security beginning January 1, 1988. This rule also applies to certain legislative branch employees who first become covered under FERS on or after January 1, 1988.

Pensions based wholly on service performed as a member of a uniformed service, whether on active or inactive duty, are excluded from the offset.

E-93. When do a widow(er)'s benefits end?

Widow(er)'s benefits end when: (1) the widow(er) dies, or (2) the widow(er) becomes entitled to a retirement benefit which is as large as or larger than the deceased worker's primary insurance amount, or (3) the widow(er)'s disability ceases.

If a widow(er)'s disability ceases, the last month of entitlement is the second month after the month in which the disability ceased, except that entitlement continues if the widow(er) becomes age 65 on or before the last day of the third month after the disability ends.

DISABLED WIDOW(ER)'S BENEFIT

E-94. Is a disabled widow(er) entitled to benefits starting before age 60?

A disabled widow(er) (or surviving divorced widow(er)) who otherwise qualifies for a widow(er)'s benefit can start receiving a disabled widow(er)'s benefit at any time after attaining age 50 and before attaining age 60. The monthly benefit will be based on 100% of the deceased spouse's PIA, but will be reduced by 28.5% so that the benefit equals 71.5% of the deceased spouse's PIA at age 60. The monthly benefit remains at 71.5% of the deceased spouse's

PIA for disabled widow(er)'s between ages 50 and 59. Once established, the benefit rate remains the same; it will not be increased when the widow(er) reaches age 60 or normal retirement age.

Disabled widow(er)'s benefits are payable to a disabled widow(er) or surviving divorced spouse age 50-59 if the individual: (1) meets the definition of disability for disabled workers, (2) became disabled no later than seven years after the month the worker died or seven years after the last month the widow(er) was previously entitled to benefits on the worker's earnings record, (3) has been disabled throughout a waiting period of five consecutive full calendar months, except that no waiting period is required if the widow(er) was previously entitled to disabled widow(er)'s benefits, and (4) meets the nondisability requirements for a surviving spouse or a surviving divorced spouse.

The first month of entitlement to disabled widow(er)'s benefits is the *latest* of the following months: (1) either the sixth consecutive calendar month of disability, where a waiting period is required, or the first full calendar month of disability, if a waiting period is not required; (2) the month the insured spouse died; (3) the twelfth month before the month the widow(er) applied for benefits; or (4) the month the widow(er) attains age 50.

Widow(er)s must meet the definition of disability used to determine if workers are entitled to disability benefits. In other words, the widow(er) must be unable to engage in any substantial gainful activity by reason of physical or mental impairment. The impairment must be medically determinable and expected to last for at least 12 months or result in death.

If benefits to a widow(er) who is disabled based on drug addiction or alcoholism are terminated after 36 months of benefits, that person cannot become entitled again to widow(er)'s benefits if drug addiction or alcoholism is a contributing factor material to the later determination of disability. See E-26.

PARENT'S BENEFITS

E-95. Under what circumstances is a deceased worker's parent entitled to benefits?

The parent of a deceased insured person is entitled to a parent's benefit if: (1) the insured person was fully insured at the time of death, (2) the parent files an application for parent's benefits, (3) the parent has reached age 62, (4) the parent is not entitled to a retirement benefit that is equal to or larger than the amount of the unadjusted parent's benefit after any increase to the minimum benefit, (5) the parent was receiving at least one-half support from the insured person, (6) evidence that the support requirement was met has been filed with the Social Security Administration within the appropriate time limit, and (7) the parent has not remarried since the insured person's death.

The support requirement must be met at: (1) the time that the insured person died, or (2) the beginning of a period of disability that was established for the deceased if it continued up until the month in which he or she died. Evidence of support must be filed within the two-year period: (1) after the date of the death of the insured person, if that point is being used or (2) after the month in which the insured person had filed an application to establish a period of disability if that point is being used. Evidence of support must be filed within the appropriate period even though the parent may not be eligible for benefits at that time (e.g., has not reached retirement age). The time limit may be extended for good cause.

The insured provides one-half of a parent's support if: (1) the insured makes regular contributions for the parent's ordinary living costs, (2) the amount of these contributions equals or exceeds one-half of the parent's ordinary living costs, and (3) any income (from sources other than the insured person) for support purposes is one-half or less of the parent's ordinary living costs.

The insured is not providing at least one-half of the parent's support unless the insured has done so for a reasonable period of time. Ordinarily, the Social Security Administration will consider a reasonable period to be the 12-month period immediately preceding the time when the one-half support requirement must be met.

E-96. Who is a parent for the purpose of receiving a parent's benefit?

One of the following conditions must be met: (1) the parent is a natural parent and would be eligible under the law of the state of the worker's domicile to share in the intestate property of the worker as the worker's father or mother; (2) the parent has legally adopted the insured person before the insured person attained age 16; or (3) the person claiming benefits became the deceased's stepparent by a marriage entered into before the deceased had attained age 16.

E-97. What is the amount of a parent's monthly benefit?

A parent's benefit is equal to 82.5% of the deceased worker's primary insurance amount (PIA), if there is only one eligible parent. If two parents are entitled to benefits, the benefit for each is 75% of the worker's PIA. The full benefit is payable at age 62. However, because of the maximum family limit, the monthly benefit actually received by a parent may be less. If total monthly benefits payable on the basis of one worker's earnings record exceeds the family maximum, all benefits are reduced proportionately to bring the total within the family maximum (see Maximum Family Benefits, F-15 to F-18).

113

E-98. Can a parent receive benefits even if the worker's widow(er) and children are eligible for benefits?

Yes. (But see E-99.)

E-99. May benefits payable to a parent reduce the benefits payable to the worker's widow(er) and children?

Yes, because the total amount of monthly benefits based on one worker's Social Security account is limited by a maximum family benefit ceiling. If total benefits computed separately exceed this limit, all benefits are reduced proportionately to bring the total within the family maximum. (See Maximum Family Benefits, F-15 to F-18.)

E-100. Is a parent's benefit starting at age 62 smaller than one starting at age 65?

No, the full parent's benefit is payable (to a father or mother) at age 62.

E-101. If a person is entitled to a parent's benefit and a retirement benefit, will he receive both full benefits?

If the parent is also eligible for a retired worker's benefit based on his own earnings record, he will receive the retired worker's benefit if it equals or exceeds the parent's benefit. However, he is not compelled to take a reduced retired worker's benefit before normal retirement age (see E-4). He can receive the parent's benefit and then switch to a full retired worker's benefit at normal retirement age.

E-102. Can a person lose a parent's benefit by working?

Yes, a person will lose some or all benefits if the person is under normal retirement age for the entire year and his earnings exceed $10,680 in 2001. In the year the person reaches normal retirement age (see E-4), he will lose some or all benefits if his earnings exceed $25,000 in 2001. However, only earnings earned before the month that he reaches normal retirement age count toward the $25,000 limit. (See LOSS OF BENEFITS BECAUSE OF EXCESS EARNINGS, SECTION H.)

E-103. When do a parent's benefits end?

When the parent dies, marries (but see E-104), or when the parent becomes entitled to a retirement benefit or disability benefit equal to or larger than the amount of the unadjusted parent's benefit.

E-104. If a parent remarries after the worker's death, will the parent lose benefits?

Yes, unless the marriage is to a person entitled to monthly Social Security benefits as a divorced spouse, widow(er), mother, father, parent, or a disabled child age 18 or over.

LUMP-SUM DEATH PAYMENT

E-105. What is the amount of the Social Security lump sum death payment?

A lump sum death benefit of $255 is paid upon the death of an insured worker, provided he is survived by a spouse who was living in the same household as the deceased at the time of death, or a spouse or dependent child eligible to receive Social Security benefits for the month of death based on his earnings record.

Also, the lump sum death benefit is paid to a spouse when the widow(er) and the deceased customarily lived together as husband and wife in the same residence. While temporary separations do not necessarily preclude the Social Security Administration from considering a couple to be living in the same household, extended separations (including most that last six months or more) generally indicate the couple was not living in the same household.

"Living in the same household" requires a male and female living together as husband and wife in the same residence. The couple may be considered to be living in the same household although one of them is temporarily absent from the residence. An absence is considered temporary if:

(1) It was due to service in the United States Armed Forces.

(2) It was six months or less and neither spouse was outside of the United States during this time and the absence was due to business, employment, or confinement in a hospital, nursing home, other medical institution, or a penal institution.

(3) It was for an extended separation, regardless of the duration, due to the confinement of either spouse in a hospital, nursing home, or other medical institution, if the evidence indicates that the spouses were separated solely for medical reasons and the spouses otherwise would have resided together.

(4) It was based on other circumstances, and it is shown that the spouses could have expected to live together in the near future.

The lump-sum death payment is paid in the following order of priority:

(1) The widow(er) of the deceased wage earner who was living in the same household as the deceased wage earner (or customarily lived together as husband and wife in the same residence) at the time of death;

115

(2) The widow(er) (excluding a divorced spouse) who is eligible for or entitled to benefits based on the deceased wage earner's record for the month of death;

(3) Children who are eligible for or entitled to benefits based on the deceased wage earner's record for the month of death.

If no surviving widow(er) or child as defined above survives, no lump sum is payable.

However, if an otherwise eligible widow(er) dies before making application for the lump-sum death payment or before negotiating the benefit check, the legal representative of the estate of the deceased widow(er) may claim the lump-sum payment. Where the legal representative of the estate is a state or political subdivision of a state, the lump-sum death benefit is not payable.

The lump-sum death benefit is not payable to an otherwise ineligible child of the wage earner after the wage earner's widow, who applied for the benefit, died before it could be paid. (*Social Security Ruling 85-24a*, October 1985).

E-106. Is the lump-sum death benefit payable only if the worker was fully insured at death?

No, it is payable if the worker was either fully or currently insured.

E-107. Must an application be made for the lump-sum death benefit?

An application need not be made by the widow(er) if he or she was receiving a spouse's benefit when the insured person died. Otherwise, an application must be filed within two years after the insured person's death unless good cause can be shown why the application was not filed within the two-year period.

COMPUTING BENEFITS

F-1. In general, how are Social Security benefits determined?

Benefits payable under the retirement, survivors, and disability benefits program are almost always based on the insured's Social Security earnings since 1950. (Under some circumstances—where an individual has little or no earnings since 1950—benefits may be computed based on earnings since 1937.)

The wage indexing formula is used to compute benefits if disability, death or age 62 occurs after 1978. (See F-4.)

If disability, death or age 62 occurred before 1979, benefits are determined using the simplified old-start benefit computation method. (See F-2.)

A transition period took place from 1979 through 1983. A worker who became 62, or a worker who died after reaching age 62 during this period, is guaranteed that the method producing the larger benefit will be used.

To be eligible for the guarantee the worker must: (1) have had income credited for one year prior to 1979, and (2) must not have been disabled prior to 1979.

The transitional guarantee does not apply to disability computations—even if disability occurs after reaching age 62. It does, however, apply to benefits for survivors if the insured becomes 62—then dies—during the transition period. (See F-19.)

THE SIMPLIFIED OLD-START BENEFIT COMPUTATION METHOD

F-2. How are benefits computed under the simplified old-start benefit computation method?

The simplified old-start benefit computation method must be used if disability, death, or age 62 occurred before 1979.

Step I. Count the number of years elapsed after 1950 (or after year the insured reached age 21, if later) and before (not including) the year of death, disability, or year of attaining age 62 (65 for a worker born before 1911—64 if born in 1911—63 if born in 1912).

117

Step II. Subtract five. (Also subtract any years that fell wholly or partly in a period of disability.) The result is the number of years of earnings (but not less than two) to be used in computing Average Monthly Earnings (AME).

Step III. List earnings for each year starting with 1951 and including the year in which the worker died—or the year *prior* to disability or application for old-age benefits. Earnings listed cannot exceed $3,600 (1951-1954); $4,200 (1955-1958); $4,800 (1959-1965); $6,600 (1966-1967); $7,800 (1968-1971); $9,000 (1972); $10,800 (1973); $13,200 (1974); $14,100 (1975); $15,300 (1976); $16,500 (1977); $17,700 (1978); $22,900 (1979); $25,900 (1980); $29,700 (1981); $32,400 (1982); $35,700 (1983); $37,800 (1984); $39,600 (1985); $42,000 (1986); $43,800 (1987); $45,000 (1988); $48,000 (1989); $51,300 (1990); $53,400 (1991); $55,500 (1992); $57,600 (1993); $60,600 (1994); $61,200 (1995); $62,700 (1996); $65,400 (1997); $68,400 (1998); $72,600 (1999); $76,200 (2000); and $80,400 (2001).

Step IV. From this list, select years of highest earnings (same number found in step I).

Step V. Total the earnings in the selected years—divide by the number of months in those years (drop cents). This is the worker's Average Monthly Earnings.

A worker's Average Monthly Earnings are subject to recalculation if earnings in his year of retirement or year of disability are higher than the lowest year of earnings used in the original calculation. Earnings in the last year are substituted for earnings in the lowest year if this results in higher Average Monthly Earnings.

Step VI. Determine the insured's Primary Insurance Amount (PIA) from Table 13.

PRIMARY INSURANCE AMOUNT

F-3. What is the "primary insurance amount?"

The primary insurance amount (PIA) is the basic unit used to determine the amount of each monthly benefit payable under Social Security. It applies to both the old and new method of computing benefits.

A disabled worker—or a retired worker whose retirement benefits start at normal retirement age—receives monthly benefits equal to the PIA. Retired workers who are fully insured and whose retirement benefits start *after* normal retirement age also receive an additional delayed retirement credit. (See F-27.)

Monthly benefits for members of an insured worker's family (dependent's and survivor's benefits) are all figured as percentages of the worker's PIA. (See Table 1.)

The total amount of monthly benefits payable on a worker's Social Security account is limited by a "maximum family benefit" which is also related to the worker's PIA.

In some instances, monthly benefits will be reduced if the insured elects to receive benefits before a specified age. (See F-29.)

The retirement benefit is reduced if the retired worker elects to start receiving a benefit at or after age 62 but before normal retirement age. The benefit for the spouse of a retired worker is also reduced if received before normal retirement age. (See F-29, F-30 and Table 10.)

The benefit for a widow(er) is reduced if he or she elects to start receiving benefits at or after age 60 but before normal retirement age. (See F-31 and Table 11.)

Disabled widow(er)'s benefits are payable beginning at age 50 for disability occurring before age 60, and are always reduced from what would have been payable at normal retirement age. (See E-94.)

The law provides a minimum benefit for insured workers and for survivors of insured workers when the worker had many years of coverage. (See F-20 and F-21.)

THE "WAGE INDEXING" BENEFIT COMPUTATION METHOD

F-4. Why did Congress require a new method for computing benefits in 1979 and after?

Benefits had traditionally been based on a worker's average earnings during the worker's working life. As the worker's earnings increased, potential future benefits also increased. Since the 1972 amendments, benefits for future beneficiaries had also been increased whenever the Consumer Price Index had risen, and price rises exceeded the rates expected by Congress. Thus, as wages increased to reflect price increases and as prices have increased to reflect wage increases, there was an upward spiraling of benefit levels which placed a much heavier burden on the Social Security trust funds than was intended by Congress.

The benefit computation method used prior to the 1977 amendments was flawed under certain economic conditions. As a result, over the years, benefit amounts would increase greatly in relative terms, *and* eventually many workers would have received retirement benefits greater than their wage levels when they retired.

F-5. How is the relationship between earnings levels and benefit levels stabilized under the "wage indexing" method?

The method for stabilizing the relationship between benefit levels and earnings levels is known as "decoupling." Decoupling means that cost-of-living increases will continue to apply to keep benefits inflation-proof, but only after a person either becomes eligible for benefits, or dies before becoming eligible.

F-6. In general, how is the PIA computed under the "wage indexing" method?

It is based on "indexed" earnings over a fixed number of years after 1950. (Indexing is a mechanism for expressing prior years' earnings in terms of their current dollar value.) Previous computations used actual earnings and a PIA Table. The "wage indexing" method uses a formula to determine the PIA.

Step I. Index the earnings record

Step II. Determine the Average Indexed Monthly Earnings (AIME)

Step III. Apply the PIA formula to the AIME.

F-7. Who should use the "wage indexing" benefit computation method?

The "wage indexing" method applies where first eligibility is after 1978. First eligibility is the earliest of: (1) the year of death, (2) the year disability begins, or (3) the year the insured becomes 62.

However, if the worker was entitled to a disability benefit before 1979, and that benefit terminated more than 12 months before death, another disability, or age 62, then the new method will be used in determining the PIA for the subsequent entitlement. (See F-14.)

F-8. What earnings are used in computing a person's "average indexed monthly earnings" (AIME)?

The AIME is based on Social Security earnings for years after 1950. This includes wages earned as an employee and/or self-employment income. (For an explanation of the terms wages and self-employment income, see WAGES AND SELF-EMPLOYMENT INCOME, SECTION C.)

Only earnings credited to the person's Social Security account can be used and the maximum earnings creditable for specific years are as follows:

$80,400 for 2001
$76,200 for 2000
$72,600 for 1999
$68,400 for 1998
$65,400 for 1997
$62,700 for 1996
$61,200 for 1995
$60,600 for 1994
$57,600 for 1993
$55,500 for 1992
$53,400 for 1991
$51,300 for 1990
$48,000 for 1989
$45,000 for 1988
$43,800 for 1987
$42,000 for 1986
$39,600 for 1985
$37,800 for 1984
$35,700 for 1983
$32,400 for 1982
$29,700 for 1981
$25,900 for 1980
$22,900 for 1979
$17,700 for 1978
$16,500 for 1977
$15,300 for 1976
$14,100 for 1975
$13,200 for 1974
$10,800 for 1973
$9,000 for 1972
$7,800 for years 1968-1971
$6,600 for years 1966-1967
$4,800 for years 1959-1965
$4,200 for years 1955-1958
$3,600 for years 1951-1954

F-9. How is the earnings record indexed for the AIME computation?

The AIME is based on the earnings record after wages have been indexed. Indexing creates an earnings history that more accurately reflects the value of the individual's actual earnings in comparison to the national average wage level at the time of eligibility. Earnings for each year are indexed up to the "indexing year," the second year before the worker reaches age 62, or dies or becomes disabled before age 62.

Wages are indexed by applying a ratio to the worker's earnings for each year beginning with 1951. The ratio is the "indexing average wage" for the second year before the year of the worker's eligibility for benefits or death, divided by the "indexing average wage" for the year being indexed. Thus, indexed earnings for each year are computed as follows:

Worker's Actual Earnings (Up to the Social Security Maximum) for Year to be Indexed	X	Average Earnings of All Workers in Indexing Year (Second year before Eligibility or Death) / Average Earnings of All Workers for Year being Indexed

Example. Mr. Martin earned $10,000 in 1980 and reached age 62 in 2001. The indexing average wage for 1999 (his "indexing year") was $30,469.84 and the indexing average wage for 1980 was $12,513.46. Indexed earnings for 1980 are computed as follows:

$$\$10,000 \quad X \quad \frac{\$30,469.84}{\$12,513.46} \quad = \quad \$24,349.65$$

Indexed earnings of $24,349.65 are used in place of actual earnings for 1970 in Mr. Martin's AIME computation.

The indexing formula must be applied to earnings in each year after 1950 —up to, but not including, the "indexing year." Actual earnings are used for the indexing year and all later years.

The list below shows the indexing average wages for each year beginning with 1951. These amounts must be used in 2001 to index earnings from 1951 through the "indexing year."

Year	Amount	Year	Amount
1951	$2,799.16	1976	$9,226.48
1952	$2,973.32	1977	$9,779.44
1953	$3,139.44	1978	$10,556.03
1954	$3,155.64	1979	$11,479.46
1955	$3,301.44	1980	$12,513.46
1956	$3,532.36	1981	$13,773.10
1957	$3,641.72	1982	$14,531.34
1958	$3,673.80	1983	$15,239.24
1959	$3,855.80	1984	$16,135.07
1960	$4,007.12	1985	$16,822.51
1961	$4,086.76	1986	$17,321.82
1962	$4,291.40	1987	$18,426.51
1963	$4,396.64	1988	$19,334.04
1964	$4,576.32	1989	$20,099.55
1965	$4,658.72	1990	$21,027.98
1966	$4,938.36	1991	$21,811.60
1967	$5,213.44	1992	$22,935.42
1968	$5,571.76	1993	$23,132.67
1969	$5,893.76	1994	$23,753.53
1970	$6,186.24	1995	$24,705.66
1971	$6,497.08	1996	$25,913.90
1972	$7,133.80	1997	$27,426.00
1973	$7,580.16	1998	$28,861.44
1974	$8,030.76	1999	$30,469.84
1975	$8,630.92		

Each year, before November 1, the Social Security Administration publishes the indexing average wage for the next indexing year. The indexing average wage for 2000 — the "indexing year" for those reaching age 62, or dying or becoming disabled before age 62 in 2002—will be published by November 2001.

It is important to remember that the "indexing year" is related to the year of first *eligibility* and not necessarily to the year of *entitlement*. A person filing for a retirement benefit in 2001 at age 64 is first *eligible* in 1999 (at age 62) and the earnings record will be indexed based on the indexing year 1997 (two years prior to first eligibility).

F-10. How do you determine a person's Average Indexed Monthly Earnings (AIME)?

Earnings listed in the records of the Social Security Administration—up to the annual wage limitation—are the basis for computing the AIME.

Step I. Count the *number* of years *after* 1950 (or after year person reached age 21, if later) and *up to* (not including) the year of attaining age 62 (or the year of disability or death, if before age 62). The number of years counted is the number of *computation elapsed years.*

Step II. Subtract five from the number of computation elapsed years when computing the AIME for *retirement* or *death benefits.* The number remaining (if less than two, use two) is the *number of computation base years* to be used in computing the AIME.

Example. An insured worker attained age 62 on December 2, 2000, and filed his application for retirement benefits on January 3, 2001. There are 40 elapsed years, counting the years from age 22 (1960) through 1999. The number of computation years is 35 (40 minus 5).

Example. An insured worker died on November 3, 2000, at the age of 59. The widow filed a claim for mother's benefits on November 10, 2000. There are 37 elapsed years beginning with 1963 (age 22) through 1999. There are 32 computation years (37 minus 5).

The number of years to be subtracted for *disability benefits* is scaled accordingly to the worker's age, under the following schedule:

Worker's Age in year of disability	Number of dropout years
Under 27	0
27 through 31	1
32 through 36	2
37 through 41	3
42 through 46	4
47 and over	5

Example. An insured woman attained age 40 in January 2001 and is found entitled to disability benefits. It is determined that her waiting period began on March 1, 2001. The elapsed years run from 1983 (age 22) through 2000 and total 18. Because the woman is 40 years old, there are 15 computation years (18 minus 3).

Step III. List Social Security earnings in the *computation base years* (See F-8 for Social Security earnings limits.) Computation base years are years *after* 1950, up to and *including* the year of death, or the year *before* entitlement to retirement or disability benefits. (A person is not entitled to benefits until an application for benefits is filed.)

Notice that the year of death is included as a computation base year, but the year in which an application is made for retirement or disability benefits is not included. However, for benefits payable for the next year after an application is made for retirement or disability benefits, the AIME for retirement or disability benefits will be recomputed, and earnings for this final year substituted for the lowest year if the result is a higher AIME.

Where benefits are being estimated for entitlement at some future time, use anticipated earnings (but not over the Social Security maximum) for future computation base years.

Step IV. Index earnings in each computation elapsed year up to but not including the "indexing year." (See F-9 for instructions on how to index earnings.)

Step V. From the list of indexed earnings (and nonindexed earnings for and after the "indexing year"), select years of highest earnings (same number as found in Step II). Selected years need not be in consecutive order.

Step VI. Total indexed and nonindexed earnings for the selected years are divided by the number of months in the number of years found in Step II, dropping cents. This is the person's Average Indexed Monthly Earnings (AIME).

If a person does not have earnings covered by Social Security in as many years as are required to be used as benefit computation years, total earnings must nevertheless be divided by the number of months in the required number of years. In other words, one or more years of zero earnings must be used. (See F-11.)

AIME for Widow(er)'s Benefits. In computing aged widow(er)'s benefits for the spouse of a worker who died before age 62, the deceased worker's earnings are indexed to wages up to the earliest of: (1) two years before the worker would have reached age 62; (2) two years before the survivor becomes eligible for aged widow(er)'s benefits; or (3) two years before the survivor becomes eligible for disabled widow(er)'s benefits. This computation applies only if it results in a higher benefit than the standard computation above (including applicable cost-of-living adjustments for the deferred period before benefits start). It will provide higher benefits for many widow(er)s whose spouses died before age 62 and will assure that the widow(er)'s initial benefit reflects wage levels prevailing nearer the time that she (or he) comes on the rolls.

EXAMPLES

In each of the three examples provided below, the worker earned at least the Social Security maximum each year. Therefore, Social Security earnings in the computation base years are as follows: $3,600 (1951-1954); $4,200 (1955-1958); $4,800 (1959-1965); $6,600 (1966-1967); $7,800 (1968-1971); $9,000 (1972); $10,800 (1973); $13,200 (1974); $14,100 (1975); $15,300 (1976); $16,500 (1977); $17,700 (1978); $22,900 (1979); $25,900 (1980); $29,700 (1981); $32,400 (1982); $35,700 (1983); $37,800 (1984); $39,600 (1985); $42,000 (1986); $43,800 (1987); $45,000 (1988); $48,000 (1989); $51,300 (1990); $53,400 (1991); $55,500 (1992); $57,600 (1993); $60,600 (1994); $61,200 (1995); $62,700 (1996); $65,400 (1997); $68,400 (1998); $72,600 (1999); $76,200 (2000); and $80,400 (2001).

Example I. Computation of AIME for person entitled to retirement benefits.

Mr. Smith, born 1939, reaches age 62 on November 1, 2001. On November 1st he retires and applies for retirement benefits. Earnings and months in 35 years must be used in computing his AIME (40 computation elapsed years, 1961-2000, minus 5). Mr. Smith has worked in covered employment and earned at least the Social Security maximum in every year after 1960. Earnings are indexed from 1960-1998. Mr. Smith's earnings in 1999, his "indexing year" and the next two years are not indexed.

Indexed earnings which apply to each example in-whole or in-part are as follows:

1951	$39,187.26	1968	$42,655.24	1985	$71,725.66
1952	$36,891.90	1969	$40,324.81	1986	$73,879.84
1953	$34,939.81	1970	$38,418.29	1987	$72,427.12
1954	$34,760.44	1971	$36,580.24	1988	$70,918.59
1955	$38,762.88	1972	$38,440.74	1989	$72,765.43
1956	$36,228.85	1973	$43,412.58	1990	$74,334.42
1957	$35,140.90	1974	$50,082.67	1991	$74,597.44
1958	$34,834.05	1975	$49,777.40	1992	$73,732.08
1959	$37,931.23	1976	$50,527.24	1993	$75,869.44
1960	$36,498.84	1977	$51,409.12	1994	$77,734.65
1961	$35,787.58	1978	$51,090.81	1995	$75,478.83
1962	$34,081.01	1979	$60,783.29	1996	$73,723.33
1963	$33,265.23	1980	$63,065.60	1997	$72,658.34
1964	$31,959.14	1981	$65,704.47	1998	$72,211.82
1965	$31,393.87	1982	$67,937.49	1999	$72,600.00
1966	$40,722.21	1983	$71,379.76	2000	$76,200.00
1967	$38,573.56	1984	$71,382.40	2001	$80,400.00

Mr. Smith's highest AIME is obtained by selecting the 35 years, 1966-2000. His AIME is $5,126 ($2,153,124 ÷ 420).

His AIME will later be recomputed to include earnings in 2001, and if this results in a higher AIME, the higher benefit will be paid beginning the following year. Thus, if Mr. Smith earned at least $80,400 in 2001, the recomputation will be based on the 35 years 1966-1970, and 1972-2000, giving him an AIME of $5,230 ($2,196,944 ÷ 420).

Example II. Computation of AIME for disability benefits.

Mr. Jones, born in February 1955, is disabled as a result of an accident on October 15, 2001. He applies for disability benefits on December 1, 2001. In computing his AIME for disability benefits, 20 benefit computation years must be used (24 years in 1977-2000, less 4). Mr. Jones has worked in covered employment every year since 1977 and in each year (including the year in which he became disabled) was paid at least the maximum Social Security earnings base for that year.

Earnings in 1977-1998 are indexed. Earnings in 1999-2000 are not adjusted because they were paid in and after his "indexing year" (1999).

Mr. Jones' highest AIME is obtained by selecting the 20 years, 1981-2000. His AIME is $6,071 ($1,457,261 ÷ 240).

The AIME will be recomputed to include earnings in 2001, and if this results in a higher AIME, the higher benefit will be paid beginning the following year. If Mr. Jones earned at least $80,400 in 2001, the recomputation will be based on the 20 years 1982-2001, giving him an AIME of $6,133 ($1,471,956 ÷ 240).

Example III. Computation of AIME for person who dies before retirement age.

Mr. Martin dies in November, 2001, at age 60 (he was born in February 1941). In computing his AIME, 33 benefit computation years must be used (38 years in 1963-2000, less 5). Mr. Martin has worked in covered employment every year since 1962 and in each year (including the year of death) was paid at least the maximum Social Security earnings base for that year. Earnings in Mr. Martin's computation base years through 1998 are indexed. Actual earnings in 1999-2001 are not adjusted since 1999 is his "indexing year."

Mr. Martin's highest AIME is obtained by selecting the following 33 years of highest earnings: 1967-1969 and 1972-2001. Mr. Martin's AIME is $5,347 ($2,117,804 ÷ 396).

F-11. How are Average Indexed Monthly Earnings (AIME) computed for a self-employed individual whose self-employment came under Social Security after 1951?

The same formula and starting date (1951) are used as in the computation for employees. In many cases, this will mean that years of zero earnings must be used in the AIME contribution.

Example. Dr. Smith, a physician, came under Social Security in 1965. He applies for retirement benefits in 1995 when he reaches age 62. Earnings and months in 35 years must be used in computing his AIME (40 elapsed years, 1955-1994, less 5). Social Security earnings in his elapsed years are at the maximum creditable amount in 1965-1994.

Although Dr. Smith has covered earnings in only 30 years before 1995, the total earnings for these 30 years must be divided by the number of months in 35 years (420). His AIME is computed by indexing his earnings from 1965-1992, adding actual earnings in 1993 and 1994 to total indexed earnings, and dividing by 420. Thus, his AIME is $3,127 ($1,313,559 ÷ 420).

Recomputation to include Dr. Smith's earnings in 1995 (assuming they are at least $61,200) will give him an AIME of $3,273.

F-12. How do you determine the primary insurance amount (PIA) for a person who first becomes eligible in 2001?

The primary insurance amount is determined by applying a formula to the person's average indexed monthly earnings (AIME). Where first eligibility is in calendar year 2001, the PIA is the sum of three separate percentages of portions of the AIME. It is found by taking 90% of the first $561 or less of the AIME, 32% of the AIME in excess of $561 through $3,381, and 15% of the AIME in excess of $3,381.

If the resulting PIA is not an even multiple of 10¢, it is rounded to the next lower multiple of 10¢.

The percentage figures and the dollar figures in the PIA formula will remain constant for computations and recomputations where first eligibility is in 2001, no matter when entitlement is established.

The PIA is subject to cost-of-living increases beginning with the year of first eligibility. (See F-23.)

Example. Mr. Bell, born May 18, 1939, filed an application for retirement benefits on March 31, 2001. His AIME is $3,500. His PIA is calculated as follows:

$$90 \text{ percent of } \$561 = \$504.90$$
$$32 \text{ percent of } \$2,820 = \$902.40$$
$$15 \text{ percent of } \$119 = \$17.85$$

$$\$504.90 + \$902.40 + \$17.85 = \$1,425.15 = \text{PIA of } \$1,425.10$$

Example. Mr. Jones, born February 13, 1939, filed an application for retirement benefits on February 10, 2001. His AIME is $450. His PIA is $405 (90% of $450 = $405).

Note, however, that the Primary Insurance Amount is calculated differently for each year eligibility begins prior to 2001. The percentages in the PIA formula remain constant but the dollar amounts differ each year. The dollar amounts in the formula since 1979 are as follows:

Eligibility Begins	AIME Dollar Amounts
1979	$180 and $1,085
1980	$194 and $1,171
1981	$211 and $1,274
1982	$230 and $1,388
1983	$254 and $1,528
1984	$267 and $1,612
1985	$280 and $1,691
1986	$297 and $1,790
1987	$310 and $1,866
1988	$319 and $1,922
1989	$339 and $2,044
1990	$356 and $2,145
1991	$370 and $2,230
1992	$387 and $2,333
1993	$401 and $2,420
1994	$422 and $2,545
1995	$426 and $2,567
1996	$437 and $2,635
1997	$455 and $2,741
1998	$477 and $2,875
1999	$505 and $3,043
2000	$531 and $3,202
2001	$561 and $3,381

Example. Mr. Smith, born March 12, 1934, filed an application for retirement benefits on August 19, 1999. His AIME is $2,700. Since he became eligible for retirement benefits in 1996 (the year he reached age 62), his PIA is calculated as follows:

$$90 \text{ percent of } \$437 = \$393.30$$
$$32 \text{ percent of } \$2,198 = \$703.36$$
$$15 \text{ percent of } \$65 = \$9.75$$

$$\$393.30 + \$703.36 + \$9.75 = \$1,106.41 = \text{PIA of } \$1,106.40$$

This amount is subject to a 2.9% cost-of-living increase in December 1996, a 2.1% increase in December 1997, a 1.3% increase in December 1998, a 2.4%

increase in December 1999, and a 3.5% increase in December 2000. Thus, his PIA for December 1996 is $1,138.40, while it is $1,162.30 for December 1997, $1,177.40 for December 1998, $1,205.60 for December 1999, and 1247.80 for December 2000.

Formula For Workers Receiving A Pension From Work Not Covered By Social Security

If a worker receives a pension from a job not covered by Social Security, and the worker also has enough Social Security credits to be eligible for retirement or disability benefits, a different formula may be used to figure the Social Security benefit. This formula results in a lower benefit. But the worker's pension from the job not covered by Social Security is not affected by this change.

The reason a different formula is used is that Social Security benefits are weighted in favor of low earners (i.e., low earners' benefits represent a higher percentage of their prior earnings than do the benefits of workers with higher earnings). If the benefits of people who work for only a portion of their careers in jobs covered by Social Security were computed as if they had been long-term, low-wage workers, these individuals would receive the advantage of the weighted benefit formula. Instead, a modified formula eliminates this unintended windfall.

The modified formula does not affect survivor benefits. It affects only workers who reach age 62 or become disabled after 1985 and first become eligible after 1985 for a monthly pension based in whole or in part on work not covered by Social Security. A worker is considered eligible to receive a pension if he meets the requirements of the pension, even if he continues to work.

The modified formula does not apply if:

- The worker is a federal worker hired after December 31, 1983.

- The worker was employed on January 1, 1984, by a nonprofit organization that was mandatorily covered under Social Security on that date.

- The worker has 30 or more years of substantial earnings under Social Security.

- The worker's only pension from work not covered by Social Security is based solely on railroad employment.

- The worker's only work not under Social Security was before 1957.

The modified formula is used in figuring the Social Security benefit beginning with the first month for which the worker receives both a Social Security benefit and a pension from work not covered under Social Security.

Social Security benefits are normally based on the worker's Average Indexed Monthly Earnings (AIMEs). In figuring benefits, the first part of the average earnings is multiplied by 90%; the second part is multiplied by 32%; and any part of the AIME remaining is multiplied by 15%. In the modified benefit formula, the 90% used in the first factor is reduced.

Benefits for workers first eligible in 2001 who use the modified formula are determined by taking 40% of the first $561 of Average Indexed Monthly Earnings; 32% of AIME from $561 to $3,381; and 15% of AIME above $3,381.

The reduction was phased in gradually for workers who reached 62 or became disabled in 1986 through 1989. The phase-in applies as follows:

Year You Became 62 or Disabled	First Factor
1986	80 percent
1987	70 percent
1988	60 percent
1989	50 percent
1990 or later	40 percent

Workers with 30 or more years of substantial Social Security coverage are not affected by the modified benefit formula. Workers with 21-29 years of Social Security coverage (as defined in F-20) will have the first factor reduced as follows:

Years of Coverage	First Factor
30 or more	90 percent
29	85 percent
28	80 percent
27	75 percent
26	70 percent
25	65 percent
24	60 percent
23	55 percent
22	50 percent
21	45 percent
20 or less	40 percent

In this formula, a worker is credited with a year of coverage if earnings equal or exceed the figures shown for each year in the following chart.

Year	Earnings	Year	Earnings
1937-50	$ 900	1984	7,050
1951-54	900	1985	7,425
1955-58	1,050	1986	7,875
1959-65	1,200	1987	8,175
1966-67	1,650	1988	8,400
1968-71	1,950	1989	8,925
1972	2,250	1990	9,525
1973	2,700	1991	9,900
1974	3,300	1992	10,350
1975	3,525	1993	10,725
1976	3,825	1994	11,250
1977	4,125	1995	11,325
1978	4,425	1996	11,625
1979	4,725	1997	12,150
1980	5,100	1998	12,675
1981	5,550	1999	13,425
1982	6,075	2000	14,175
1983	6,675	2001	14,925

A guarantee is provided to protect workers with relatively low "noncovered" pensions. It provides that the reduction in the Social Security benefit under the modified formula cannot be more than one-half of that part of the pension attributable to earnings after 1956 not covered by Social Security. Effective for benefits based on applications filed in or after November 1989, the amount of the pension considered when determining the windfall guarantee is the amount payable in the first month of concurrent entitlement to both Social Security and the pension from noncovered employment.

F-13. How do you determine the primary insurance amount (PIA) after 2001?

For individuals who attain age 62, or become disabled or die before age 62 in any calendar year after 2001, the PIA will be determined by formulas using the same percentage amounts listed in F-12 above. However, the bend points (dollar amounts) will be adjusted yearly as average wages rise or fall.

On or before November 1 of each year the Social Security Administration must publish in the Federal Register the bend points (dollar amounts) that will be used in computing the PIA for those eligible in the year after publication. The bend points for 2001 are $561 and $3,381.

Remember that the bend points used in calculating an individual's PIA are determined from the year the individual first became *eligible* for the benefits and not necessarily the year first *entitled* to benefits.

F-14. How is the PIA computed for an individual who was previously entitled to a disability benefit?

The PIA is not always computed under the "wage indexing" benefit computation method when a worker reaches age 62 or becomes disabled. Other benefit computations may be required if the worker was previously entitled to a disability benefit.

The PIA will be computed or recomputed under the simplified old-start benefit computation method if the individual was entitled to a disability benefit before 1979 and fewer than 12 months have passed between the prior entitlement to the disability benefit and current entitlement to benefits.

If an individual has been entitled to a disability benefit either before or after 1979—but within 12 months of current entitlement to retirement, disability, or death benefits—the PIA is the largest of the following:

(1) The PIA (including one computed under the simplified old-start benefit computation method) that was used in figuring the individual's previous disability benefit—increased by any cost-of-living or general benefit increases that occurred since the individual was last entitled;

(2) The special minimum PIA; or

(3) A recomputation of the former PIA to take into account earnings after the disability entitlement ended.

If an individual's entitlement to a disability benefit ended more than 12 months before his current entitlement to benefits, a new PIA must be computed under the "wage indexing" method. The PIA will be the higher of the recalculated PIA or the individual's PIA during the last month of his former entitlement to disability benefits (without regard to any interim cost-of-living increases).

MAXIMUM FAMILY BENEFITS

F-15. How do you determine the Maximum Family Benefit under the wage indexing method in 2001?

The following formula determines the Maximum Family Benefit for those reaching age 62 or dying before age 62 in 2001:

(1) 150% of the first $717 of PIA, plus

(2) 272% of PIA over $717 through $1,034, plus

(3) 134% of PIA over $1,034 through $1,349, plus

(4) 175% of PIA over $1,349.

The result is the family maximum. (The final figure should be rounded to the next lower multiple of $.10 if not an even multiple of $.10.) The Maximum Family Benefit is subject to cost-of-living increases beginning with the year of first eligibility. (See F-23.)

The Maximum Family Benefit is calculated differently for each year eligibility begins prior to 2001. The percentages in the Maximum Family Benefit formula remain constant, but the dollar amounts differ each year. The dollar amounts in the formula since 1979 are as follows:

Eligibility Begins	PIA Dollar Amounts
1979	$230, $332, and $433
1980	$248, $358, and $467
1981	$270, $390, and $508
1982	$294, $425, and $554
1983	$324, $468, and $610
1984	$342, $493, and $643
1985	$358, $517, and $675
1986	$379, $548, and $714
1987	$396, $571, and $745
1988	$407, $588, and $767
1989	$433, $626, and $816
1990	$455, $656, and $856
1991	$473, $682, and $890
1992	$495, $714, and $931
1993	$513, $740, and $966
1994	$539, $779, and $1,016
1995	$544, $785, and $1,024
1996	$559, $806, and $1,052
1997	$581, $839, and $1,094
1998	$609, $880, and $1,147
1999	$645, $931, and $1,214
2000	$679, $980, and $1,278
2001	$717, $1,034 and $1,349

DISABILITY

For a disabled worker and family, benefits may not exceed the lesser of 85% of the Average Indexed Monthly Earnings (AIME) on which the worker's disability benefit is based, or 150% of the disability benefit payable to the worker alone. However, in no case will a family's benefit be reduced below 100% of the benefit that would be payable to the worker alone.

This limit on family disability benefits applies to workers who first become entitled to disability benefits after June 30, 1980. A worker who first becomes entitled to disability benefits in the first six months of 1980 will compute the maximum family benefit in the same manner as those who reach age 62 or die in 1980.

Example. Mr. Smith becomes entitled to disability benefits on October 1, 2001. His AIME is $1,800 and he would be eligible to receive $901.30 a month in disability payments on his own. However, Mr. Smith has a wife and a 10 year-old child. His maximum family benefit is the lesser of 85% of his AIME (85% x $1,800 = $1,530.00), or 150% of his disability benefit (150% x $901.30 = $1,351.95). Since 150% of his benefit is less than 85% of his AIME, his maximum family benefit is $1,351.95.

F-16. How is the Maximum Family Benefit determined under the simplified old-start benefit computation method?

Maximum Family Benefits applicable under the law in December 1978 remain in effect for those individuals who attained age 62, became disabled, or died before January 1979. Maximum Family Benefits—based on the worker's Average Monthly Earnings (AME)—are listed in the June 1978 benefit table of the Social Security Administration. (See Table 13—Consumer Price Index increases after June 1978 must be applied to Maximum Family Benefits listed in Table 13.)

F-17. How are individual benefit rates reduced to bring the total amount payable within the family maximum limit?

Adjustment of individual benefit rates because of the family maximum limit is required whenever the total monthly benefits of all the beneficiaries payable on *one* Social Security account exceed the family maximum that can be paid on that record for the month. All the benefit rates, except the retirement or disability benefit and benefits payable to a divorced spouse or surviving divorced spouse, must be reduced to bring the total monthly benefits payable within the family maximum. This means that even though a beneficiary's benefit rate is originally set by law as a percentage of the insured person's PIA, the actual benefit paid may be less when the total monthly benefits payable on one earnings record exceed the family maximum prescribed by law.

The entitlement of a divorced spouse to a spouse's benefit or a surviving divorced spouse's benefit does not result in reducing the benefits of other categories of beneficiaries. Likewise, the entitlement of a legal spouse where a deemed spouse is also entitled will not affect the benefit of other beneficiaries entitled in the month. The other dependents or survivors benefits are reduced for the maximum, not taking into account the existence of the divorced spouse, surviving divorced spouse, or the legal spouse. Nor are the benefits of the divorced spouse, surviving divorced spouse, or the legal spouse ever reduced because of the family maximum. (See E-33 and E-87.)

Adjustment for the family maximum is made by proportionately reducing all the monthly benefits subject to the family maximum on the Social Security earnings record (except for retired worker's or disabled worker's benefits) to bring the total monthly benefits payable within the limit applicable in the particular case.

The individual reduced benefit rates are figured as follows:

(1) If the insured person is alive, the insured person's benefit is subtracted from the applicable family maximum amount. Any remainder is divided among the other persons entitled to benefits on the insured person's Social Security earnings record.

(2) If the insured worker is dead and all monthly benefits are based on the same percentage (e.g., all are based on 100% of the PIA, or all are based on 75%), the applicable family maximum is divided equally among all those who are entitled to benefits on the Social Security earnings record.

(3) If the insured person is deceased and some benefits are based on 100%, some on 82.5%, and some on 75% of the PIA, each beneficiary is paid a proportionate share of the applicable family maximum based on that beneficiary's original benefit rate.

This adjustment is made after any deductions which may be applicable. Thus, where: (1) reduction for the family maximum is required, and (2) a benefit payable to someone other than the worker must be withheld, the reapportionment for the maximum is made as if the beneficiary whose benefit must be withheld were not entitled to the amounts withheld.

Example. Mr. Edwards dies before age 62 in 2001, leaving a widow age 35 and two small children. His AIME is $2,000, and his PIA is $965.30. The full benefit for the widow and each child is $723.90 (75% of $965.30). However, the sum of the full benefits is $2,171.70 (3 x $723.90), which exceeds $1,750.80—the maximum family benefit for a PIA of $965.30. Thus, the benefit actually payable to each beneficiary is $583.00 (1/3 of $1,750.80, rounded to the next lower dollar).

When a person is entitled to benefits based on two different earnings records, only the amount of benefits actually paid on a record is considered in determining how much to reduce monthly benefits because of the family maximum. Any amount not paid because of a person's entitlement on another earnings record is not included. The effect of this provision is to permit payment of up to the full maximum benefits to other beneficiaries who are not subject to a deduction or reduction.

135

Example. Mr. Smith, his wife, and 2 children are entitled to benefits. Mr. Smith's PIA is $1,250 and his family maximum (for purposes of this example) is $2,180. Due to the maximum limit, the monthly benefits for his wife and children must be reduced to $310 each ($930 ÷ 3). Their original rates (50% of Mr. Smith's benefit) are $625 each. Mr. Smith's children are also entitled to benefits on their own records. One child is entitled to $390 per month and the other child is entitled to $280 per month. This causes a reduction in the benefit to the first child to $0, and the benefit to the second child to $30.

In computing the total benefits payable on Mr. Smith's record, only the benefits actually paid to the children, or $30, are considered. This allows payment of an additional amount to Mrs. Smith, increasing her benefit to $625.00 (50% of her husband's benefit). This is how the calculation works: (1) The amount available under the family maximum for the wife and children is $930 ($2,180 - $1,250 = 930); (2) Subtract the amount that is due the children after a reduction due to entitlement to their own benefits, which is $30; (3) The amount available for Mrs. Smith is $900 ($930 - $900 = $30); and (4) The amount payable to Mrs. Smith is $625, which is the lesser of $625 and $900.

F-18. If one or more members of a family cease to be entitled to benefits, will the benefits of the remaining beneficiaries be increased?

Yes, if their benefits have been reduced because of the family maximum limit.

Example. Mr. Jones dies in 2001, leaving a widow and two children aged 6 and 12 entitled to survivor's benefits. His AIME is $1,800; his PIA, $901.30; and the maximum family benefit is $1,576.80. Since the full benefit for each family member is $675.90 (75% of $901.30), the total of all three benefits exceeds the family maximum of $1,576.80 because 3 x $675.90 = $2,027.70. Initially, then, each beneficiary receives only $525.00 (1/3 of $1,576.80, rounded down to the next lower dollar). Eventually, the older child reaches age 18, and his benefits end. The widow and younger child then receive their full benefits (the widow until the child attains age 16, and the child until attaining age 18 or, if enrolled in a full-time elementary or secondary school program, upon attaining age 19) since the sum of these two benefits does not exceed the maximum family benefit.

TRANSITIONAL GUARANTEE BENEFIT METHOD

F-19. What is the transitional guarantee benefit method?

To provide a degree of protection for workers nearing retirement when decoupling was implemented, those who reach age 62 after 1978 and before 1984 are guaranteed a retirement benefit no lower than they would have received under the simplified old-start benefit computation method as of December 1978. The benefit computed under this method is known as the transitional guarantee PIA.

Those eligible for retirement benefits in the transition period are eligible for the larger of the PIA under the "wage indexing" benefit computation method or the transitional guarantee method.

The PIA under the transitional guarantee method is based on the June 1978 benefit table. (See Table 13.) The benefit table will not be subject to future automatic benefit increases, but an individual's retirement benefits will automatically increase beginning with age 62 for cost-of-living adjustments.

To be eligible for the guarantee, an individual must: (1) have had income credited for one year prior to 1979, and (2) must not have been disabled prior to 1979.

The transitional guarantee does not apply to disability computations even when the disability begins after age 62. It does apply to survivors of individuals who attain age 62 in the transition period and who die in or after the month they reach age 62.

The transitional guarantee method is basically the same as the simplified old-start benefit computation method, but earnings in the year in which the worker reached age 62 and any year thereafter may not be included in the benefit computation.

Example. Mr. White, born 1917, reaches age 62 on October 7, 1979. He retires one day later and applies for retirement benefits. Earnings and months in 23 years must be used in computing his AME (28 computation elapsed years, 1951-1978, less 5). Mr. White has worked in covered employment and earned at least the social security maximum in every year after 1950. Social Security earnings in his computation base years are therefore as follows: $3,600 (1951-1954); $4,200 (1955-1958); $4,800 (1959-1965); $6,600 (1966-1967); $7,800 (1968-1971); $9,900 (1972); $10,800 (1973); $13,200 (1974); $14,100 (1975); $15,300 (1976); $16,500 (1977); $17,700 (1978). Mr. White's highest AME is obtained by selecting the 23 years 1956-1978. His AME is $678 ($187,200 ÷ 276), and his PIA is $486.10.

The PIA computed above under the transitional guarantee method will be used if it is higher than Mr. White's PIA computed under the "wage indexing" method.

The PIA under the transitional guarantee method is subject to cost-of-living increases beginning with the month applicable for the year of first eligibility. A worker who attains age 62 in 1982, is entitled to a transitional guarantee PIA determined from the PIA Table printed in 1978. The PIA will not be affected by cost-of-living benefit increases in 1979, 1980 or 1981, but the June 1982 cost-of-living increase and subsequent ones will apply.

MINIMUM AND MAXIMUM SINGLE BENEFITS

F-20. What is the special minimum benefit?

The special minimum benefit, which applies to individuals who worked for many years under Social Security for very low (but not insignificant) wages, guarantees a benefit of at least $11.50 for each "year of coverage" over 10 and up to 30, adjusted for cost-of-living increases in 1979 and after. The special minimum benefit is used if it is higher than the one the worker's AIME would produce.

A "year of coverage" is defined as having earnings equal to at least 25% of the maximum taxable earnings base for years in 1951-1978, about 18.7% of such base in 1979-90, and about 11.2% of such base in subsequent years.

The maximum special minimum PIA is $230 ($11.50 x 20 Years), before adjustment for cost-of-living increases in 1979 and after, and is $600.90 for benefits for December 2000 through November 2001. A worker and spouse, if both are 65 at initial claim, are entitled to a maximum special minimum benefit of $902.00 per month in 2001.

The special-minimum benefit was recomputed in January 1979 for pre-1979 beneficiaries to take into account the increase in the base figure from $9.00 to $11.50. Cost-of-living increases apply automatically each year, so that the special minimum applicable for December 2000 through November 2001 is at a rate of approximately $30 per year of coverage in excess of 10 years (up to 30 years).

F-21. What is the frozen minimum PIA?

Legislation in 1981 eliminated the frozen minimum PIA for workers first eligible for benefits on or after January 1, 1982.

The frozen minimum PIA is $122 a month for workers first eligible for benefits on or before December 31, 1981. Hence, $122 is the minimum amount payable as a disability benefit or as a retirement benefit if the worker is 65 or over when benefits commence. The minimum benefit for a sole survivor of an insured worker is also $122. Benefits based on the minimum have been updated for increases in the cost-of-living (as measured by the Consumer Price Index) beginning with the year the person became entitled to benefits and will continue to be so updated in the future.

F-22. What is the maximum benefit payable for retirement at the normal retirement age under present law?

The maximum benefit payable in 2001 at 65 (person born in January 1936) who did not have a prior period of disability is $1,536 a month. This benefit amount is computed under the "wage indexing" computation method.

The maximum benefit at the normal retirement age in the future *before* any cost-of-living increases using 2001 figures as a base is $1,905 a month. A person born in January 1969 who earns the Social Security maximum each year after 2000 for 35 years up through age 66 (assuming it remains at $80,400 each year after 2001 and that the 2001 PIA formula does not change) would be entitled to this amount at age 67 under the "wage indexing" computation method. Increases in the Social Security earnings base after 2001 and future revisions in the bend points in the AIME computation method will increase this amount dramatically before the worker reaches normal retirement age.

INCREASE IN BENEFITS

F-23. Do benefits increase when the cost-of-living increases?

The Social Security Act provides for automatic increases in benefits and in the maximum earnings base (earnings subject to Social Security taxes) due to changing economic conditions.

The automatic increases in benefits are determined by increases in the Consumer Price Index for All Urban Wage Earners and Clerical Workers prepared by the Department of Labor. (But see F-25.) The increases in the maximum earnings base are determined from increases in average nationwide wages, if there has been a cost-of-living increase in benefits for the preceding December. (See C-2.)

Benefits have been raised by the following percentages since 1977:

Month/Year	Increase in Benefits
July 1977	5.9%
July 1978	6.5%
July 1979	9.9%
July 1980	14.3%
July 1981	11.2%
July 1982	7.4%
January 1984	3.5%
January 1985	3.5%
January 1986	3.1%
January 1987	1.3%
January 1988	4.2%
January 1989	4.0%
January 1990	4.7%
January 1991	5.4%
January 1992	3.7%
January 1993	3.0%
January 1994	2.6%
January 1995	2.8%
January 1996	2.6%
January 1997	2.9%
January 1998	2.1%
January 1999	1.3%
January 2000	2.4%
January 2001	3.5%

There can be no cost-of-living computation quarter in any calendar year if in the year prior to that year a general benefit increase has been enacted or become effective.

The amount of excess earnings that results in loss of benefits will be increased whenever there is an automatic cost-of-living benefit increase and nationwide average wages have risen (the increase is based on the rise in average wages). (See H-2.)

F-24. Who is entitled to a cost-of-living benefit increase?

Individuals using the "wage indexing" benefit computation method are entitled to cost-of-living increases beginning with the year of first eligibility (the year of attaining age 62, or disability or death before age 62). The PIA is calculated for the year of first eligibility and the cost-of-living increases in that year and subsequent years will be added. As long as eligibility exists in any month of the year, the PIA will be increased by the automatic benefit increase percentage applicable to the check sent in January of the following year.

Example. Mr. Johnson attains age 62 in November 1999, and waits until January 2001 to apply for benefits. The PIA is calculated and will be increased by the automatic cost-of-living benefit increases applicable to December 1999 and December 2000. The resultant PIA will be payable in the benefit paid for January 2001.

The automatic cost-of-living increase provisions in effect in December 1978 continue to apply for those who reached age 62, became disabled, or died before January 1979. A revised benefit table is published each year by the Social Security Administration. These revised tables are *not* applicable to individuals who become eligible for benefits *after 1978*, except those using the transitional guarantee.

Beneficiaries using the transitional guarantee will also receive cost-of-living increases beginning with the year of first eligibility. (See F-19.)

F-25. How will the cost-of-living stabilizer affect future cost-of-living benefit increases?

The Social Security Amendments of 1983 include a provision designed to protect the system from the kinds of trust-fund depletions that occur when price increases outpace wage gains. This stabilizer provision goes into effect if reserves in the trust fund providing retirement, disability and survivor benefits fall below 20% of what is needed to provide benefits for a year. When the stabilizer takes effect, automatic cost-of-living benefit increases are based on the lower of the percentage increase in the

Consumer Price Index or the percentage rise in the nationwide average wage.

Later, if the fund reserves exceed 32% of what is estimated to be needed for a year, recipients will be entitled to extra cost-of-living increases to compensate for losses in inflation protection resulting from having benefit increases tied to wage levels in the past (if this occurred).

YEAR OF RETIREMENT

F-26. If age 62 is the computation age, is there any advantage to waiting until normal retirement age to collect benefits?

Yes, remember that the full PIA is payable at age 65 for those attaining age 65 before 2003, with a reduced amount paid in case of an earlier retirement age. Age 62 is used to determine the computation elapsed years but earnings are counted to age 65. Thus, early retirement usually affects the benefit in two ways. The PIA usually will be smaller (because fewer years of possibly higher earnings will be used in computing the AIME), and the lower PIA will be subject to reduction (5/9 of 1% per month for the first 36 months under the normal retirement age and 5/12 of 1% per month for any additional months under the normal retirement age).

F-27. Can a person obtain higher retirement benefits by working past retirement age?

Yes, in two ways.

First, workers who continue on the job receive an increase in retirement benefits for each year they work between normal retirement age and 70. Note that this is *not* an increase in the worker's PIA. Other benefits based on the PIA, such as those payable to a spouse, are not affected.

This delayed retirement credit is also payable to a worker's surviving spouse receiving a widow(er)'s benefit.

Beginning in 1990, the delayed retirement credit payable to workers who attain age 62 after 1986 and who delay retirement past the normal retirement age, the full-benefit age (gradually rising from age 65 to age 67) is gradually increased. The delayed retirement credit is increased by one-half of 1% every other year until reaching 8% per year in 2009 or later. The higher delayed retirement credits are based on the year of attaining age 62 and are payable only at and after normal retirement age.

141

Delayed Retirement Credit Rates		
Attain Age 62	Monthly Percentage	Yearly Percentage
1979-1986	1/4 of 1%	3%
1987-1988	7/24 of 1%	3.5%
1989-1990	1/3 of 1%	4%
1991-1992	3/8 of 1%	4.5%
1993-1994	5/12 of 1%	5%
1995-1996	11/24 of 1%	5.5%
1997-1998	1/2 of 1%	6%
1999-2000	13/24 of 1%	6.5%
2001-2002	7/12 of 1%	7%
2003-2004	5/8 of 1%	7.5%
2005 or after	2/3 of 1%	8%

For workers who became age 65 before 1990 (and after 1981) and continued on the job received an increase in retirement benefits usually equal to 3% for each year (1/12 of 3% for each month) they worked between age 65 and 70. (The factor was only 1% for workers who became age 65 before 1982.)

Second, work past the normal retirement age frequently results in a higher AIME. The reason: In figuring the *number* of years to be used in the computation, the year in which the person reaches age 62 and succeeding years are not counted. (See F-10). But those years can be selected as years of highest earnings.

F-28. Will the retirement age when unreduced benefits are available (currently age 65) ever be increased?

Yes, the Social Security Amendments of 1983 increase the retirement age when unreduced benefits are available by two months per year for workers reaching age 62 in 2000-2005—to age 66; maintains age 66 for workers reaching age 62 in 2006-2016; increases by two months a year the retirement age for workers reaching age 62 in 2017-2022; and maintains age 67 for workers reaching age 62 after 2022. It does not change the age of eligibility for Medicare.

The 1983 amendments do not change the availability of reduced benefits at 62 (60 for widow(er)s) but revise the reduction factors so that there is a further reduction (up to a maximum of 30% for workers entitled at age 62 after the normal retirement age is increased to age 67, rather than only up to 20% for entitlement at age 62 under prior rules). There is no increase in the maximum reduction in the case of widow(er)s, but some increases in the reduction occur at ages above 60 and below normal retirement age.

142

Effects of Retirement-Age Provision in Social Security Amendments of 1983*

Year of Birth	Attainment of Age 62	Normal Retirement Age (Year/ Months)	Date of Attainment of Normal Retirement Age[1]	Age-62 Benefit as Percent of PIA[2]
1938	2000	65/2	March 1, 2003	79.2
1939	2001	65/4	May 1, 2004	78.3
1940	2002	65/6	July 1, 2005	77.5
1941	2003	65/8	September 1, 2006	76.7
1942	2004	65/10	November 1, 2007	75.8
1943	2005	66/0	January 1, 2009	75.0
1943-1954	2005-2016	66/0	January 1, 2009-2020	75.0
1955	2017	66/2	March 1, 2021	74.2
1956	2018	66/4	May 1, 2022	73.3
1957	2019	66/6	July 1, 2023	72.5
1958	2020	66/8	September 1, 2024	71.7
1959	2021	66/10	November 1, 2025	70.8
1960 and after	2022 and after	67/0	January 1, 2027 and after	70.0

* Normal Retirement Age is for worker and spouse benefits only. Normal Retirement Age for widow(er)s is based on attainment of age 60 in 2000 or later, so that Normal Retirement Age is age 67 beginning 2029.

[1] Birth date assumed to be January 2 of year (for benefit-entitlement purposes, Social Security Administration considers people born on the first day of a month to have attained a given age in the prior month). For later months of birth, add number of months elapsing after January up to birth month.

[2] Applies present-law reduction factor (5/9 of 1 percent per month) for the first 36 months' receipt of early retirement benefits and new reduction factor of 5/12 of 1 percent per month for additional months.

REDUCTION IN BENEFITS

F-29. When a person elects to start receiving a retirement benefit before normal retirement age, how is the benefit reduced?

A fully insured worker can start receiving retirement benefits the month after he reaches age 62 (or the month he reaches age 62 if his birthday is on the first or second of the month), or for any month thereafter. (See E-7.) However, if the worker elects to start receiving benefits before normal retirement age, the benefit is reduced.

In making the reduction, the worker's PIA must first be determined. The PIA is then reduced by 5/9 of 1% (1/180) for each of the first 36 months that the worker is under normal retirement age when the benefits commence and by 5/12 of 1% (1/240) for each such month in excess of 36. (The amount of the reduction, if not an even multiple of 10¢, is increased to the next higher multiple of 10¢.) For example, if the worker's PIA is $1,000, and he elects to retire and start receiving benefits 24 months before his normal retirement age, his benefit will be reduced by $133.40 (24 x 1/180 x $1,000), giving him a monthly benefit of $866.60. Ordinarily, he will continue to receive the reduced benefit even after normal retirement age (but see Recomputation of Benefits, F-34).

F-30. If the spouse of a retired worker starts receiving a spouse's benefit before normal retirement age, how is the benefit reduced?

First, the spouse's full benefit is determined. This is one-half of the retired worker's PIA. (Where the retired worker is receiving a reduced retirement benefit starting before normal retirement age, the spouse's full benefit is computed as 50% of the retired worker's PIA, not 50% of the reduced benefit.) The spouse's full benefit is then reduced by 25/36 of 1% (1/144) for each of the first 36 months that the spouse is under normal retirement age when benefits commence and by 5/12 of 1% (1/240) for each month in excess of 36. (The amount of the reduction, if not an even multiple of 10¢, is increased to the next higher multiple of 10¢.)

For example, suppose that the retired worker's PIA is $1,000, and the spouse's full benefit is $500 (1/2 of $1,000). If the spouse takes the benefit exactly 24 months before his or her normal retirement age, the full benefit will be reduced by $83.40 (24 x 1/144 x $500), giving the spouse a monthly benefit of $416.60 ($500 - $83.40). If a spouse starts receiving benefits for the month 36 months before normal retirement age, the benefit under this formula will be 75% of the full benefit, or 37.5% of the retired worker's PIA. Ordinarily, the spouse will continue to receive the reduced benefit even after normal retirement age (but see Recomputation of Benefits, F-34). (See also Table 10.)

F-31. If a widow(er) elects to start receiving a widow(er)'s benefit before normal retirement age, how is the benefit reduced?

The widow(er)'s full benefit must first be determined. The full benefit (to which he or she would be entitled by waiting until normal retirement age) is 100% of the deceased spouse's PIA. This benefit was reduced by 19/40 of 1% (19/4000) for each month that the widow(er) was under normal retirement age when benefits begin.

For example, suppose that the deceased spouse's PIA was $1,000. The widow(er)'s full benefit would have been $1,000. However, if the widow(er) elected to receive benefits starting with the month of his or her 60th birthday (60 months before age 65), the full widow(er)'s benefit would have been reduced by $285 (60 x 19/4000 x $1,000), resulting in a benefit of $715 ($1,000 - $285). The amount of the reduction, if not an even multiple of 10¢, is increased to the next higher multiple of 10¢. A benefit beginning with the month of a widow(er)'s 60th birthday accordingly will equal 71.5% of the spouse's PIA.

When the normal retirement age is more than 65, the 71.5% reduction at age 60 remains unchanged, but the reduction factor will be different (based on 71.5% at age 60 and 100% at normal retirement age). Ordinarily, the widow(er) will continue to receive the reduced benefit even after normal retirement age (but see Recomputation of Benefits, F-34). (See Table 11 for widow(er)'s reduced benefits.)

If the widow(er)'s deceased spouse retired before normal retirement age, the widow(er)'s benefit cannot exceed the deceased spouse's reduced benefit or, if larger, 82.5% of his or her PIA.

The benefit of a disabled widow(er) who starts receiving benefits before age 60 is equal to 71.5% of his or her spouse's PIA. (See E-94.)

F-32. How are a beneficiary's benefits figured when he is entitled to a reduced retirement benefit and a larger spouse's benefit simultaneously?

The beneficiary will receive the retirement benefit, reduced in the regular manner. (See F-29.) That is, the PIA is reduced by 5/9 of 1% (1/180) for each of the first 36 months that he is under normal retirement age when benefits commence and 5/12 of 1% (1/240) for each month in excess of 36. The beneficiary will also receive a spouse's benefit based on the difference between the full spouse's benefit (1/2 of his or her spouse's PIA) and his or her PIA. This spouse's benefit is reduced by 25/36 of 1% (1/144) for each of the first 36 months that he is under normal retirement age when benefits commence and 5/12 of 1% (1/240) for each month in excess of 36. (See F-30.)

F-33. How are benefits figured if a beneficiary starts receiving a reduced retirement benefit and later becomes entitled to a larger spouse's benefit?

The beneficiary will continue to receive the retirement benefit reduced in the regular manner. (See F-29.) When he becomes entitled to the larger spouse's benefit, he will receive, in addition, a partial spouse's benefit. This benefit will be based on the difference between a spouse's full benefit (1/2 of his or her spouse's PIA) and the beneficiary's PIA. If he becomes entitled to the spouse's benefits at or after normal retirement age, the spouse's benefit will equal this difference. If he becomes entitled to the spouse's benefit before normal retirement age, this difference must be reduced by 25/36 of 1% (1/144) for each of the first 36 months that he is under normal retirement age when the spouse's benefits commence and 5/12 of 1% (1/240) for each month in excess of 36.

RECOMPUTATION OF BENEFITS

F-34. Under what circumstances are benefits recomputed?

Automatic recomputation of benefits is provided each year to take account of

145

any earnings a beneficiary might have that would increase his benefit amount. Also, the recomputation takes into account the final year's earnings in the case of retirement and disability benefits. The recomputation for a living beneficiary is effective with January of the year following the one in which the earnings were received. A recomputation affecting survivor's benefits is effective with the month of death.

The "wage indexing" computation method must be used to recompute the PIA for an individual who has earnings after 1978, if the PIA was originally computed or could have been computed under this method.

The actual dollar amounts in the records of the Social Security Administration for the year of entitlement and each later year will annually be compared with the earnings in the base years which were used in the last computation. Higher earnings in any year that was not used in the last computation will be substituted for one or more years of lower earnings that were used, and the PIA will be recomputed.

The PIA will be recomputed using the same "bend points" and "indexing year" that applied when current eligibility was established. (See F-12.) Recomputation must result in a PIA increase of at least $1 to be effective.

A PIA computed using the transitional guarantee benefit computation method or the simplified old-start benefit computation method—based on eligibility after 1978—cannot be recomputed to include earnings in or after the year of current eligibility.

F-35. If a person is simultaneously entitled to two or more benefits, which benefit will be paid?

A person may be entitled to more than one Social Security benefit at the same time. For example, a woman may be entitled to a parent's benefit on her deceased child's account and to a spouse's benefit on her husband's account. However, only the highest benefit will be paid, except when one of the benefits is a retirement or disability benefit. The lower benefit cannot be paid even though the higher benefit is not payable for one or more months. But if the higher benefit is terminated, the lower benefit will be reinstalled automatically.

If a person is entitled to retirement or disability benefits and to a higher benefit, he will receive the retirement or disability benefit plus the difference between this benefit and the higher one. Payment, however, may be made in a single check. If one benefit is not payable for one or more months, the other may be payable. For example, if a spouse's benefit is not payable for some months because of the worker's excess earnings, he or she will nevertheless receive a retirement benefit.

A child may be entitled to child's benefits on more than one earnings record, for example, his father's record and his mother's record. A child can receive the benefit based on the PIA which will result in the highest original benefit. However, if the highest original benefit is payable on the lowest PIA, he is paid on this account only if it would not reduce (after the reduction for the family maximum) the benefit of any beneficiary because of his entitlement.

DISABILITY FREEZE

F-36. How does a period of disability affect retirement and survivor's benefits?

A person who has an established period of disability will have his earnings record "frozen" during the period of disability. This means that the years of disability need not be included in computing his AIME. Otherwise, if the worker died or recovered and returned to work before he reached retirement age, the years of zero earnings in his period of disability might reduce his PIA for retirement or survivors' benefits. In figuring the number of years that must be used in computing the worker's AIME, a year which fell wholly or partly within a period of disability is not counted. However, a year which is partly within a period of disability will be used as a computation base year if inclusion of earnings for that year will produce a higher AIME.

CALCULATING THE EXACT BENEFIT AMOUNT

F-37. In calculating the exact amount of each monthly benefit, how must the figures be rounded?

Benefits for members of a worker's family, if not an even multiple of $1, are rounded (after deducting the premium for Medical Insurance under Medicare, if any) to the next lower multiple of $1. For example, if the PIA of a deceased worker is $444.30, a child's survivor benefit is figured as $333.20 (75% of $444.30). However, this amount will be rounded to $333.00 (the next lower multiple of $1).

TAXATION OF SOCIAL SECURITY BENEFITS

G-1. Are Social Security benefits subject to federal income taxation?

Social Security retirement, survivor, and disability benefits may be taxable in some cases. The person who has the legal right to receive the benefits must determine if the benefits are taxable. For example, if a parent and child both receive benefits, but the check for the child is made out in the parent's name, the parent must use only the parent's portion of the benefits in figuring if benefits are taxable. The portion of the benefits that belongs to the child must be added to the child's other income to see if any of those benefits are taxable.

If the only income a person receives is Social Security benefits, the benefits generally are not taxable and he probably docs not need to file a return. However, if a person has other income in addition to benefits, he may have to file a return even if none of the benefits are taxable.

If the total of a person's income plus half of his benefits is more than the *base amount*, some of the benefits are taxable. Included in the person's total income is any tax-exempt interest income, excludable interest from United States savings bonds, and excludable income earned in a foreign country, United States possession, or Puerto Rico.

Voluntary federal income tax withholding is allowed on Social Security benefits. Recipients may submit a Form W-4V if they want federal income tax withheld from their benefits. Beneficiaries are able to choose withholding at 7%, 15%, 28%, or 31% of their total benefit payment.

G-2. What are the base amounts?

The base amount is as follows depending upon a person's filing status:

- $32,000 for married couples filing jointly.

- $-0- for married couples filing separately and who lived together at any time during the year.

- $25,000 for other taxpayers.

If a person is married and files a joint return, the person and his spouse must combine their incomes and their Social Security benefits when figuring if any of their combined benefits are taxable. Even if the spouse did not receive any

149

benefits, the person must add the spouse's income to his when figuring if any of his benefits are taxable.

Example. Jim and Julie Smith are filing a joint return for 2000 and both received Social Security benefits during the year. Jim received net benefits of $6,600, while Julie received net benefits of $2,400. Jim also received a taxable pension of $10,000 and interest income of $500. Jim did not have any tax-exempt interest income. Jim and Julie's Social Security benefits are not taxable for 2000 because the sum of their income ($10,500) and one-half their benefits ($9,000 ÷ 2 = $4,500) is not more than their base amount ($32,000).

Any repayment of Social Security benefits a person made during the year must be subtracted from the gross benefits received. It does not matter whether the repayment was for a benefit the person received in that year or in an earlier year.

G-3. How much of someone's benefits are subject to income taxes?

The amount of benefits to be included in taxable income depends on the person's total income plus half his Social Security benefits. The higher the total, the more benefits a person must include in taxable income. Depending upon a person's income he may be required to include either up to 50% or up to 85% of benefits in income.

50 Percent Taxable

If a person's income plus half of his Social Security benefits is more than the following *base amount* for his filing status, up to 50% of his benefits will be included in his gross income.

- $32,000 for married couples filing jointly.

- $-0- for married couples filing separately and who lived together at any time during the year.

- $25,000 for all other taxpayers.

85 Percent Taxable

If a person's income plus half of his Social Security benefits is more than the following *adjusted base amount* for his filing status, up to 85% of his benefits will be included in his gross income.

- $44,000 for married couples filing jointly.

- $-0- for married couples filing separately and who lived together at any time during the year.

- $34,000 for other taxpayers.

If a person is married filing separately and *lived with* his spouse at any time during the year, up to 85% of his benefits will be included in his gross income.

G-4. Why is non-taxable interest income included in the taxpayer's adjusted gross income?

Nontaxable interest income is included in income to limit opportunities for manipulation of tax liability on benefits. Individuals whose incomes consist of different mixes of taxable and nontaxable income are treated the same as individuals whose total income is taxable for federal income tax purposes.

G-5. Are workers' compensation benefits included in the definition of Social Security benefits for tax purposes?

Yes, also included in the definition of Social Security benefits for tax purposes are workers' compensation benefits to the extent they cause a reduction in Social Security and railroad retirement tier 1 disability benefits. This is intended to assure that these social insurance benefits, which are paid in lieu of Social Security payments, are treated similarly for purposes of taxation.

G-6. How are overpayments and lump-sum retroactive benefits taxed?

Special rules are provided for dealing with overpayments and lump-sum retroactive benefit payments. Benefits paid to an individual in any taxable year are reduced by any overpayments repaid during the year. Taxpayers who received a lump-sum payment of retroactive benefits may treat the benefits as wholly payable for the year in which they receive them or may elect to attribute the benefits to the tax years in which they would have fallen had they been paid timely. No benefits for months before 1984 are taxable, regardless of when they are paid.

Example. Ms. Jones is single and in 1999 she applied for Social Security disability benefits but was told she was ineligible to receive them. She appealed the decision and won her appeal. In 2000, she received a lump-sum payment of $6,000 which included $2,000 for 1999. She has two choices. She can use her 2000 income to figure the taxable part of the entire $6,000 payment, or she can use her 1999 income to figure the taxable part of the $2,000 received for 1999. In the latter case, her 2000 income would include the sum of the taxable benefits for each year as figured under the lump-sum election method.

Example. Assume that Mr. Jackson receives a $1,000 Social Security benefit in 2000, $400 of which is attributable to 1999. Assume also that the $1,000 benefit would increase Mr. Jackson's 2000 gross income by $500 (i.e., by the full 50%), but that the $400 would have increased his 1999 gross income by only $150, and the remaining $600 would have increased his 2000 gross income by $300. He may limit the increase in 2000 gross income to only $450, the sum of the increases in gross income that would have occurred had the $400 been paid in 1999.

G-7. What reporting requirements must be met by the Social Security Administration?

The Commissioner of Social Security must file annual returns with the Secretary of the Treasury setting forth the amounts of benefits paid to each individual in each calendar year, together with the name and address of the individual. The Commissioner of Social Security must also furnish similar information to each beneficiary by January 31 of the year following the benefit payments. The statement will show the total amount of Social Security benefits paid to the beneficiary, the total amount of Social Security benefits repaid by the beneficiary to the Social Security Administration during the calendar year, and the total reductions in benefits to offset workers' compensation benefits received by the beneficiary.

G-8. Are Social Security benefits subject to income tax withholding?

Voluntary federal income tax withholding on Social Security benefits is allowed. Recipients may submit a Form W-4V if they want federal income tax withheld from their benefits. Recipients may choose withholding at 7%, 15%, 28%, or 31% of their total benefit payment.

G-9. If a recipient of Social Security benefits elects Medical Insurance (Part B) under Medicare and the premiums are deducted from the individual's benefits, is the whole benefit, before the deduction, a Social Security benefit?

Yes, the individual is treated as if he received the whole benefit and later paid separately for the Medical Insurance (Part B) coverage. Both the Commissioner of Social Security and the Railroad Retirement Board will include the entire amount as paid to the individual in the statements they furnish.

LOSS OF BENEFITS BECAUSE OF "EXCESS" EARNINGS

"RETIREMENT TEST"

H-1. Can a person lose some or all Social Security benefits by working?

Yes, if the person is under normal retirement age (see E-4) for all of 2001 and earns over $10,680; or in the year the person reaches normal retirement age he earns over $25,000, except that only earnings earned before the month he reaches normal retirement age count towards the $25,000 limit. An alternative test applies in the initial year of retirement if it produces a more favorable result (see the last "bullet" of H-2). See F-28 for a discussion of the normal retirement age.

The exempt amount applicable to an individual who reaches normal retirement age before the close of the taxable year involved will be $30,000 in 2002.

The annual exempt amount for beneficiaries under the normal retirement age ($10,680 in 2001) will be increased each year as wage levels rise.

A beneficiary who is older than the normal retirement age can earn any amount without losing benefits. Regardless of how much earnings are in the year of attaining normal retirement age, no benefits are withheld for the month in which normal retirement age is reached, or for any subsequent month. Also, earnings in and after the month in which a person attains normal retirement age will not be included in determining total earnings for the year.

The retirement test does not apply to individuals entitled to benefits because of their disability or to beneficiaries outside the United States whose work is not covered by Social Security.

The Senior Citizens' Freedom to Work Act of 2000 repealed the retirement test for those over normal retirement age. Prior to this repeal, benefits could be lost for those aged 65-69 who were receiving benefits. The repeal is effective for tax years ending after 1999.

Annual Exempt Amounts		
Year	Age 65 through Age 69	Under Age 65
1985	$ 7,320	$5,400
1986	7,800	5,760
1987	8,160	6,000
1988	8,400	6,120
1989	8,880	6,480
1990	9,360	6,840
1991	9,720	7,080
1992	10,200	7,440
1993	10,560	7,680
1994	11,160	8,040
1995	11,280	8,160
1996	12,500	8,280
1997	13,500	8,640
1998	14,500	9,120
1999	15,500	9,600
2000	17,000	10,080
2001	25,000	10,680
2002	30,000	**

** Annual exempt amount for beneficiaries under age 65 will increase each year after 2001 as wage levels rise.

H-2. What are the general rules for loss of benefits because of excess earnings?

When the beneficiary is older than the normal retirement age (see E-4), no benefits are lost because of his earnings. If he is under the normal retirement age, the following rules apply:

• If no more than $25,000 is earned in 2001 by a beneficiary who reaches the normal retirement age in 2001, no benefits will be lost for that year.

• If more than $25,000 is earned in 2001 before the month the beneficiary reaches normal retirement age, $1 of benefits will ordinarily be lost for each $3 of earnings over $25,000.

• If not more than $10,680 is earned in 2001 by a beneficiary who is under the normal retirement age for the entire year, no benefits will be lost for that year.

• If more than $10,680 is earned in 2001 by a beneficiary who is under the normal retirement age for the entire year, $1 of benefits will ordinarily be lost for each $2 of earnings over $10,680.

- But, no matter how much is earned during 2001, no *retirement* benefits in the *initial year of retirement* will be lost for any month in which the beneficiary neither: (1) earns over $890 as an employee if retiring in a year prior to the year he reaches normal retirement age, nor (2) renders any substantial services in self-employment.

The initial year of retirement is the first year in which he is both entitled to benefits and has a month in which he does not earn over the monthly exempt wage amount (as listed above) and does not render substantial services in self-employment.

When the monthly earnings test applies, regardless of the amount of annual earnings, the beneficiary gets full benefits for any month in which earnings do not exceed the monthly exempt amount, and the beneficiary does not perform substantial services in self-employment.

The attainment of normal retirement age in a year determines which test applies. The normal retirement age test applies if the beneficiary attains normal retirement age on or before the last day of the taxable year involved. The under normal retirement age test applies if the beneficiary does not attain normal retirement age on or before the last day of the taxable year. See F-28 for a discussion of the increase in the normal retirement age.

Example. Dr. James, who reports his earnings on a calendar year basis, turns age 65 on July 18, 2001. The under normal retirement age test ($10,080 for 2000) applies for calendar year 2000, and the normal retirement age test ($25,000) applies for calendar year 2001. However, none of Dr. James earnings earned in July through December, 2001 count towards the $25,000 limit.

Example. Miss Norton, who reports her earnings on the basis of a fiscal year ending June 30, attains age 65 on August 15, 2001. The under normal retirement age test ($10,680) applies for her fiscal year July 1, 2000 through June 30, 2001. The normal retirement age test ($25,000) applies for her next fiscal year; however, only earnings earned in July, 2001 count towards the $25,000 limit.

H-3. How are "excess" earnings charged against benefits?

In determining the amount of benefits for a given year that will be lost, two factors must be taken into consideration: (1) the amount of the person's "excess" earnings for the year, and (2) the months in the year that can actually be charged with all or a portion of the excess earnings potentially chargeable in the initial year of retirement.

Both wages earned as an employee and net earnings from self-employment are combined for purposes of determining the individual's total earnings for the year. Only "excess earnings" are potentially chargeable against benefits. If a person is under the normal retirement age for the entire year and earns $10,680 or less (in 2001) for the year, there are no "excess earnings." If earnings for the year are more than $10,680, then one-half of the amount over $10,680 is "excess earnings." In the year a person reaches the normal retirement age, he can earn up to $25,000 (in 2001) before losing benefits. However, only earnings earned before the month the person reaches normal retirement age count toward the $25,000 limit. See F-28 for a discussion of the normal retirement age.

Excess earnings are charged against retirement benefits in the following manner. They are charged first against all benefits payable on the worker's account for the first month of the year. If any excess earnings remain, they are charged against all benefits payable for the second month of the year, and so on until all the excess earnings have been charged, or no benefits remain for the year. However, a month cannot be charged with any excess earnings and must be skipped if the individual: (1) was not entitled to benefits for that month, (2) was over normal retirement age in that month, or (3) in the initial year of retirement he did not earn over $890 (using 2001 figures) if he retires in a year before the year he reaches normal retirement age, or (4) he did not render substantial services as a self-employed person in that month.

If the excess earnings chargeable to a month are less than the benefits payable to the worker and to other persons on his account, then the excess is chargeable to each beneficiary in the proportion that the original entitlement rate of each bears to the sum of all their original entitlement rates.

Example. Dr. Brown partially retires in January 2001 at the age of 62. Based on his earnings history and the age he starts receiving benefits, his Social Security benefit is $1,200 per month. He practices for three months in 2001 and earns $30,000. The remainder of his initial year of retirement is spent in Florida playing golf. Despite the fact that Dr. Brown has excess earnings in 2001 which would, under the annual test, cause a benefit loss of $9,660, he will lose only the $3,600 in benefits for the three months during which he performed substantial services in self-employment because 2001 is his initial year of retirement.

Example. Dr. Smith, who partially retired in 2000 at age 62, practices for four months in 2001 and earns $32,000. Since 2001 is his second year of retirement, the monthly earnings test does not apply. His benefit will be reduced by $1 for each $2 of earnings over $10,680. This means that Dr. Smith's benefits in 2001 will be reduced by $10,660 (1/2 of the amount in excess of $10,680).

Example. Mr. Martin is 66 years old and has not retired. He earns $35,000 a year. Mr. Martin receives Social Security retirement benefits of $700 a month. Because he is over the normal retirement age, he loses none of his benefits by working.

The annual exempt amount is not prorated in the year of death. In addition, the higher exempt amount applies to persons who die before their date of birth in the year that they otherwise would have attained normal retirement age.

H-4. Can a person who is receiving dependent's or survivor's benefits lose benefits by working?

Yes, if the person is under the normal retirement age for the entire year and earns over $10,680 (in 2001), or in the year the person reaches normal retirement age he earns over $25,000. Only earnings earned in before the month the person reaches normal retirement age count toward the $25,000 limit. The same "retirement test" applies as applies to retirement beneficiaries (see H-2). However, the excess earnings of a person receiving dependent's or survivor's benefits are not charged against the benefits payable to other dependents or survivors. For example, a child's excess earnings are not chargeable against mother's benefits. A retirement beneficiary's excess earnings, on the other hand, are chargeable against dependent's benefits because those benefits are based on the retirement beneficiary's Social Security account. See F-28 for a discussion of the normal retirement age.

H-5. If a widow's benefits are withheld because of work, will this necessarily reduce the total amount of benefits payable to the family?

No. Where there are several children, all survivor benefits may have to be reduced to come within the maximum family benefit. Even though the mother works and loses her benefits, the maximum may still be payable to the children. In many cases, however, loss of the mother's benefits will reduce the total amount of benefits payable to the family.

Example. Mr. Apple dies in 2001, leaving a widow and four small children. His PIA is $700. If it were not for the maximum family limit, the widow and each child would be entitled to a survivor's benefit of $525 (75% of $700). However, since the maximum family benefit for a PIA of $700 is $1,050, each beneficiary receives only $210 (1/5 of $1,050, rounded to the next lower even dollar). Mrs. Apple goes to work and earns an amount sufficient to eliminate her mother's benefits ($1 is withheld for every $2 of excess earnings). Nevertheless, the family still receives $1,050 in benefits because each child's benefit is raised to $262 (1/4 of $1,050, rounded to the next lower even dollar).

Example. Mr. Berry dies in 2001, leaving a widow and two small children; his PIA is $800; and the maximum family benefit is $1,301. If it were not for the maximum family limit, the widow and each child would be entitled to a monthly benefit of $600 (75% of $800). Because of the family maximum limit, however, each receives only $433 (1/3 of $1,301, rounded to the next lower even dollar). Mrs. Berry goes to work and earns an amount sufficient to eliminate her widows' benefits. Each child then receives a full benefit of $600.

H-6. How is the loss of benefits figured for the year in which the worker reaches normal retirement age?

In the year in which a person reaches normal retirement age, his earnings in and after the month in which he reaches normal retirement age will not be included in determining his total earnings for the year.

H-7. What kinds of earnings will cause loss of benefits?

Wages received as an employee and net *earnings* from self-employment. Bonuses, commissions, fees, and earnings from all types of work, whether or not covered by Social Security, count for the retirement test. For example, earnings from family employment are counted even though such employment is not covered by Social Security (see B-27). Earnings above the Social Security "earnings base" are counted. Income as an absentee owner counts as "earnings" for the retirement test. If the person renders substantial services as a self-employed person (even in another business), such income also will count as "earnings" for the taxable year in the initial year of retirement.

The following types of income are *not* counted as "earnings" for purposes of the retirement test:

• Any income from employment earned in or after the month the individual reaches normal retirement age. (Self-employment income earned in the year is not examined as to when earned, but rather is pro-rated by months, even though actually earned after normal retirement age.) See F-28 for a discussion of normal retirement age.

• Any income from self-employment which is received in a taxable year after the year the individual becomes entitled to benefits, but which is not attributable to significant services performed after the first month of entitlement to benefits. This income is excluded from gross income only for purposes of the earnings test.

• Damages, attorneys' fees, interest, or penalties paid under court judgment or by compromise settlement with the employer based on a wage claim. However, back pay recovered in such proceedings counts for the earnings test.

- Payments to secure release of an unexpired contract of employment.

- Certain payments made under a plan or system established for making payments because of the employee's sickness or accident disability, medical or hospitalization expenses, or death.

- Payments from certain trust funds that are exempt from income tax.

- Payments from certain annuity plans that are exempt from income tax.

- Pensions and retirement pay.

- Sick pay if paid more than six months after the month the employee last worked.

- Payments-in-kind for domestic service in the employer's private home, for agricultural labor, for work not in the course of the employer's trade or business, or the value of meals and lodging furnished under certain conditions.

- Rentals from real estate that cannot be counted in earnings from self-employment because, for instance, the beneficiary did not materially participate in production work on the farm, the beneficiary was not a real estate dealer, etc.

- Interest and dividends from stocks and bonds (unless they are received by a dealer in securities in the course of business).

- Gain or loss from the sale of capital assets, or sale, exchange, or conversion of other property which is not stock in trade nor includable in inventory.

- Net operating loss carry-over resulting from self-employment activities.

- Loans received by employees unless the employees repay the loans by their work.

- Workers' compensation and unemployment compensation benefits.

- Veterans' training pay.

- Pay for jury duty.

- Prize winnings from contests, unless the person enters contests as a trade or business.

- Tips paid to an employee which are less than $20 a month or are not paid in cash.

- Payments by an employer which are reimbursements specifically for travel expenses of the employee and which are so identified by the employer at the time of payment.

- Payments to an employee as a reimbursement or allowance for moving expenses, if they are not counted as wages for Social Security purposes.

- Royalties received in or after the year in which a person reaches normal retirement age, to the extent that they flow from property created by the person's own personal efforts which he copyrighted or patented before the taxable year in which he reached normal retirement age. These royalties are excluded from gross income from self-employment only for purposes of the earnings test.

- Retirement payments received by a retired partner from a partnership provided certain conditions are met.

- Certain payments or series of payments paid by an employer to an employee or any of his dependents on or after the employment relationship has terminated because of death, retirement for disability, or retirement for age and paid under a plan established by the employer.

- Payments *from* Individual Retirement Accounts (IRAs) and Keogh Plans.

In other words, a person can receive most any amount of "investment" or passive income without loss of benefits.

H-8. What is meant by "substantial services" in self-employment?

Whether a self-employed beneficiary is rendering "substantial services" in the initial year of retirement is determined by the actual services rendered in the month. The test is whether the person can reasonably be considered retired in the month. In applying the test, consideration is given to such factors as: (1) the amount of time devoted to the business (including all time spent at the place of business or elsewhere) in any activity related to the business (including the time spent in planning and managing as well as doing physical work), (2) the nature of the services, (3) the relationship of the activities performed before retirement to those performed after retirement, and (4) other circumstances, such as the amount of capital the beneficiary has invested in the business, the type of business establishment, the presence of a paid manager, partner, or family member who manages the business, and the seasonal nature of the business.

Generally, services of 45 hours or less in a month are not considered substantial. However, as few as 15 hours of service a month could be substantial if, for instance, they involved management of a sizeable business or were spent in a highly skilled occupation. Services of less than 15 hours a month are never considered substantial.

The amount of earnings is not controlling. High earnings do not necessarily mean that substantial services were rendered, nor do low or no earnings mean that they were not rendered.

NOTE: The "substantial services" test is used only for the initial year of retirement. After that, the amount of earnings alone determines whether benefits will be lost.

H-9. Must a Social Security beneficiary report earnings to the Social Security Administration?

The annual report of earnings that must be filed by beneficiaries with earnings over the earnings limit has been eliminated.

The Social Security Administration now uses earnings information for workers that has been reported by employers on the W-2 income tax form — or income reported by the self-employed on their tax form. Until recently it was impossible to use the W-2 information that the Social Security Administration received from employers for beneficiary annual reporting because there was a lag of several years in receiving and processing the millions of earnings items annually.

Improvements in employer reporting practices and in the Social Security Administration's own processing of the reports make elimination of the annual report of earnings possible. For most beneficiaries, the process will be totally automated, with the Social Security Administration receiving and processing earnings information reported for tax purposes and using that information to adjust the Social Security benefits payable accordingly.

Benefits will be stopped for the number of months necessary to offset excess earnings. If too much has been withheld, the beneficiary will receive a check for the underpayment. If too little, the overpayment will be withheld from future benefits or must be refunded.

H-10. How are a life insurance agent's first-year and renewal commissions treated for purposes of the Retirement Test?

Whether original (first year) and renewal commissions from the sale of life insurance policies are wages or earnings from self-employment depends upon the status of the agent when the sale of the policy was completed. If the agent was an employee when the sale of the policy was consummated, both original and renewal commissions from that policy are wages. If the agent was self-employed when the sale of the policy was completed, both the original and renewal commissions from the policy are earnings from self-employment.

Each insurance company normally furnishes its agents with sufficient information identifying policies on which commission payments are made, amounts of payments which are regular commissions, the commuted value of the renewals, service fees, efficiency income, etc., to enable a beneficiary to figure how much the earnings are for Social Security purposes.

A life insurance agent will receive retirement benefits for the month in which normal retirement age is reached, and for every month thereafter regardless of whether still working, and regardless of how much is earned.

Moreover in the *initial year of retirement*, and regardless of the amount of earnings for the taxable year, benefits will not be lost for any month in which the individual neither: (1) earns more than $890 (if under normal retirement age) as an employee, nor (2) renders substantial services in self-employment. See F-28 for a discussion of the normal retirement age.

It is necessary to determine whether the agent was an employee or a self-employed person when the policy was sold. (For status of a life insurance agent as an employee or as a self-employed person under Social Security, see B-11.) The reason is that, for retirement test purposes, "wages" of an **employee** are treated as earnings in the year in which they are **earned**. But net earnings for **self-employment** are treated as earnings in the year in which they are **received**.

Original (first-policy-year) commissions are earnings for purposes of the retirement test for the month and year in which an **employee-agent** completed the sale of the policy. As a rule an employee-agent is paid the original commission on a policy according to the way the insured person pays the premium. The entire original commission is earnings for the month in which the agent completed the sale of the policy regardless of whether the commission is received on a monthly, quarterly, semi-annual, or annual basis.

Renewal commissions of an employee-agent are earnings for purposes of the retirement test for the month in which the employee completed the sale of the life insurance policy and are includable in total earnings for the taxable year. They are deferred compensation for services rendered in completing the sale.

All of the renewal commissions which an employee-agent anticipates receiving from a life insurance policy sold while an employee must be reported as earnings for purposes of the retirement test for the month and year in which the original sale of the policy was completed. If the anticipated renewal commissions fail to materialize, thus making incorrect the total annual or monthly earnings, any benefit previously withheld but now due the beneficiary will be paid.

An employee-agent beneficiary must include the following in figuring total earnings for purposes of the retirement test for a taxable year:

* All original commissions on life insurance policies sold during the year.

* All anticipated renewal commissions on life insurance policies sold in the year. If the agent-beneficiary cannot determine the exact amount of anticipated renewals from such policies, as a last resort it should be assumed that they equal the amount of the original commission.

* Insurance service fees, persistency fees, and the like earned during the year.

* All renewal commissions received in the taxable year from policies sold in prior years while self-employed.

* All remuneration classified as earnings from other jobs, trades, or business.

Thus, renewal commissions on business in past years are not "earnings" for retirement test purposes when received by the agent-beneficiary if an **employee** when the policies were sold.

An employee-agent earns commission on a life insurance policy in the month in which the last act required for entitlement to the commission is performed. The acts to be performed before entitlement to commissions are usually set out in the agent's contract with the company or can be determined from the company's regulations, rules, or practices. The agent should submit a copy of the contract or other evidence if there is any doubt about the last act required.

The month in which the company approves the policy is not the month in which the commission was earned unless it happens to coincide with the last act required of the agent, as, for instance, if later in that month the agent forwarded the first premium due on the approved policy and this qualified for the commission. Similarly, the month in which the agent delivered the policy and collected the initial premium is not the month in which the commission was earned if the agent qualified for commission when the customer signed the policy application.

This same rule applies to converted policies. If the conversion of the life insurance policy resulted in new commissions, the commissions are earned in the month in which the agent performed the last act which qualified for those new commissions. In the latter case, it is immaterial that the conversion was accomplished with the help of another agent through the insistence of the purchaser of the policy; some action (even if it is only the signature) was required of the selling agent in order to be entitled to the new rate of commissions.

If the life insurance agent is a **self-employed** person when the policy is sold, first-year and renewal commissions are treated as earnings for purposes of Social Security taxes for the taxable year in which they are **received**. When a policy is sold, there should be reported in the year of sale only the first-year commission received on the policy in that year. Renewal commissions on such a policy will be treated as earnings for purposes of Social Security taxes in the year when received. Renewal commissions received in a year after the year of entitlement to Social Security benefits are not included as earnings for purposes of the retirement test if they were the result of services rendered in or prior to the initial month of entitlement.

A self-employed agent includes the following in figuring total earnings for a particular taxable year for purposes of the retirement test:

- Original commissions received during the year.

- Renewal commissions received during the year from policies sold while a self-employed agent if the policies were sold after the initial month of entitlement to Social Security benefits, but not for such policies sold in or before such initial month. Further, there will be excluded all renewal commissions received from policies sold in prior years while an employee. Also, excluded will be anticipated renewal commissions on policies sold during the current year while self-employed.

- All net earnings from self-employment derived during the year in the form of insurance service fees, persistency fees, etc.

- All remuneration classified as earnings from other jobs, trades, or businesses.

- Any net loss from other self-employment during the year.

Are Self-Employed Earnings Subject to Social Security Retirement Test?

| | Commissions Received In | |
| | Year of First | Years After Year |
Time of Sale	Entitlement*	of First Entitlement*
Prior to Year of First		
Entitlement	Yes	No
In Year of First Entitlement		
(1) Sold in months through		
month of First Entitlement	Yes	No
(2) Sold in months after		
month of First Entitlement	Yes	Yes
After Year of First Entitlement	Yes	Yes

*Entitlement means (a) being eligible by virtue of age and insured status (i.e., having the required number of Quarters of Coverage) and (b) having filed a claim for benefits.

The receipt of renewal commissions in the initial year of retirement on policies sold by a self-employed agent will not necessarily result in a loss of benefits even though they exceed the earnings limit for the taxable year. The reason is that such "self-employment" earnings cannot be charged against benefits for any month in the initial year of retirement in which the agent-beneficiary does not render any substantial services in self-employment. Even large amounts of renewal commissions will not cause loss of any benefits if the agent-beneficiary renders no substantial services in self-employment during the taxable year in which the commissions are received.

Generally, repeat commissions paid on **casualty insurance policies** (e.g., accident and health) differ from renewal commissions in the life insurance field. This is true even though the repeat commissions are sometimes called "renewal" commissions. Each repeat commission is, in fact, for a policy written for a new and different term.

Ordinarily, the rate of commission on these repeats is the same regardless of how many times the insurance is extended for a new term. In life insurance renewals, on the other hand, there is a limit on the number of years for which renewal commissions are paid on the same life insurance policy. Regardless of the amount of work done by an agent when a casualty insurance policy is extended, the commission paid is for the new term only. It is not additional compensation for the original term of the policy. For these reasons, repeat commissions from accident and health policies are normally earned in the month in which the policy is extended. Thus, they are wages for the month and year if the agent then was an employee. If the agent then was self-employed, they may be included as earnings from self-employment for the year in which they are received.

165

MEDICARE

I-1. What is Medicare?

Medicare is a federal health insurance program for persons 65 or older, persons of any age with permanent kidney failure, and certain disabled persons. Medicare is administered by the Health Care Financing Administration within the Department of Health and Human Services. Social Security Administration offices across the country take applications for Medicare and provide general information about the program.

Medicare consists of Hospital Insurance (Part A) protection, Medical Insurance (Part B) protection, and Medicare+Choice (Part C).

Hospital Insurance (Part A) provides institutional care, including inpatient hospital care, skilled nursing home care, post-hospital home health care, and, under certain circumstances, hospice care. Part A is financed for the most part by Social Security payroll tax deductions which are deposited in the Federal Hospital Insurance Trust Fund. Medicare beneficiaries also participate in the financing of Part A by paying deductibles, coinsurance and premiums.

Medical Insurance (Part B) is a voluntary program of health insurance which covers physician's services, outpatient hospital care, physical therapy, ambulance trips, medical equipment, prosthesis, and a number of other services not covered under Part A. It is financed through monthly premiums paid by those who enroll and contributions from the federal government. The government's share of the cost far exceeds that paid by those enrolled.

Medicare+Choice (Part C) permits contracts between the Health Care Financing Administration and a variety of different managed care and fee-for-service entities. The type of entities that may be granted contracts under Medicare+Choice include:

- Coordinated care plans, including Health Maintenance Organizations (HMOs), Preferred Provider Organizations (PPOs), and Provider-Sponsored Organizations (PSOs). A PSO is defined as a public or private entity established by health care providers, which provide a substantial proportion of health care items and services directly through affiliated providers who share, directly or indirectly, substantial financial risk.

- Private fee-for-service plans which reimburse providers on a fee-for-service basis, and are authorized to charge enrolled beneficiaries up to

167

115% of the plan's payment schedule (which may be different from the Medicare fee schedule).

- Medical savings account/high deductible plans (under a demonstration in which up to 390,000 beneficiaries may enroll, with no new enrollments permitted after January 1, 2003). Under this option, beneficiaries would obtain high deductible health policies that pay for at least all Medicare-covered items and services after an enrollee meets the annual deductible of up to $6,000 (as indexed). The difference between the premiums for such high deductible policies and the applicable Medicare+Choice premium amount would be placed into an account for the beneficiary to use in meeting his deductible expenses.

The Department of Health and Human Services contracts with private insurance companies for the processing of payments to patients and health care providers. These private insurance companies are called fiscal intermediaries under Part A and are selected by the health care providers. Under Part B, these private insurance companies are called carriers and are selected by the Department of Health and Human Services.

The Health Care Financing Administration, whose central office is in Baltimore, Maryland, directs Medicare and Medicaid programs. The Social Security Administration processes Medicare applications and claims, but it does not set Medicare policy. The Health Care Financing Administration sets the standards which hospitals, skilled nursing facilities, home health agencies, and hospices must meet in order to be certified as qualified providers of services.

HOSPITAL INSURANCE

I-2. What persons are eligible for benefits under Part A Hospital Insurance?

All persons age 65 and over who are entitled to monthly Social Security cash benefits (or would be entitled except that an application for cash benefits has not been filed), or monthly cash benefits under railroad retirement programs (whether retired or not) are eligible for benefits.

Persons age 65 and over can receive Medicare benefits even if they continue to work. Enrollment in the program while working will not affect the amount of future Social Security benefits.

A dependent or survivor of a person entitled to Hospital Insurance benefits, or a dependent of a person under age 65 who is entitled to retirement or disability benefits, is also eligible for Hospital Insurance benefits if such dependent or survivor is at least 65 years old. For example, a woman age 65 or over who is entitled to a spouse's or widow's Social Security benefit is eligible for benefits under Hospital Insurance.

A Social Security disability beneficiary is covered under Medicare after entitlement to disability benefits for 24 months or more. Those covered include disabled workers at any age, disabled widows and widowers age 50 or over, beneficiaries age 18 or older who receive benefits because of disability beginning before age 22, and disabled qualified railroad retirement annuitants.

A person who becomes reentitled to disability benefits within five years after the end of a previous period of entitlement (within seven years in the case of disabled widows or widowers and disabled children) is automatically eligible for Medicare coverage without having to wait another 24 months. However, and further, if the previous period of disability ends after March 1, 1988, a person is covered under Medicare without again having to meet the 24 month waiting period requirement, regardless of not meeting the five year (or seven year) requirement if the current impairment is the same as (or directly related to) that in the previous period of disability.

End-Stage Renal Disease

Insured workers (and their dependents) with end-stage renal disease who require renal dialysis or a kidney transplant are deemed disabled for Medicare coverage purposes even if they are working. Coverage can begin with the first day of the third month after the month dialysis treatments begin. This three-month waiting period is waived if the individual participates in a self-care dialysis training course during the waiting period. Medicare coverage based on transplant begins with the month of the transplant or with either of the two preceding months if the patient was hospitalized during either of those months for procedures preliminary to transplant. If entitlement could be based on more than one of the factors the earliest date is used.

Coverage is provided under Medicare for the self-administration of erythropoietin for home renal dialysis patients.

Medicare is the secondary payer during a period (generally 30 months) for individuals who have Medicare solely on the basis of their end-stage renal disease, if they have employer group health plan coverage themselves or through a family member. During this period, if an employer plan pays less than the provider's charges, then Medicare may supplement the plan's payments.

Government Employees

Federal employees who were not covered under Social Security (e.g., temporary workers have been covered since 1951) began paying the portion of

Social Security tax that is creditable for Medicare Hospital Insurance (Part A) purposes in 1983. Those covered under Social Security, such as virtually all hired after 1983, pay the Hospital Insurance tax as well as the OASDI tax. A transitional provision provides credit for retroactive hospital quarters of coverage for federal employees who were employed before 1983 and also on January 1, 1983.

State and local government employees hired after March 31, 1986, are covered under Medicare coverage and tax provisions. A person who was performing substantial and regular service for a state or local government before April 1, 1986 is not covered provided he was a bona fide employee on March 31, 1986, and the employment relationship was not entered into in order to meet the requirements for exemptions from coverage.

State or local government employees whose employment is terminated after March 31, 1986, are covered under Medicare if they are later rehired.

Beginning after June 30, 1991, state and local government workers who are not covered by a retirement system in conjunction with their employment, and who are not already subject to the Medicare Hospital Insurance tax, are also automatically covered and must pay such taxes. A retirement system is defined as a pension, annuity, retirement, or similar fund or system established by a state or by a political subdivision of a state.

Individuals are not automatically covered under Medicare if employed by a state or local government:

(1) to relieve them of unemployment;

(2) in a hospital, home, or institution where they are inmates or patients;

(3) on a temporary basis because of an emergency such as a storm, earthquake, flood, fire or snow;

(4) if the individuals qualify as interns, student nurses or other student employees of District of Columbia government hospitals, unless the individuals are medical or dental interns or medical or dental residents in training.

State governments may voluntarily enter into agreements to extend Medicare coverage to employees not covered under the rules above.

Medicare as Secondary Payer

There are limitations on Medicare payments for services covered under group health plans. Medicare is secondary payer, under specified conditions, for services covered under any of the following:

(1) Group health plans of employers that employ at least 20 employees and that cover Medicare beneficiaries age 65 or older who are covered under the plan by virtue of the individual's current employment status with an employer or the current employment status of a spouse of any age.

(2) Group health plans (without regard to the number of individuals employed and irrespective of current employment status) that cover individuals who have end stage renal disease. Generally, group health plans are always primary payers throughout the first 30 months of end stage renal disease based on Medicare eligibility or entitlement.

(3) Large group health plans (that is, plans of employers that employ at least 100 employees) that cover Medicare beneficiaries who are under age 65, entitled to Medicare on the basis of disability, and covered under the plan by virtue of the individual's or a family member's current employment status with an employer.

Group health plans and large group health plans may not take into account that the individuals described above are entitled to Medicare on the basis of age or disability, or eligible for, or entitled to Medicare on the basis of end stage renal disease. Group health plans of employers of 20 or more employees must provide to any employee or spouse age 65 or older the same benefits, under the same conditions, that they provide to employees and spouses under 65. The requirement applies regardless of whether the individual or spouse 65 or older is entitled to Medicare. Group health plans may not differentiate in the benefits they provide between individuals who have end stage renal disease and other individuals covered under the plan on the basis of the existence of end stage renal disease, the need for renal dialysis, or in any other manner.

An employer or insurer is prohibited from offering Medicare beneficiaries financial or other benefits as incentives not to enroll in, or to terminate enrollment in, a group health plan that is, or would be, primary to Medicare. The prohibition precludes offering to Medicare beneficiaries an alternative to the employer primary plan (for example, coverage of prescription drugs) unless the beneficiary has primary coverage other than Medicare. An example would be primary coverage through his own or a spouse's employer.

An employee may reject the employer's plan and retain Medicare as the primary payer, but regulations prevent employers from offering a health plan or option designed to induce the employee to reject the employer's plan and retain Medicare as primary payer.

Medicare benefits are secondary to benefits payable by a large group health plan for services furnished during any month in which the individual: (1) is entitled to Medicare Part A benefits on the basis of disability, (2) is covered under a large group health plan, and (3) has large group health plan coverage by virtue of his own or a family member's current employment status.

Medicare becomes primary if the services are: (1) furnished to Medicare beneficiaries who have declined to enroll in the group health plan, (2) not covered under the plan for the disabled individual or similarly situated individuals, (3) covered under the plan but not available to particular disabled individuals because they have exhausted their benefits under the plan, (4) furnished to individuals whose COBRA continuation coverage has been terminated because of the individual's Medicare entitlement, or (5) covered under COBRA continuation coverage notwithstanding the individual's Medicare entitlement.

Medicare is also the secondary payer:

(1) When medical care can be paid for under no-fault insurance or liability insurance (including automobile insurance).

(2) If the individual is entitled to veterans benefits.

(3) If the individual is entitled to black lung benefits.

(4) If the individual is covered by workers' compensation.

The Health Care Financing Administration must mail questionnaires to individuals before they become entitled to Part A Hospital Insurance benefits or enroll in Part B Medical Insurance to determine whether they are covered under a primary plan. Benefits, however, will not be denied for covered services solely on the grounds that the beneficiary failed to note the existence of other health plan coverage in the questionnaire. Providers and suppliers are required to provide information on claim forms regarding potential coverage under other plans. Civil monetary penalties are established for an entity that knowingly, willfully, and repeatedly fails to complete a claim form with accurate information.

I-3. Can a person age 65 or over qualify for Part A Hospital Insurance benefits even though he cannot qualify for Social Security or Railroad Retirement benefits?

Most persons age 65 or over and otherwise ineligible for Hospital Insurance may enroll voluntarily and pay a monthly premium if they are also enrolled for Part B Medical Insurance under Medicare. (See I-6 and I-21.)

Most persons who reached age 65 before 1968 are eligible to enroll for Hospital Insurance without paying premiums even if they have no coverage under Social Security. Also eligible for enrollment under this transitional provision are persons age 65 and over with specified amounts of earnings credits less than that required for cash benefit eligibility.

Not eligible under the transitional provision are: (1) retired federal employees covered by the Federal Employees' Health Benefits Act of 1959, (2) nonresidents of the United States, and (3) aliens admitted for permanent residence (unless lawfully admitted for permanent residence in the United States continuously during the five years immediately preceding the month in which they apply for enrollment).

I-4. How is Hospital Insurance financed?

By a separate Hospital Insurance tax imposed upon employers, employees and self-employed persons. The tax must be paid by every individual, regardless of age, who is subject to the regular Social Security tax or to the Railroad Retirement tax. It must also be paid by all federal employees and by all state and local government employees: (1) hired after March 1986, or (2) not covered by a state retirement system in conjunction with their employment (beginning July 2, 1991).

The tax is imposed upon all earnings. The rates of the Hospital Insurance Tax are 1.45% for employees and employers and 2.90% for self-employed persons.

There is a special federal (and generally following through to state) income tax deduction of 50% of the OASDI/Hospital Insurance self-employment tax. This income tax deduction, which is taken directly against an individual's gross income to determine adjusted gross income, is designed to treat the self-employed in much the same manner as employees and employers are treated for Social Security and income tax purposes.

I-5. Is Part A Hospital Insurance a compulsory program?

Yes. Every person who works in employment or self-employment covered by the Social Security Act, or in employment covered by the Railroad Retirement Act, must pay the Hospital Insurance tax and will be eligible for Hospital Insurance benefits if fully insured when he reaches age 65, receives disability benefits for more than 24 months, or has end-stage renal disease. (See I-2.)

I-6. Can an individual not automatically entitled to Hospital Insurance benefits enroll by paying a special premium?

Yes, provided the individual: (1) has attained age 65, (2) is enrolled in Part B Medical Insurance (see I-21 through I-27), (3) is a resident of the United States and is either: (a) a citizen, or (b) an alien lawfully admitted for permanent residence who has resided in the United States continuously during the five years immediately preceding the month in which he applies for enrollment, and (4) is not otherwise entitled to Hospital Insurance benefits.

Disabled individuals under age 65 may also be able to obtain Hospital Insurance coverage through monthly premiums. Eligibility is extended to individuals under age 65 who qualify for Hospital Insurance benefits on the basis of a disabling physical or mental impairment, but who lose entitlement because they have earnings that exceed the eligibility limit for Social Security disability benefits and are not otherwise entitled to Hospital Insurance benefits.

The Hospital Insurance premium is $300 a month in 2001 (but see paragraph below for premium reduction exception).

The Hospital Insurance premium is reduced for individuals and their spouses with credits for 30 or more quarters paid into the Social Security system. The Hospital Insurance premium is reduced to $165 a month (in 2001). The reduction in premium payments will also apply to the surviving spouse or divorced spouse of an individual who had at least 30 quarters of coverage under Social Security.

The premium for an individual who enrolls after the close of the initial enrollment period or who reenrolls is increased by 10% if there were at least 12 months of delayed enrollment, regardless of how late the individual enrolls. The initial enrollment period starts the first day of the third month prior to eligibility and ends seven months later. The increased-premium paying period is limited to twice the number of years an individual delayed enrolling. The premium then reverts to the standard monthly premium in effect at that time.

Certain state and local government retirees are no longer required to pay the premium to receive Hospital Insurance benefits.

I-7. In general, what benefits are provided under Part A Hospital Insurance?

Over and above the "deductibles" and "coinsurance" amounts which must be paid by the patient, the following services are covered:

(1) *Inpatient hospital care* for up to 90 days in each "benefit period." The patient pays a deductible of $792 for the first 60 days and coinsurance of $198 a day for each additional day up to a maximum of 30 days. In addition, each person has a non-renewable "reserve" of 60 additional hospital days with coinsurance of $396 a day. Each of these reserve days can only be used once during someone's lifetime.

(2) *Posthospital extended care in a skilled nursing facility* for up to 100 days in each "benefit period." The patient pays nothing for the first 20 days. After 20 days the patient pays coinsurance of $99 a day for each additional day up to a maximum of 80 days.

(3) The first 100 *home health service* visits following a hospital or skilled nursing facility stay. The patient pays nothing toward home health services, except that there is 20% cost-sharing payable by the patient for durable medical equipment (other than the purchase of certain used items).

(4) *Hospice care* for terminally ill patients (see I-10).

I-8. Specifically, what inpatient hospital services are paid for under Part A Hospital Insurance?

Except for the deductible amount which must be paid by the patient, Medicare helps pay for inpatient hospital services for up to 90 days in each "benefit period." Medicare will also pay (except for a coinsurance amount) for 60 additional hospital days over each person's lifetime (applies to disabled beneficiaries at any age; others after age 65).

Medicare pays for hospital care if the patient meets the following four conditions: (1) a doctor prescribes inpatient hospital care for treatment of the illness or injury, (2) the patient requires the kind of care that can only be provided in a hospital, (3) the hospital is participating in Medicare, and (4) the Utilization Review Committee of the hospital, a Peer Review Organization (PRO), or an intermediary does not disapprove of the stay.

In 2001 the patient must pay a deductible of $792 for the first 60 days in each benefit period. If the stay is longer than 60 days during a benefit period, coinsurance of $198 a day must be paid for each additional day up to a maximum of 30 days. Thus, a 90-day stay would cost the patient $6,732. After 90 days, the patient pays the full bill unless the lifetime reserve of 60 days is drawn upon. Coinsurance of $396 a day is paid for these 60 additional lifetime reserve days.

The coinsurance amounts are based on those in effect when services are furnished, rather than on those in effect at the beginning of the beneficiary's spell of illness (benefit period).

The 90-day benefit period starts again with each spell of illness. A "benefit period" is a way of measuring the patient's use of services under Hospital Insurance. The patient's first benefit period starts the first time the patient receives inpatient hospital care after Hospital Insurance begins. A benefit period ends when the patient has been out of a hospital or other facility primarily providing skilled nursing or rehabilitative services for 60 days in a row (including the day of discharge). If a patient remains in a facility (other than a hospital) that primarily provides skilled nursing or rehabilitative services, a benefit period ends when the patient has not received any skilled care there for 60 days in a row. After one benefit period has ended, another one will start whenever the patient again receives inpatient hospital care.

There is no limit to the number of 90-day benefit periods a person can have in a lifetime (except in the case of hospitalization for mental illness). However, the lifetime reserve of 60 days is not renewable. Also, special limited benefit periods apply to hospice care. (See I-10.)

Specifically, the following inpatient services are covered:

• *Bed and board in a semi-private room* (two to four beds) or a ward (five or more beds). Hospital Insurance will pay the cost of a private room only if it is required for medical reasons. If the patient requests a private room, Hospital Insurance will pay the cost of semi-private accommodations; the patient must pay the extra charge for the private room.

• *All meals*, including special diets.

• *Nursing services* provided by or under the supervision of licensed nursing personnel (other than the services of a private duty nurse or attendant).

• Services of the hospital's medical *social workers*.

• Use of *regular hospital equipment*, supplies and appliances, such as oxygen tents, wheel chairs, crutches, casts, surgical dressings, and splints.

• *Drugs and biologicals* ordinarily furnished by the hospital. A limited supply of drugs needed for use outside the hospital is also covered, but only if medically necessary in order to facilitate the patient's departure from the hospital and the supply is necessary until the patient can obtain a continuing supply.

• *Diagnostic or therapeutic items and services* ordinarily furnished by the hospital or by others (including clinical psychologists, as defined by the Health Care Financing Administration), under arrangements made with the hospital.

• *Operating and recovery room* costs, including hospital costs for anesthesia services.

- Services of *interns and residents in training* under an approved teaching program.

- *Blood transfusions*, after the first three pints. Hospital Insurance helps pay for blood (whole blood or units of packed red blood cells), blood components, and the cost of blood processing and administration. If the patient receives blood as an inpatient of a hospital or skilled nursing facility, Hospital Insurance will pay for these blood costs, except for any nonreplacement fees charged for the first three pints of whole blood or units of packed red cells per calendar year. The nonreplacement fee is the amount that some hospitals and skilled nursing facilities charge for blood that is not replaced. The patient is responsible for the nonreplacement fees for the first three pints or units of blood furnished by a hospital or skilled nursing facility. If the patient is charged nonreplacement fees, the patient has the option of either paying the fees or having the blood replaced. If the patient chooses to have the blood replaced, the patient can either replace the blood personally or arrange to have another person or an organization replace it.

- *X-rays* and other radiology services, including radiation therapy, billed by the hospital.

- *Lab tests.*

- *Respiratory or inhalation therapy.*

- *Independent clinical laboratory services* under arrangement with the hospital.

- *Alcohol detoxification and rehabilitative services* when furnished as inpatient hospital services.

- *Dental services* when the patient requires hospitalization because of the severity of the dental procedure or because of his underlying medical condition and clinical status.

- Cost of *special care units*, such as an intensive care unit, coronary care unit, etc.

- *Rehabilitation services*, such as physical therapy, occupational therapy, and speech pathology services.

- *Appliances* (such as pacemakers, colostomy fittings, and artificial limbs) that are permanently installed while in the hospital.

- *Lung and heart-lung transplants.*

Hospital Insurance does *not* pay for:

- Services of physicians and surgeons, including the services of patholo-gists, radiologists, anesthesiologists, and physiatrists. (Nor does Hospi-tal Insurance pay for the services of a physician, resident physician or intern—except those provided by an intern or resident in training under an approved teaching program.)

- Services of a private duty nurse or attendant, unless the patient's condition requires such services and the nurse or attendant is a bona fide employee of the hospital.

- Personal convenience items supplied at the patient's request, such as television rental, radio rental, or telephone.

- The first three pints of whole blood (or packed red blood cells) received in a calendar year.

- Supplies, appliances and equipment for use outside the hospital, unless continued use is required (e.g., a pacemaker).

Medicare beneficiaries have the right to receive the hospital care necessary for the proper diagnosis and treatment of their illness or injury. A beneficiary's discharge date must be determined solely by his medical needs. Beneficiaries have the right to be fully informed about decisions affecting their Medicare coverage and payment for their hospital stay and any post-hospital services. They also have the right to request a review by a Peer Review Organization (PRO) of any written notice of noncoverage they receive from the hospital. PROs are groups of doctors who are paid by the federal government to review medical necessity, appropriateness, and quality of hospital treatment fur-nished to Medicare patients.

I-9. What is a Health Maintenance Organization?

A Medicare beneficiary eligible for Part A Hospital Insurance benefits and Part B Medical Insurance benefits (or only Medical Insurance benefits) under Medicare may choose to have covered health insurance services furnished through a Health Maintenance Organization (HMO) by enrolling in an HMO that has a Medicare contract.

Coordinated care plans are prepaid, managed care plans, most of which are HMOs or competitive medical plans (CMPs). Both HMOs and CMPs contract with Medicare and follow the same contracting rules. HMOs provide or arrange for all Medicare covered services, and generally charge the beneficiary fixed monthly premiums and only small copayments. This means that if a beneficiary joins a coordinated care plan and gets all services through the HMO, his out-of-pocket costs are usually more predictable. Also, depending on the beneficiary's health needs, those costs may be less than he would pay if he had to pay the regular Medicare deductible and coinsurance amounts.

An HMO is an organization that provides to it members, who are also Medicare beneficiaries, either directly or through arrangement with others, at least all the Medicare covered services which are available to Medicare beneficiaries who are not enrolled in the HMO who reside in the geographic area serviced by the HMO. Some HMOs also provide services not covered by Medicare, either free to the Medicare enrollee (that is, funded out of the payment Medicare makes to the HMO), or for an additional charge. HMOs typically charge a set monthly premium and nominal copayments for services instead of Medicare's coinsurance and deductibles.

Generally, services include those covered under *both* Part A Hospital Insurance and Part B Medical Insurance, and are available to all Medicare beneficiaries in the area served by the HMO. The only enrollment criteria for Medicare HMOs are: (1) the Medicare beneficiary must be enrolled in Medical Insurance and continue to pay the Medical Insurance premiums, (2) the Medicare beneficiary must live in the plan's service area, (3) the Medicare beneficiary cannot be receiving care in a Medicare-certified hospice, and (4) the Medicare beneficiary cannot have permanent kidney failure.

Only federal qualified HMOs and HMO-like organizations that the Department of Health and Human Services determines meet the Competitive Medical Plan (CMP) requirements of the law are eligible to enter into Medicare contracts. HMOs which do not meet the requirements for fully qualified HMOs can contract for Medicare participation and be paid on a reasonable cost basis for their services.

Services received by Medicare beneficiaries differ depending on the conditions of the contract between the Department of Health and Human Services and the HMO. Beneficiaries considering enrolling in an HMO should compare plans available in their respective geographic areas to ensure the best mix of services and prices to fit their individual needs.

Qualified HMO's are paid on an estimated per capita basis. Payments are made only to established HMOs, which are those: (1) with a minimum enrollment of 25,000, not more than half of whom are age 65 or older, and (2) which have been in operation for at least two years. Exception to the size requirement is provided for HMOs in small communities or sparsely populated areas (5,000 members and three years of operation).

The Department of Health and Human Services designates a single 30-day period each year in which all HMOs in an area participating in Medicare must have an open enrollment period. During this 30-day period, HMOs must accept Medicare beneficiaries up to the limits of their capacity.

Individuals may disenroll from an HMO effective on the first day of the calendar month following the date on which they requested disenrollment. Under previous law, disenrollment could not be effective until the first day of the second month following the date on which they requested disenrollment.

HMOs must provide assurances to the Health Care Financing Administration that if they cease to provide items and services for which they have contracted, they will provide or arrange for supplemental coverage of Medicare benefits relating to a preexisting condition.

HMOs are responsible for ensuring that all enrollees are informed in writing of the appeal procedures that are available to them. Medicare beneficiaries who enroll in HMOs retain all the rights to appeal which are available to other Medicare beneficiaries.

I-10. How is hospice care covered under Part A Hospital Insurance?

A hospice is a public agency or private organization that is primarily engaged in providing pain relief, symptom management, and supportive services to terminally ill people. Medicare pays for services every day and also permits a hospice to provide appropriate custodial care, including homemaker services and counseling. Hospice care under Medicare includes both home care and inpatient care, when needed, and a variety of services not otherwise covered under Medicare.

Hospice care is covered under Hospital Insurance when the beneficiary: (1) is eligible for Hospital Insurance benefits, (2) is certified by a doctor as terminally ill (i.e., life expectancy of six months or less), and (3) files a statement electing to waive all other Medicare coverage for hospice care from hospice programs other than the one chosen, and elects not to receive other services related to treatment of the terminal condition. (The beneficiary can later revoke the election.)

The following are covered hospice services:

• Nursing care provided by or under the supervision of a registered nurse.

• Medical social services provided by a social worker under a physician's direction.

• Counseling (including dietary counseling) with respect to care of the terminally ill patient and adjustment to his approaching death.

- Short-term inpatient care, including respite care, provided in a participating hospice, hospital or skilled nursing facility.

- Medical appliances and supplies.

- Services of a home health aid and homemaker services.

- Drugs, including outpatient drugs for pain relief and symptom management.

- Physical therapy, occupational therapy, and speech-language pathology services to control symptoms or to enable the patient to maintain
  activities of daily living and basic functional skills.

Up until August 5, 1997, hospices were required to provide directly for
physician services under Medicare. The Balanced Budget Act of 1997 deleted
physician services from a hospice's core services and allows hospices to
employ or contract with physicians for their services.

The benefit period consists of two 90-day periods followed by an unlimited
number of 60-day periods. The medical director or physician member of the
hospice interdisciplinary team would have to re-certify that the beneficiary is
terminally ill at the beginning of the 60-day periods. Prior to August 5, 1997,
the benefit period consisted of two 90-day periods and one 30-day period.

The amount paid by Medicare is equal to the reasonable costs of providing
hospice care or based on other tests of reasonableness as prescribed by
regulations. No payment may be made for bereavement counseling, and no
reimbursement may be made for other counseling services (including nutri-
tional and dietary counseling) as separate services.

There are no deductibles under the hospice benefit. The beneficiary does
not pay for Medicare-covered services for the terminal illness, except for
small coinsurance amounts for outpatient drugs and inpatient respite care. The
patient is responsible for 5% of the cost of outpatient drugs or $5 toward each
prescription, whichever is less. For inpatient respite care, the patient pays $5
per day such care is provided.

Respite care as an inpatient in a hospice (to give a period of relief to the
family providing home care for the patient) is limited to no more than five days
in a row.

Persons must be certified as terminally ill within two days after hospice
care is initiated. However, beginning January 1, 1990, if verbal certification
is provided within two days, certification may occur within eight days after
care is initiated.

I-11. Are inpatient hospital benefits provided for care in a psychiatric hospital?

Yes, but benefits for psychiatric hospital care are subject to a lifetime limit of 190 days. Furthermore, if the patient is already in a mental hospital when he becomes eligible for Medicare, the time he has spent there in the 150-day period before becoming eligible will be counted against the maximum of 150 days available in such cases (including any later period of such hospitalization when he has not been out of a mental hospital for at least 60 consecutive days between hospitalizations). However, this latter limitation does not apply to inpatient service in a general hospital for other than psychiatric care.

I-12. What special provisions apply to care in a Christian Science sanatorium?

Benefits are payable for services provided by a Christian Science sanatorium operated or certified by the First Church of Christ Scientist in Boston. In general, these institutions can participate in the plan as a hospital and the regular coverages and exclusions relating to inpatient hospital care apply. Thus, in 2001, the patient pays a $792 deductible for the first 60 days, and coinsurance of $198 a day for the next 30 days (plus $396 a day for the 60 lifetime reserve days). A Christian Science sanatorium may also be paid as a skilled nursing facility. However, extended care benefits will be paid for only 30 days in a calendar year (instead of the usual 100 days), and the patient must pay the coinsurance amount ($99 a day) for each day of service (instead of only for each day after the 20th day).

In response to a federal district court ruling, Congress deleted any reference to Christian Science sanatoriums in the Social Security Act and replaced them with the term "religious nonmedical health care institutions." The Balanced Budget Act of 1997 includes detailed eligibility criteria for facilities to protect the health and safety of patients, and limits the total amount of expenditures that can be paid to religious nonmedical health care institutions.

I-13. Must a doctor certify that hospitalization is required?

Initial certification is no longer required except for inpatient psychiatric hospital services and inpatient tuberculosis hospital services. For prolonged hospital stays, however, certification by a doctor will be required as often, and with such supporting material, as will be stipulated in the regulations under the law.

I-14. What must a hospital or Health Maintenance Organization do to qualify for Medicare payments?

It must meet certain standards and must enter into a Medicare agreement with the federal government. However, provision is made for paying nonparticipating hospitals in cases of emergency.

I-15. What provisions are made Part A under Hospital Insurance for post-hospital care in a skilled nursing facility or other such facility?

Except for a coinsurance amount payable by the patient after the first 20 days, Hospital Insurance will pay the reasonable cost of post-hospital care in a skilled nursing facility for up to 100 days in a benefit period. The following items and services are covered:

- Bed and board in a semi-private room (two to four beds in a room), unless the patient's condition requires isolation or no semi-private rooms are available.

- Nursing care provided by, or under the supervision of, a registered nurse (but not private-duty nursing).

- Drugs, biologicals, supplies (such as splints and casts), appliances (such as wheelchairs), and equipment for use in the facility.

- Medical social services.

- Medical services of interns and residents in training under an approved teaching program of a hospital.

- Other diagnostic or therapeutic services provided by a hospital with which the facility has a transfer agreement.

- Rehabilitation services, such as physical, occupational, and speech therapy.

- All meals, including special diets furnished by the facility.

- Blood transfusions.

- Such other health services as are generally provided by a skilled nursing facility.

The patient pays nothing for the first 20 days of covered service in each spell of illness; after 20 days, coinsurance is payable for each additional day, up to a maximum of 80 days. For a patient in the skilled nursing facility in 2001, the coinsurance is $99 a day. Thus, a 100-day stay during 2001 will cost the patient $7,920.

There is no lifetime limit on the amount of skilled nursing facility care provided under Hospital Insurance. Except for the coinsurance (which must be paid after the first 20 days in each spell of illness), the plan will pay the cost of 100 days' post-hospital care in each benefit period, regardless of how many benefit periods the person may have. After 100 days of coverage, the patient must pay the full cost of skilled nursing facility care.

In order to qualify for skilled nursing facility benefits, the patient must meet all five of the following conditions:

(1) The patient's condition requires daily skilled nursing or skilled rehabilitative services, which, as a practical matter, can only be provided in a skilled nursing facility.

(2) The patient has been in a hospital at least three days in a row (not counting the day of discharge) before being admitted to a participating skilled nursing facility.

(3) The patient is admitted to the skilled nursing facility within a short time (generally within 30 days) after leaving the hospital.

(4) The patient's care in the skilled nursing facility is for a condition that was treated in the hospital, or for a condition that arose while receiving care in the skilled nursing facility for a condition which was treated in the hospital.

(5) A medical professional certifies that the patient needs, and receives, skilled nursing or skilled rehabilitative services on a daily basis.

Exception. Skilled nursing facility coverage is permitted without regard to the three-day prior hospital stay requirement if there is no increase in cost to the program involved, and the acute care nature of the benefit is not altered. Persons covered without a prior hospital stay may be subject to limitations in the scope of or extent of services. The Department of Health and Human Services will decide when to lift the three-day hospital stay requirement but has not done so yet (and is not likely to do so).

If a patient leaves a skilled nursing facility and is readmitted within 30 days, the patient does not need to have a new three-day stay in a hospital for care to be covered.

I-16. What is a qualified skilled nursing facility?

A skilled nursing facility is a specially qualified facility that specializes in skilled care. It has the staff and equipment to provide skilled nursing care or skilled rehabilitative services and other related health services.

A skilled nursing facility may be a skilled nursing home, or a distinct part of an institution, such as a ward or wing of a hospital, or a section of a facility another part of which is an old-age home. Not all nursing homes will qualify; those which offer only custodial care are excluded. The facility must be primarily engaged in providing skilled nursing care or rehabilitation services for injured, disabled or sick persons. Skilled nursing care means care that can only be performed by, or under the supervision of, licensed nursing personnel. Skilled rehabilitative services may include such services as physical therapy performed by, or under the supervision of, a professional therapist.

At least one registered nurse must be employed full-time and adequate nursing service (which may include practical nurses) must be provided at all times. Every patient must be under the supervision of a doctor, and a doctor must always be available for emergency care. Generally, the facility must be certified by the state. It also must have a written agreement with a hospital that is participating in the Medicare program for the transfer of patients.

Many residents of nursing homes will not qualify for Medicare coverage because coverage is restricted to patients in need of skilled nursing and rehabilitative services on a daily basis. Most nursing homes are *not* skilled nursing facilities and many skilled nursing facilities are not certified by Medicare. Medicare does not pay for custodial care when it is the only kind of care needed. Custodial care includes help in walking, getting in and out of bed, bathing, dressing, eating, and taking medicine.

An institution which is primarily for the care and treatment of mental diseases or tuberculosis is not a skilled nursing facility.

I-17. What post-hospital home health services are provided under the basic hospital insurance plan?

Part A Hospital Insurance covers the cost of 100 home health visits made on an "intermittent" basis during a home health spell of illness under a plan of treatment established by a physician. Coverage includes only home health visits following a hospital or skilled nursing facility stay.

A home health agency is a public or private agency that specializes in giving skilled nursing services and other therapeutic services, such as physical therapy, in the home.

Hospital Insurance pays for home health visits if all six of the following conditions are met:

(1) The care is post-institutional home health service.

(2) The care provided includes intermittent skilled nursing care, physical therapy, or speech therapy.

(3) The person is confined at home.

(4) The person is under the care of a physician who determines the need for home health care and sets up a home health plan for the person.

(5) The home health agency providing services participates in Medicare.

(6) The services are provided on a visiting basis in the person's home, or if it is necessary to use equipment that cannot be readily made available in the home, on an outpatient basis in a hospital, skilled nursing facility, or licensed rehabilitation center.

A patient can receive home health services indefinitely if the services are provided seven days a week for four hours per day. As an alternative, the patient can receive home health services for 21 days if services are provided seven days a week for eight hours a day.

A doctor must certify that the person is under a doctor's care, under a plan of care established and periodically reviewed by a doctor, confined to the home, and in need of: (1) skilled nursing care on an intermittent basis, or (2) physical or speech therapy, or has a continued need for (3) occupational therapy when eligibility for home health services has been established because of a prior need for intermittent skilled nursing care, speech therapy, or physical therapy in the current or prior certification period.

Home health aids, whether employed directly by a home health agency or made available through contract with another entity, must successfully complete a training and competency evaluation program or competency evaluation program approved by the Department of Health and Human Services.

Generally, a doctor may *not* make the determination in item 4 above for a patient of any agency in which the doctor has a significant ownership interest or a significant financial or contractual relationship. However, a doctor who has a financial interest in an agency which is a sole community health agency may carry out certification and plan of care functions for patients served by the agency.

Part A Hospital Insurance will pay for these services:

• Part-time or intermittent skilled nursing care.

• Physical therapy.

• Speech therapy.

If a person needs part-time or intermittent skilled nursing care, physical therapy, or speech therapy, Medicare also pays for:

- Part-time or intermittent services of home health aides.

- Medical social services.

- Medical supplies.

- Durable medical equipment (80% of approved cost; patient pays remaining 20%).

- Occupational therapy.

The patient pays nothing for the first 100 home health visits. Medicare pays the full approved cost of all covered home health visits. The patient may be charged only for any services or costs that Medicare does not cover. However, if the patient needs durable medical equipment, the patient is responsible for a 20% coinsurance payment for the equipment. Durable medical equipment includes iron lungs, oxygen tents, hospital beds and wheelchairs. The home health agency will submit claims for payment. The patient does not send in any bills.

Beginning January 1, 1998, both Part A Hospital Insurance and Part B Medical Insurance cover home health visits, but Hospital Insurance pays for the first 100 visits following a hospital or skilled nursing facility stay while Medical Insurance only pays for home health services that are unassociated with a hospital or skilled nursing facility stay.

Medicare does not cover home care services furnished primarily to assist people in meeting personal, family, and domestic needs. These non-covered services include general household services, preparing meals, shopping, or assisting in bathing, dressing, or other personal needs.

Home health services *not* covered by Medicare also include:

- 24-hour-a-day nursing care at home.

- Drugs and biologicals.

- Blood transfusions.

- Meals delivered to the home.

- Homemaker services.

While the patient must be homebound to be eligible for benefits, payment will be made for services furnished at a hospital, skilled nursing facility, or rehabilitation center if the patient's condition requires the use of equipment that ordinarily cannot be taken to the patient's home. However, Medicare will not pay the patient's transportation costs.

A patient is considered "confined to the home" if he or she has a condition, due to an illness or injury, that restricts his or her ability to leave home except with the assistance of another person or the aid of a supportive device (such as crutches, a cane, a wheelchair, or a walker), or if the patient has a condition such that leaving home is medically contraindicated. While a patient does not have to be bedridden to be considered "confined to home," the condition should be such that there exists a normal inability to leave home, that leaving home requires a considerable and taxing effort, and that absences from home are infrequent or of relatively short duration, or are attributable to the need to receive medical treatment.

I-18. Does Hospital Insurance pay any of the cost of outpatient hospital services?

No, outpatient diagnostic services are covered under Medicare Medical Insurance (Part B) (see I-26).

I-19. Will the amounts to be paid by patients as deductible and coinsurance remain the same in future years?

No. The $792 initial deductible for inpatient hospital care for 2001 will be increased based upon the expected expenditures for Medicare Part A for the next year. The daily coinsurance for inpatient hospital care for the 61st to 90th days in a benefit period is 1/4 of the initial deductible ($198 in 2001). The daily coinsurance for post-hospital extended care after 20 days is 1/8 of this initial deductible ($99 in 2001). The lifetime reserve days' coinsurance is 1/2 of the initial deductible ($396 in 2001).

I-20. Does a person have to be in financial need to receive the Part A Hospital Insurance benefits?

No, benefits are payable to rich and poor alike.

MEDICAL INSURANCE

I-21. Who is eligible for benefits under Part B Medical Insurance?

All persons entitled to premium-free Hospital Insurance (Part A) or premium Hospital Insurance (Part A) for the working disabled under Medicare may enroll in Medical Insurance (Part B). Social Security and Railroad Retirement beneficiaries, age 65 or over, are, therefore, automatically eligible. However, any other person age 65 or over may enroll provided only that he is a resident of the United States and is either: (1) a citizen of the United States, or (2) an alien lawfully admitted for permanent residence who has resided in the United States continuously during the five years immediately prior to the month in which he applies for enrollment.

Disabled beneficiaries (workers under age 65, widows aged 50-64, and children aged 18 or over disabled before age 22) who have been on the disability benefit roll for at least two years are covered in the same manner as persons age 65 or over. This includes disabled railroad retirement beneficiaries.

I-22. How does a person enroll in Medical Insurance (Part B)?

Those who are receiving Social Security or Railroad Retirement benefits will be enrolled automatically at the time they become entitled to premium-free Hospital Insurance unless they elect not to be covered for Medical Insurance. Others may enroll at their nearest Social Security office.

The initial enrollment period is a period of seven full calendar months, the beginning and end of which is determined for each person by the day on which he is first eligible to enroll. The initial enrollment period begins on the first day of the third month before the month a person first becomes eligible to enroll and ends with the close of the last day of the third month following the month a person first becomes eligible to enroll. For example, if a person's 65th birthday is April 10, 2001, the initial enrollment period begins January 1, 2001 and ends July 31, 2001.

If a person decides not to enroll in the initial enrollment period, he may enroll during a special enrollment period. The special enrollment period is a period of seven full calendar months beginning with the first month during which a person's employer plan coverage ends, or employment ends, whichever occurs first. In the case of an individual entitled to Medicare because of a disability, the special enrollment period begins: (1) when the individual is no longer enrolled as an active individual in a large group health plan (one that covers 100 or more employees), (2) when the employment status ends, or (3) when the plan coverage is terminated. For example, if a 67 year-old retires on July 1, 2001, the special enrollment period will begin on July 1, 2001, and run through January 31, 2002.

In order to obtain coverage at the earliest possible date, a person must enroll before the beginning of the month in which age 65 is reached. For a person who enrolls during the initial enrollment period, the effective date of coverage is as follows:

(1) If the person enrolls before the month in which age 65 is reached, coverage will commence the first day of the month in which age 65 is reached.

(2) If the person enrolls during the month in which age 65 is reached, coverage will commence the first day of the following month.

(3) If the person enrolls in the month after the month in which age 65 is reached, coverage will commence the first day of the second month after the month of enrollment.

(4) If the person enrolls more than one month (but at least within three months) after the month in which age 65 is reached, coverage will commence the first day of the third month following the month of enrollment.

A 7-month special enrollment period is provided if Medicare has been the secondary payer of benefits for individuals age 65 and older who are covered under an employer group health plan because of current employment. The special enrollment period generally begins with the month in which coverage under the private plan ended. Coverage under Medical Insurance will begin with the month after coverage under the private plan ends, if the individual enrolls in such month, or with the month after enrollment, if the individual enrolls during the balance of the special enrollment period.

I-23. What if someone declines to enroll during the automatic enrollment period?

Anyone who declines to enroll during his initial enrollment period may enroll during a general enrollment period. There are general enrollment periods each year from January 1st through March 31st. Coverage begins with the following July.

The premium will be higher for a person who fails to enroll within 12 months, or who drops out of the plan and later reenrolls. The monthly premium will be increased by 10% for each full 12 months during which he could have been, but was not, enrolled (see I-24).

If a person declines to enroll (or terminates enrollment) at a time when Medicare is secondary payer to an employer group health plan, the months in which he is covered under the employer group health plan (based on current employment) and Hospital Insurance will not be counted as months during which he could have been but was not enrolled in Medical Insurance for the purpose of determining if the premium amount should be increased above the basic rate.

I-24. How is Part B Medical Insurance financed?

Medical Insurance is voluntary and is financed through premiums paid by the people who enroll and through funds from the federal government. Each person who enrolls must pay a basic monthly premium of $50 per month in 2001. Premium rates may be increased from time to time if program costs rise. In September of each year, the government announces the premium rate for the 12-month period starting the following January. The Part B premium is set so that it will cover 25% of the program's costs for the year.

Basic Monthly Premium
Medical Insurance (Part B)

Year	Monthly Premium
1986	$15.50
1987	17.90
1988	24.80
1989	27.90
1990	28.60
1991	29.90
1992	31.80
1993	36.60
1994	41.10
1995	46.10
1996	42.50
1997	43.80
1998	43.80
1999	45.50
2000	45.50
2001	50.00

The premium rate for a person who enrolls after the first period when enrollment is open, or who reenrolls after terminating coverage, will be increased by 10% for each full 12 months the person stayed out of the program.

These monthly premiums are, of course, in addition to the "deductible" and "coinsurance" amounts which must be paid by the patient (see I-27).

I-25. How are premiums paid for under Medical Insurance?

Persons covered will have the premiums deducted from their Social Security, railroad retirement or federal civil service retirement benefit checks. Persons who are not receiving any of these government benefits will pay the premiums directly to the government.

I-26. What benefits are provided under Medical Insurance?

Under Medical Insurance, Medicare usually pays 80% of the approved charges for doctors' services and the cost of other services that are covered under Medical Insurance after the patient pays the first $100 of such covered services in each calendar year.

Medical Insurance covers: (1) medical and surgical services, including anesthesia, (2) diagnostic tests and procedures that are part of the patient's treatment, (3) radiology and pathology services by doctors while the patient is a hospital inpatient or outpatient, (4) treatment of mental illness (Medicare payments are limited), (5) X-rays, (6) services of the doctor's office nurse, (7) drugs and biologicals that cannot be self-administered, (8) transfusions of blood and blood components, (9) medical supplies, and (10) physical/occupational therapy and speech-language pathology services.

Medical Insurance does *not* cover: (1) most routine physical examinations, and tests directly related to such examinations (except some Pap smears and mammograms), (2) most routine foot care and dental care, (3) examinations for prescribing or fitting eyeglasses and hearing aids, (4) immunizations (except flu shots, pneumococcal pneumonia vaccinations or immunizations required because of an injury or immediate risk of infection, and hepatitis B for certain persons at risk), (5) cosmetic surgery, unless it is needed because of accidental injury or to improve the function of a malformed part of the body, and (6) most prescription drugs.

Specifically, the following fees and services are covered by Medical Insurance:

- *Doctors' services* wherever furnished in the United States. This includes the cost of house calls, office visits, and doctors' services in a hospital or other institution. It includes the fees of physicians, surgeons, pathologists, radiologists, anesthesiologists, physiatrists, and osteopaths.

- Beginning January 1, 1998, *home health services* not directly related to hospital or skilled nursing facility stays will gradually be covered and paid by Part B Medical Insurance.

- Services of *clinical psychologists* are covered if they would otherwise be covered if furnished by a physician (or as an incident to a physician's service).

- Services by licensed *chiropractors* for manual manipulation of the spine to correct a subluxation that is demonstrated by X-ray. Medical Insurance does not pay for any other diagnostic or therapeutic services, including X-rays, furnished by a chiropractor. Beginning January 1, 2000, Medicare pays for manual manipulation of the spine to correct a subluxation without requiring an X-ray to prove that subluxation exists.

- Fees of *podiatrists* are covered, including fees for the treatment of plantar warts, but not routine foot care. Common problems covered by Medical Insurance include ingrown toenails, hammer toe deformities, bunion deformities, and heel spurs. Care *not* covered by Medical Insurance includes cutting or removal of corns and calluses, trimming of nails, and other hygienic care. Medical Insurance does help pay for some routine foot care if the patient is being treated by a medical doctor for a medical condition affecting the patient's legs and feet (such as diabetes or peripheral vascular disease) which requires that a podiatrist or doctor of medicine or osteopathy perform the routine care. The cost of treatment of debridement of mycotic toenails (i.e., the care of toenails with a fungal infection) is not included if performed more frequently than once every 60 days. Exceptions are authorized if medical necessity is documented by the billing physician. Medical Insurance also helps pay for therapeutic shoes and shoe inserts for people who have severe diabetic foot disease.

- Services from certain *specially qualified practitioners* who are not physicians but are approved by Medicare.

- The cost of routine physicals, most vaccine shots, and examinations for eyeglasses and hearing aids is *not* covered. But the cost of diagnosis and treatment of *eye and ear ailments* is covered. Also covered is an optometrist's treatment of *aphakia.*

- *Plastic surgery* for purely cosmetic reasons is excluded; but plastic surgery for repair of an accidental injury, an impaired limb or a malformed part of the body is covered.

- *Radiological or pathological services* furnished by a physician to a hospital inpatient are covered.

- The cost of *blood clotting factors* and supplies related to their administration for hemophilia patients.

- *Outpatient physical therapy and speech-language pathology services* received as part of a patient's treatment in a doctor's office or as an outpatient of a participating hospital, skilled nursing facility, or home health agency; or approved clinic, rehabilitative agency, or public health agency, if the services are furnished under a plan established by a physician or physical therapist. A physician is required to review all plans of care. A podiatrist (when acting within the scope of his practice) is a physician for purposes of establishing a plan for outpatient physical therapy. A dentist and podiatrist are also within the definition of a physician for purposes of outpatient ambulatory surgery in a physician's office. Services of *independent physical therapists* are limited to a maximum of $1,500 in approved charges in any one year. Services of *independent occupational therapists* are covered up to a maximum of $1,500 in approved charges for such services in a calendar year.

- *Services and supplies relating to a physician's services and hospital services rendered to outpatients*; this includes drugs and biologicals which cannot be self-administered.

- A physician who includes charges for *independent clinical laboratory services* in his bill is entitled to the lesser of: (1) the approved charge of the laboratory, or (2) the amount actually charged by the physician. The physician's charge can include a small fee for handling the specimen.

- *Dentists' bills* for jaw or facial bone surgery, whether required because of accident or disease, are covered. Also covered are hospital stays warranted by the severity of the noncovered dental procedure, and services provided by dentists which would be covered when provided by a physician. However, bills for ordinary dental care are not covered.

- The cost of *psychiatric treatment* outside a hospital for mental, psycho-neurotic or personality disorders is covered, but with 50% coinsurance instead of the usual 20% (except that the latter applies when services are provided on a hospital-outpatient basis if, in the absence of treatment outside a hospital, hospitalization would have been required).

- *Radiation therapy* with X-ray, radium or radioactive isotopes.

- *Surgical dressings, splints, casts* and other devices for reduction of fractures and dislocations; rental or purchase of *durable medical equipment*, such as iron lungs, oxygen tents, hospital beds and wheel chairs, for use in the patient's home; *prosthetic devices*, such as artificial heart valves or synthetic arteries, designed to replace part or all of an internal organ (but not false teeth, hearing aids, or eye-glasses); braces, artificial limbs, artificial eyes (but not orthopedic shoes).

- *Ambulance service* if the patient's condition does not permit the use of other methods of transportation.

- Comprehensive *outpatient rehabilitation facility service* performed by a doctor or other qualified professionals in a qualified facility. Therapy and supplies are covered.

- Under certain circumstances, *antigens* prepared for the patient by a doctor.

- The cost of *pneumococcal, hepatitis B, and flu vaccines* through 2002.

- *Liver transplants* when reasonably and medically necessary.

- Certified *nurse-midwife services* and such services and supplies as are incident to nurse-midwife service. The service must be authorized under state law. Coverage includes services outside the maternity cycle. The amount paid by Medical Insurance is based upon a fee schedule but cannot exceed 65% of the prevailing charge allowed for the same service performed by a physician.

- *Partial hospitalization services* incident to a physician's services. Partial hospitalization services are items and services prescribed by a physician and provided in a program under the supervision of a physician pursuant to an individualized written plan of treatment.

- *Screening pap smears* for early detection of cervical cancer. Coverage is provided for a screening pap smear, but only once every three years, except in cases where the Health Care Financing Administration has established shorter time periods for testing women at high risk of developing cervical cancer. Beginning January 1, 1998, the patient is not required to pay the deductible for pap smears.

- *Screening mammography* and *Diagnostic mammography* are covered. Beginning January 1, 1998, Medicare covers an annual screening mammogram for all women age 40 and over. The Part B deductible for screening mammography is waived.

- The cost of an *injectable drug* approved for the treatment of a bone fracture related to *post-menopausal osteoporosis* under the following conditions: (1) the patient's attending physician certifies that the patient is unable to learn the skills needed to self-administer or is physically or mentally incapable of self-administering the drug, and (2) the patient meets the requirements for Medicare coverage of home health services.

- One pair of conventional *eyeglasses* or conventional *contact lenses* that replace the natural lens of the eye following cataract surgery with insertion of an intraocular lens.

- Services of *nurse practitioners* and *clinical nurse specialists* in rural areas for the services that nurse practitioners and clinical nurse specialists are authorized to perform under state law and regulations.

- *Oral cancer drugs* if they are the same chemical entity as those administered intravenously and covered prior to 1994. In addition, off-label anti-cancer drugs are covered in some cases.

- *Lung transplants* for beneficiaries with progressive end-stage pulmonary disease when performed by facilities that: (1) make an application to the Health Care Financing Administration, (2) supply documentation showing their compliance with federal regulations on lung transplants, and (3) are approved by the Health Care Financing Administration under criteria based on federal regulations. Medicare also covers lung transplantation for end-stage cardiopulmonary disease when it is expected that transplant of the lung will result in improved cardiac function.

- *Heart-lung transplants* for beneficiaries with progressive end-stage cardiopulmonary disease when they are provided in a facility that has been approved by Medicare for both heart and lung transplantation.

- *Prescription drugs used in immunosuppressive therapy* that have been approved by the Federal Drug Administration for preventing or treating the rejection of a transplanted organ or tissue. Coverage is available only for prescription drugs used in immunosuppressive therapy, furnished to an individual who receives an organ or tissue transplant for which Medicare payment is made, for 36 months for drugs furnished after 1997.

- *Prostate cancer screening*, including digital rectal exams and prostate specific blood antigen (PSA) tests, effective January 1, 2000.

- *Colorectal screening* procedures, including fecal occult blood test, flexible sigmoidoscopy for persons at high risk for colorectal cancer, screening colonoscopy.

- *Diabetes screening*, including coverage of diabetes outpatient self-management services to individuals with diabetes. Medicare also pays for blood glucose monitoring strips as inexpensive DME.

- *Bone mass measurement* for certain individuals.

- *Screening pelvic exams.* There is no deductible.

- *Rural health clinic services.*

- *Ambulatory surgical services.*

Charges imposed by an immediate relative (e.g., a doctor who is the son/daughter or brother/sister of the patient) are *not* covered.

I-27. What portion of the cost must be borne by the patient?

The patient pays the first $100 of covered expenses incurred in each calendar year. Medicare pays 80% of the balance of the approved charges (50% generally for out-of-hospital psychiatric or mental health services) over the $100 deductible. However, there is no cost-sharing for the following services:

(1) the cost of second opinions for certain surgical procedures when Medicare requires a second opinion, (2) the cost of home health services except the 20% coinsurance charge applies for durable medical equipment (except for the purchase of certain used items), (3) pneumococcal and flu vaccines, and (4) outpatient clinical diagnostic laboratory tests performed by physicians who take assignments, or by hospitals or independent laboratories that are Medicare-certified.

MEDICARE+CHOICE

I-28. What is Medicare+Choice?

The Balanced Budget Act of 1997 established Medicare Part C, the Medicare+Choice program. The Act permits contracts between the Health Care Financing Administration and a variety of different managed care and fee-for-service entities. Most Medicare beneficiaries may choose to receive benefits through the original Medicare fee-for-service program or through one of the following Medicare+Choice plans:

- Coordinated care plans, including Health Maintenance Organizations (HMOs), Preferred Provider Organizations (PPOs), and Provider-Sponsored Organizations (PSOs).

- Private fee-for-service plans that reimburse providers on a fee-for-service basis, and are authorized to charge enrolled beneficiaries up to 115% of the plan's payment schedule (which may be different from the Medicare fee schedule).

- Medical Savings Account/High Deductible Plans (under a demonstration in which up to 390,000 beneficiaries may enroll, with no new enrollments permitted after January 1, 2003). Under this option, beneficiaries would obtain high deductible health policies that pay for at least all Medicare-covered items and services after the enrollee meets the annual deductible of up to $6,000 (as indexed). The difference between the premiums for such high deductible policies and the applicable Medicare+Choice premium amount would be placed into an account for the beneficiary to use in meeting deductible expenses.

I-29. What is the Medical Savings Account option under Medicare+Choice?

Up to 390,000 beneficiaries will have the choice (on a demonstration basis ending January 1, 2003) of enrolling in a Medical Savings Account (MSA) option. Under this option, beneficiaries would obtain high deductible health policies that pay for at least all Medicare-covered items and services after the enrollee meets the annual deductible of up to $6,000 (as indexed). The difference between the premiums for such high deductible policies and the applicable Medicare+Choice premium amount will be placed into an account for the beneficiary to use in meeting deductible expenses. Currently, no private company offers Medicare+Choice MSAs.

I-30. Who can enroll in Medicare+Choice?

Beneficiaries entitled to Medicare Part A and enrolled in Medicare Part B are eligible to enroll in a plan that services the geographic area in which they reside, except beneficiaries with end-stage renal disease (although beneficiaries who develop end-stage renal disease may remain in the plan if already enrolled). Medicare Part B only enrollees are ineligible for Medicare+Choice.

I-31. What must Medicare+Choice plans cover?

Medicare+Choice plans must provide all current Medicare-covered items and services. They may incorporate extra benefits in a basic package or they may offer supplemental benefits priced separately from the basic package. A Medicare+Choice plan is a secondary payer to any employer-provided health coverage.

I-32. When may beneficiaries enroll or disenroll in Medicare+Choice plans?

Beneficiaries may enroll or disenroll in Medicare+Choice at any time of the year through 2001. In 2002, beneficiaries will be permitted to enroll or disenroll from Medicare+Choice only during the first six months of the year. After 2002, beneficiaries may enroll or disenroll only during the first three months of the year.

GENERAL

I-33. Is there any over-all limit to the benefits a person can receive under Medicare?

Under the Part A Hospital Insurance plan, benefits begin anew each "benefit period." In addition, there are no dollar limits under Part B Medical Insurance except for psychiatric care and independent physical and occupational therapy. Under Hospital Insurance, care in a psychiatric hospital is subject to a lifetime limit of 190 days (see I-11). (The time a patient has spent in a hospital for psychiatric care immediately prior to becoming eligible for Medicare counts against the special 150-day limit in the first hospitalization period, but not against the 190-day life-time limit.) Under Medical Insurance, coverage of psychiatric treatment outside a hospital is subject to an annual benefit limit of $1,100 and services of independent physical therapists are reimbursable to no more than

$1,500 per calendar year (as also applies to the services of independent occupational therapists).

Medicare may limit benefit payments for services for which other third party insurance programs (e.g., workers' compensation, auto or liability insurance, and employer health plans) may ultimately be liable. Medicare has the right to: (1) bring an action against any entity which would be responsible for payment with respect to such item or service, (2) bring an action against any entity (including any physician or provider) which has been paid with respect to such item or service, or (3) join or intervene in an action against a third party.

I-34. What are some of the medical items and services *not covered* by Medicare?

(1) Private rooms in a hospital or nursing home—(unless required for medical reasons)—see I-8, (2) private nursing, (3) routine physical check-ups, eyeglasses (except after cataract surgery), hearing aids (and examinations for same), (4) most immunizing vaccines, (5) ordinary dental care and dentures, (6) orthopedic shoes, (7) cosmetic plastic surgery (but see I-27), (8) custodial care, (9) services required as a result of war, (10) services covered by workers' compensation, (11) acupuncture, (12) drugs and medicines the patient buys with or without a doctor's prescription.

I-35. Is the spouse of a 65-year-old Social Security beneficiary entitled to Medicare if he or she is under age 65?

No, no one is entitled to Medicare who is not eligible as a result of being either age 65 or disabled. (See I-2.)

I-36. Who makes the payments under Medicare?

The government has appointed organizations engaged in the health insurance field (mainly insurance companies or Blue Cross and Blue Shield organizations) to act as contractors in administering Medicare. Using federal guidelines, a contractor determines the approved charges and makes payments, either directly or by way of reimbursement, to participants and suppliers of services.

I-37. Who receives the payments from Medicare?

Hospitals, skilled nursing facilities, and home health agencies are paid directly by the contractors. However, a hospital may collect deductibles and coinsurance amounts directly from the patient. Payment of a doctor's fees (or charges of another individual supplier of services) may be handled in either of two ways. The patient may submit an itemized bill (receipted or unpaid) to the contractor and receive payment (or the doctor may do this for the patient). Or, with the doctor's approval, the patient may assign his right to payment to the doctor or other supplier of services (and such doctor or other supplier agrees to limit the charges to what Medicare determines). This is called the "assignment" method.

Under the first method, the patient will receive 80% of what the contractor determines is an approved charge for the services after the $100 deductible—regardless of the actual charge. If the doctor or other suppliers of services accepts an assignment, his combined charge to Medicare and the patient cannot exceed what the contractor determines is an approved charge for his services.

Benefits are permitted to be paid to a health benefits plan, provided the beneficiary agrees and the physician or other supplier accepts the plan's payment as payment in full. This indirect payment procedure is available to group, as well as non-group, employments and non-employment health benefits plans such as employers, unions and insurance companies.

I-38. How are approved charges for covered medical services determined?

Before January 1 of each year, the Health Care Financing Administration must establish fee schedules for payment amounts for physicians' services in all fee schedule areas. The fee schedule must include national uniform relative values for all physicians' services. The relative value of each service must be the sum of relative value units (RVUs) representing physician work, experience, and the cost of malpractice insurance. Nationally uniform relative values are adjusted for each locality by a geographic adjustment factor (GAF).

I-39. Can patients choose their own doctor or hospital?

Generally, patients are free to choose their own doctor or other supplier of services. However, except for hospital care in emergency cases, Medicare will pay only to "qualified" hospitals, extended care facilities and home health agencies.

Use of a foreign hospital by a U.S. resident is authorized when such hospital is closer to the patient's residence or more accessible than the nearest United States hospital. But such hospitals must be approved. Medicare also authorizes payment for emergency care in a foreign hospital when the emergency occurred in the United States or in transit between Alaska and other continental states. Necessary physicians' services in connection with such foreign hospitalization are authorized under Medical Insurance.

TABLE OF HOSPITAL INSURANCE (PART A) BENEFITS
Effective January 1, 2001

Service	Benefit	Medicare Pays	A Person Pays
HOSPITALIZATION Semiprivate room and board, general nursing, and other hospital services and supplies	First 60 days	All but $792	$792
	61st to 90th day	All but $198 a day	$198 a day
	91st to 150th day[1]	All but $396 a day	$396 a day
	Beyond 150 days	Nothing	All costs
SKILLED NURSING FACILITY CARE Semiprivate room and board, skilled nursing and rehabilitative services and other services and supplies.[2]	First 20 days amount	100% of approved	Nothing
	Additional 80 days	All but $99 a day	$99 a day
	Beyond 100 days	Nothing	All costs
POST-HOSPITAL HOME HEALTH CARE Part-time or intermittent skilled care, home health aid services, durable medical equipment and supplies and other services.	First 100 days in spell of illness	100% of approved amount; 80% of approved amount for durable medical equipment	Nothing for services; 20% of approved amount for durable medical equipment
HOSPICE CARE Pain relief, symptom management and support services for the terminally ill.	For as long as the doctor certifies need	All but limited costs for outpatient drugs and inpatient respite care	Limited costs for outpatient drugs and inpatient respite care
BLOOD When furnished by a hospital or skilled nursing facility during covered stay.	Unlimited if medically necessary	All but first 3 pints per calendar year	For first 3 pints[3]

1. 60 Reserve days benefit may be used only once in a lifetime.
2. Neither Medicare nor private Medigap insurance will pay for most nursing home care.
3. Blood paid for or replaced under Part B of Medicare during the calendar year does not have to be paid for or replaced under Part A.

TABLE OF MEDICAL INSURANCE (PART B) BENEFITS
Effective January 1, 2001

Services	Benefit	Medicare Pays	You Pay
MEDICAL EXPENSES Doctors' services, inpatient and outpatient medical and surgical services and supplies, physical and speech therapy, diagnostic tests, durable medical equipment and other services.	Unlimited if medically necessary.	80% of approved amount (after $100 deductible). Reduced to 50% for most outpatient mental health services.	$100 deductible,[1] plus 20% of approved amount and limited charges above approved amount.[2]
CLINICAL LABORATORY SERVICES Blood tests, urinalyses, and more	Unlimited if medically necessary.	Generally 100% of approved amount.	Nothing for services.
HOME HEALTH CARE Part-time or intermittent skilled care, home health aide services, durable medical equipment and supplies and other services.	Unlimited but covers only home health care not covered by Hospital Insurance (Part A)	100% of approved amount; 80% of amount for durable medical equipment.	Nothing for services; 20% of approved amount for durable medical equipment
OUTPATIENT HOSPITAL TREATMENT Services for the diagnosis or treatment of illness or injury.	Unlimited if medically necessary.	Medicare payment to hospital based on hospital cost.	20% of whatever the hospital charges (after $100 deductible).[1]
BLOOD	Unlimited if medically necessary.	80% of approved amount (after $100 deductible and starting with 4th pint).	First 3 pints plus 20% of approved amount for additional pints (after $100 deductible).[3]
AMBULATORY SURGICAL SERVICES	Unlimited if medically necessary.	80% of pre-determined amount (after $100 deductible)	$100 deductible plus 20% of predetermined amount

1. Once a person has had $100 of expense for covered services in 2001, the Part B deductible does not apply to any further covered services received for the rest of the year.
2. A person pays for charges higher than the amount approved by Medicare unless the doctor or supplier agrees to accept Medicare's approved amount as the total charge for services rendered.
3. Blood paid for or replaced under Part A of Medicare during the calendar year does not have to be paid for or replaced under Part B.

SOCIAL SECURITY TAXES

J-1. What are the Social Security and Medicare tax rates for employers and employees?

The tax rate is the same for both the employer and the employee. Every employer who employs one or more persons and every employee in covered employment is subject to the tax imposed under the Federal Insurance Contributions Act (FICA).

The tax consists of two taxes: the OASDI tax (the tax for old-age, survivors and disability insurance) and the Hospital Insurance (HI) tax (for Medicare Part A).

For 2001, the maximum earnings base (the maximum amount of annual earnings subject to the tax) for the OASDI tax is $80,400.

There is no maximum earnings base for the Hospital Insurance (HI) tax. Beginning in 1994, all wages and self-employment income are subject to the Hospital Insurance tax. The maximum earnings base for the Hospital Insurance tax was $135,000 in 1993.

For employees and employers, the rate of the OASDI tax is 6.20%, and the rate of the HI tax is 1.45%. Thus, the maximum OASDI tax for an employee in 2001 (with maximum earnings of $80,400) is $4,984.80. The maximum HI tax is unlimited because all wages and self-employment income are subject to the tax.

The OASDI maximum earnings base and maximum tax are subject to automatic adjustment in 2001 and after based on changes in wage levels.

Not all earnings are subject to Social Security taxes. A person can be an employee but be exempt from the Social Security tax. An example is an individual hired by a federal agency on a temporary basis as an emergency firefighter to help fight forest fires. The individual performed the service for three months, 12 hours a day, and the federal agency supplied the necessary equipment and gave him directions on a daily basis. The Internal Revenue Service ruled that although the individual was an employee under common law rules, he was exempt from Social Security taxes because the Internal Revenue Code exempts from the definition of employment those services performed for the United States by an individual serving on a temporary basis in case of fire or other emergencies.

203

OASDI TAX ON EMPLOYEES AND EMPLOYERS			
Year	% Rate (OASDI)	Max. Wage Base	Max. Tax (each)	Max Tax (both)
1986	5.70	$42,000	$2,394.00	$4,788.00
1987	5.70	$43,800	$2,496.60	$4,993.20
1988	6.06	$45,000	$2,727.00	$5,454.00
1989	6.06	$48,000	$2,908.80	$5,817.60
1990	6.20	$51,300	$3,180.60	$6,361.20
1991	6.20	$53,400	$3,310.80	$6,621.60
1992	6.20	$55,500	$3,441.00	$6,882.00
1993	6.20	$57,600	$3,571.20	$7,142.40
1994	6.20	$60,600	$3,757.20	$7,514.40
1995	6.20	$61,200	$3,794.40	$7,588.80
1996	6.20	$62,700	$3,887.40	$7,774.80
1997	6.20	$65,400	$4,054.80	$8,109.60
1998	6.20	$68,400	$4,240.80	$8,481.60
1999	6.20	$72,600	$4,501.20	$9,002.40
2000	6.20	$76,200	$4,724.40	$9,448.80
2001	6.20	$80,400	$4,984.80	$9,969.60

Note: The 1.45% Medicare tax applies to all wages

J-2. If an employee works for two employers during the year and more than the maximum tax is paid on his wages, will the overpayment be refunded to the employee and his employers?

Each employer is required to withhold the employee's tax, and to pay the employer's tax, on wages up to the maximum earnings base for the year. Consequently, if an employee works for more than one employer during the year, the taxes paid may exceed the maximum payable for the year. In this case, the employee is entitled to a refund of his overpayment, or the overpayment will be credited to his income tax for the year. His employers, however, are not entitled to any refund or credit. Each employer is liable for tax on his wages up to the maximum earnings base.

However, a group of corporations concurrently employing an individual will be considered a single employer if one of the group serves as a common paymaster for the entire group. This will result in such corporations having to pay no more in Social Security taxes than a single employer pays.

J-3. Does an employer get an income tax deduction for Social Security tax payments?

Yes, the employer's Social Security tax is deductible as a business expense, but only if wages upon which taxes are paid are also deductible.

J-4. Must Social Security taxes be paid on cash tips?

Yes, an employee must pay Social Security taxes on cash tips of $20 or more a month from one employer. Such tips will be treated as wages for Social

Security and income tax withholding purposes and must be reported. Cash tips of less than $20 a month are not reported.

The employee is required to report tips to an employer within 10 days following the month in which the tips equal or exceed $20.

The employer must pay the usual employer tax on such tips.

The employer must withhold income tax and deduct the employee Social Security and Hospital Insurance (HI) tax on tips reported to him. The withholding is to be made from any wages (other than tips) that are under the employer's control. Employers may deduct the tax due on tips during a calendar quarter on an estimated basis and adjust the amount deducted from wages paid to the employee either during the calendar quarter or within 30 days thereafter. If these wages are not sufficient to cover the employee tax due, the employee may (but is not required to) furnish the employer with additional funds to cover the tax.

The employee is directly responsible for paying any portion of the employee tax which the employer cannot collect from wages or from funds furnished by the employee. The employer is required to give statements to both the employee and the Internal Revenue Service showing the difference between the amount of the employee tax due and the amount collected by the employer.

Food or beverage establishments are provided with a business tax credit equal to the amount of the employer's Social Security tax obligation (7.65%) attributable to reported tips in excess of those treated as wages for purposes of satisfying the minimum wage provisions of the Fair Labor Standards Act (FLSA). An employer must pay a Social Security tax on the tip income of employees, and tips can be counted as satisfying one-half of the minimum wage requirement.

The credit also applies to tips received from customers in connection with the delivery or serving of food or beverages, regardless of whether the food or beverages are for consumption on an establishment's premises. The credit is available even if the employee failed to report the tips.

For further information regarding income and employment taxes on tips, see *IRS Publication 531 (Reporting Income from Tips)*.

J-5. How does an individual report Social Security taxes on domestic help?

The threshold amount for Social Security coverage of a domestic worker is $1,000 annually, effective for calendar year 1994. This threshold amount is indexed in future years for increases in average wages in the economy. Indexing occurs in $100 increments, rounded down to the nearest $100.

The threshold amount is $1,300 for calendar year 2001.

Exempt from Social Security taxes are any wages paid to a worker for domestic services performed in any year during which the worker is under age 18, except for workers under age 18 whose principal occupation is household employment. Being a student is considered to be an occupation for purposes of this test. Thus, for example, the wages of a student who is 16 years-old who also babysits will be exempt from the reporting and payment requirements, regardless of whether the amount of wages paid is above or below the threshold. On the other hand, the wages of a 17 year-old single mother who leaves school and goes to work as a domestic to support her family will be subject to the reporting and payment requirements.

Employers may satisfy their tax obligations through regular estimated tax payments or increased tax withholding from their own wages. Estimated tax penalties apply in and after 1998. Employers received refunds for payroll taxes on wages paid in 1994 when the total wages that an employee received from the employer were below the $1,000 threshold.

There was no loss of Social Security wage credits for domestic employees with respect to amounts refunded for 1994. Employees received Social Security wage credits for domestic work in 1994 even though they did not earn over the $1,000 threshold.

Example (1). Assume an employer pays a domestic employee $500 in wages for calendar year 2001. Because the amount of these taxes is below the $1,300 threshold, the employer is not subject to reporting.

Example (2). Assume an employer pays a domestic employee $1,500 in wages for calendar year 2001. Because the amount of these wages is above the $1,300 threshold, the employer is subject to reporting.

J-6. What is the rate of Social Security and Medicare tax for a self-employed person?

The tax on self-employed persons is imposed under the Self-Employment Contributions Act.

The self-employment tax consists of two taxes: the OASDI tax (the tax for old-age, survivors, and disability insurance) and the Hospital Insurance (HI) tax (for Medicare Part A).

For 2001, the maximum earnings base (the maximum amount of net earnings subject to the tax) for the OASDI tax is $80,400. There is no maximum earnings base for the Hospital Insurance (HI) tax. In other words, all earnings from self-employment are subject to the HI tax.

The rate of the OASDI tax is 12.40%, and the rate of the HI tax is 2.90%. Thus, the maximum OASDI tax for a self-employed person in 2001 (with maximum earnings of $80,400) is $9,969.60. The maximum HI tax for a self-employed person is unlimited because all self-employment earnings are subject to the tax.

There is a special federal (and generally following through to state) income tax deduction of 50% of the Social Security and Medicare self-employment tax. This income tax deduction is designed to treat the self-employed in much the same manner as employees and employers are treated for Social Security, Medicare, and income tax purposes under present law.

OASDI TAX ON SELF-EMPLOYED PERSONS*			
Year	% Rate (OASDI)	Max. Earnings Base	Max. Tax
1986	11.40	$42,000	$4,788.00
1987	11.40	43,800	4,993.20
1988	12.12	45,000	5,454.00
1989	12.12	48,000	5,817.60
1990	12.40	51,300	6,361.20
1991	12.40	53,400	6,621.60
1992	12.40	55,500	6,882.00
1993	12.40	57,600	7,142.40
1994	12.40	60,600	7,514.40
1995	12.40	61,200	7,588.80
1996	12.40	62,700	7,774.80
1997	12.40	65,400	8,109.60
1998	12.40	68,400	8,481.60
1999	12.40	72,600	9,002.40
2000	12.40	76,200	9,448.80
2001	12.40	80,400	9,969.60

*There is a special income tax deduction of 50% of the self-employment tax.
Note: The 2.90% Medicare tax applies to all self-employment earnings.

The OASDI maximum earnings base and maximum tax are subject to automatic adjustment in 2002 and after based on changes in wage levels.

If a self-employed person reports earnings on a fiscal year basis, the tax rate to be used is the one that applies to the calendar year in which the fiscal year began.

J-7. If a self-employed person also receives wages as an employee, what portion of income is subject to tax as self-employment income?

Only the difference between the maximum earnings base for the year and the wages received as an employee is subject to tax as self-employment income.

Example (1). Mr. Smith, an attorney, is employed as a part-time instructor for a law school, and his salary is $30,000 a year. During 2001, Mr. Smith earned an additional $65,000 from his private practice, which counts as $60,027.50 for Social Security purposes (i.e., 92.35% of $65,000). Only $50,400 of his net earnings from self-employment is subject to the OASDI self-employment tax ($80,400 - $30,000). Note, however, that all of Mr. Smith's wages and $60,027.50 of his self-employment income are subject to the HI self-employment tax because all wages and self-employment income are subject to the HI tax.

No self-employment tax is due unless net earnings from self-employment are at least $434 for the taxable year (because of the 92.35% factor). Nevertheless, in some cases, the amount of income subject to OASDI self-employment tax may be less than $400.

Example (2). Assume the same facts as in Example (1), except that Mr. Smith's salary as a law instructor is $80,200. Mr. Smith's net earnings from self-employment after application of the 92.35% factor ($60,027.50) exceed $400 and, hence, must be reported. However, only $200 is subject to the OASDI self-employment tax ($80,400 - $80,200 = $200), but the entire $60,027.50 is subject to the HI tax.

J-8. Must a Social Security beneficiary who works pay Social Security and Medicare taxes?

Yes, even though receiving Social Security benefits, the beneficiary must pay taxes at the same rate as other individuals. Social Security and Medicare taxes must be paid even if the earnings are too small to increase the Social Security benefits the beneficiary will receive in the future.

Example. Mr. Anderson, age 73, receives $800 a month in Social Security retirement benefits. He also works part-time and earns $4,000 for the year. Mr. Anderson must pay $306 in Social Security and Medicare HI taxes.

J-9. How does a life insurance agent pay Social Security taxes on first-year and renewal commissions?

If the agent is an *employee* when the policy is sold, both first-year and renewal commissions are *wages* at the time they are paid. (For status of a life insurance agent as an employee, see B-11.) Consequently, they are subject to the employer-employee tax in the year they are received by him. It does not matter whether, at the time of payment, the agent is an employee or a self-employed person. If the agent is a self-employed individual when the policy is sold, first-year and renewal commissions are treated as net earnings from self-employment in the year they are received.

Renewal commissions paid to the estate (or other beneficiary) of a deceased life insurance agent in a year after death are not subject to the employer-employee tax. Renewal commissions paid to a disabled life insurance agent are not subject to the Social Security tax if he became entitled to disability insurance benefits before the year in which the renewal commission is paid and did not work for the employer during the period for which the payment is made. The renewal commissions of a self employed agent do not constitute net earnings from self-employment to a widow(er) (they were not derived from a trade or business carried on by the widow(er)).

J-10. Must the self-employment tax be included in a person's estimated tax return?

Yes.

J-11. What is the federal income tax deduction for medical expense insurance premiums?

No premiums other than those for medical expense insurance will qualify for the deduction. If the taxpayer itemizes deductions, he may deduct the full amount of the medical expense insurance premiums subject to the 7.5% adjusted gross income floor. A self-employed individual may be able to deduct up to 60% (in 2001) of medical expense insurance premiums. The monthly premium for Medicare Part B is treated as a medical expense insurance premium for this purpose.

FILING FOR BENEFITS

GENERAL INFORMATION

K-1. What procedure should be followed to determine if a person is eligible for Social Security benefits?

An application must be filed for a person to become entitled to benefits, including Medicare, or to establish a period of disability under the retirement, survivors, and disability programs. The application should be made on a form prescribed by the Social Security Administration. A person can apply for Social Security via the mail, telephone, or by visiting one of the Social Security Administration's 1,300 field offices.

Since a person age 65 or older who is entitled to monthly benefits under Social Security or railroad retirement is automatically entitled to Medicare Part A Hospital Insurance and Part B Medical Insurance, no separate application for these is required. However, a person who is *eligible* for monthly Social Security benefits and is at least age 65 may apply for Hospital Insurance and Medical Insurance without applying for Social Security benefits. Also, an application is necessary for persons age 65 or older who have no Social Security coverage or other entitlement but who wish to file for Hospital Insurance and Medical Insurance, and who are willing to pay the monthly premiums involved.

Prompt filing of an application is generally advantageous even if the person is still working. Delay may result in fewer payments since monthly benefits cannot be paid retroactively in some instances and not for more than 12 months (depending on the situation) before the month in which the application is filed.

A person may be entitled to monthly benefits retroactively for months before the month in which he filed an application for benefits. Retirement and survivor claims may be paid for up to six months retroactively and benefits may be paid in certain cases involving disability up to 12 months retroactively. The claimant is entitled to benefits beginning with the first month in the retroactive period in which all the requirements for entitlement to benefits are met except for the filing of an application. For example, if a man reaches age 66 in March 2001 and is then fully insured but does not file an application for retirement benefits until March 2002, he may be entitled retroactively beginning with the month of September 2000.

Retroactive benefits for months prior to attainment of age 65 are not payable to a retired worker, a spouse, or a widow(er) if this would result in a permanent reduction of the monthly benefit amount. However, there are exceptions to this rule which permit payment of retroactive benefits even though it causes an actuarial reduction in benefits. This limitation does not apply if the applicant is a surviving spouse or surviving divorced spouse who is under a disability and could be entitled to retroactive benefits for any month before attaining age 60.

A widow(er) or surviving divorced spouse who files an application in the month after the month of the worker's death may be entitled to benefits in the month of his or her death if otherwise eligible in that month.

Regulations issued by the Social Security Administration establish deemed filing dates for applications filed by persons who have received misinformation about eligibility from the Social Security Administration. The Social Security Administration may establish an earlier filing date when there is evidence that the Social Security Administration gave the claimant misinformation which caused the claimant not to file an application at the appropriate time.

Example. Mr. Smith contacts a Social Security office at age 62 to inquire about applying for retirement benefits. He is told by an employee of the Social Security Administration that he must be age 65 to be eligible for retirement benefits. This information is incorrect and causes Mr. Smith to delay filing an application for retirement benefits for three years. When he reaches age 65, he contacts the Social Security Administration and is told that he could have received reduced retirement benefits at age 62. After filing an application for retirement benefits, Mr. Smith provides information to show that a Social Security Administration employee provided misinformation, and requests a deemed filing date based on the misinformation he received when he was age 62.

If the Social Security Administration determines that a person failed to apply for monthly benefits because it gave the person incorrect information about eligibility for such benefits, the Social Security Administration will deem an application for such benefits to have been filed with the Social Security Administration on the later of: (1) the date on which the misinformation was provided to the person, or (2) the date on which the person met all of the requirements for entitlement to the benefits, other than the requirement for filing an application for benefits.

Preferred evidence that misinformation was given by the Social Security Administration includes a notice, letter or other document issued by the Social Security Administration and addressed to the claimant, or the Social Security Administration's record of the claimant's letter, phone call, or visit to an office of the Social Security Administration. In the absence of preferred evidence, the Social Security Administration will consider statements by the claimant about possible misinformation and other evidence. The claimant's statements, however, must be supported by other evidence in order for the Social Security Administration to find that the claimant was given misinformation.

A person may make a claim for benefits based on misinformation at any time. The claim must be in writing and must contain the information that was provided by the Social Security Administration and why this information resulted in the person not filing an application for Social Security benefits.

A person cannot receive more than one full monthly benefit. If eligible for more than one monthly benefit, the amount payable will be equal to the largest one for which the person is eligible.

Each application form is clearly worded to show its scope as an application for one or more types of benefits. For example, the present applications for entitlement to Medicare Part A Hospital Insurance protection, or for monthly Social Security benefits, may be applications for all benefits that a claimant may be entitled to on any Social Security earnings record. The scope of any application may, however, be expanded or restricted as the claimant desires if appropriate remarks are added in writing prior to adjudication. The Social Security Administration will use the application to make an *initial determination* regarding the amount of benefits, if any.

When the application for benefits has been approved, the U.S. Treasury mails a check to the applicant. The benefit *for* a month is paid *in* the next month. Monthly benefit payments to a husband and wife who are entitled to benefits on the same Social Security account and are living at the same address are usually combined into one check made out to them jointly. However, individual checks will be sent if either prefers to have a separate check. Benefit payments to children in one family unit are usually combined in one check. Where the children are members of different households, separate checks will be issued to each family group.

Benefit notices from the Social Security Administration must: (1) use clear and simple language, (2) include the local office telephone number and address (in notices generated by local Social Security offices), and (3) include the address and telephone number of the Social Security office serving the recipient (in notices generated by central offices of the Social Security Administration).

K-2. When should a person file for retirement benefits?

A person should get in touch with a Social Security office two or three months before reaching age 62. The Social Security office will furnish the information needed to decide whether or not to file an application for retirement benefits at that time. Because of the rules regarding retroactive benefits, a person should consider filing for benefits on January 1 of the year that he attains normal retirement age (NRA) (see E-4).

If a worker does not file an application, he should contact the Social Security office again: (1) two or three months before retirement, (2) as soon as the worker knows that he will neither earn more than the monthly exempt amount in wages nor render substantial services in self-employment in one or more months of the year, regardless of expected total annual earnings, or (3) two or three months before the worker reaches NRA, even if still working.

It may be advantageous to delay filing an application for benefits where: (1) the person is under the NRA and wishes to wait and receive an unreduced benefit at NRA, (2) the person is at the NRA but benefits are not payable because of earnings (application at or near retirement may provide higher benefits in the year of retirement), or (3) the person would lose benefits payable under some other program.

A Social Security Ruling (SSR 96-10p) issued in 1996 initiates the Social Security Administration's policy for allowing customers to communicate with the Social Security Administration electronically through access methods such as the Internet, video conferencing, and dial-up phone systems. The Social Security Administration will be able to use these access methods to accept reports, requests, applications, and other information. The Ruling also sets out policy making electronic and digital signatures the functional equivalent of traditional handwritten signatures in certain situations.

K-3. At what time should the survivors of a deceased worker file for survivor's benefits?

An application should be filed immediately in the month of death by or for *each* person who is entitled to a benefit as a survivor of a deceased worker.

An application for the lump-sum death payment must be filed within the two-year period after the worker's death by the person eligible for the lump-sum, unless the eligible person is the widow(er) of the deceased worker, and was entitled to spouse's benefits for the month before the month in which the worker died. In the latter case, no application for the lump-sum is required.

K-4. When should a person file an application for disability benefits?

An application for the establishment of a period of disability may be filed before the first day this period can begin. In these circumstances, the application will be effective if the person actually becomes eligible for the benefit, or for the period of disability, at some time before a final decision on the application is made.

When a person applies for monthly disability benefits, he simultaneously applies for a "disability freeze" (see F-36).

K-5. When should a person file an application for the lump-sum death payment?

An application for the lump-sum death payment must be filed within a two-year period by the person eligible for the lump sum unless the eligible person is the widow(er) of the deceased worker, and was entitled to spouse's benefits for the month before the month in which the worker died. In the later case, no application for the lump sum is required.

An application filed after the two-year period will be deemed to have been filed within the two-year period if there is good cause for a failure to file the application in time. Good cause means that the claimant did not file the lump sum death payment application within the time limit because of: (1) circumstances beyond the claimant's control, such as extended illness, communication difficulties, etc., (2) incorrect or incomplete information given the claimant by the Social Security Administration, (3) efforts to get the evidence to support the claim, not realizing he could file the application within the time limit and submit the supporting evidence later, or (4) unusual or unavoidable circumstances which show that the claimant could not reasonably be expected to have been aware of the need to file the application within a specified period.

PROOF REQUIRED

K-6. What proofs are required before survivors' and retirement benefits can be paid?

Social Security survivors' and retirement benefits cannot be paid until satisfactory proofs have been furnished. Claimants must prove their identity and that they have met all the requirements to be entitled to the benefits which are being claimed. Evidence usually required to be submitted to the Social Security Administration in claims for monthly benefits is summarized below:

- *Insured person*: evidence of age. If disability is involved, evidence to establish disability.

- *Spouse (62 or over)*: evidence of age and marriage.

- *Spouse under 62 (child in care)*: evidence of marriage and child in care.

- *Divorced spouse (62 or over)*: evidence of age, marriage and divorce.

- *Child*: evidence of age, parent-child relationship, dependency or support, school attendance (if 18-19 years old and not disabled), and death of the worker in survivor claims. If disability is involved, evidence to establish disability.

- *Widow(er) (60 or over, 50 or over if disabled)*: evidence of age, marriage, and death of worker. If disability is involved, evidence to establish disability.

- *Surviving divorced spouse*: evidence of age, marriage, divorce, and death of worker. If disability is involved, evidence to establish disability.

- *Widow(er) under 62 or surviving divorced mother or father (child in care)*: evidence of marriage, divorce (surviving divorced mother or father only), parent-child relationship, child in care, and death of worker.

- *Parent*: evidence of age, parent-child relationship, dependency or support, and death of worker.

K-7. What are acceptable proofs of death?

Evidence of death may consist of:

(1) A certified copy of a public record of death.

(2) A statement of death by the funeral director.

(3) A statement of death by the attending physician or the superintendent, physician or intern of the institution where the person died.

(4) A certified copy of the coroner's report of death or the verdict of the coroner's jury.

(5) A certified copy of an official report of death or finding of death made by an agency or department of the United States government which is authorized or required to make such report or finding in the administration of any law of the United States.

Recent court cases have held that a claimant had to show only that the missing person had been absent for seven years, and that the Social Security Administration had the burden of proving that the individual was still alive, or an explanation to account for the individual's absence in a manner consistent with continued life.

Social Security Administration regulations conform with these court cases by providing that the presumption of death arises when a claimant establishes that an individual has been absent from his residence and not heard from for seven years. Once the presumption arises, the burden then shifts to the Social Security Administration to rebut the presumption either by presenting evidence that the missing individual is still alive or by providing an explanation to account for the individual's absence in a manner consistent with continued life rather than death.

The regulations also state that the presumption of death can be rebutted by evidence that establishes that the person is still alive or explains the individual's absence in a manner consistent with continued life. Two examples are provided. In one, evidence in a claim for surviving child's benefits showed that the worker had wages posted in his earnings record in the year following his disappearance. It was established that the wages belonged to the worker and were for work done after he was supposed to have disappeared. The presumption of death is rebutted by evidence (wages belonging to the worker) that the worker is still alive. In a second example, evidence showed that the worker left the family home shortly after a woman, whom he had been seeing, also disappeared. The worker phoned his wife a few days after he left home to tell her he was starting a new life in California. The presumption of death is rebutted in this case because the evidence explains the worker's absence in a manner consistent with continued life.

No one *convicted* of the felonious and intentional homicide of the worker can be entitled to benefits on the worker's earnings record. Further, the convicted person is considered not to exist in deciding the rights of other persons to benefits on the worker's record.

K-8. What are the best forms of proof of age and family relationship?

Proof of age is required when age is a factor in determining benefit rights. A public record of birth or a religious record of birth or baptism established or recorded before the individual's 5th birthday must be submitted as proof of age, if available. Where such a document is unavailable, the individual must submit another document or documents which may serve as the basis for a determination of date or birth, provided the evidence is corroborated by other evidence or by information in the records of the Social Security Administration.

Some records that may be submitted are listed below; these records must show the individual's date of birth or age:

(1) School record.

(2) Census record.

(3) Bible or other family record.

(4) Religious record of confirmation or baptism in youth or early adult life.

(5) Insurance policy.

(6) Marriage record.

(7) Employment record.

(8) Labor union record.

(9) Fraternal organization record.

(10) Military record.

(11) Voting record.

(12) Vaccination record.

(13) Delayed birth certificate

(14) Birth certificate of child showing age of parent.

(15) Physician's or midwife's record of birth.

(16) Passport.

(17) Immigration record.

(18) Naturalization record.

A person should obtain, and file among his valuable papers, the most acceptable form of proof of the ages and relationships of all members of his family. This will save time, effort and money later when Social Security benefits become payable.

A natural legitimate parent-child relationship may be shown by the child's birth or baptismal certificate if it shows the worker to be the child's parent. If the child is illegitimate, he may be considered the worker's child for Social Security purposes if he is legitimated or can inherit the worker's intestate personal property under applicable state law. The evidence required would depend on state law requirements for legitimation or inheritance rights.

The legal adoption of a child may be provided by an amended birth certificate issued as the result of an adoption.

A step-relationship is proved by: (1) first proving the relationship between the child and the natural (or adopting) parent, and (2) then proving the marriage between the natural (or adopting) parent and the stepparent.

Evidence of full-time school attendance is required if a child age 18-19 is not under a disability. Necessary information is obtained from the child and verified by the school or schools involved.

A ceremonial marriage may be proved by: (1) a certified copy of the public record of the marriage, (2) a certified copy of the religious record of the marriage, or (3) the original marriage certificate.

Evidence to prove a common-law marriage in those states which recognize such marriages must, where obtainable, include: (1) If the husband and wife are living, a statement from each and a statement from a blood relative of each, (2) If either the husband or wife is dead, a statement from the surviving widow or widower and statements from two blood relatives of the decedent, and (3) If both a husband and wife are dead, a statement from a blood relative of the husband and from a blood relative of the wife.

Evidence of termination of a marriage may be required if the claimant's right to benefits depends upon the validity of a subsequent marriage or the termination of a prior marriage. The termination of a marriage may be established by: (1) a certified copy of the divorce decree, (2) a certified copy of the annulment decree, (3) a certified copy of the death certificate, or (4) if none of the above is available, any other evidence of probative value.

Evidence that a child is in a claimant's care usually consists of: (1) statements by the claimant, (2) where the claimant and the child are living apart, statements by the person with whom the child is living or by an official of the school which the child is attending, or both, and (3) statements of other people who know the facts, if necessary.

Evidence of support includes a statement from the claimant and whatever other evidence may be necessary to substantiate the claimant's statements concerning support.

Evidence of United States citizenship may be required in certain cases, for instance, to determine coverage status of people working in foreign countries or the applicability of the alien nonpayment provision. The most acceptable evidence is a birth certificate showing birth within the United States. Other acceptable evidence includes: (1) Certificate of Naturalization, (2) Citizenship Certificate issued by the Immigration and Naturalization Service to United States citizens who derived their citizenship through another person, (3) a United States passport issued by the Department of State, (4) Consular report of birth issued by the Department of State, (5) proof of marriage to a male United States citizen before September 22, 1922, (6) a card of identity and registration as a United States citizen, or an official communication from an American Foreign Service post indicating the individual is registered there as a United States citizen, or (7) Form I-197 (United States Citizen Identification Card).

RIGHT TO APPEAL

K-9. Is there a review procedure available if a person is disappointed with the Social Security Administration's initial determination regarding benefits?

There is an administrative review process for a person who is dissatisfied with the Social Security Administration's action concerning a claim for benefits. After the Social Security Administration makes an initial determination, further review may be requested by the person or his representative. The administrative review process consists of several steps which must be requested in writing, usually within specified time periods, and in the following order:

(1) The person or representative may request that the initial determination be reconsidered. A reconsideration is a reexamination of the administrative records which results in another determination.

(2) If there is still disagreement with the reconsidered determination, the person or representative may request a hearing before an administrative law judge of the Office of Hearings and Appeals.

(3) If the person disagrees with the administrative law judge's decision or dismissal, he may request a review by the Appeals Council of the Office of Hearings and Appeals, which has the authority to deny or grant review or dismiss the request for any reason for which the administrative law judge could have dismissed. Also, the Appeals Council may, on its own motion, review an administrative law judge's decision.

(4) After Appeals Council review (or denial of review) a person who is still dissatisfied may file a civil action in a federal district court.

An initial determination becomes final unless reconsideration is requested within 60 days from the date notice of the initial determination is received by the person or the person's representative.

Reconsideration is the first step in the administrative review process that is provided if there is dissatisfaction with the initial determination. The request for reconsideration may be made by the claimant, by another person whose benefit rights are affected by the determination, or by the appointed representative of either. The reconsideration must be requested in writing by the person (or the person's representative).

The reconsideration process is an independent reexamination of all evidence on record related to the case by the Social Security Administration. It is based on evidence submitted for the initial determination plus any additional information that the claimant or representative may submit in connection with the reconsideration. The reconsideration is not limited to the issues raised by the claimant. A reconsideration is made by a member of a different staff from the one that made the initial determination and who is specially trained in the handling of reconsiderations. The claimant receives a personalized notice detailing the basis for the determination in his case.

When a person can demonstrate that he failed to appeal an adverse decision because of reliance on incorrect, incomplete, or misleading information provided by the Social Security Administration, his failure to appeal may not serve as the basis for denial of a second application for any Social Security benefit. This protection applies to both initial denials and reconsiderations. The Social Security Administration is required to include in all notices of denial a clear, simple description on the effect of reapplying for benefits rather than filing an appeal.

The Social Security Administration issued a ruling in 1995 on establishing good cause for late filing of a request for administrative review for a claimant who received an initial or reconsideration determination notice that did not state that filing a new application instead of a request for administrative review could result in the loss of benefits. The Social Security Administration will make a finding of good cause for late filing of a request for administrative review for a claim if the claimant received an initial or reconsideration determination notice and demonstrates that, as a result of the notice, he did not timely request such review. Notices covered by this Ruling include only those dated prior to July 1, 1991, that did not state that filing a new application for benefits instead of a request for review could result in the loss of benefits. If the adjudicator determines that good cause exists, the Social Security Administration will extend the time for requesting administrative review and take the action which would have been appropriate had the claimant filed a timely request for administrative review. *Social Security Ruling SSR 95-1p.*

K-10. What is the appeals process for disability under the disability redesign plan?

The Social Security Administration has approved a new plan for the disability claims process. The first phase will test the procedures followed when a person files a request for a hearing before an administrative law judge in connection with a claim for benefits based on disability. The new procedures make an adjudication officer the primary point of contact after a person files a hearing request and before the person has a hearing with an administrative law judge. The adjudication officer will identify issues in dispute, develop evidence, conduct informal conferences, and conduct any other prehearing proceeding as may be necessary.

The adjudication officer has the authority to make a decision wholly favorable to the person if the evidence so warrants. If the adjudication officer does not make a decision on the claim, the hearing request will be assigned to an administrative law judge for further proceedings.

When a person files a request for a hearing before an administrative law judge in connection with a claim or benefits based on disability where the question of whether the person is under a disability is at issue, the adjudication officer will conduct an interview with the person. The interview may take place in person, by telephone, or by video conference. The adjudication officer will provide the person with information regarding the hearing process, including the right to representation. As may be appropriate, the adjudication officer will provide the person with referral sources for represen-tation, and give the person copies of necessary documents to facilitate the appointment of a representative. If the person has a representative, the adjudication officer will conduct an informal conference with the representa-tive to identify the issues in dispute and prepare proposed written agreements for approval of the administrative law judge regarding those issues which are not in dispute and those issues proposed for the hearing. If a person obtains representation after the adjudication officer has concluded that the case is ready for a hearing, the administrative law judge will return the case to the adjudication officer who will conduct an informal conference with the person and his representative.

A person, or representative, may submit, or may be asked to obtain and submit, additional evidence to the adjudication officer. The adjudication officer may refer the claim for further medical or vocational evidence.

The adjudication officer will refer the claim to the administrative law judge for further proceedings when the development of evidence is complete, and the person or representative agree that a hearing is ready to be held. If the parties are unable to agree that a hearing is ready to be held, the adjudication officer will note the disagreement and refer the claim to the administrative law judge for further proceedings. At this point, the administrative law judge conducts all further hearing proceedings, including scheduling and holding a hearing, considering any additional evidence or arguments submitted, and issuing a decision or dismissal of the request for a hearing.

If, after a hearing is requested but before it is held, the adjudication officer decides that the evidence in the case warrants a decision which is wholly favorable to the person, the adjudication officer may issue such a decision.

The decision must be in writing and must give the findings of fact and the reasons for the decision. A decision by the adjudication officer in favor of the person is binding on all parties to the hearing and not subject to further review unless: (1) the person or another party requests that the hearing continue, (2) the Appeals Council decides to review the decision on its own motion, (3) the decision is revised under special procedures, or (4) in a case remanded by a federal court, the Appeals Council assumes jurisdiction.

The adjudication officer must be an employee of the Social Security Administration or a state agency that makes disability determinations for the Social Security Administration.

The Social Security Administration is testing elimination of the final step in the administrative review process used in determining claims for benefits based on disability. The right of appeal for a claimant who is included in the test procedures and who is dissatisfied with the decision of an administrative law judge will be able to file a civil action in federal district court, rather than to request a review of the decision by the Appeals Council.

K-11. How can a person appeal the reconsideration determination?

A hearing before an administrative law judge may be requested by the person or appointed representative who disagrees with the reconsidered determination, or by a person who can show that the reconsidered determination will harm the person's rights under the Social Security Act.

The person and/or person's representative may appear in person, submit new evidence, examine the evidence used in making the determination under review, give testimony, and present and question witnesses. If a person properly waives the right to an oral hearing, the administrative law judge will ordinarily make a decision on the basis of the evidence already submitted or otherwise obtained by the person or any other party to the hearing.

If the claim is about the amount of Part A Hospital Insurance benefits under Medicare, the amount in question must be $100 or more. Carriers review complaints about the amount of Medical Insurance benefits under Medicare.

A person may also be able to use the expedited appeals procedure if he has no dispute with the findings of fact of the reconsideration determination beyond a contention that a section of the applicable statute is unconstitutional. (For further details, see K-14.)

Notice of time and place of the hearing is sent by the administrative law judge to the parties to the hearing at least 20 days before the date set for the hearing. The hearing is usually held in the area where the person requesting the hearing resides, although the person may be required to travel up to 75 miles. (Travel expenses are paid by the government if travel over 75 miles is required.)

At times, the administrative law judge will examine the evidence and certify a case to the Appeals Council with a recommended decision. (See K-14.)

K-12. How is a hearing request made?

A request for a hearing is made by filling out Form HA-501, "Request for Hearing," or by writing a letter to the nearest Social Security office, a presiding officer, or with the Appeals Council. The request for a hearing must be made within 60 days after the date that the notice of the reconsidered decision is received and must include: (1) the name and Social Security number of the individual, (2) the reason for disagreeing with the reconsidered or revised determination, (3) a statement of additional evidence which will be submitted, and (4) the name and address of the individual's representative, if any. The 60 day time limit can be extended if there is a good reason.

A beneficiary of disability benefits has the option of having his benefits continued through the hearing stage of appeal. If the earlier unfavorable determinations are upheld by the administrative law judge, the benefits are subject to recovery by the Social Security Administration. (If an appeal is made in good faith, recovery may be waived.) Medicare eligibility is also continued, but Medicare benefits are not subject to recovery.

K-13. What will a hearing cost?

There is no charge for a hearing. Of course, if a person is represented by a lawyer, he must pay that fee. A person must pay for all travel expenses also unless the hearing is held more than 75 miles from home. If this happens, a person is reimbursed for reasonable travel expenses.

K-14. If a person disagrees with the hearing decision, may he ask for a review?

Yes. A review of the hearing by the Appeals Council of the Office of Hearings and Appeals must be in writing and must be filed within 60 days from the date the person or the person's representative receives notice of the administrative law judge's action.

Within 60 days from the date of the administrative law judge's decision or dismissal, the Appeals Council may on its own initiative decide to review the action that was taken. Notice of this review is mailed to all parties at the last known address.

The Appeals Council will review a hearing decision or dismissal where: (1) there appears to be an abuse of discretion by the administrative law judge, (2) there is an error of law, (3) the presiding officer's action, findings, or conclusions are not supported by substantial evidence, or (4) there is a broad policy or procedural issue which may affect the general public interest.

The Appeals Council will notify the person whether it will review the case. If the Appeals Council decides to review the case, the claimant or representative may request an appearance before the Appeals Council for the presentation of oral arguments. If the Appeals Council determines that a significant question of law or policy is presented, or that oral arguments would be beneficial in rendering a proper decision, the appearance will be granted. The claimant may also file written statements in support of his claim. The Appeals Council will notify the claimant of its action in the case.

The Appeals Council may deny or dismiss a party's request for review, or it may grant the request and either issue a decision or remand the case to an administrative law judge. If the Appeals Council denies a request for review of a decision by an administrative law judge, the administrative law judge's decision becomes a final decision of the Social Security Administration subject to judicial review (except when judicial review is precluded in certain Medicare cases). If the Appeals Council grants a request for review and issues a decision, that decision also becomes a final decision of the Social Security Administration subject to judicial review except in certain Medicare cases.

If an administrative law judge makes a decision in favor of a person in a disability case and the Appeals Council does not render a final decision within 110 days, interim disability benefits are provided to the person. (Delays in excess of 20 days caused by or on behalf of the claimant do not count in determining the 110-day period.) These benefits begin with the month before the month in which the 110-day period expires, and are not considered overpayments if the final decision is adverse, unless the benefits are fraudulently obtained.

K-15. May a person file a civil action in the United States District Court?

Yes, a person dissatisfied with the decision of the Appeals Council or denial of the request for review of the administrative law judge's decision by the Appeals Council may bring suit in a federal district court. To file a civil action regarding the amount of Part A Hospital Insurance benefits under Medicare, however, the amount in question must be $1,000 or more. The Social Security Act does not provide for court review of a determination concerning the amount of benefits payable under Medicare Part B Medical Insurance.

The civil action in the court must be filed within 60 days from the date notice of the Appeals Council decision or denial of the request for review is received by the person or appointed representative. This time limit may be extended by the Appeals Council for good reason.

The court may issue a decision on the record or remand for further development. There is no right to court action where the Appeals Council has dismissed a request for review, or denied a request for review of an administrative law judge's dismissal.

A person may be able to advance directly from a reconsideration determination to a federal district court by filing a claim contending that the applicable statute of the Social Security Act is unconstitutional. This procedure, known as expedited appeals process, is allowable when: (1) the individual has presented a claim at the reconsideration level, (2) the only issue is the constitutionality of the statutory requirement, (3) the claim is neither invalid or cognizable under a different section of the Social Security Act, and (4) the amount in controversy is $1,000 or more.

In order to reach a federal district court after a reconsideration determination, the Social Security Administration must determine that the claim raises a constitutional question and is appropriate for treatment under the expedited appeals procedure. After this is done, the Social Security Administration and the person must sign an agreement that identifies the constitutional issue involved and explains the final reconsideration determination.

A person must file for expedited judicial review within 60 days after the date of receipt of notice of the reconsideration determination. An extension of time is available if good cause is established for not filing on time.

Should the Social Security Administration determine that a claim is not appropriate for expedited judicial review before a federal district court, its decision is final and not subject to administrative or judicial review. It is required, however, to notify the person filing the claim of its decision, and to treat the person's request as a request for a reconsideration, a hearing, or an Appeals Council review (whichever is appropriate).

The Supreme Court has held that the Social Security Act does not permit a person to have subject-matter jurisdiction to the federal district courts to review a decision of the Social Security Administration not to reopen a previously adjudicated claim for Social Security benefits. The Court found that unless the claim was based on a constitutional challenge, the Act did not authorize judicial review to reopen a final decision on disability benefits after the 60 day limit for a review by civil action had terminated. *Califano v. Sanders*, 430 U.S. 99 (1977).

K-16. Are there situations where the Social Security Administration may not recover an overpayment to a beneficiary?

Yes, the Social Security Administration is barred from recovering an overpayment if recovery is "against equity and good conscience." According to the Social Security regulations, recovery of an overpayment is "against equity and good conscience" under three conditions: (1) if the beneficiary has changed his or her position for the worse, (2) if the beneficiary relinquished a valuable right because of reliance upon a notice that a payment would be made or because of the overpayment itself, or (3) if the beneficiary was living in a separate household from the overpaid person or the eligible spouse and did not receive the overpayment.

The Ninth Circuit Court of Appeals has broadened the definition of "against equity and good conscience." *Quinlivan v. Sullivan*, 916 F.2nd 524 (9th Cir. 1990). The case involved a former inmate who had been in prison from 1963 to 1985 on a felony conviction, and who had been receiving Social Security disability benefits while in prison. Although the Social Security Act was amended in 1980 to prohibit payment of disability benefits to certain incarcerated felons, he continued to receive benefits until 1982 and was unaware of the change in the law. After learning about the change in the law, the inmate informed the Social Security Administration of his situation. The Social Security Administration requested repayment. The inmate requested a waiver of recovery for the overpayment and a personal conference with a government representative was held in 1984, but no decision was issued at that time. The inmate was released from prison in 1985 and spent his overpayment.

The Ninth Circuit held that requiring the former inmate to repay the overpayment was against equity and good conscience because Congress intended a broad concept of fairness to apply to waiver requests, one that takes into account the facts and circumstances of each case. The court noted that the former inmate had no material goods, no means of transportation, no income, and had only worked in a few temporary jobs. Also, the court pointed to the presence of a psychological impairment as a factor in favor of waiver of recovery of the overpayment.

Social Security regulations address the rights of individuals regarding overpayment and waiver determinations. The rules follow policy established as a result of a series of court decisions. Whenever an initial determination is made that more than the correct amount of payment has been made, and the Social Security Administration seeks adjustment or recovery of the overpayment, the individual involved must be immediately notified.

The notice must include: (1) the overpayment amount and how and when it occurred, (2) a request for full, immediate refund, unless the overpayment can be withheld from the next month's benefit, (3) the proposed adjustment of benefits if refund is not received within 30 days after the date of the notice and adjustment of benefits is available, (4) an explanation of the availability of a different rate of withholding, (5) an explanation of the right to request waiver of adjustment or recovery and the automatic scheduling of a file review and pre-recoupment hearing if a request for waiver cannot be approved after initial paper review, (6) an explanation of the right to request reconsideration of the fact and/or amount of the overpayment determination, (7) instructions about the availability of forms for requesting reconsideration and waiver, (8) an explanation that if the individual does not request waiver or reconsideration within 30 days of the date of the overpayment notice, adjustment or recovery of the overpayment will begin, (9) a statement that a Social Security Administration office will help the individual complete and submit forms for appeal or waiver requests, and (10) a statement that the individual receiving the notice should notify the Social Security Administration promptly if reconsideration, waiver, a lesser rate of withholding, repayment by installments, or cross-program adjustment is wanted.

There can be no adjustment or recovery in any case where an overpayment has been made to an individual who is without fault if adjustment or recovery would either defeat the purpose of the Social Security Act or be against equity and good conscience.

If an individual requests waiver of adjustment or recovery within 30 days after receiving a notice of overpayment, no action will be taken until after the initial waiver determination is made. If an individual requests waiver of adjustment or recovery more than 30 days after receiving a notice of overpayment, the Social Security Administration will stop any adjustment or recovery actions until after the initial waiver determination is made.

When waiver is requested, the individual provides the Social Security Administration with information to support the contention that the individual is without fault in causing the overpayment and that adjustment or recovery would either defeat the purpose of the Social Security Act or be against equity and good conscience. That information, along with supporting documentation, is reviewed to determine if waiver can be approved. If waiver cannot be approved after this review, the individual is notified in writing and given the dates, times and place of the file review and personal conference. The file review is always scheduled at least five days before the personal conference.

At the file review, the individual and the individual's representative have the right to review the claims file and applicable law and regulations with the decision maker or another Social Security Administration representative who is prepared to answer questions.

At the personal conference, the individual is given the opportunity to: (1) appear personally, testify, cross-examine any witnesses, and make arguments, (2) be represented by an attorney or other representative, although the individual must be present at the conference, and (3) submit documents for consideration by the decision maker.

The decision maker: (1) explains the provisions of law and regulations applicable to the issue, (2) briefly summarizes the evidence already on file, (3) ascertains from the individual whether the information presented is correct and understandable, (4) allows the individual and the individual's representative to present the individual's case, (5) allows each witness to present information and allows the individual and the individual's representative to question each witness, (6) ascertains whether there is any further evidence, (7) reminds the individual of any evidence promised by the individual which has not been presented, (8) allows the individual and the individual's representative to present a proposed summary or closing statement, (9) explains that a decision will be made and the individual will be notified in writing, and (10) explains repayment options and further appeal rights in the event the decision is adverse to the individual.

The Social Security Administration will issue a written decision, specifying the findings of fact and conclusions in support of the decision to approve or deny waiver and advising of the individual's right to appeal the decision. If waiver is denied, adjustment or recovery of the overpayment begins even if the individual appeals.

If the individual is dissatisfied with the initial determination, reconsideration is the first step in the administrative review process. If dissatisfied with the reconsidered determination, the individual may request a hearing before an administrative law judge.

K-17. What is the appeals procedure for civil monetary penalty cases?

The Social Security Administration may impose a civil monetary penalty of up to $5,000 and additional assessments against any individual, organization, agency, or other entity that makes or causes to be made a false or misleading statement or representation of a material fact for use in determining initial or continuing rights to Social Security benefits. (See A-11 for additional information.)

Social Security regulations provide that an individual or organization imposed with a civil monetary penalty or assessment may request a hearing with an administrative law judge. The hearing must be requested within 60 days of receiving notice of the civil monetary penalty and assessment from the Social Security Administration. All parties may be advised by an attorney and may participate in any conference held by the administrative law judge. The parties have the right to present evidence, present and cross-examine witnesses, and present oral arguments at the hearing. The burden of proof is on the Social Security Administration to prove an individual or organization made or caused to be made a false or misleading statement or representation of a material fact used in determining Social Security benefits.

Either party may appeal the decision of the administrative law judge to the Departmental Appeals Board of the Department of Health and Human Services by filing a notice of appeal within 30 days of the date of service of the initial decision. The Departmental Appeals Board may extend the initial 30-day period for up to 30 days if a party files a request for an extension within the initial 30-day period and shows good cause. When the Departmental Appeals Board reviews the case, it limits the review to whether the administrative law judge's initial decision is supported by substantial evidence on the whole record or contained error of law.

No party has the right to appeal personally to the Departmental Appeals Board. A notice of appeal must be accompanied by a written brief specifying exceptions to the initial decision and reasons supporting the exceptions, and identifying which findings of fact and conclusions of law the party is taking exception to.

Within 60 days after the time for submission of briefs, the Departmental Appeals Board must issue to each party a copy of its decision and a statement describing the right of any respondent who is found liable to seek judicial review upon a final decision.

Except with respect to any penalty or assessment remanded to the administrative law judge, the Departmental Appeals Board's recommended decision becomes final 60 days after the parties to the appeal receive a copy of the recommended decision, unless the Commissioner of the Social Security Administration reverses or modifies the recommendation decision within that 60-day period. If the Commissioner reverses or modifies the recommended decision, the Commissioner's decision is final and binding on the parties.

Any petition for judicial review must be filed within 60 days after the parties are served with a copy of the final decision.

BENEFITS FOR FEDERAL GOVERNMENT EMPLOYEES

INTRODUCTION

L-1. What are the two retirement systems for federal employees?

There are over 2.7 million full-time civilian federal employees. About 2.4 million Americans currently receive some form of benefits under the retirement systems for federal employees.

There are two retirement systems for federal employees: the Civil Service Retirement System (CSRS) and the Federal Employees' Retirement System (FERS).

The CSRS, created in 1920, was the only retirement system for federal employees until the FERS became public law in 1986. FERS created a new federal retirement program coordinated with Social Security retirement benefits for federal employees hired after 1983. Federal employees in FERS are automatically covered by Social Security and must pay Social Security taxes, while federal employees who remain in CSRS are exempt from Social Security taxes. FERS also provides a guaranteed basic annuity and a tax-deferred savings plan similar to a Section 401(k) retirement plan.

FEDERAL EMPLOYEES' RETIREMENT SYSTEM

L-2. Who is covered under the Federal Employees' Retirement System?

The Federal Employees' Retirement System (FERS) is a three-tier retirement system for federal workers who began work with the government after 1983. In addition, a number of federal employees hired before 1984 elected to transfer from the Civil Service Retirement System (CSRS) to FERS during a 1987 transfer period.

The following are excluded from FERS coverage:

- A person not covered by Social Security, including a person covered by full CSRS.

- A person who has served without a break in service of more than 365 days since December 31, 1983, in the position of: (a) Vice

231

President, (b) member of Congress, (c) a senior executive Service or Senior Foreign Service noncareer appointee, or (d) persons appointed by the President or Vice President to positions where the maximum rate of basic pay is at or above the rate for Level V of the Executive Schedule.

- An employee who is rehired after December 31, 1986, who has had a break in service and who, at the time of the last separation from the service, had at least five years of civilian service creditable under CSRS rules, any part of which was covered by CSRS or the Foreign Service Retirement system.

- An employee who has not had a break in service of more than three days ending after December 31, 1986, and who, as of December 31, 1986, had at least five years of creditable civilian service under CSRS rules (even if none of this service was covered by CSRS).

L-3. Who is eligible for FERS benefits?

Unreduced retirement benefits are provided at age 60 with 20 or more years of service, at age 62 with five or more years of service, and at "minimum retirement age" with 30 years of service. The minimum retirement age is currently 55.

The "minimum retirement age" for employees with 30 or more years of service is gradually increasing. Until the year 2003, an employee with 30 years of service may retire at age 55. Beginning in the year 2003, the minimum retirement age increases by two months every year until year 2009. Thus, at 2009 the employee must be age 56 to retire with 30 or more years of service. Age 56 continues to be the minimum retirement age until 2020. Beginning in the year 2021, the minimum retirement age again increases by two-month increments until the year 2027. The minimum retirement age for employees with 30 or more years of service is 57 in the year 2027 and after. The minimum retirement age for reduced benefits is also being gradually increased from 55 to 57. An employee must have at least 10 years of service to be eligible for reduced retirement benefits. For an employee retiring with less than 30 years of service, a reduction of 5% per year for each year under age 62 is imposed. Thus, benefits for an employee retiring at age 55 are reduced 35%.

An employee can leave government employment prior to the date that he is eligible for a retirement benefit and still be eligible for a Basic Annuity at a later date. If the employee has five years of creditable service and does not withdraw contributions when he terminates government service, he may receive a deferred, unreduced annuity when he attains age 62 with at least five years of civil service employment; age 60 with at least

20 years of service; or at minimum retirement age (currently age 55) with at least 30 years of service.

An employee is entitled to a Basic Annuity at age 50 with 20 years of service or at any age after completing 25 years of service, if: (1) his retirement is involuntary (except by removal by cause for misconduct or delinquency) and he did not decline a reasonable offer for a position which is not lower than two grades below his present position; or (2) his retirement is voluntary because his agency is undergoing a major reduction in employees, reorganization, or a transfer of function in which a number of employees are separated or downgraded.

Basic Annuity

L-4. What is the Basic Annuity?

The Basic Annuity is the second tier of benefits under FERS. Social Security is the first tier of benefits. Social Security includes retirement, disability and survivor benefits, and health insurance benefits under Medicare. The Basic Annuity provides retirement, disability and survivor benefits in addition to those provided by Social Security. The Basic Annuity guarantees a specific monthly retirement payment based on the employee's age, length of creditable service, and "high-3" years' average salary. An employee must have five years of creditable service and be subject to FERS at separation in order to be eligible for a Basic Annuity.

L-5. How much must an employee contribute to the Basic Annuity?

An employee contributes 0.8% of his basic pay to the Basic Annuity. Certain FERS members pay an additional 0.5% to the Basic Annuity. These members include firefighters, law enforcement personnel, air traffic controllers, members of Congress and Congressional employees. Basic pay does not include bonuses, overtime pay, military pay, holiday pay, cash awards or special allowances given in addition to basic pay. The federal government makes a contribution to the Basic Annuity plan pursuant to a formula.

L-6. What annuities are available to a retiring employee?

The following annuities are available to a retiring federal employee:

- an annuity with no survivor benefit.

- a lump-sum credit of the employee's contributions (excluding interest) with a reduced annuity.

- an annuity to the employee for life, with a survivor annuity payable for the life of the surviving spouse.

233

- a lump-sum credit of the employee's contributions (excluding interest) with a reduced annuity which is further reduced to provide a survivor benefit.

- a reduced annuity with a survivor benefit to a person with an insurable interest, provided the employee is in good health.

Note, however, that an employee cannot elect against providing survivor benefits to his spouse unless his spouse consents to the election in writing.

L-7. What is the amount of the Basic Annuity?

The amount of the Basic Annuity depends on the employee's years of service and highest three-year ("high-3") average salary. It also depends on whether an annuity supplement is added into the Basic Annuity formula.

For employees under age 62, or age 62 or older with less than 20 years of FERS service, the formula, not including the supplement where applicable, is:

- 1.0% x "high-3" average salary x length of service

For employees age 62 or older with at least 20 years of FERS service, the formula is:

- 1.1% x "high-3" average salary x length of service

(No annuity supplement is payable if the employee is age 62 or older.)

For law enforcement officers, firefighters, air traffic controllers, employees of Congress, foreign service employees, and certain CIA employees, the formula is:

(1) 1.7% x "high-3" average salary x years of service up to 20 years, plus

(2) 1.0% x "high-3" average salary x years of service over 20 years, plus

(3) the annuity supplement, where applicable.

All periods of creditable service are totaled to determine length of service. Years and months of creditable service (extra days are dropped) are then used in the annuity computation formula.

"High-3" average salary is the highest pay obtainable by averaging an employee's rates of basic pay in effect over any three consecutive years of service. The three years need not be continuous, but they must consist of consecutive periods of service. In other words, two or more separate periods of employment which follow each other can be joined to make up the three consecutive years.

Example. Steve James retires at age 65 after 30 years of civil service employment. His "High-3" average salary is $31,000 ($30,000 + $31,000 + $32,000 ÷ 3 = $31,000). His FERS benefit is computed as follows:

(1) 1.1% x $31,000 = $341

(2) $341 x 30 years of service = $10,230 Basic Annuity.

L-8. How is the Basic Annuity adjusted for cost-of-living increases?

The Basic Annuity for employees age 62 or older is adjusted for cost-of-living increases pursuant to the following schedule:

(1) Where the change in the Consumer Price Index for All Urban Wage Earners and Clerical Workers (CPI) for the year is less than 2.0%, the annuity is increased by the full amount of the CPI increase.

(2) Where the change in the CPI for the year is at least 2.0% but is not more than 3.0%, the annuity is increased by 2.0%.

(3) Where the change in the CPI for the year is more than 3.0%, the annuity is increased by the CPI less 1%. For example, if the CPI increases 4.5%, the Basic Annuity will increase 3.5%.

The cost-of-living increase for 2001 is 2.5%.

L-9. What is the Annuity Supplement?

An Annuity Supplement is added to the Basic Annuity as a substitute for Social Security when the employee is receiving the Basic Annuity and is under age 62. It is equal to the estimated amount of Social Security benefits that the employee would be eligible to receive at age 62 based on civil service employment earnings. The Supplement ends when the employee first becomes eligible for a Social Security retirement benefit (age 62).

The Supplement is payable to: (1) employees who retire after the minimum retirement age (currently age 55) with 30 years of service; (2) employees who retire at age 60 with 20 years of service; and (3) employees who retire involuntarily and have reached minimum retirement age (currently age 55).

The Supplement is not subject to cost-of-living increases, and is reduced for excess earnings after retirement in much the same way that Social Security benefits are reduced for excess earnings. In 2001, the Supplement is reduced by $1 for every $2 that the beneficiary earns over $10,680.

Survivor Benefits

L-10. What survivors' benefits are payable under FERS?

Survivor benefits are paid upon the death of an employee or retired civil service employee. Benefits are paid on a monthly basis or in a lump-sum to eligible survivors. The spouse, former spouse and dependent children of a deceased employee may be entitled to a survivor annuity.

A spouse may be entitled to a "post-retirement survivor benefit." The annuity of a married employee who retires is generally reduced by 10% to provide a survivor annuity for the spouse, unless the employee and his spouse both waive the survivor annuity. A surviving spouse is entitled to 50% of the employee's unreduced annuity increased by cost-of-living benefit adjustments. There is also a 5% reduction in the annuity of a married employee who retires and selects a 25% survivor annuity.

There is a permanent actuarial reduction in the retiree's annuity in the case of a retiree who marries after retirement and elects a survivor benefit. The reduction may not be more than 25% of the retiree's annuity. The reduction is permanent and unaffected by any future termination of the marriage.

The surviving spouse: (1) must have been married to the employee for at least nine months; (2) must be the parent of a child of the marriage at the time of death, or (3) the death of the retired employee must have been accidental.

If the survivor is under age 60 and Social Security survivor benefits are *not* payable, benefits are the lesser of: (1) current CSRS survivor benefits; or (2) 50% (25% if elected) of accrued annuity plus a Social Security "equivalent." When Social Security survivor benefits are payable, FERS pays 50% (25% if elected) of the deceased retiree's annuity.

If the employee was unmarried at the time of retirement and then married after retirement, he may elect a reduced annuity with a survivor benefit for his spouse. Such an election must take place within two years after the marriage.

If the spouse dies before the retired employee, and the retired employee remarries, the new spouse is eligible to receive the same survivor benefits as the former spouse. The retired employee must elect to take a reduced annuity with a survivor benefit for his new spouse.

A retired employee and spouse who have elected against a survivor benefit can change their election within 18 months. The retired employee must pay the full cost of providing the survivor annuity if an election is made during this second election period.

There is also a survivor benefit for the spouse of an employee who dies prior to retirement. The surviving spouse is entitled to a guaranteed amount of $23,386.98 (in 2001), plus 50% of the employee's final salary or, if higher, his "high-3" average. In addition, if the deceased employee completed 10 or more years of service, the surviving spouse is entitled to an annuity equal to 50% of the unreduced annuity the employee would have been entitled to had he reached retirement age. Survivor benefits are subject to cost-of-living adjustments.

The $23,386.98 payment, which is indexed to the Consumer Price Index, can be in a lump-sum or in monthly installments.

The surviving spouse: (1) must have been married to the employee for at least nine months, or (2) must be the parent of a child of the marriage, or (3) the death of the employee must have been accidental. The deceased employee must also have at least 18 months of creditable service while subject to FERS.

L-11. Is the former spouse of a deceased employee entitled to a survivor benefit?

The former spouse of a deceased employee may be entitled to a survivor benefit if he or she: (1) was married to the deceased employee for at least nine months; (2) has not remarried prior to age 55; and (3) a court order or court-approved property settlement agreement provides for payment of a survivor annuity to the former spouse.

The survivor annuity is payable to a former spouse when: (1) the deceased employee has at least 18 months of creditable service under FERS; or (2) the deceased former employee has title to a deferred annuity and has 10 years of service.

A former spouse who does not meet the requirements listed above may still be entitled to an annuity if the retiree, at the time of retirement, elected to provide the former spouse with a survivor annuity.

The amount of the survivor annuity for a former spouse is the same as that for a spouse, except that the Guaranteed Amount ($23,386.98, see L-10) is not payable unless payment is required under a court order or agreement.

L-12. Is there a survivor benefit for the children of a deceased employee?

If a retiree or an employee has 18 months of creditable service under FERS before he dies, his dependent children are entitled to monthly annuities reduced by the amount of any Social Security survivor benefits they receive. The annuity begins on the day after the death and ends on the last day of the month before the one in which the child dies, marries, reaches age 18, or if over 18, becomes capable of self-support. The annuity of a child who is a student ends on the last day of the month before he: (1) marries; (2) dies; (3) ceases to be a student; or (4) attains the age of 22. If a student drops out of school or his annuity is terminated, it can be restored if he later returns to school and is still under age 22 and unmarried.

Annuity payments restart again if the child's marriage has ended and he or she is still eligible for benefits because of disability or enrollment as a full-time student while under age 22. If a child's marriage ends because of divorce or death, the child's annuity and health benefits coverage is restored beginning the first day of the month in which dissolution of the marriage occurs.

The amount of the benefit depends on whether the child is eligible to receive Social Security benefits and whether the deceased worker's spouse is still living.

If the retiree or employee is survived by a spouse or the child has a living parent, each eligible child is entitled to receive an annuity in 2001 equal to the lessor of:

(1) 60% of the employee's "high-3" average pay, divided by the number of qualified children.

(2) $1,107 per month, divided by the number of qualified children.

(3) $369 per month.

If the retiree or employee is *not* survived by a spouse or the child has *no* living parent, each eligible child is entitled to receive an annuity in 2001 equal to the lessor of:

(1) 75% of the employee's "high-3" average pay, divided by the number of qualified children.

(2) $1,326 per month, divided by the number of qualified children.

(3) $442 per month.

L-13. Is a person with an insurable interest in a retiree or employee eligible for a survivor benefit?

A retiree or employee can designate that a survivor annuity be paid to a person with an insurable interest in the life of the retiree or employee. The benefit is equal to 50% of the retiree's benefit, but is reduced depending on the difference in the age of the person with the insurable interest and the age of the retiring employee.

If the age difference is 30 years or more, the annuity is reduced 40%; if the age difference is 25 to 29 years, the reduction is 35%; if the age difference is 20 to 24 years, the reduction is 30%; if the age difference is 15 to 19 years, the reduction is 25%; if the age difference is 10 to 14 years, the reduction is 20%; if the age difference is five to nine years, the reduction is 15%; if the age difference is less than five years, the reduction is 10%.

L-14. When is a lump-sum survivor benefit paid?

A lump-sum survivor benefit is payable immediately after the death of an employee if the employee: (1) has *less* than 18 months of creditable service; or (2) leaves *no* widow(er), former spouse or children who are eligible for a survivor annuity.

The lump-sum survivor benefit is the amount paid into the Civil Service Retirement and Disability Fund by the employee. It also includes accrued interest.

The employee, former employee or annuitant has the right to name the lump-sum survivor benefit beneficiary. If no beneficiary is named, the lump-sum is payable to the widow(er); if there is no widow(er), it is paid to his living children in equal shares; if no children, it is paid to his parents; if no parents, it is paid to the executor or administrator of his estate; if none of the above, it is paid to the next of kin under the laws of the state where the deceased was domiciled.

Disability Benefits

L-15. What disability benefits are paid under FERS?

Disability benefits are payable to an employee with 18 months of creditable service who, because of injury or disease, can no longer perform his job in a useful and efficient manner. The beneficiary is entitled to a benefit equal to 60% of his "high-3" average pay during the first year of disability, reduced dollar for dollar by any Social Security disability benefit. After the first year, the beneficiary is entitled to 40% of his "high-3" average pay, reduced by 60% of the Social Security disability benefit. The benefit is further adjusted at age 62 to equal the *lesser* of: (1) a retirement benefit computed as if he had worked during his years of disability; or (2) the disability benefit he would receive after the benefit is offset by any Social Security disability benefit. Disability benefits are adjusted after the first year of disability by the increase in the Consumer Price Index for All Urban Wage Earners and Clerical Workers

(CPI). Where the change in the CPI for the year is less than 2.0%, the benefit is increased by the full amount of the CPI increase. Where the change in the CPI for the year is at least 2.0% but is not more than 3.0%, the benefit is increased by 2%. Where the change in the CPI for the year is more than 3.0%, the benefit is increased by the CPI less 1%. Periodic medical examinations are required until the beneficiary reaches age 60.

Thrift Savings Plan

L-16. What is the Thrift Savings Plan for FERS employees?

The Thrift Plan creates a third tier of benefits under FERS. A thrift plan account is set up automatically for every employee covered under FERS.

The government contributes 1% of pay to an account for each employee even if the employee declines to contribute to the plan. In addition, the government matches employee contributions as follows:

(1) Contributions up to the first 3% of pay, dollar for dollar;

(2) Contributions that are more than 3% but not more than 5% of pay, 50 cents per dollar.

Until July 2001, a FERS employee may contribute up to 10% of his salary towards the Thrift Plan.

Beginning in July 2001, allowable employee contributions are increased by 1% per year until the limit is 15% in 2005. After 2005, the percentage contribution limits are lifted entirely.

In any case, the maximum amount that a FERS employee can contribute is $10,500 in 2001.

Contributions, and earnings on contributions, are not subject to federal income taxation until distributed to the employee at retirement. In addition, contributions reduce the employee's gross income for federal income tax purposes. (Contributions are subject to Social Security taxes, however.)

Contributions can be directed by employees to three investment funds:

(1) Government securities fund (G Fund);

(2) Fixed-income fund (F Fund); and

(3) Stock index fund (C Fund).

Beginning in May 2001, employees may invest in two additional funds:

(1) Small Capitalization Stock index Investment Fund (S Fund); and

(2) International Stock Index Investment (I Fund).

All government contributions through 1992 must be held in the government securities fund (G Fund). FERS employees may elect to invest any portion of their current account balances and/or future contributions in the G Fund, F Fund, C Fund, S Fund, or I Fund. Participants may make four interfund transfers in any calendar year, subject to a one-transfer per month limit.

Thrift Plan payments may be made in the following manner:

(1) At retirement or disability, if eligible for a Basic Annuity, the payment may be made as an immediate or deferred annuity, a lump-sum payment, a fixed-term payment, or by transfer to an IRA or other qualified pension plan.

(2) At death, funds in the Thrift Plan are paid to eligible survivors or to beneficiaries as specified by FERS.

(3) At termination of employment, if eligible for a deferred Basic Annuity, the payment may be made as an immediate or deferred annuity, a transfer to an IRA or other qualified pension plan, or over a fixed term after the employee retires with a Basic Annuity.

(4) At termination of employment, if not eligible for a deferred Basic Annuity, the payment must be transferred to an IRA or qualified pension plan.

(5) At age 59½ or during a period of financial hardship. (See below.)

A participant must withdraw his account balance in a single payment or begin receiving his Thrift Savings Plan account balance in monthly payments (or in the form of a Thrift Savings Plan annuity) by April 1 of the later of: (1) the year following the year in which the participant reaches age 70½, or (2) the year following the year in which the participant separates from federal service. If the participant does not make an election so that payment can be made by this deadline, the Federal Retirement Thrift Investment Board must use the Thrift Savings Plan to purchase an annuity for the participant.

A participant who has turned age 59½ can withdraw an amount up to his vested Thrift Savings Plan account balance before separating from government employment. A participant is allowed only one withdrawal under this provision. In addition, a participant can obtain a withdrawal before separating from government employment on the basis of financial hardship. A financial hardship withdrawal is limited to the amount the participant contributed to the Thrift Savings Plan (plus the earnings attributed to those contributions). There is no limit on the number of such withdrawals. The participant may ask the Thrift Savings Plan to transfer all or a portion of the withdrawal to an IRA or other eligible retirement plan.

A participant can continue to contribute to the Thrift Savings Plan after obtaining an aged-based withdrawal, but is not eligible to contribute to the Thrift Savings Plan for a period of six months after obtaining a financial hardship withdrawal. After six months ineligibility to contribute, the participant can resume Thrift Savings Plan contributions only by making a new Thrift Savings Plan election on Form TSP-1.

The spouse of a FERS participant must consent to an in-service withdrawal and the spouse of a CSRS participant is entitled to notice when the participant applies for an in-service withdrawal.

Federal employees who separate or enter leave-without-pay status to serve in the military may make up contributions to the Thrift Plan missed because of military service. A federal employee would be permitted to contribute an amount equal to what an employee would have been eligible to contribute. The federal government must give such an employee two to four times the length of his military service to make up the Thrift Plan contributions. The government would match employee contributions in the same manner as regular matching contributions under the Thrift Plan.

Twice a year there are Thrift Savings Plan open seasons when federal employees may begin participation, end participation, or change contribution amounts or the way future contributions are invested. The 2001 open season is from May 15, 2001 to July 31, 2001 and from November 15, 2001 to January 31, 2002.

L-17. Can members of the Civil Service Retirement System take advantage of the Thrift Plan?

Yes, but there are two differences:

(1) The government does not contribute to the employee's plan, no matter how much the employee contributes.

(2) CSRS employees may contribute no more than 5% of base pay to the Thrift Plan. This percentage will increase in July 2001 by 1% per calender year until the CSRS limit is 10% in 2005. After 2005, the percentage limited will be lifted entirely.

CIVIL SERVICE RETIREMENT SYSTEM

L-18. Which federal employees are covered under the Civil Service Retirement System?

The Civil Service Retirement System (CSRS) covers employees of the U.S. government and the District of Columbia who were hired before January 1, 1984, unless coverage is specifically excluded by law. Among the exclusions from CSRS coverage are employees who are subject to another federal retirement system. Employees subject to the Federal Employees' Retirement System (FERS) are excluded from participation in CSRS.

CSRS coverage for pre-1984 employees is automatic for all federal employees except those who are employed by Congress. Congressional employees had to elect coverage.

L-19. Who is eligible for a CSRS retirement annuity?

An employee must meet two requirements in order to be eligible for a CSRS retirement annuity. First, the employee must complete at least five years of civilian service with the government. Second, the employee, unless retiring on account of total disability, must have been employed under the CSRS for at least one year out of the last two years before separation from service.

The total service of an employee or member of Congress is measured in full years and months. Anything less than a full month is not counted. An employee's service is credited from the date of original employment to the date of separation. No credit is allowed for a period of separation from service in excess of three calendar days.

An employee is allowed credit for periods of military service if performed prior to the date of separation from his civilian position.

L-20. How are CSRS benefits paid for?

CSRS benefits are funded by deductions from the basic pay of covered employees, matching contributions from their employing agencies, and by payments from the General Treasury for the balance of the cost of the system. Under the current law, the employee and the employing agency *each* contribute:

- 8.0% of basic pay for Members of Congress,

- 7.5% of basic pay for Congressional employees, law enforcement officers and firefighters, and

- 7.0% of basic pay for other employees.

The portion of compensation withheld and contributed to the retirement and disability fund is includable in the employee's gross income in the same taxable year in which it would have been included if it had been paid to the employee directly. No refund is allowed for taxes attributable to mandatory contributions from the employee's salary to the Civil Service Retirement Fund.

L-21. Who is entitled to an immediate annuity?

An immediate annuity begins no later than one month after separation from the service. This includes an annuity for an employee who retires optionally — for age, for disability, or due to involuntary separation from the service. It does not include an annuity for a separated employee who is entitled to a deferred retirement annuity at a future date.

An employee who is separated from the service is entitled to an annuity:

(1) at age 55 with 30 years of service,

(2) at age 60 with 20 years of service,

(3) at age 62 with five years of service,

(4) at age 50 with 20 years of service as a law enforcement officer or firefighter, or a combination of such service totaling at least 20 years.

An employee whose separation is involuntary, except for removal for cause on charges of misconduct or delinquency, is entitled to a reduced annuity after 25 years of service or after age 50 and 20 years of service. However, no annuity is payable if the employee has declined a reasonable offer of another position in the employee's agency for which the employee is qualified, which is not lower than two grades (pay levels) below the employee's grade, and which is within the employee's commuting area.

Also entitled to this reduced annuity is an employee who, while serving in a geographic area designated by the Office of Personnel Management, is voluntarily separated during a period in which: (1) the agency in which the employee is serving is undergoing a major reorganization, a major reduction in force, or a major transfer of function, and (2) a significant percentage of employees serving in this agency will be separated or subject to an immediate reduction in the rate of basic pay.

Such early retirements must be approved by the Office of Personnel Management. The annuities are reduced by 2% for each year the employee is under age 55.

L-22. Are there alternative forms of CSRS retirement annuities?

Yes, an employee may, at the time of retirement, elect the following alternative forms of annuities:

(1) payment of an annuity to the employee for life,

(2) payment of an annuity to the employee for life, with a survivor annuity payable for the life of a surviving spouse,

(3) payment of an annuity to the employee for life, with benefit to a named person having an insurable interest,

(4) election of lump-sum credit option and reduced monthly annuity.

L-23. What is an annuity for life?

The annuitant has a right to receive monthly payments during his lifetime unless he is convicted of certain offenses against the United States. Upon the annuitant's death, any accrued annuity that remains unpaid will be paid to: (1) the deceased annuitant's executor or administrator, or (2) if there is no executor or administrator, to the decedent's next of kin under state law, after 30 days have passed from the date of death.

L-24. What are the features of an annuity with a survivor benefit?

An annuity with survivor benefit entitles the survivor to an annuity equal to 55% of the annuity amount prior to reduction for the election of the survivor benefit. An annuity for a married employee will automatically include an annuity for a surviving spouse unless the employee and spouse waive the spouse's annuity in writing. The written waiver requirement can be overcome only in instances where the employee's spouse cannot be located or where other exceptional circumstances are present.

Generally, the survivor benefit is paid until the survivor dies or remarries. However, remarriage of a widow or widower who is at least age 55 does not terminate the survivor annuity. Where the survivor annuity is terminated because the survivor had remarried prior to reaching age 55, the annuity may be restored if the remarriage is dissolved by death, annulment, or divorce.

Where the spouse properly consents, an employee may elect to reduce that portion of the annuity that is to be treated as a survivor annuity.

The portion of the employee's annuity treated as a survivor annuity will be reduced according to a formula. The reduction is 2.5% of the first $3,600 chosen as a base, plus 10% of any amount over $3,600. For example, if the employee chooses $4,800 as a base, the reduction in the annual annuity would be 2.5% of the first $3,600 ($90 a year), plus 10% of the $1,200 balance ($120 a year), making a total reduction of $210 ($90 + $120) a year.

If marriage is terminated after retirement by the divorce, annulment or death of the spouse named as beneficiary, the retiree may elect to have the annuity recomputed and payment at the single-life unreduced rate will be made for each full month the employee is not married. Should the employee remarry, he has two years from the date of remarriage to notify the Office of Personnel Management in writing that he wants the annuity reduced again to provide a survivor annuity for the new spouse.

If a retired employee dies, absent a waiver of benefits by the survivor, the surviving spouse will receive 55% of the yearly annuity which the deceased employee had earned at the time of death. This earned annuity is computed in the same manner as if the deceased employee had retired, but with no reduction for being under age 55, and no increase for voluntary contributions.

The surviving spouse's annuity begins on the day after the employee's death and terminates on the last day of the month before the surviving spouse dies or remarries before age 55.

L-25. How does an annuity with benefit to a named person having an insurable interest work?

If the employee is in good health at retirement, he may elect an Annuity With Benefit to Named Person Having an Insurable Interest. A disabled dependent relative or former spouse is considered as having an insurable interest. An employee electing this annuity will have his annuity reduced by a percentage amount as follows:

Age of Named Person In Relation to Retiring Employee's Age	Reduction in Annuity of Retiring Employee
Older, same age, or less than 5 years younger	10%
5 but less than 10 years younger	15%
10 but less than 15 years younger	20%
15 but less than 20 years younger	25%
20 but less than 25 years younger	30%
25 but less than 30 years younger	35%
30 or more years younger	40%

Upon the employee's death after retirement, the named beneficiary will receive an annuity equal to 55% of the employee's reduced annuity rate. The survivor's annuity begins on the day after the retired employee's death and terminates on the last day of the month before the survivor dies. However, if the person named as having an insurable interest dies before the employee, the employee's annuity will be restored to life rate upon written request.

L-26. Is there a lump-sum credit option upon retirement under CSRS?

Beginning in 1986, employees were allowed to receive a payment equal to the value of the contributions they made to the retirement program over their working years. The lump-sum payments were paid in one payment at first and then in two installments of equal amounts.

Prior to October 1, 1994, there were two categories of employees eligible for the lump-sum payments: (1) workers who are "involuntarily separated," and (2) workers eligible to voluntarily retire who are certified as having a life-threatening or certain other critical illness. Workers who are involuntarily separated can receive a lump-sum payable in two installments of 50% each. One payment is made shortly after retirement and the next is made a year later. Workers eligible to voluntarily retire who have a critical illness can receive the lump-sum in one payment.

The Omnibus Budget Reconciliation Act of 1993 eliminated the lump-sum option for involuntarily separated workers, beginning October 1, 1994. Workers with life-threatening conditions remain eligible for the lump-sum option.

L-27. How is the reduced annuity computed?

You need to know the amount of the member's contributions into the plan. You will also need to compute the member's regular annuity. To determine the amount of monthly reduction of the annuity, the computation is as follows:

- LS/PV = monthly reduction in annuity

- where LS equals the lump-sum credit and PV equals the present value factor of the annuity

The present value factors of CSRS and FERS appear below.

To obtain the amount of the reduced monthly annuity, subtract the monthly reduction figure obtained above from the amount of the regular (unreduced) monthly annuity.

Example. Mr. Edwards, a member of the CSRS, is 64 at the time he retires from government service. His contributions to CSRS total $25,000. His present value factor (from the table) is 166.5. Using the formula above, $25,000 ÷ 166.5 = $150.15. Mr. Edwards' monthly annuity would therefore be reduced by $150.15.

REDUCED ANNUITY TABLES
CSRS

Present Value Factors

Age at Retirement	Factor	Age at Retirement	Factor
40	294.4	66	156.0
41	290.0	67	150.7
42	285.5	68	145.4
43	280.8	69	140.2
44	276.2	70	134.7
45	270.4	71	129.4
46	264.7	72	124.0
47	259.2	73	118.8
48	253.5	74	113.6
49	247.2	75	108.5
50	240.4	76	103.5
51	235.0	77	98.7
52	229.8	78	93.9
53	224.4	79	89.4
54	218.6	80	84.9
55	212.6	81	80.5
56	207.5	82	76.3
57	202.4	83	72.3
58	197.0	84	68.4
59	192.3	85	64.7
60	188.3	86	61.2
61	182.9	87	57.9
62	177.0	88	54.7
63	171.9	89	51.8
64	166.5	90	48.9
65	161.1		

FERS

Present Value Factors for Most Employees

Age at Retirement	Present Value Factor	Age at Retirement	Present Value Factor
40	169.2	66	143.6
41	168.8	67	139.1
42	168.4	68	134.6
43	168.1	69	130.1
44	167.7	70	125.4
45	166.9	71	120.7
46	166.1	72	116.0
47	165.4	73	111.4
48	164.7	74	106.8
49	163.7	75	102.2
50	162.4	76	97.8
51	161.9	77	93.5
52	161.6	78	89.2
53	161.2	79	85.0
54	160.6	80	80.9
55	160.0	81	77.0
56	160.0	82	73.1
57	160.2	83	69.4
58	160.4	84	65.8
59	161.2	85	62.4
60	162.7	86	59.1
61	163.5	87	56.0
62	161.3	88	53.0
63	157.1	89	50.2
64	152.5	90	47.5
65	148.0		

Computing The CSRS Annuity

L-28. How is the amount of the CSRS annuity determined?

The amount of an annuity depends primarily on the employee's length of service and "high-3" average pay. These two factors are used in a formula to determine the basic annuity which may then be reduced or increased for various reasons.

The "high-3" average pay is the highest pay obtainable by averaging the rates of basic pay in effect during any three consecutive years of service, with each rate weighted by the time it was in effect. The three years need not be continuous, but they must consist of consecutive periods of service. Thus, two or more separate periods of employment which follow each other may be joined to make up the three consecutive years of service on which the "high-3" average pay is based. The pay rates for each period of employment are weighted on an annual basis.

Example. Mr. Smith's final three years of government service included pay rates of:

6	months at $14,500	—	$^1/_2$ year	X	$14,500	=	$ 7,250	
18	months at $15,000	—	$1^1/_2$ years	X	$15,000	=	22,500	
12	months at $15,000	—	1 year	X	$15,000	=	15,500	
							$45,250	

Mr. Smith's average pay is computed as:

$$\frac{\$45,250}{3} = \$15,083 = \text{(Average Pay)}$$

A three-step formula is used to determine the basic annuity.

*   *Step I.* 1.5% x Average Pay x number of years of service up to five years, plus

*   *Step II.* 1.75% x Average Pay x number of years of service over five and up to 10 years, plus

*   *Step III.* 2.0% x Average Pay x number of years of service over 10.

Note that for employees with over 10 years of service, all three steps apply. For those with less than 10 years of service, only steps I and II apply.

Example. Mr. Martin retires from civil service employment with 30 years of service. The three consecutive years of service with the highest rates of basic pay were his last three years before retirement.

Rate of pay during 28th year of service · $14,500
Rate of pay during 29th year of service   15,000
Rate of pay during 30th year of service   <u>15,500</u>
$45,000 (total)

$$\frac{\$45,250}{3} = \$15,000 = \text{(Average Pay)}$$

The general formula, using Mr. Martin's $15,000 average pay and 30 years of service, is applied as follows:

1. $1\frac{1}{2}\%$ X $15,000 X 5 years = $1,125.00
2. $1\frac{3}{4}\%$ X $15,000 X 5 years = 1,312.50
3. 2% X $15,000 X 20 years = <u>6,000.00</u>
Basic Annuity $8,437.50

The employee's basic annuity may not exceed 80% of his average pay. If the formula produces an amount exceeding the 80% maximum, it must be reduced to an amount which equals 80% of the average pay.

L-29. What is the substitute computation method?

A substitute computation method is provided as an alternative for employees with a "high-3" of under $5,000. Instead of taking the 1.5%, 1.75%, and 2% of the "high-3" average pay, the employee may substitute 1% of the "high-3" average pay plus $25 for all parts of the general formula. If the "high-3" average pay is between $2,500 and $3,333, substitute the 1% plus $25 for the 1.5% and 1.75% in the first and second parts of the general formula. If the "high-3" average pay is between $3,334 and $4,999, substitute the 1% plus $25 for the 1.5% in the first part of the general formula.

L-30. How is the benefit determined for disability retirement?

An employee under age 60 who retires on account of total disability will receive no less than the guaranteed minimum annuity which is the *lesser* of:

(1) 40% of the employee's "high-3" average pay, or

(2) the amount obtained under the general formula after adding to years of actual service the number of years he is under age 60 on the date of separation.

An employee must have completed at least five years of government service in order to be eligible for disability benefits. The provision for a minimum disability annuity does not apply to employees over age 60. The disability annuity rate for an employee over age 60 is always computed by using actual service in the general formula.

L-31. Can an employee obtain a larger retirement annuity by making voluntary contributions?

An employee can obtain a larger retirement annuity by making voluntary contributions, in multiples of $25, to purchase an additional annuity. Total voluntary contributions may not exceed 10% of the employee's total basic pay.

Voluntary contributions are interest-bearing. The interest rate is determined at the end of each year by the Treasury Department. Each $100 in the account provides an additional annuity in the amount of $7, plus 20 cents for each full year the employee is over age 55 at retirement.

Death Benefits

L-32. Is there a death benefit under the CSRS?

Death benefits are of two kinds: survivor annuities and lump-sum payments. Survivor annuities are payable to an employee's surviving spouse and children upon the death of the employee. A lump-sum benefit is payable upon the death of the employee if there is no spouse or dependent children entitled to an annuity, or, if one is payable, after the right of the last person entitled thereto has been terminated.

While not formally called a "death benefit," where the employee has retired, annuities are payable to the surviving spouse (unless the spouse had waived survivor benefit entitlement) and, where applicable, payable to a named person with an insurable interest.

Annuity Eligibility Requirements

L-33. Who is eligible for a survivor annuity?

Employee's Spouse. In order for the surviving spouse to qualify for a survivor annuity:

(1) The spouse must have been married to the employee for at least nine months before death, or

(2) The spouse must be the parent of the deceased's child born of the marriage.

However, these requirements are waived where: (1) the employee dies as a result of an accident, or (2) the employee had previously married and subsequently divorced the surviving spouse, and the aggregate time married is at least nine months.

Employee's Child. Generally, for a deceased employee's child to qualify for the survivor annuity, the child must be unmarried, under 18 years of age, and a dependent of the employee. The following rules also apply:

(1) An adopted child is considered to be the employee's child.

(2) A stepchild is considered to be the employee's child even if the child did not live with the deceased employee. An illegitimate child, however, must prove he was dependent upon the deceased employee.

(3) An illegitimate child is considered to be the employee's child even if the child did not live with the deceased employee. An illegitimate child, however, must prove he was dependent upon the deceased employee.

(4) A child who lived with the employee and for whom the employee had filed an adoption petition is considered to be the employee's child, but only where the surviving spouse did in fact adopt the child following the employee's death.

Notwithstanding the age requirement above, each of the following persons is considered to be a child for purposes of the survivorship annuity:

(1) An unmarried dependent child, regardless of age, who is incapable of self-support because of a mental or physical disability incurred before age 18.

(2) An unmarried dependent child between 18 and 22 who is a "student" (pursuing a full-time course of study or training in residence in a high school, trade school, college, university, or comparable recognized educational institution.

Benefits for a child end upon marriage. However, annuity payments restart again if the child's marriage has ended and he or she is still eligible for benefits because of disability or enrollment as a full-time student while under age 22. If a child's marriage ends because of divorce or death, the child's annuity and health benefits coverage is restored beginning the first day of the month in which dissolution of the marriage occurs.

Computing The Survivor Annuity

L-34. How do you compute the survivor annuity?

If an employee dies after completing at least 18 months of civilian service, there is a guaranteed minimum survivor annuity based upon the employee's average pay over the total civilian service. The annuity, however, is at least 55% of the smaller of: (1) 40% of the deceased employee's "high-3" average pay, or (2) the regular computation obtained after increasing service by the period of time between the date of death and the date the employee would have become age 60.

This guaranteed minimum does not apply if 55% of the employee's earned annuity produces a higher benefit than the guaranteed minimum. Also, since active service cannot be projected beyond age 60 in any case, the guaranteed minimum does not apply where the employee dies after reaching age 60.

Where an employee is survived by a spouse and is survived by children who qualify for survivor benefits, each surviving child is entitled to a benefit equal to whichever of the following amounts is the least: (1) 60% of the employee's high-3 average pay, divided by the number of qualified children, (2) $1,107 per month, divided by the number of qualified children, or (3) $369 per month.

When an employee leaves no surviving spouse but leaves children who qualify for survivor benefits, each child will be paid the least of: (1) 75% of the employee's high-3 average pay, divided by the number of qualified children, (2) $1,326 per month, divided by the number of qualified children, or (3) $442 per month.

A child's annuity begins on the day after the employee or annuitant dies and continues until the last day of the month before the child marries, dies or reaches age 18, except in the following cases:

(1) For a child age 18 or over who is incapable of self-support because of a disability which began before age 18, payments stop at the end of the month before the child becomes capable of self-support, marries or dies.

(2) The annuity of a student age 18 or over stops at the end of the month before the child ceases to be a student, reaches age 22, marries, or dies, whichever occurs first.

Lump-Sum Death Benefit

L-35. When does the lump-sum death benefit become payable?

The lump-sum death benefit becomes payable to the estate of the proper party where the employee dies:

(1) without a survivor, or

(2) with a survivor, but the survivor's right to an annuity terminates before a claim for a survivor annuity has been filed.

The lump-sum benefit consists of the amount paid into the Civil Service Retirement and Disability Fund by the employee, plus any accrued interest.

If all rights to a CSRS annuity cease before the total annuity paid equals the lump-sum credit, the difference between the lump-sum credit and the total annuity paid becomes payable to the estate of the proper party. Thus, if an employee leaves a spouse or children who are eligible for a survivor annuity, a lump-sum death benefit may be payable after all survivors' annuities have been paid. The lump-sum benefit would consist of that portion of the employee's lump-sum credit which has not been exhausted by the annuity payments to survivors.

Annuity Payments

L-36. How are annuity payments made?

Annuities are paid by monthly check. The Office of Personnel Management authorizes the payment, and the Treasury Department issues the check. After the initial check, each regular check is dated the first workday of the month after the month for which the annuity is due. For example, the annuity payment for the month of April will be made by a check dated May 1.

An employee annuity begins on the first day of the month after: (1) separation from the service, or (2) pay ceases and the service and age requirements for entitlement to an annuity are met. Any other annuity payable begins on the first day of the month after the occurrence of the event on which payment is based.

Disability Retirement

L-37. When is an annuity payable for disability retirement?

An immediate annuity is payable to an employee for disability retirement when each of the following conditions are met:

(1) The employee has completed five years of civilian service.

(2) The employee has become totally disabled for useful and efficient service in the position occupied, or the duties of a similar position at the same grade or level.

A claim for disability retirement must be filed with the Office of Personnel Management before separation from the service or within one year thereafter. The one-year requirement may be waived in cases of incompetency.

The annuity payable will be the earned annuity based on the high-3 average salary, the years of actual service, and the three-part formula (see L-28), but not less than: (1) 40% of the high-3 average salary, or (2) the amount computed under the general formula after adding to years of actual service the number of years he is under age 60 on the date of separation.

Unless the disability is permanent in nature, an employee receiving a disability retirement annuity must be medically examined annually until age 60. The Government pays for the examination.

Upon recovery before reaching age 60, the annuity is continued temporarily (not to exceed one year) to give the individual an opportunity to find a position. If reemployed in Government service within the year, the annuity stops on reemployment. If the individual is not reemployed, the annuity stops at the expiration of the 180 day period.

Cost-of-Living Adjustments

L-38. Is there a cost-of-living adjustment to CSRS annuities?

Annuities for retirees and survivors are subject to a cost-of-living adjustment in December of each year. The increases are reflected in the annuity payment received the following month. The percentage of the cost-of-living increase each year is determined by the average price index for the third quarter of each year over the third quarter average of the Consumer Price Index for Urban Wage Earners and Clerical Workers of the previous year.

Annuitants receive a 3.5% cost-of-living adjustment in 2001.

Refund Of Contributions

L-39. Is there a refund of contributions if an employee leaves government service?

Yes, an employee who leaves government service or transfers to government work under another retirement system may withdraw his retirement lump-sum credit (contributions plus any interest payable) so long as the employee: (1) is separated from the job for at least 31 consecutive days, (2) is transferred to a position that is not subject to CSRS or FERS and remains in that position for at least 31 consecutive days, (3) files an application for a refund of retirement deductions, (4) is not reemployed in a position subject to CSRS or

FERS at the time the application is filed, *and* (5) will not become eligible to receive an annuity within 31 days after filing the application.

LIFE INSURANCE BENEFITS

L-40. In general, what life insurance benefits are available to federal civil service employees?

All federal civil service employees — whether CSRS or FERS members — and employees of the District of Columbia are automatically insured under the provisions of a group policy purchased by the U.S. Office of Personnel Management.

Basic insurance coverage may be declined by written notice only. If coverage has been declined, the employee cannot obtain coverage for at least one year and then only if the applicant is in good health. Special rules apply if the employee has experienced a break in service of at least 180 days. Under this exception, all previous waivers of life insurance coverage are canceled, but any of the optional coverages must be affirmatively elected within 31 days after the employee's return. Each insured receives a certificate setting forth the group insurance benefits, to whom benefits are payable, to whom claims are submitted, and summarizing the provisions of the policy. The group insurance is underwritten by a large number of private insurance companies and claims are settled by the Office of Federal Employees' Group Life Insurance, 200 Park Avenue, New York, N.Y. 10166-0188.

Group insurance includes: (1) group term life coverage without a medical examination, and (2) accidental death and dismemberment insurance protection. The amount of each type of insurance is based on the employee's "basic insurance amount," which is determined by rounding the employee's annual salary to the next higher multiple of $1,000 and adding $2,000. However, in no case may the basic insurance amount be less than $10,000.

The group accidental death and dismemberment insurance provides payment for: (1) loss of life or loss of two or more members, and (2) loss of one hand or one foot or for permanent and total loss of sight in one eye. The accidental death benefit equals the employee's basic insurance amount and is paid in addition to the group life insurance.

An insured individual who is certified by a doctor as terminally ill may elect to receive a lump-sum payment of Basic Insurance. Optional insurance is not available for payment as a Living Benefit. The effective date of a Living Benefit election is the date on which the Living Benefit payment is cased or deposited. Once an election becomes effective, it can't be revoked. No further election of Living Benefits can be made. If the insured individual has assigned his insurance, he cannot elect a Living Benefit; nor can an assignee elect a

Living Benefit on behalf of an insured individual. If an individual has elected a Living Benefit, he may assign his remaining insurance. An individual may elect to receive either a full Living Benefit (all of the Basic Insurance) or a partial Living Benefit (a portion of the Basic Insurance, in a multiple of $1,000). The amount of Basic Insurance elected as a Living Benefit will be reduced by an actuarial amount representing the amount of interest lost to the fund because of the early payment of benefits.

An individual may assign ownership of all life insurance, except Option C (which covers family members). If an individual wishing to make an assignment owns more than one type of coverage, he must assign all the insurance; an individual cannot assign only a portion of the coverage. Option C cannot be assigned. If the insurance is assigned to two or more individuals, corporations, or trustees, the insured individual must specify percentage shares, rather than dollar amounts or types of insurance, to go to each assignee.

L-41. How does an employee designate the beneficiary or beneficiaries?

An employee's designation of beneficiary or beneficiaries is made in a signed and witnessed writing which is received before the employee's death by his employing office. If no beneficiary is designated when the employee dies, payment is made in the following order: to the employee's widow or widower; or, if none, to the child or children of the employee in equal shares and descendants of deceased children by representation; or, if none, to the parents of the employee in equal shares or the entire amount to the surviving parent; or, if none, to the duly appointed executor or administrator of the employee; or, if none, to the next of kin of the employee under the law of the employee's domicile at the time of death.

Beneficiaries receiving insurance proceeds in excess of $7,500 receive a money market account instead of a check from the government. Beneficiaries entitled to less than $7,500 receive a single check from the government for the full amount of insurance coverage. Insurance proceeds earn interest in the money market account. Beneficiaries receive special checkbooks and can write checks on the money market account for $250 up to the full amount of the insurance payment.

L-42. When does insurance coverage cease?

Subject to the exceptions below, an employee's group insurance coverage ceases on the earliest of: (1) the date of separation from the service, (2) the date on which a period of 12 months of continuous non-pay status ends, or (3) the date of any other change in employment which results in the employee's ineligibility for insurance coverage. In addition, coverage may be terminated at the end of the pay period in which it is determined that periodic pay, after all other deductions, is insufficient to cover the required withholdings (such as court-ordered child support) to a point at which deductions for federal employee group life insurance cannot be made.

An exception to the termination rule occurs where: (1) the employee retires on an immediate annuity, or (2) the employee becomes entitled to workers' compensation.

An employee who does not want insurance may waive group insurance coverage. In such a case, coverage ceases on the last day of the pay period in which the agency receives the employee's waiver of coverage.

L-43. Can an employee convert to an individual policy?

If coverage ceases as a result of one of the occurrences described in L-42 above, the employee may apply for an individual life insurance policy. The employee's coverage may not exceed the amount for which he was insured at the time of the terminating event. The conversion excludes the Option C coverage. (See L-45.)

The employee's request for conversion information must be submitted to the Office of Federal Employee's Group Life Insurance and postmarked within 31 days following the date of the terminating event or within 31 days of the date the employee received notice of loss of the group coverage and right to convert, whichever is later. Detailed information concerning how to apply for the policy may be obtained from the Office of Federal Employees' Group Life Insurance, 200 Park Avenue, New York, N.Y. 10166-0188.

L-44. What is the cost of basic insurance?

The employee pays two-thirds, by means of salary withholding, of the cost of that amount of group term life and accidental death and dismemberment which equals his basic insurance amount. The cost of the additional group term life (i.e., that amount in excess of his basic insurance amount) is paid entirely by the government. Thus, the amount withheld from the bi-weekly pay of an employee is 15.5 cents for each $1,000 of his basic insurance amount. The amount withheld from the pay of an employee who is paid on other than a bi-weekly basis is determined at a proportionate rate, adjusted to the nearest cent. The following table shows the amount withheld from pay to meet the employees' share of the cost.

INSURANCE WITHHOLDINGS

Amount of Withholdings Per Pay Period

Basic Insurance Amount*	Biweekly	Semimonthly	Monthly
$18,000	$2.79	$3.02	$6.05
$19,000	$2.95	$3.19	$6.38
$20,000	$3.10	$3.36	$6.72
$21,000	$3.26	$3.53	$7.05
$22,000	$3.41	$3.69	$7.39
$23,000	$3.57	$3.86	$7.72
$24,000	$3.72	$4.03	$8.06
$25,000	$3.88	$4.20	$8.40
$26,000	$4.03	$4.37	$8.73
$27,000	$4.19	$4.53	$9.07
$28,000	$4.34	$4.70	$9.40
$29,000	$4.50	$4.87	$9.74
$30,000	$4.65	$5.04	$10.08
$31,000	$4.81	$5.21	$10.41
$32,000	$4.96	$5.37	$10.75
$33,000	$5.12	$5.54	$11.08
$34,000	$5.27	$5.71	$11.42
$35,000	$5.43	$5.88	$11.75
$36,000	$5.58	$6.05	$12.09
$37,000	$5.74	$6.21	$12.43
$38,000	$5.89	$6.38	$12.76
$39,000	$6.05	$6.55	$13.10
$40,000	$6.20	$6.72	$13.43
$41,000	$6.36	$6.88	$13.77
$42,000	$6.51	$7.05	$14.11
$43,000	$6.67	$7.22	$14.44
$44,000	$6.82	$7.39	$14.78
$45,000	$6.98	$7.56	$15.11
$46,000	$7.13	$7.72	$15.45
$47,000	$7.29	$7.89	$15.78
$48,000	$7.44	$8.06	$16.12
$49,000	$7.60	$8.23	$16.46
$50,000	$7.75	$8.40	$16.79
$51,000	$7.91	$8.56	$17.13
$52,000	$8.06	$8.73	$17.46
$53,000	$8.22	$8.90	$17.80
$54,000	$8.37	$9.07	$18.14
$55,000	$8.53	$9.24	$18.47
$56,000	$8.68	$9.40	$18.81
$57,000	$8.84	$9.57	$19.14
$58,000	$8.99	$9.74	$19.48
$59,000	$9.15	$9.91	$19.81
$60,000	$9.30	$10.08	$20.15
$61,000	$9.46	$10.24	$20.49
$62,000	$9.61	$10.41	$20.82
$63,000	$9.77	$10.58	$21.16

INSURANCE WITHHOLDINGS (continued)

Amount of Withholdings Per Pay Period

Basic Insurance Amount*	Biweekly	Semimonthly	Monthly
$64,000	$9.92	$10.75	$21.49
$65,000	$10.08	$10.91	$21.83
$66,000	$10.23	$11.08	$22.17
$67,000	$10.39	$11.25	$22.50
$68,000	$10.54	$11.42	$22.84
$69,000	$10.70	$11.59	$23.17
$70,000	$10.85	$11.75	$23.51
$71,000	$11.01	$11.92	$23.84
$72,000	$11.16	$12.09	$24.18
$73,000	$11.32	$12.26	$24.52
$74,000	$11.47	$12.43	$24.85
$75,000	$11.63	$12.59	$25.19
$76,000	$11.78	$12.76	$25.52
$77,000	$11.94	$12.93	$25.86
$78,000	$12.09	$13.10	$26.20
$79,000	$12.25	$13.27	$26.53
$80,000	$12.40	$13.43	$26.87
$81,000	$12.56	$13.60	$27.20
$82,000	$12.71	$13.77	$27.54
$83,000	$12.87	$13.94	$27.87
$84,000	$13.02	$14.11	$28.21
$85,000	$13.18	$14.27	$28.55
$86,000	$13.33	$14.44	$28.88
$87,000	$13.49	$14.61	$29.22
$88,000	$13.64	$14.78	$29.55
$89,000	$13.80	$14.94	$29.89
$90,000	$13.95	$15.11	$30.23
$91,000	$14.11	$15.28	$30.56
$92,000	$14.26	$15.45	$30.90
$93,000	$14.42	$15.62	$31.23
$94,000	$14.57	$15.78	$31.57
$95,000	$14.73	$15.95	$31.90
$96,000	$14.88	$16.12	$32.24
$97,000	$15.04	$16.29	$32.58
$98,000	$15.19	$16.46	$32.91
$99,000	$15.35	$16.62	$33.25
$100,000	$15.50	$16.79	$33.58
$101,000	$15.66	$16.96	$33.92
$102,000	$15.81	$17.13	$34.26
$103,000	$15.97	$17.30	$34.59
$104,000	$16.12	$17.46	$34.93
$105,000	$16.28	$17.63	$35.26
$106,000	$16.43	$17.80	$35.60
$107,000	$16.59	$17.97	$35.93
$108,000	$16.74	$18.14	$36.27
$109,000	$16.90	$18.30	$36.61
$110,000	$17.05	$18.47	$36.94

INSURANCE WITHHOLDINGS (continued)

Amount of Withholdings Per Pay Period

Basic Insurance Amount*	Biweekly	Semimonthly	Monthly
$111,000	$17.21	$18.64	$37.28
$112,000	$17.36	$18.81	$37.61
$113,000	$17.52	$18.97	$37.95
$114,000	$17.67	$19.14	$38.29
$115,000	$17.83	$19.31	$38.62
$116,000	$17.98	$19.48	$38.96
$117,000	$18.14	$19.65	$39.29
$118,000	$18.29	$19.81	$39.63
$119,000	$18.45	$19.98	$39.96
$120,000	$18.60	$20.15	$40.30
$121,000	$18.76	$20.32	$40.64
$122,000	$18.91	$20.49	$40.97
$123,000	$19.07	$20.65	$41.31
$124,000	$19.22	$20.82	$41.64
$125,000	$19.38	$20.99	$41.98
$126,000	$19.53	$21.16	$42.32
$127,000	$19.69	$21.33	$42.65
$128,000	$19.84	$21.49	$42.99
$129,000	$20.00	$21.66	$43.32
$130,000	$20.15	$21.83	$43.66
$131,000	$20.31	$22.00	$43.99
$132,000	$20.46	$22.17	$44.33
$133,000	$20.62	$22.33	$44.67
$134,000	$20.77	$22.50	$45.00
$135,000	$20.93	$22.67	$45.34
$136,000	$21.08	$22.84	$45.67
$137,000	$21.24	$23.00	$46.01
$138,000	$21.39	$23.17	$46.35
$139,000	$21.55	$23.34	$46.68
$140,000	$21.70	$23.51	$47.02

L-45. What optional insurance coverages are available to the civil service employee?

Optional insurance coverages currently available include: (1) optional life insurance (termed Option A — Standard Insurance), (2) additional optional life insurance (Option B — Additional Insurance), and (3) optional life insurance on family members (Option C — Family Coverage). Beneficiary provisions for optional insurances on the life of the employee are the same as for basic (regular) insurance.

Option A — Standard Insurance

Employees covered under the basic life insurance program may purchase $10,000 of optional group term life insurance. This coverage includes accidental death and dismemberment.

The premium is paid entirely by the employee through withholding, and the bi-weekly cost is as follows:

Age Group	Withholding for $10,000 Insurance Biweekly	Monthly
Under age 35	$ .30	$ .65
35 through 39	.40	.87
40 through 44	.60	1.30
45 through 49	.90	1.95
50 through 54	1.40	3.03
55 through 59	2.70	5.85
60 and over	6.00	13.00

Where Option A insurance has been declined, the employee is eligible to enroll for this coverage only by meeting the two requirements for canceling a waiver of basic life insurance. Neither a retiree nor an employee receiving basic life insurance while receiving workers' compensation may cancel a previous declination of Option A — Standard.

Option B — Additional Optional Insurance

An employee with basic life insurance may purchase Option B — additional optional life insurance on himself — without regard to whether he has purchased Option A insurance.

The cost of Option B insurance, like Option A, is paid entirely by the employee through withholdings. The bi-weekly rates per $1,000 of coverage are as follows:

Age Group	Withholding per $1,000 Insurance Biweekly	Monthly
Under age 35	$ .03	$ .065
35 through 39	.04	.087
40 through 44	.06	.130
45 through 49	.10	.217
50 through 54	.15	.325
55 through 59	.31	.672
60 and over	.70	1.517

Retiring employees or compensationers may elect to continue Option B coverage on an unreduced basis by continuing to pay premiums after age 65. Annuitants and compensationers who elect unreduced Option B may later cancel that election and have the full reduction. Annuitants and compensationers who had Option B coverage on a reduction schedule as of October 30, 1998, were offered the opportunity to elect an unreduced schedule on a prospective basis.

Option C — Family Coverage

Option C — life insurance coverage on the life of spouse and dependents — is available in either one, two, three, four, or five multiples of coverage. One multiple is equal to $5,000 for a spouse and $2,500 for each dependent child. The cost of this insurance is paid entirely by the employee through withholding. The bi-weekly rates for coverage of the spouse and child (or children) are as follows:

Age of Employee	Withholding per Multiple Biweekly	Monthly
Under age 35	$ .27	$ .59
35 through 39	.34	.74
40 through 44	.46	1.00
45 through 49	.60	1.30
50 through 54	.90	1.95
55 through 59	1.45	3.14
60 through 64	2.60	5.63
65 through 69	3.00	6.50
70 and over	3.40	7.37

Retiring employees may choose to elect unreduced Option C coverage by continuing to pay premiums after age 65. Annuitants and compensationers who elect unreduced Option C may later cancel that election and have the full reduction.

Foster children are covered under Option C. Dependency of the foster child must be established before the child is approved for coverage under Option C.

L-46. May a retiring employee continue life insurance coverage?

With respect to basic (regular) life insurance, an employee who retires on an immediate annuity may continue his basic life insurance (excluding accidental death and dismemberment) so long as he satisfies the "five or less five" rule. This requires that the retiree be insured either: (1) through the five years of service immediately preceding his retirement, or (2) if less than five years, then throughout the period or periods of service during which he was entitled to coverage. An additional requirement for continuing basic insurance is that the employee may not have converted the policy to an individual life policy.

The retiring employee's basic life options are as follows:

Election	Monthly Cost
1. 75% REDUCTION — Amount of insurance reduces 2% per month after age 65 to a minimum of 25% of Basic Insurance Amount at retirement.	No Cost
2. 50% REDUCTION — Amount of insurance reduces 1% per month after age 65 to a minimum of 50% of Basic Insurance Amount at retirement.	$.59 per $1,000* *of Basic Insurance Amount at retirement
3. NO REDUCTION — 100% of Basic Insurance Amount at retirement is retained after age 65.	$2.04 per $1,000* *of Basic Insurance Amount at retirement

Where the employee chooses the 75% Reduction and retired before December 31, 1989, there is no cost to the individual after retirement, regardless of age. If the employee retires after December 31, 1989 and elects the 75% Reduction, the life insurance withholdings will be at the same rate to age 65 as for active employees and withholdings will be deducted from his annuity. After the individual reaches age 65, withholdings will stop.

Where the employee chooses the 50% Reduction or No Reduction, the full cost of the additional protection is deducted from the retiree's monthly annuity check. The withholdings begin at retirement and continue for life or until the election is canceled or coverage is otherwise discontinued.

Where the employee elected Option A — Standard Insurance, the retiree may continue the insurance so long as it was in force during the "five or less than five" period explained earlier. The cost of the Option A life insurance will be withheld from the annuity until the end of the calendar month in which he attains age 65. After that time the Option A life insurance will be continued without cost to the retiree.

Option A life insurance, in all cases, is subject to a reduction of 2% at the end of each full calendar month following the date on which the employee attains age 65 or retires, whichever occurs later. These reductions continue until a minimum (but in no event less than 25% of the amount of Option A life in force before the first reduction) is reached.

An employee who retires on an immediate annuity may continue the amount of Option B — Additional Life Insurance so long as it was in force for the required "five or less than five" period explained above. The full cost of

264

the Option B life that is continued will be withheld from the retiree's annuity until the calendar month in which the retiree attains age 65. Beginning with the end of that calendar month, Option B life insurance will be continued without cost to the retiree. The amount of Option B life insurance is subject to a reduction of 2% each month beginning with the second calendar month after the date on which the employee attains age 65 or retires, whichever occurs later. These reductions continue for 50 months at which time the Option B life coverage ends.

Retiring employees or compensationers may elect to continue Option B coverage on an unreduced basis by continuing to pay premiums after age 65. Annuitants and compensationers who elect unreduced Option B may later cancel that election and have the full reduction. Annuitants and compensationers who have Option B coverage on a reduction schedule will be offered the opportunity to elect an unreduced schedule on a prospective basis.

An employee who retires on an immediate annuity may continue his Option C — Family Coverage that was in force during the "five or less than five" period. The full cost of the optional family coverage which is continued will be withheld from the retiree's annuity until the calendar month in which the retiree attains age 65. Beginning with the end of that calendar month, the optional family life coverage will be continued without cost to the retiree. Optional family life coverage which is continued after retirement is subject to the same method of reduction as is the additional optional life insurance (see above). Thus, coverage of optional family life will end following the expiration of the same 50 months.

Retiring employees may choose to elect unreduced Option C coverage by continuing to pay premiums after age 65. Annuitants and compensationers who elect unreduced Option C may later cancel that election and have the full reduction.

A recipient of federal workers' compensation avoids a termination of federal employee group life insurance so long as he has met the "five or less than five" rule. This rule applies to basic life insurance as well as any of the optional coverages. No accidental death and dismemberment insurance is available to the workers' compensation recipient.

BENEFITS FOR SERVICEMEMBERS AND VETERANS

MILITARY RETIREMENT

M-1. In general, who is entitled to military retirement benefits?

Members of the armed forces may retire after a certain amount of active service. Monthly retirement pay is based on a percentage of base pay of the highest rank held, as well as number of years of service.

Servicemembers who become disabled while in service may be placed on either temporary or permanent disability retirement, depending on the degree and length of disability, and also on whether they satisfy certain other conditions of eligibility.

Reservists are entitled to receive retirement benefits if they meet certain eligibility requirements.

All benefit payments to veterans, their dependents, and survivors are electronically deposited into their bank accounts.

M-2. What retirement benefits are available for those who first became members before August 1, 1986?

An immediate annuity is available to a servicemember who completes 20 years of service. No benefit is available to a servicemember who does not complete 20 years of service.

The retirement annuity is based in part on the servicemember's retirement "pay base," as well as the date on which the individual became a member of the uniformed service.

For those becoming members of a uniformed service for the first time *on or before September 7, 1980*, the retired pay base equals the servicemember's final monthly basic pay to which he was entitled the day before retirement.

For persons becoming members of a uniformed service for the first time *after September 7, 1980*, the monthly retired pay base is one thirty-sixth of the total amount of the monthly basic pay which the servicemember received for the highest thirty-six months (whether or not consecutive) of active duty.

In order to compute the monthly retirement benefit, the monthly retired pay base is multiplied by an amount equaling 2.5% for each year of service up to a maximum of thirty years. The benefits range from 50% at 20 years of service to 75% at 30 or more years of service.

Retired pay is adjusted annually by the increase in the cost-of-living as measured by the Consumer Price Index for All Urban Wage Earners and Clerical Workers (CPI).

The uniformed services retirement system is noncontributory. However, the servicemember contributes, while on active duty, to the Social Security system and, thereby, earns eligibility for a Social Security retirement benefit.

M-3. What is the retirement system for those who first become members on or after August 1, 1986?

Under the Military Retirement Reform Act of 1986, anyone who becomes a member of a uniformed service on or after August 1, 1986 is subject to a new retirement system.

The average monthly basic pay for the highest three years of pay during service becomes the pay base for servicemembers. This is known as "high-3." The multiplier, or percentage, for each year of service which is multiplied by the pay base, remains unchanged at 2.5% for each year of service. The maximum number of years creditable toward retirement is 30 — or 75% of pay base.

Under this system, where the servicemember has retired and has completed fewer than 30 years of service, the percent reached above is reduced by one percentage point for each year between 30 years and the number of years completed.

This means that a 20-year retiree will receive 40% of the pay base, as opposed to 50% under the system for those who became servicemembers before August 1, 1986. A 30-year retiree, however, will receive the full 75% of the pay base, the same as under the old system.

Years of Service	Multiplier	
	Before 62	After 62
20	40.0	50.0
21	43.5	52.5
22	47.0	55.0
23	50.5	57.5
24	54.0	60.0
25	57.5	62.5
26	61.0	65.0
27	64.5	67.5
28	68.0	70.0
29	71.5	72.5
30	75.0	75.0

Cost-of-living adjustments to retirement benefits are guaranteed in years of inflation. Annual benefit increases will equal the increase in the Consumer Price Index (CPI), less one percentage point. This formula is known as "CPI Minus 1."

There is a one-time recomputation of retirement pay at age 62 in recognition of the fact that at about age 62 military retirement pay becomes the primary source of retirement income for career military personnel. At the point when a retiree reaches age 62, retirement pay is recomputed as if the one percentage point penalty for retirement at less than 30 years of service had not been applied. Additionally, at the same time, the retirement pay is increased to the level it would have reached if cost-of-living adjustments had been made under the full CPI rather than the "CPI Minus 1" formula.

In short, at age 62, the level of military retirement pay is restored to the level at which it would have been under the law for military members who entered the service prior to August 1, 1986. Note, however, that all cost-of-living adjustments after age 62 are under the "CPI Minus 1" formula. Thus, military retirees will lose 1% to inflation each year after age 62.

A servicemember retiring after 30 years of service will receive 75% of basic pay both before and after age 62. His retirement pay will be affected only by the change in the cost-of-living adjustment formula.

Survivor Annuity

M-4. What is the Survivor Benefit Plan?

The Survivor Benefit Plan provides survivor benefits for eligible widows, widowers and dependent children of eligible military personnel. Benefits are essentially the same as those provided federal government employees.

Those eligible to participate in the Survivor Benefit Plan (SBP) must be: (1) entitled to retired or retainer pay, or (2) eligible for retired pay but for the fact that they are under 60 years of age. The standard annuity is paid to those entitled to retired or retainer pay. The reserve-component annuity is paid to those who are eligible but under age 60. If a person entitled to retired or retainer pay is married or has a dependent child, he is automatically covered by the SBP *with maximum coverage* unless he elects lessor coverage or declines participation before the first day he becomes eligible for the retired or retainer pay. Unmarried service personnel who have no dependent children may elect a survivor annuity in favor of someone who has an insurable interest in their life. Retired pay is, of course, reduced for Plan participants.

A retiree who has a spouse and a child (or children) at retirement may elect survivor benefits for the *spouse only* or for the *child (or children) only*. Absent some election, coverage for both the spouse and child (or children) is automatic. The spouse must concur in: (1) an election not to participate in the plan, (2) an election to provide the spouse with an annuity at less than the maximum level, and (3) an election to provide an annuity for a dependent child but not the spouse.

An election not to participate in the Plan by a person eligible for retired pay is irrevocable unless revoked before the date on which the person first becomes entitled to that pay. An election by a person under age 60 not to participate in the Plan becomes irrevocable if not revoked by the end of the 90-day period beginning on the date he receives notification that he has completed the required years of service.

M-5. Who is eligible to receive Survivor Benefit Plan benefits?

The Survivor Benefit Plan provides a monthly annuity payment effective the first day after the death of the retiree. The annuity is paid to one of the following:

- The eligible surviving widow or widower;

- The surviving dependent children in equal shares, if the eligible widow or widower or eligible former spouse is dead, dies, or otherwise becomes ineligible;

- The dependent children in equal shares if the retiree elected to provide an annuity for dependent children but not for the spouse or former spouse; or

- The former spouse under certain conditions.

The following criteria apply for the purposes of determining eligible beneficiaries:

- A *widow* is the surviving wife of a person who, if not married to the retiree at the time he became eligible for retired pay, was married to him for at least one year immediately before his death, or is the mother of issue by that marriage.

- A *widower* is the surviving husband of a retiree who, if not married to the person at the time she became eligible for retired pay, was married to her for at least one year immediately before her death, or is the father of issue by that marriage.

- A *former spouse* is the surviving former husband or wife of a person who is eligible to participate in the Plan.

- A *dependent child* is a person who is: (1) unmarried, (2) under 18 years of age; or at least 18, but under 22 years of age, and pursuing a full-time course of study or training in a high school, vocational school or college; or incapable of self-support because of a mental or physical incapability existing before age 18 or incurred on or after that birthday, but before age 22, while pursuing such a full-time course of study or training, (3) the child of a retiring participant, including an adopted child, a step-child, foster child, or recognized natural child who lived with the retiree in a regular parent-child relationship.

- A *person with an insurable interest* is any person who has a bona fide financial interest in the continued life of the retiree. The relationship of the person to the retiree normally does not extend beyond the mother, father, brother, sister or single child of the retiree.

The annuity payable to a surviving spouse of the retiree is paid for life, except that if the annuitant remarries before age 55, the remarriage terminates the annuity. If the remarriage is terminated by death, annulment or divorce, payment of the annuity is resumed upon the termination of the remarriage.

M-6. What is the amount of the Survivor Benefit Plan annuity?

The amount of a Survivor Benefit Plan annuity payable to a widow, widower, former eligible spouse or dependent children is based on a figure known as the *base amount*. The base amount is: (1) the amount of monthly retired pay to which a retiree became entitled when first eligible or later became entitled to by being advanced on the retired list, performing active duty, or being transferred from the temporary disability retired list to the permanent disability retired list, or (2) any lesser amount designated by the retiree on or before the first day of eligibility for retired pay, but not less than $300.

A retiree who wants maximum survivor benefits for a spouse and children (at the cost of maximum reduction in retirement pay), will designate as the base amount on which survivor benefits are figured the full amount of retired pay. For a lower level of survivor benefits (in exchange for a smaller reduction in retirement pay), a base amount less than full retirement pay will be designated.

The following are categories of dependents and the rules for determining the amount of annuity payable:

(1) In the case of a standard annuity for a widow, widower or child, the monthly annuity is an amount equal to 55% of the base amount, if the beneficiary is under 62 years of age or is a dependent child when becoming entitled to the annuity. If the beneficiary (other than a dependent child) is 62 years of age or older when becoming entitled to

the annuity, the monthly annuity is an amount equal to 35% of the base amount.

(2) In the case of a standard annuity for an ex-spouse or person with an insurable interest in the annuitant (other than a widow, widower or dependent child), the monthly annuity payable to the beneficiary is an amount equal to 55% of the retired pay of the person who elected to provide the annuity.

(3) An annuity is also payable to a surviving spouse of a member who dies on active duty after: (a) becoming eligible to receive retired pay, (b) qualifying for retired pay except that he has not applied for or been granted that pay, or (c) completing 20 years of active service but before he is eligible to retire as a commissioned officer because he has not completed 10 years of active commissioned service. An annuity is payable to the dependent child of the servicemember if there is no surviving spouse or if the servicemember's surviving spouse subsequently dies.

If a person receiving an annuity in (3) above is under 62 or is a dependent child when the servicemember or former servicemember dies, the monthly annuity is an amount equal to 55% of the retired pay to which the servicemember or former servicemember would have been entitled if the servicemember or former servicemember had been entitled to that pay based upon his years of active service when he died.

If a person receiving an annuity in (3) above (other than a dependent child) is 62 or older when the servicemember or former servicemember dies, the monthly annuity is an amount equal to 35% of the retired pay to which the servicemember or former servicemember would have been entitled if the servicemember or former servicemember had been entitled to that pay based upon his years of active service when he died.

M-7. Are Survivor Benefit Plan annuities subject to cost-of-living increases?

Whenever retirees receive a cost-of-living increase in their retired pay, Survivor Benefit Plan annuities are increased at the same time by the same total percent. The percentage is applied to the monthly annuity payable before any reduction is made in consideration of the annuitant's eligibility for Dependency and Indemnity Compensation or Social Security survivor benefits.

M-8. How does the Survivor Benefit Plan reduce the regular retirement annuity?

The Survivor Benefit Plan reduces the regular retirement annuity according to the following formulas:

Where the individual first becomes a member of the uniformed service before March 1, 1990, the reduction is the lesser of:

(1) an amount equal to 2.5% of the first $364 of the base amount of the annuity subject to the survivor benefit, plus 10% of the remainder, or

(2) an amount equal to 6.5% of the base amount of the annuity subject to the survivor benefit.

Where the individual first becomes a member of the uniformed service on or after March 1, 1990, the reduction for the Survivor Benefit Plan is a flat 6.5% of the base amount of the annuity.

"Base amount" does not include cost-of-living increases.

Disability Retirement

M-9. When is a servicemember entitled to retire on permanent disability?

When he has been called or ordered to active duty for a period of more than 30 days (excluding Ready Reserve training duty), and:

(1) He is unfit to perform his duties because he has incurred a physical disability while entitled to basic pay;

(2) The disability is of a permanent and stable nature based on commonly accepted medical principles;

(3) The disability is not due to intentional or willful neglect, and not incurred during a period of unauthorized absence; and

(4) One of the following applies: (a) the disability is rated at least 30% under the Department of Veterans Affairs disability rating schedule, or (b) the servicemember has completed at least 20 years of service.

Where the servicemember has not completed 20 years of service but has a disability of at least 30% as explained in (a) above, one of the following tests must additionally be satisfied:

(1) The disability must be incurred in the line of duty.

(2) The disability must be the proximate result of performing active duty.

273

(3) The servicemember must have completed at least eight years of service.

Where the active-duty or inactive training period is 30 days or less, a regular servicemember or reservist is entitled to permanent disability based on *injury* where the following conditions are met:

(1) He is unfit to perform his duties because he has incurred a physical disability while entitled to basic pay;

(2) The disability is of a permanent and stable nature based on commonly accepted medical principles;

(3) The disability is the proximate result of performing active duty or inactive training;

(4) The disability is not due to intentional misconduct or willful neglect, and not incurred during a period of unauthorized absence; and

(5) One of the following applies: (a) the disability is rated at least 30% under the Department of Veterans Affairs disability rating schedule, or (b) the servicemember has completed at least 20 years of service.

M-10. How is disability retirement pay determined?

Disability retirement pay is figured by either of two methods, at the retiree's option, up to a maximum of 75% of basic pay: (1) 2.5% of monthly basic pay multiplied by the number of years of active service, or (2) the percentage rating of disability.

A servicemember who meets the requirements of temporary disability may be placed on temporary disability retirement for up to five years. Retired pay for temporary disability is no less than 50% of basic pay. A servicemember will be permanently retired for physical disability if still disabled after five years.

Social Security

M-11. Are servicemembers entitled to Social Security benefits in addition to military benefits?

Servicemembers are entitled to Social Security retirement, disability and survivor benefits in addition to military benefits. Beginning in 1957, they are credited with an additional $300 for each calendar quarter when calculating their Average Indexed Monthly Earnings (AIMEs) for determining Social Security benefits. This is done as an allowance for the value of quarters and subsistence.

Reservists' Retirement Pay

M-12. Are Reservists entitled to retired pay?

To qualify for retired pay in the Reserves, a person must complete at least 20 years of "satisfactory Federal service" as a member of the armed forces. He meets this requirement for a year by earning at least 50 points each year. Points are earned for both inactive duty and active duty. The branch of service will advise the reservist of point totals and the number of years of satisfactory federal service he has completed. The last eight qualifying years must have been spent in a Reserve unit. Entitlement to Reserve retired pay begins at age 60.

The Reserve point system is an element used in computing retirement pay. In totalling points, there is no limit to the number of active points that may be earned in a year, but no more than 60 inactive duty points may be counted for any one year.

M-13. How is Reserve retired pay computed?

Generally, reserve retired pay is computed by:

(1) Dividing the reservist's cumulative active and inactive point total by 360 to convert the points into years of service;

(2) Taking the monthly basic pay rate for the member's grade and length of service at the time he becomes entitled to retired pay at age 60;

(3) Multiplying that rate by 2.5% x the years of service that are credited to him through the point conversion process (but not in excess of 30 years).

Where the reservist first became a member after September 7, 1980, instead of using his actual pay rate as described in (2) above, he uses an average of the basic monthly pay to which he would have been entitled had he been on active duty for the three years in which he was a member of an armed force.

M-14. How does the Survivor Benefit Plan work for Reservists?

Generally, the Survivor Benefit Plan for Reservists follows the rules for the regular servicemember's Survivor Benefit Plan. With respect to the amount of reduction in retired pay of the reserve component annuity, the reduction, effective March 1, 1991, is the lesser of:

(1) an amount equal to 2.5% of the first $364 of the base amount of the annuity subject to the survivor benefit, plus 10% of the remainder, or

(2) an amount equal to 6.5% of the base amount of the annuity subject to the survivor benefit.

VETERANS

Dependency And Indemnity Compensation

M-15. What is Dependency and Indemnity Compensation?

Dependency and Indemnity Compensation (DIC) is the benefit program providing monthly payments to a surviving spouse, child or parent of the veteran due to a *service-connected* death that occurs after 1956. (Where the death occurred prior to 1957, certain survivors could have elected to take benefits under DIC.)

Generally, DIC is payable to survivors of servicemembers or reservists who died from: (1) disease or injury incurred or aggravated in the line of duty while on active or inactive duty training, or (2) disability compensable under laws administered by the Department of Veterans Affairs.

Veterans and dependents may obtain information on benefits by calling the toll-free number 1-800-827-1000. Callers are automatically connected to the Department of Veterans Affairs regional office serving the area from which their call originates.

M-16. Who is eligible for DIC benefits?

DIC benefits are payable to an eligible *surviving spouse* regardless of the survivor's income or employment status. The survivor's death or remarriage terminates the benefit. Benefit eligibility is not reestablished if the survivor's remarriage is terminated by death or divorce. A surviving spouse may receive DIC payments as well as Social Security survivor benefits.

The surviving spouse must have been married: (1) before expiration of 15 years after the end of the period of active duty, active duty for training, or inactive training duty, in which the injury or disease causing death was incurred or aggravated, (2) for one or more years, or (3) for any period of time if a child was born of or before the marriage.

The surviving spouse's benefit is increased when the spouse has children under age 18. Where there is no surviving spouse eligible to receive DIC, children under 18 are eligible to receive DIC benefits.

The definition of *"child"* includes the veteran's legitimate child, legally adopted child, stepchild who is a member of the veteran's household or was a member at the time of the veteran's death, and illegitimate child (provided a number of requirements are met).

DIC payments are made to children who are unmarried and who: (1) are under age 18, or (2) before attaining age 18, become permanently incapable of self-support, or (3) after attaining age 18 and until completion of education or training (but not after attaining age 23), are pursuing a course of instruction at an approved educational institution.

Eligibility of *parents* to receive DIC is measured by an annual income test rather than by dependency. A remarriage of a parent does not terminate the benefits. Parent's DIC benefits continue until death.

M-17. How is the amount of the DIC benefit determined?

The Veterans' Benefits Act of 1992 standardizes the DIC payment to surviving spouses of veterans whose service-connected deaths occur on or after January 1, 1993, by eliminating the schedule of benefits which had been based on the military rank of the deceased veteran. Effective December 1, 2000, a monthly base rate of $911 will be payable to the surviving spouses of all such veterans. That rate is increased by $197 a month if the veteran was totally disabled due to service-connected disabilities continuously for at least eight years prior to death.

If there is a surviving spouse with one or more children below the age of 18 of a deceased veteran, the DIC paid monthly to the surviving spouse is increased by $229 for each child for benefits payable on or after December 1, 2000.

In addition to an annual limitation, the amount of DIC payable monthly to a *parent* depends upon whether there is only one parent, whether two surviving parents are or are not living together, and whether a parent has remarried and is living with a spouse.

The maximum monthly benefit payable to *one parent only* is $445. No DIC is payable if annual income exceeds $10,584. *Two parents not living together* are entitled to a maximum monthly benefit of $320 each. No DIC is paid to a parent whose annual income exceeds $10,584. *Two parents living together* (or remarried parents living with spouses, when both parents are alive) are entitled to a maximum monthly benefit of $300 each. No DIC is paid to a parent if total combined annual income exceeds $14,228. The monthly rate of DIC payable to a parent is increased by $239 if such parent is: (1) a patient in a nursing home, or (2) helpless or blind, or so nearly helpless and blind as to need or require the regular aid and attendance of another person.

Death Prior to January 1, 1993

For surviving spouses of veterans who died prior to January 1, 1993, monthly payments are made according to the veteran's pay grade at the time of death or under the new formula, whichever provides the highest benefit. (See Table 4, Servicemembers and Veterans Tables, for benefits based on pay grade.)

If the veteran did not die in active service, the pay grade will be determined as of: (1) the time of last discharge or release from active duty, or (2) the time of discharge or release from any period of active duty for training or inactive duty training, if death results from service-connected disability incurred during such period. The discharge must have been other than dishonorable.

The monthly rate of DIC is increased by $229 if the surviving spouse is: (1) a patient in a nursing home, or (2) helpless and blind, or so nearly helpless and blind as to need the regular aid and attendance of another person.

The monthly rate of DIC will be increased by $110 if the surviving spouse is permanently housebound by reason of disability, and does not qualify for the aid and attendance allowance described above.

DIC Benefits for Children

If a *child* is under age 18, and there is no surviving spouse entitled to DIC, DIC is paid in equal shares to the children of the deceased veteran at the following monthly rates: one child, $386; two children, $556; three children, $723; more than three children, $723 plus $140 for each child in excess of three.

If a child is 18 or over, and the child became permanently incapable of self-support while under 18 and eligible for DIC, the child's DIC is continued past age 18 and increased by $229 per month. If DIC is payable to a surviving spouse with a child, age 18 or older, who became permanently incapable of support while under 18, the Department of Veterans Affairs will pay an additional sum of $386 for such child.

If DIC is payable to a spouse with a child, age 18 or over and under age 23, who is attending an approved educational institution, DIC is paid to the child, concurrently with the payment of DIC to the spouse, in the amount of $194 per month.

Disability Benefits — Service-Connected

M-18. What benefits are available for service-connected disability?

There are three kinds of benefits for a service-connected disability: (1) compensation paid by Department of Veterans Affairs, (2) severance pay, and (3) disability retirement pay. Disability retirement is discussed in SECTION L.

Monthly compensation is paid by the Department of Veterans Affairs without regard to other income on the basis of average impairments of earning capacity in civilian employment. A person eligible for both disability retirement pay and this compensation may elect which to receive but cannot receive full benefits from both sources.

The veteran must be disabled by injury or disease incurred in or aggravated by active service in line of duty. Discharge or separation must be other than dishonorable, and the injury cannot have resulted from willful misconduct. Reservists disabled while on active training duty may qualify for compensation.

The monthly compensation amount depends on the veteran's degree of disability.

Degree of Disability	Rate
10%	$ 101
20	194
30	298
40	427
50	609
60	769
70	969
80	1,125
90	1,266
100	2,107

A service-connected disability rating may be increased or decreased in accordance with medical findings of changes in the affected condition. However, once a condition has been rated at or above a particular evaluation for 20 continuous years, the rating is protected by law and may not be changed unless the rating was established by fraud.

Any veteran entitled to monthly compensation whose disability is rated not less than 30% is entitled to additional compensation for dependents. The current rates listed below are based upon 100% disability. If the disability rating is at least 30% but less than 100%, the amount of dependent benefits will be approximately the same percent of these rates as the percent of disability rating.

The monthly compensation rates for dependents are as follows:

Spouse and —	Amount
no children	$121
1 child	208
2 children	271
3 children	334
additional children, each	63

If no surviving spouse —	
1 child	82
2 children	145
3 children	208
additional children, each	63

Dependent parent(s)	
each parent	98

A child's benefit usually ends at age 18. However, each dependent child between ages 18 and 23 who is attending an approved school is eligible for $192 monthly if the veteran is totally disabled, and a proportionate amount if the veteran is partially disabled.

The spouse of a totally disabled veteran is entitled to $229 a month if: (1) a patient in a nursing home, or (2) helpless and blind, or so nearly helpless and blind as to need or require the regular aid and attendance of another person. The spouse of a veteran who is not totally disabled, but at least 30% disabled, is entitled to a proportionate monthly benefit.

These dependency allowances are not payable if the serviceman receives any other allowance for dependents under any other law with the exception of Social Security benefits. The higher of the two amounts may be elected but not both. Social Security benefits for total and permanent disability will not be reduced by the amount of any service-connected disability compensation received from the Department of Veterans Affairs.

Service personnel are entitled to *disability severance pay* when separated from service for physical disability but are not eligible for disability retirement pay where: (1) the rated disability is less than 30%, or (2) length-of-service credits are insufficient.

Disability severance pay is a lump-sum equal to twice the monthly base and longevity pay multiplied by years of service, but not exceeding the amount of two years' basic pay, and is payable by the member's branch of service.

Veterans with a 10% disability rating may be entitled to a program of vocational rehabilitation if the Department of Veterans Affairs finds that the veteran has a "serious employment handicap" and needs rehabilitative services to prepare for, obtain, or retain suitable employment.

Any veteran receiving a pension awarded between January 30, 1985, and December 31, 1995, can apply for a vocational rehabilitation evaluation. If an evaluation shows the veteran can achieve a vocational goal if provided the appropriate rehabilitative services, the Department of Veterans Affairs will help develop a plan of services which can lead to employment. There is no requirement that a pensioner participate in an evaluation or training and, if the veteran elects to enter a rehabilitative program, the pension benefit is protected until the veteran is employed.

The Department of Veterans Affairs makes disability payments based on a presumption that veterans who served in Vietnam were exposed to Agent Orange and other herbicides. The conditions the Department of Veterans Affairs recognizes on this basis are soft-tissue sarcoma, non-Hodgkin's lymphoma, chloracne, Hodgkin's disease, porphyria cutanea tarda (PCT), multiple myeloma (a cancer involving the bone marrow) and respiratory cancers (lung, bronchus, larynx and trachea). All Department of Veterans Affairs medical centers provide a special examination to assist Vietnam veterans who were exposed to Agent Orange in determining their current health status.

Death Benefits — Service-Connected

M-19. What other service-connected death benefits are available?

The Department of Veterans Affairs reimburses survivors up to $1,500 (or more, in the case of a federal employee who dies in the performance of duty) for the burial expenses of a veteran who dies as a result of service-connected disability or disabilities.

When a member of the armed forces dies while on active duty, active or inactive training duty, or while receiving hospital treatment for a service-connected ailment, his branch of service will provide for the disposition of his remains. Additional costs of transportation of the remains of the deceased may be allowed if the veteran died while hospitalized or residing in a Department of Veterans Affairs facility, or while in transit, at Department of Veterans Affairs' expense, to or from a hospital, domiciliary, or a Department of Veterans Affairs regional office.

Other allowances include burial in a national cemetery, American flag, and transportation from place of death to place of burial. The next of kin is also entitled to a headstone, or a headstone monetary allowance in the event the veteran purchased a headstone prior to death.

A lump-sum of $6,000 is paid to the survivors of a servicemember who dies on active duty, active or inactive training duty, or within 120 days after separation from active duty if death is from a service-connected cause. This death gratuity is paid by the branch of service of the deceased to the spouse, if living; otherwise to any children in equal shares; otherwise to parents, brothers or sisters as designated by the deceased.

Dependents of a servicemember may remain in government housing for 90 days without charge after the servicemember's death.

Survivors and dependents may also be eligible for the survivors and dependents educational assistance program. The purpose of this program is: (1) to enable children to obtain an education they might not otherwise have had an opportunity to obtain, and (2) to enable surviving spouses to prepare to support themselves and their families at a standard of living which the veteran, but for death or disability, could have expected to provide.

Pension, Disability And Death Benefits Not Service-Connected

M-20. When is a veteran eligible for non-service-connected pension, disability and death benefits?

Veterans with limited income who are discharged under conditions other than dishonorable may be eligible for: (1) an Improved Pension, (2) Section 306 pension, or (3) old law pension. The old law pension is for veterans who died before July 1, 1960.

The pension-eligible veteran must have:

(1) had 90 days active service during the Mexican border period, World War I, World War II, the Korean Conflict, or Vietnam Era,

(2) been discharged because of service-connected disability, or

(3) at the time of death been receiving (or entitled to receive) compensation or retirement pay based on a service-connected disability incurred during wartime.

M-21. When is a surviving spouse and dependents eligible for non-service-connected pension, disability and death benefits?

A surviving spouse must have lived continuously with the veteran from the time of marriage until the veteran's death, except where there was a separation due to the misconduct of, or caused by, the veteran, without fault on the surviving spouse's part. The surviving spouse's valid remarriage or death permanently terminates the benefit. However, if the remarriage is annulled, or is terminated by death or divorce (unless the divorce was secured by fraud or collusion), the surviving spouse is not barred from receiving benefits.

The surviving spouse must have been married to the veteran: (1) for at least one year, or (2) for any period if a child was born either before or after the marriage. For Vietnam Era veterans, the marriage must have taken place before May 8, 1985.

M-22. Are children entitled to benefits?

Unmarried children and surviving spouses under 18 of a deceased veteran may be eligible for a pension. The pension is based on need. Regardless of the income limit, however, benefits will be denied a child or surviving spouse who owns capital which, in the Department of Veterans Affairs' judgment, should be consumed for his or her support.

Unmarried children and surviving spouses over 18 may qualify for pension in their own right if they are: (1) permanently incapable of self-support since prior to age 18, or (2) under 23 and attending a Department of Veterans Affairs-approved educational institution.

M-23. What is the amount of the Improved Pension?

Under the "Improved Pension Program," which went into effect on January 1, 1979, the maximum annual rates payable (effective December 1, 2000) are as follows:

Veterans and Dependents

Veteran without dependent spouse or child	$9,304
Veteran with one dependent (spouse or child)	$12,186
Veteran in need of regular aid and attendance without dependents	$15,524
Veteran in need of regular aid and attendance with one dependent	$18,405
Veteran permanently housebound without dependents	$11,372
Veteran permanently housebound with one dependent	$14,253
Two veterans married to one another, one of which is in need of aid and attendance	$18,405
Two veterans married to one another, both of which are in need of aid and attendance	$23,979
Two veterans married to one another, one of which is housebound	$14,253
Two veterans married to one another, both of which are housebound	$16,322
Two veterans married to one another, one housebound and the other in need of aid and attendance	$20,470

Mexican border period and
World War I veteran .... add $2,109 to the
applicable annual rate

Increase for each additional dependent child $1,586

Spouse and Dependents

Surviving spouse without dependent children $6,237

Surviving spouse with one dependent child $8,168

Surviving spouse in need of regular aid and
attendance without dependent child $9,973

Surviving spouse in need of regular aid and
attendance with one dependent child $11,900

Surviving spouse permanently housebound
without dependent child $7,625

Surviving spouse permanently housebound
with one dependent child $9,551

Increase for each additional dependent child $1,586

Child not in custody of veteran's surviving
spouse, or child if no living surviving spouse
of the veteran $1,586

Benefits are generally paid monthly and are reduced by the annual countable income of the claimant and any dependent of the claimant. Generally, all non-pension income is included for this purpose, but income paid for certain educational or medical expenses is excluded from the computation.

In addition, the pension may be denied or discontinued if the claimant's net worth is such that it is reasonable that some portion of the estate be used for his support. Additional pension for a child may be denied if the child's net worth is excessive.

Pensioners must provide income and net worth reports to the Department of Veterans Affairs on an annual basis.

M-24. What is the Section 306 Pension?

The veteran, surviving spouse, and children who came on the pension rolls on or after July 1, 1960 but prior to January 1, 1979 may continue to receive a pension at the monthly rate in effect as of December 31, 1978. The pension will be paid so long as the veteran remains permanently and totally disabled, there is no charge in dependency, and income does not exceed the adjusted income limitation. The income limitation is Consumer Price Index (CPI) sensitive.

Pensions range from $5 to $197 monthly for veterans with no dependents and up to $222 per month for veterans with dependents. If the annual income of a veteran with no children exceeds $10,584, no pension is paid. Where there is one child and annual income exceeds $14,228, no pension is paid.

A surviving spouse with no minor children may receive up to $139 a month, but if annual income exceeds $10,584, no pension is paid. Where there is one child and annual income exceeds $14,228, no pension is paid.

Where there is no eligible surviving spouse, a child may receive $61 a month with $26 added for each additional child and the total divided among them. A child is not entitled if the income, not counting his or her own earnings, exceeds $8,651.

M-25. What is the Old Law Pension?

Eligible veterans, their surviving spouses and children of certain deceased veterans who died before July 1, 1960, may be entitled to an Old Law pension or death benefit. Where the veteran's surviving spouse or children are claiming Old Law death benefits, it must be shown that the veteran died of causes not due to service. The veteran must have served during World War I, World War II or the Korean conflict.

The monthly rates: Surviving spouse, no child — $50.40. Surviving spouse, one child — $63 (each additional child, $7.56). No surviving spouse, one child — $27.30. No surviving spouse, two children — $40.95. No surviving spouse, three children — $54.60 (each additional child, $7.56).

These pensions are not payable to a veteran or surviving spouse without children, or to an entitled child, if the claimant receives other income over $9,265 annually, or to a veteran or surviving spouse with child if his or her other income is in excess of $13,357.

GOVERNMENT LIFE INSURANCE

Servicemembers' Group Life Insurance

M-26. Who is eligible to be insured automatically under Servicemembers' Group Life Insurance?

Any member of the uniformed service (Army, Navy, Air Force, Marine Corps, Coast Guard, commissioned Corps of the National Oceanic and Atmospheric Administration) on active duty, active duty for training, or inactive duty training in a commissioned, warrant, or enlisted rank or grade, or as a cadet or midshipman of the U.S. Naval, Air Force or Coast Guard Academy. Also, any member of the Ready Reserve in a unit or position which may require active duty or active duty for training and each year performs at least 12 periods of inactive duty training that is creditable for retirement purposes.

M-27. What is the amount and nature of the coverage?

The maximum amount of SGLI is $200,000. Members on active duty in the Uniformed Services of the Army, Navy, Air Force, Marine Corps, Coast Guard, Commissioned Corps of the United States Public Health Service and the National Oceanic and Atmospheric Administration are automatically insured for $200,000.

Automatic insurance coverage is $200,000 unless the member elects in writing: (1) not to be insured, or (2) to be insured for less than $200,000. Members may elect coverage in increments of $10,000 between $10,000 and $200,000. Any person who elects not to be insured or to be insured in an amount less than $200,000 may thereafter be insured for $200,000 upon written application, proof of good health, and compliance with such other terms and conditions as may be prescribed by the Administrator.

The coverage under SGLI is group term life insurance evidenced by a certificate issued to the insured and is entirely separate from and in addition to any other government life insurance the insured may have or later acquire. The insurance is underwritten by a pool of commercial insurers, with one acting as the primary insurer and the others participating as reinsurers.

The program is administered by the Office of Servicemembers' Group Life Insurance, 213 Washington Street, Newark, New Jersey, 07102-2999, and is supervised by the Department of Veterans Affairs. The phone number of the Office of Servicemembers' Group Life Insurance is 1-800-419-1473.

M-28. When is coverage terminated and can the policy be converted?

The day after SGLI coverage ceases for any member on active duty, active duty for training, or inactive duty training, the policy is automatically converted to five-year renewable term coverage under Veterans' Group Life Insurance (VGLI). This automatic conversion is subject to the timely payment of the initial premium. Members may choose to be covered in $10,000 increments up to the amount of SGLI they had while on active duty. Veterans' Group Life Insurance is renewable for life.

In the case of a member on active duty or active duty for training under a call or order to duty that does not specify a period of less than 31 days, SGLI coverage ceases 120 days after the separation or release from active duty or active duty for training, unless the member is totally disabled. If the member is disabled, SGLI ceases one year after the date of separation or release, or on the date total disability ceases, whichever date is earlier, but in no event prior to expiration of 120 days after separation or release.

M-29. Who pays the cost of SGLI?

The government pays, from a revolving fund in the U.S. Treasury, the administrative expenses of the SGLI program and costs traceable to the extra hazard of duty in the uniformed services. The balance is paid by the insured members. At present, a serviceman pays, by deduction, 80 cents a month per $10,000, or $16.00 a month for $200,000 of insurance. A Ready Reservist (one who is assigned to a unit or position that requires at least 12 periods of inactive duty training that is creditable for retirement purposes) pays the same rates as those servicemen on active duty. Reservists with part-time coverage (duty for 30 days or less by a Reservist) pay a premium at an annual rate of 10 cents per $1,000, or $20.00 a year for $200,000.

M-30. How does a person designate a beneficiary?

Death proceeds are paid to the beneficiary or beneficiaries designated by the insured in writing. If no named beneficiary survives, payment is made in the following order of preference: (1) surviving spouse, (2) child or children of the insured and descendants of deceased children by representation, (3) insured parents or their survivors, (4) executor or administrator of insured's estate, or (5) insured's other next of kin entitled under laws of the insured's domicile at time of his death.

An adopted child may qualify for SGLI based on the death of both his natural and adopted parents. But no person who consents to the adoption of a child may be recognized as a parent for SGLI purposes. A child, in other words, cannot claim from more than one father or one mother in an adoption case. An illegitimate child is considered the child of its natural mother.

If a person otherwise entitled to payment does not make claim within one year after insured's death, or if payment to that person is prohibited by federal law, payment may be made in the order of precedence as if the person had not survived the insured, and any such payment is a bar to recovery by any other person.

If a person entitled to benefits does not file a claim for benefits within two years after the insured's death, and there is no notice that a claim will be made, the Department of Veterans Affairs may pay the benefit to someone it deems is appropriate. Such payment is a bar to recovery by any other person.

The insured may elect settlement of the proceeds either in a lump sum or in 36 equal monthly installments. If no election is made by the insured, the beneficiary or beneficiaries may elect settlement either in a lump sum or in 36 equal monthly installments. If the insured has elected settlement in a lump sum, the beneficiary or beneficiaries may elect settlement in 36 equal monthly installments.

Veterans' Group Life Insurance

M-31. Who is eligible for Veterans' Group Life Insurance?

Servicemembers leaving active duty can convert their SGLI to Veterans' Group Life Insurance (VGLI) without medical examination. The day after SGLI coverage ceases for any member on active duty for training, or inactive duty training, the policy is automatically converted to VGLI, subject to timely payment of the initial premium. Reservists performing active duty or inactive duty for training under a call or orders specifying a period of less than 31 days who are injured or disabled and become uninsurable at standard rates are eligible for VGLI. Also, members of the Individual Ready Reserve and Inactive National Guard are eligible for SGLI. An application for coverage must be filed by a member of these groups.

All Retired Reserve SGLI policyholders will have their policies automatically exchanged for policies under the VGLI program. Retired reservists may retain lifetime coverage under VGLI instead of being cut off from coverage at age 61 or when receiving retired pay, as is the case with Retired Reserve SGLI.

In addition, VGLI is extended generally to reservists and National Guard members who decide to separate prior to reaching 20-year retirement.

Veterans who were granted a service-connected disability but are otherwise in good health, may apply to the Department of Veterans Affairs for up to $10,000 life insurance coverage at standard insurance rates within two years from the date the Department of Veterans Affairs notifies the veteran that the disability has been rated as service-connected. This applies even if the disability rating is 0%.

M-32. What is the amount of Veterans' Group Life Insurance?

The maximum amount of VGLI is $200,000. No one may carry a combined amount of SGLI and VGLI in excess of $200,000 at any one time. Also, the amount is limited to an amount equal to or less than the amount of the veteran's terminating SGLI. VGLI is available only in increments of $10,000.

VGLI is *renewable* five-year term. It has no cash, loan, paid-up, or extended values, and lapses for nonpayment of premiums (except in the case of a mental incompetent who dies within one year after becoming insured).

VGLI has a reinstatement period of five years after a policy has lapsed.

M-33. How is the beneficiary designated under Veterans' Group Life Insurance?

VGLI proceeds are paid to the designated beneficiary or beneficiaries when a valid claim is established. If no beneficiary survives, or the insured fails to designate a beneficiary, payment is made in the following order of preference: (1) surviving spouse, (2) child or children of the insured and descendants of deceased children by representation, (3) insured's parents or survivor of them, (4) executor or administrator of insured's estate, or (5) insured's other next of kin entitled under laws of the insured's domicile at the time of death.

There are no restrictions on beneficiary designations, and the insured may change the designation without the knowledge or consent of the beneficiary. This right cannot be waived or restricted. The Department of Veterans Affairs does not recognize state court divorce decrees that require veterans to keep their ex-spouses as beneficiaries on their Department of Veterans Affairs life insurance policies. The forms required for a change of beneficiary may be obtained from the Office of Servicemembers' Group Life Insurance, any Department of Veterans Affairs office, or by calling the Department of Veterans Affairs Insurance Center at 1-800-669-8477.

Any designation of beneficiary or beneficiaries for SGLI filed with a uniformed service is considered a designation for VGLI, but only for 60 days after the VGLI becomes effective. Where the insured is incompetent at the end of the 60-day period, the designation made for SGLI may continue in force until the disability is removed, but not for more than five years after the effective date of the insured's VGLI.

The designation of beneficiary or beneficiaries, except for a designation by an incompetent, must be in writing signed by the insured and received by the administrative office to be effective.

No claim for VGLI will be denied because of a failure to file a claim within four years of the insured's death.

If the insured, in the application for VGLI, does not limit the beneficiary's payments, the beneficiary can elect to receive the insurance in a single payment or in 36 equal monthly installments.

Payment of benefits under VGLI made to or on account of a beneficiary are exempt from taxation and the claims of creditors. The benefits are not liable to attachment, levy or seizure by or under any legal or equitable process.

M-34. What are the premium rates for Veterans' Group Life Insurance?

Premium rates depend on age. Premium payment options include the use of automatic payments by deductions from Department of Veterans Affairs benefits or retirement checks and an option to take a one-month discount for annual payments.

Veterans' Group Life Insurance						
Amount of Insurance	**Monthly Premium Rate**					
	Age 29 & Below	Age 30-34	Age 35-39	Age 40-44	Age 45-49	Age 50-54
$200,000	$16.00	$24.00	$32.00	$48.00	$84.00	$130.00
190,000	15.20	22.80	30.40	45.60	79.80	123.50
180,000	14.40	21.60	28.80	43.20	75.60	117.00
170,000	13.60	20.40	27.20	40.80	71.40	110.50
160,000	12.80	19.20	25.60	38.40	67.20	104.00
150,000	12.00	18.00	24.00	36.00	63.00	97.50
140,000	11.20	16.80	22.40	33.60	58.80	91.00
130,000	10.40	15.60	20.80	31.20	54.60	84.50
120,000	9.60	14.40	19.20	28.80	50.40	78.00
110,000	8.80	13.20	17.60	26.40	46.20	71.50
100,000	8.00	12.00	16.00	24.00	42.00	65.00
90,000	7.20	10.80	14.40	21.60	37.80	58.50
80,000	6.40	9.60	12.80	19.20	33.60	52.00
70,000	5.60	8.40	11.20	16.80	29.40	45.50
60,000	4.80	7.20	9.60	14.40	25.20	39.00
50,000	4.00	6.00	8.00	12.00	21.00	32.50
40,000	3.20	4.80	6.40	9.60	16.80	26.00
30,000	2.40	3.60	4.80	7.20	12.60	19.50
20,000	1.60	2.40	3.20	4.80	8.40	13.00
10,000	.80	1.20	1.60	2.40	4.20	6.50

Veterans' Group Life Insurance (continued)				
	Monthly Premium Rate				
Amount of Insurance	Age 55-59	Age 60-64	Age 65-69	Age 70-74	Age 75 & Over
$200,000	$176.00	$225.00	$300.00	$450.00	$900.00
190,000	167.20	213.75	285.00	427.50	855.00
180,000	158.40	202.50	270.00	405.00	810.00
170,000	149.60	191.25	255.00	382.50	765.00
160,000	140.80	180.00	240.00	360.00	720.00
150,000	132.00	168.75	225.00	337.50	675.00
140,000	123.20	157.50	210.00	315.00	630.00
130,000	114.40	146.25	195.00	292.50	585.00
120,000	105.60	135.00	180.00	270.00	540.00
110,000	96.80	123.75	165.00	247.50	495.00
100,000	88.00	112.50	150.00	225.00	450.00
90,000	79.20	101.25	135.00	202.50	405.00
80,000	70.40	90.00	120.00	180.00	360.00
70,000	61.60	78.75	105.00	157.50	315.00
60,000	52.80	67.50	90.00	135.00	270.00
50,000	44.00	56.25	75.00	112.50	225.00
40,000	35.20	45.00	60.00	90.00	180.00
30,000	26.40	33.75	45.00	67.50	135.00
20,000	17.60	22.50	30.00	45.00	90.00
10,000	8.80	11.25	15.00	22.50	45.00

These premium rates are subject to change depending on emerging experience.

M-35. How is Veterans' Group Life Insurance converted to an individual policy?

VGLI may be converted to an individual policy at any time upon written application for conversion to the participating company selected and payment of the required premiums. The individual policy will be issued without medical examination on a plan currently written by the company.

On request, the administrative office will furnish a list of life insurance companies participating in the program and companies (not participating in the program) which meet qualifying criteria, terms, and conditions established by the administrator and which agree to sell insurance to former members in accordance with the rules described.

RAILROAD RETIREMENT

EMPLOYEE AND SPOUSE ANNUITIES

N-1. Who is eligible for an employee annuity?

The Railroad Retirement Act provides annuities for employees who have reached a specific age and have been credited with a specified number of years of service. The Act also provides annuities for employees who become disabled. The basic requirement for a regular employee retirement annuity is 120 months (10 years) of creditable railroad service. Service months need not be consecutive, and in some cases military service may be counted as railroad service.

Benefits are based on months of service and earnings credits. Earnings are creditable up to certain annual maximums on the amount of compensation subject to railroad retirement taxes.

(1) *Annuities based on 10 years of service.* An employee with 10 years of railroad service but less than 30 years of service is eligible for an annuity if he: (1) has attained retirement age, or (2) has attained age 62 (the annuity cannot begin prior to the first full month during which the employee is age 62) but is less than retirement age. Early retirement annuity reductions are applied to annuities awarded before retirement age.

(2) *Annuities based on 30 years of service.* An employee who has been credited with 30 years of railroad service is eligible for a regular annuity based on age and service the first full month he is age 60. Early retirement reductions are applied to annuities awarded before age 62.

Starting in the year 2000, the age at which full benefits are payable increases in gradual steps until it reaches age 67. This affects people born in 1938 and later. Reduced annuities will still be payable at age 62 but the maximum reduction will be 30% rather than 20% by the year 2022. Part of an annuity is not reduced beyond 20% if the employee had any creditable railroad service before August 12, 1983. These reductions do not affect those who retire at age 62 with 30 years service.

There are two types of disability annuities for employees who have been credited with at least 10 years of railroad service. An employee may receive an *occupational disability*, at age 60, if he has at least 10 years of railroad

293

service or at any age if the employee has at least 20 years (240 months) of service, when the employee is permanently disabled for his *regular railroad occupation*. An employee who cannot be considered for a disability annuity based on ability to work in his regular railroad occupation may receive a *total disability* annuity at any age if he is permanently disabled for *all regular work* and has at least 10 years (120 months) of creditable railroad service.

A five-month waiting period beginning with the month after the month of the onset of disability is required before disability annuity payments can begin.

While an annuity based on disability is not paid until the employee has stopped working for a railroad, employment rights need not be relinquished until the employee attains age 65.

N-2. Who is entitled to a supplemental annuity?

An employee with a current connection with the railroad industry at the time of retirement may qualify for a supplemental annuity in addition to the regular employee annuity. Supplemental annuities are paid from a separate account funded by employer taxes in addition to those assessed for regular annuities. The supplemental annuity is reduced if the employee receives a private pension based on contributions from a railroad employer.

An employee is entitled to a supplemental annuity if he: (1) has been credited with railroad service in at least one month before October 1981, (2) is entitled to the payment of an employee annuity awarded after June 30, 1966, (3) has a current connection with the railroad industry when the employee annuity begins, (4) has given up the right to return to work, and either (5) is age 65 or older and has completed 25 years of service, or (6) is age 60 or older and under age 65, has completed 30 years of service, and is awarded an annuity on or after July 1, 1974.

A supplemental annuity that begins after December 21, 1974, does not affect the payment of the regular employee annuity. The payment of a supplemental annuity does not affect the amount of a spouse or survivor annuity.

N-3. What is a current connection with the railroad industry?

An employee who worked for a railroad in at least 12 of the 30 consecutive months immediately preceding the month his annuity begins will meet the current connection requirement. If the employee has 12 months' service in an earlier 30 consecutive month period, he may still meet the current connection requirement. This alternative generally applies if the employee did not have any regular employment outside the railroad industry after the end of the 30 consecutive month period which included 12 months of railroad service.

If an employee died before retirement, railroad service in at least 12 of the 30 consecutive months before death will meet the current connection requirement for the purpose of paying survivor benefits.

N-4. When is a spouse eligible for spouse annuities?

The Railroad Retirement Act provides annuities for the spouse (and divorced spouse) of an employee who is entitled to an employee annuity. A spouse may receive an annuity based on age, or on having a child of the employee in his or her care. A divorced spouse may only receive an annuity based on age. No spouse or divorced spouse annuity may be paid based upon disability.

To be eligible for an annuity, a spouse must: (1) be the husband or wife of an employee who is entitled to an annuity, and (2) stop working for any railroad employer.

Where the employee has completed 10 years but less than 30 years of railroad service, and has attained age 62, the spouse must be: (1) retirement age or older, (2) less than retirement age and have in his or her care a disabled child or a minor child (a child under 18 years old if the spouse claimant is a wife or under 16 years old if the spouse claimant is a husband) of the employee, or (3) age 62 or older but under retirement age. (In such case, all annuity components are reduced for each month the spouse is under retirement age at the time the annuity begins.)

Where the employee has completed 30 years of railroad service and is age 60 or older, the spouse must be: (1) age 60 or older, (2) less than age 60 and have in his or her care a disabled or minor child of the employee, or (3) age 60 but less than retirement age.

To be eligible for a *divorced spouse annuity*, the employee annuitant must be at least age 62, must have been married for at least 10 years, and the divorced spouse must: (1) be the divorced wife or husband of an employee, (2) stop work for a railroad employer, (3) not be entitled to a retirement or disability benefit under the Social Security Act based on a Primary Insurance Amount (PIA) that is equal to or greater than one-half of the employee's tier I PIA, and either (4) have attained retirement age, or (5) have attained age 62 but be under retirement age. (The annuity is reduced for each month the spouse is under retirement age at the time the annuity begins.)

The amount of the divorced spouse's annuity is, in effect, equal to what Social Security would pay in the same situation and therefore less than the amount of the spouse annuity otherwise payable.

SURVIVOR BENEFITS

N-5. What survivor benefits are payable under the Railroad Retirement Act?

The Railroad Retirement Act provides annuities for the widow(er), surviving divorced spouse, or remarried widow(er) of an employee. The deceased employee must have completed 10 years of railroad service and have had a current connection with the railroad industry at the time of his death. A widow(er), surviving divorced spouse, or remarried widow(er) may receive an annuity based on age, on disability, or on having a child of the employee in his care.

A *widow(er)* of an employee who has completed 10 years of railroad service and had a current connection with the railroad industry at death is eligible for an annuity if he or she has not remarried, and (1) has attained retirement age, (2) is at least 50 but less than 60 years of age and becomes disabled (this results in a reduced annuity), (3) is less than retirement age but has in his or her care a child who either is under age 18 (16 with respect to the tier I component) or is disabled and who is entitled to a child's annuity, or (4) is at least 60 years of age but has not attained retirement age. If eligibility is based on (4), all components of the annuity are reduced for each month the widow(er) is age 62 or over but under retirement age when the annuity begins. For each month the widow(er) is at least 60 but under age 62, all components of the annuity are reduced as if the widow(er) were age 62.

A *surviving divorced spouse* of an employee who completed 10 years of railroad service and had a current connection with the railroad industry at death, is eligible for an annuity if he or she: (1) is unmarried, (2) was married to the employee for at least 10 years, and (3) is not entitled to a Social Security retirement benefit that is equal to or higher than the surviving divorced spouse's annuity before any reduction for age. In addition, the divorced spouse must meet one of the following requirements: (1) have attained retirement age, (2) be at least 50 years old but less than retirement age and disabled (this results in a reduced annuity), (3) be less than retirement age but have in his or her care a child who either is under age 16 or is disabled and who is entitled to a child's benefit, or (4) is at least 60 years of age but has not attained retirement age. In this case, the annuity is reduced for each month the surviving spouse is under retirement age when the annuity begins.

If a surviving divorced spouse marries after attaining age 60 (or age 50 if he or she is a disabled surviving divorced spouse), the marriage is deemed not to have occurred.

A widow(er) of an employee who completed 10 years of railroad service and had a current connection with the railroad industry at death is eligible for an annuity as a *remarried widow(er)* if he or she: (1) remarried either after having attained age 60 (after age 50 if disabled) or before age 60 but the marriage terminated, and (2) is not entitled to a Social Security retirement benefit that is equal to or higher than the full amount of the remarried widow(er) annuity before any reduction for age. In addition, the remarried widow(er) must meet one of the following requirements: (1) have attained retirement age, (2) be at least 50 but less than 60 years of age and disabled (this results in a reduced annuity), (5) have not attained retirement age but have in his or her care a child who either is under age 16 or is disabled, and who is entitled to a child's annuity, or (6) be at least age 60 but have not attained retirement age. (In this case, the annuity is reduced for each month the remarried widow(er) is under retirement age when the annuity begins.)

N-6. Are children and other dependents eligible for survivor benefits?

Other survivor annuities are payable to:

- A *child under age 18.*

- A *child age 18 in full-time attendance at an elementary or secondary school*, until the student attains age 19 or the end of the school term after the student attains age 19.

- A *disabled child* over age 18 if the child became totally and permanently disabled before age 22.

- A *dependent grandchild* meeting any of the requirements described above for a child, if both the grandchild's parents are deceased or disabled.

- A *parent* at age 60 who was dependent on the employee for at least half of the parent's support. If the employee was also survived by a widow(er) or child who can qualify for an annuity, the parent's annuity is limited to the amount that Social Security would pay.

In order to be eligible for a child's annuity, the child must be: (1) a child of an employee who has completed 10 years of railroad service and had a current connection with the railroad industry when he died, (2) unmarried at the time the application was filed, and (3) dependent upon the employee.

N-7. What happens to survivors with dual benefits?

Survivor annuities, like retirement annuities, consist of Tier I and Tier II components. Tier I is based on the deceased employee's combined railroad retirement and Social Security credits, and is generally equivalent to the amount that would have been payable under Social Security. Tier II amounts are percentages of the deceased employee's tier I amount.

The tier I portion is reduced by the amount of any Social Security benefits received by a survivor annuitant, even if the Social Security benefits are based on the survivor's own earnings. This reduction follows the principles of Social Security law under which only the higher of a retirement or survivor benefit is, in effect, payable to a beneficiary. When both railroad retirement annuities and Social Security benefits are payable, the payments are generally combined into a single check issued through the Railroad Retirement Board.

The tier I annuity portion of a widow's or widower's annuity may be reduced for receipt of any federal, state, or local government pension based on the widow(er)'s own earnings. The reduction does not apply if the employment on which the public pension is based was covered under Social Security as of the last day of the individual's employment.

Military service pensions based entirely on active duty before 1957 will cause a reduction. However, payments from the Department of Veterans Affairs will not cause a reduction. For those subject to the government pension reduction, the tier I reduction is equal to two-thirds of the amount of the government pension.

If a widow or widower is qualified for a railroad retirement employee annuity as well as a survivor annuity, a special guarantee applies in some cases. If both the widow and widower and the deceased employee started railroad employment after 1974, only the railroad retirement employee annuity or the survivor annuity chosen by the annuitant is payable. If either the deceased employee or the survivor annuitant had some service before 1975 but had not completed 120 months of railroad service before 1975, the employee annuity and the tier II portion of the survivor annuity would be payable to the widow or widower. The tier I portion of the survivor annuity would be payable only to the extent that it exceeds the tier I portion of the employee annuity. If either the deceased employee or the survivor annuitant completed 120 months of railroad service before 1975, the widow or dependent widower would receive both an employee annuity and a survivor annuity, without a full dual benefit reduction.

N-8. Are there work and earnings limitations for those receiving survivor annuities?

A survivor annuity is not payable for any month in which the survivor works for a railroad or railroad union.

Survivors who are receiving Social Security benefits have their railroad retirement annuity and Social Security benefit combined for earnings limitation purposes. The combined annuity and benefits are reduced by $1 for every $2 of earnings over $10,680 (in 2001) if the survivor is under the normal retirement age; benefits are reduced by $1 for every $3 of earnings over $25,000 (for 2001) in the year an annuitant reaches normal retirement age, however, only earnings earned prior to the month the normal retirement age is reached count toward the $25,000 limit. The earnings limitation does not apply to annuitants who are older than the normal retirement age, starting with the month they reach normal retirement age. See F-28 for a discussion of the normal retirement age.

If the annuitant is under the normal retirement age, in the first year benefits are payable, if the individual earns more than the annual exempt amount, work deductions apply only if monthly earnings are greater than 1/12 of the annual exempt amount ($890 in 2001).

These earnings restrictions do not apply to disabled widows or widowers under age 60 or to disabled children. However, any work or earnings by a disability annuitant is reviewed to determine whether it indicates recovery from the disability.

N-9. When do survivor benefits end?

Payment stops upon death, and no annuity is payable for the month of death.

A *widow(er)'s annuity* or *surviving divorced spouse's* benefit stops if: (1) the annuity was based on caring for a child under age 18 (16 for a surviving divorced spouse) or a disabled child and the child is no longer under age 18 (16 for a surviving divorced spouse) or disabled, or (2) the annuity was based on disability and the beneficiary recovers from the disability before age 60. A disability annuity can be reinstated if the disability recurs within seven years. Remarriage will reduce a widow(er)'s annuity rate, and, in some cases, prevent payment.

A *child's* or *grandchild's annuity* will stop if the child: (1) marries, (2) reaches age 18, or (3) recovers from the disability on which the annuity was based. If the child is 18 and a full-time elementary or high school student, the annuity stops upon graduation from high school, attainment of age 19, or the end of the first school term after attainment of age 19.

A *parent's survivor annuity* may stop upon remarriage; in certain cases, a remarried parent is entitled to a tier I benefit.

RAILROAD RETIREMENT TAXES

N-10. What are the railroad retirement tax rates for employees and employers?

Railroad retirement tier I taxes are coordinated with Social Security taxes and increase automatically when Social Security taxes rise. Employees and employers pay tier I taxes which are the same as Social Security taxes. In addition, both employees and employers pay tier II taxes to finance railroad retirement benefit payments over and above Social Security levels.

Tier I is the first level of the regular annuity for employees. It is calculated in generally the same way as a Social Security benefit.

Tier II is the second tier of a regular annuity and is computed under a separate formula. Tier II is based on railroad service alone. Tier II benefits are equal to seven-tenths of 1% of the employee's average monthly earnings using the tier II tax base in the 60 months of highest earnings, times his years of service in the rail industry.

The tier I tax rate for employees and employers is 7.65%. The tier II tax rate for employers is 16.10% and tier II tax rate for employees is 4.90%.

Tax Rate For Employees And Employers

Employers and employees each		Tier II tax rate	
Hospital insurance (HI) tax rate	Tier I tax rate including HI tax	Employers	Employees
1.45	7.65	16.10%	4.90%

*Medicare Hospital Insurance (HI) tax applies to all annual earnings.

2001 Regular Railroad Retirement Taxes

	Tax rate	Taxable earnings
Tier I		
Employees	7.65%	$80,400
Employers	7.65%	80,400
Tier II		
Employees	4.90%	$59,700
Employers	16.10%	59,700

*Taxes on Someone Earning $80,400**

	Tier I	*Tier II*	*Total*
Employees	$6,150.60	$2,925.30	$9,075.90
Employers	6,150.60	9,611.70	15,762.30

*Medicare Hospital Insurance (HI) tax applies to all annual earnings.

Railroad employees who also worked for a Social Security covered employer in the same year may, under certain circumstances, receive a tax credit or refund equivalent to any excess Social Security taxes withheld.

Employees who worked for two or more railroads in a year, or who had tier I taxes withheld from their Railroad Retirement Board sickness insurance benefits in addition to their railroad earnings, may be eligible for a tax credit or refund of any excess tier I or tier II railroad retirement taxes withheld. Such tax credits or refunds may be claimed on an employee's federal income tax return.

TABLE 1 — BENEFITS AS PERCENTAGE OF PIA

RETIREMENT BENEFIT
Starting at normal retirement age (NRA)
(gradually rising from 65 to 67) .... PIA
Starting age 62 or above (but below NRA) .... PIA reduced

DISABILITY BENEFIT .... PIA

SPOUSE'S BENEFIT (husband or wife
of retired or disabled worker)
Caring for child (under 16 or disabled) .... 50% of PIA
Starting at NRA
(gradually rising from 65 to 67) .... 50% of PIA
Starting age 62 or above (but below NRA) .... 50% of PIA
reduced

CHILD'S BENEFIT
Child of retired or disabled worker .... 50% of PIA
Child of deceased worker .... 75% of PIA

MOTHER'S OR FATHER'S BENEFIT (widow(er)
caring for child under 16 or disabled) .... 75% of PIA

WIDOW(ER)'S BENEFIT (widow(er)
not caring for child)
Starting at NRA
(gradually rising from 65 to 67) .... 100% of PIA
Starting age 60 or above (but below NRA) .... 100% of PIA
reduced

DISABLED WIDOW(ER)'S BENEFIT
Starting age 50-60 .... 71$\frac{1}{2}$% of PIA

PARENT'S BENEFIT (dependent parent of
deceased worker)
One dependent parent .... 82$\frac{1}{2}$% of PIA
Two dependent parents .... 75% of PIA (each)

TABLE 2
QUARTERS OF COVERAGE REQUIRED TO BE FULLY INSURED FOR RETIREMENT BENEFITS

Birth Year	Men	Women
1892 or earlier	6	6
1893	7	6
1894	8	6
1895	9	6
1896	10	7
1897	11	8
1898	12	9
1899	13	10
1900	14	11
1901	15	12
1902	16	13
1903	17	14
1904	18	15
1905	19	16
1906	20	17
1907	21	18
1908	22	19
1909	23	20
1910	24	21
1911	24	22
1912	24	23
1913	24	24
1914	25	25
1915	26	26
1916	27	27
1917	28	28
1918	29	29
1919	30	30
1920	31	31
1921	32	32
1922	33	33
1923	34	34
1924	35	35
1925	36	36
1926	37	37
1927	38	38
1928	39	39
1929 or after	40	40

TABLE 3
YEARS IN WHICH PERSON REACHES AGE 21

1930	1951
1931	1952
1932	1953
1933	1954
1934	1955
1935	1956
1936	1957
1937	1958
1938	1959
1939	1960
1940	1961
1941	1962
1942	1963
1943	1964
1944	1965
1945	1966
1946	1967
1947	1968
1948	1969
1949	1970
1950	1971
1951	1972
1952	1973
1953	1974
1954	1975
1955	1976
1956	1977
1957	1978
1958	1979
1959	1980
1960	1981
1961	1982
1962	1983
1963	1984
1964	1985
1965	1986
1966	1987
1967	1988
1968	1989
1969	1990
1970	1991
1971	1992
1972	1993
1973	1994
1974	1995
1975	1996
1976	1997
1977	1998
1978	1999
1979	2000
1980	2001
1981	2002

TABLE 4
MINIMUM NUMBER OF QUARTERS OF COVERAGE NEEDED TO BE FULLY INSURED AT DEATH

Birth Year	2000	2001
1938 or before	40	40
1939	39	40
1940	38	39
1941	37	38
1942	36	37
1943	35	36
1944	34	35
1945	33	34
1946	32	33
1947	31	32
1948	30	31
1949	29	30
1950	28	29
1951	27	28
1952	26	27
1953	25	26
1954	24	25
1955	23	24
1956	22	23
1957	21	22
1958	20	21
1959	19	20
1960	18	19
1961	17	18
1962	16	17
1963	15	16
1964	14	15
1965	13	14

TABLE 5
NUMBER OF YEARS EARNINGS THAT MUST BE USED IN COMPUTING RETIREMENT BENEFITS
(less if person had an established period of disability)

Birth Year	Computation Age	Year of Computation	No. of Years	No. of Divisor Months
1915	62	1977	21	252
1916	62	1978	22	264
1917	62	1979	23	276
1918	62	1980	24	288
1919	62	1981	25	300
1920	62	1982	26	312
1921	62	1983	27	324
1922	62	1984	28	336
1923	62	1985	29	348
1924	62	1986	30	360
1925	62	1987	31	372
1926	62	1988	32	384
1927	62	1989	33	396
1928	62	1990	34	408
1929	62	1991	35	420
1930 or later	62	1992 or later	35	420

TABLE 6 — INSURED STATUS NEEDED FOR SOCIAL SECURITY BENEFITS

The worker must be FULLY insured to provide monthly benefits for:

... Retired worker (at age 62 or over)
... Spouse of retired worker (at age 62 or over)
... Spouse of retired worker (at any age if caring for a child)
... Child of retired worker
... Widow(er) of worker (at age 60 or over)
... Disabled widow(er) of worker (at age 50 or over)
... Dependent parent of deceased worker

The worker may be either FULLY or CURRENTLY insured to provide monthly benefits for:

... Child of deceased worker
... Widow(er) of worker (at any age if caring for child)

A disabled worker must be FULLY insured and (a) if disability began at or after age 31, must have worked in covered employment 5 out of the last 10 years, or (b) if disability began before age 31, must have worked in covered employment ½ of the quarters between age 21 and onset of disability (but not less than 6), to provide benefits for:

... Disabled worker (at any age)
... Child of disabled worker
... Spouse of disabled worker (at age 62 or over)
... Spouse of disabled worker (at any age if caring for a child)

A worker who is either FULLY or CURRENTLY insured qualifies for the lump-sum death benefit if he is survived by (1) a spouse who was living with him at the time of his death, or (2) a dependent child or spouse eligible to receive social security benefits based on his earnings record.

TABLE 7 — MAXIMUM AIME FOR RETIREMENT, SURVIVOR
AND DISABILITY BENEFITS*
(for workers earning $80,400 or more in 2001)

Year of Birth	Normal Retirement Age	Death in 2001	Disability in 2001	Year of Birth	Normal Retirement Age	Death in 2001	Disability in 2001
1939	5,431	5,231	5,126	1958	6,549	6,200	6,141
1940	5,530	5,291	5,188	1959	6,567	6,215	6,141
1941	5,720	5,354	5,248	1960	6,586	6,229	6,153
1942	5,810	5,421	5,312	1961	6,601	6,243	6,166
1943	5,898	5,487	5,379	1962	6,617	6,260	6,180
1944	5,971	5,557	5,447	1963	6,633	6,278	6,192
1945	6,043	5,626	5,517	1964	6,647	6,300	6,192
1946	6,114	5,698	5,588	1965	6,661	6,315	6,195
1947	6,184	5,755	5,660	1966	6,673	6,337	6,210
1948	6,253	5,816	5,719	1967	6,684	6,364	6,226
1949	6,300	5,880	5,780	1968	6,694	6,393	6,244
1950	6,341	5,948	5,846	1969	6,700	6,428	6,228
1951	6,376	6,020	5,915	1970	6,700	6,463	6,229
1952	6,406	6,063	5,989	1971	6,700	6,509	6,241
1953	6,428	6,102	6,033	1972	6,700	6,589	6,228
1954	6,450	6,133	6,033	1973	6,700	6,525	6,178
1955	6,471	6,158	6,072	1974	6,700	6,525	6,123
1956	6,492	6,172	6,103	1975	6,700	6,525	6,118
1957	6,511	6,185	6,128	1976	6,700	6,525	6,139

*Normal Retirement Age for unreduced benefits (PIA) is 65 at this time but increases by two months a year for workers reaching age 62 in 2000-2005; maintains age 66 for workers reaching age 62 in 2006-2016; increases by two months a year for workers reaching age 62 in 2017-2022; and maintains age 67 for workers reaching age 62 after 2022.

*AIME calculations assume that the worker earned the Social Security maximum earnings base in all years up to an including, respectively, the year before normal retirement ($80,400 is used for 2001 and later years), the year of death, the year before disability.

TABLE 8 — AIME FOR WORKERS EARNING $5,000-$40,000 IN 2001*

Year Born	AIME	$5,000-10,000	$11,000-16,000	$17,000-22,000	$23,000-28,000	$29,000-34,000	$35,000-40,000
1939	Retirement	512	921	1,330	1,740	2,149	2,558
	Death	502	903	1,305	1,707	2,108	2,509
	Disability	497	894	1,292	1,689	2,087	2,484
1940-1944	Retirement	531	954	1,378	1,803	2,227	2,651
	Death	506	910	1,315	1,720	2,124	2,529
	Disability	501	900	1,300	1,701	2,101	2,501
1945-1949	Retirement	549	987	1,426	1,864	2,303	2,742
	Death	507	913	1,319	1,724	2,130	2,536
	Disability	501	901	1,302	1,702	2,103	2,503
1950-1954	Retirement	566	1,019	1,472	1,925	2,378	2,831
	Death	509	916	1,323	1,730	2,137	2,544
	Disability	501	901	1,302	1,702	2,103	2,504
1955-1959	Retirement	587	1,056	1,525	1,994	2,464	2,933
	Death	517	930	1,343	1,756	2,170	2,583
	Disability	503	905	1,307	1,709	2,112	2,514
1960-1964	Retirement	611	1,099	1,588	2,076	2,565	3,054
	Death	540	971	1,403	1,834	2,266	2,697
	Disability	517	931	1,345	1,758	2,172	2,586
1965-1969	Retirement	622	1,120	1,617	2,115	2,613	3,110
	Death	567	1,020	1,474	1,927	2,380	2,834
	Disability	537	967	1,397	1,826	2,256	2,686
1970-1974	Retirement	625	1,125	1,625	2,125	2,625	3,125
	Death	607	1,093	1,579	2,065	2,551	3,037
	Disability	557	1,003	1,448	1,894	2,340	2,785

• AIMEs are approximate and based on the assumption that the worker has had 6% pay raises each year through 2001. AIME calculations for retirement assume that the worker's current earnings stay the same until Normal Retirement Age. Match AIMEs with AIMEs closest to them in Tables 10, 11, and 12 to determine benefits.

SOCIAL SECURITY TABLES

TABLE 9 — AIME FOR WORKERS EARNING $41,000-$80,000 IN 2001*

Year Born	AIME	Current Annual Earnings					
		$41,000-46,000	$47,000-52,000	$53,000-59,000	$60,000-66,000	$67,000-73,000	$74,000-80,000
1939	Retirement	2,956	3,338	3,706	4,108	4,469	4,807
	Death	2,899	3,267	3,622	3,991	4,319	4,623
	Disability	2,870	3,231	3,576	3,928	4,239	4,527
1940-1944	Retirement	3,065	3,469	3,870	4,322	4,750	5,154
	Death	2,920	3,300	3,661	4,065	4,423	4,756
	Disability	2,888	3,261	3,616	4,001	4,342	4,656
1945-1949	Retirement	3,181	3,605	4,054	4,551	5,016	5,488
	Death	2,942	3,329	3,722	4,167	4,578	4,968
	Disability	2,904	3,285	3,670	4,107	4,511	4,884
1950-1954	Retirement	3,284	3,737	4,228	4,756	5,253	5,771
	Death	2,951	3,358	3,799	4,274	4,685	5,126
	Disability	2,904	3,305	3,739	4,206	4,609	5,036
1955-1959	Retirement	3,402	3,872	4,380	4,927	5,475	6,022
	Death	2,996	3,409	3,857	4,339	4,822	5,304
	Disability	2,916	3,318	3,754	4,223	4,693	5,162
1960-1964	Retirement	3,542	4,031	4,560	5,130	5,700	6,270
	Death	3,129	3,560	4,028	4,531	5,035	5,538
	Disability	2,999	3,413	3,861	4,344	4,826	5,309
1965-1969	Retirement	3,608	4,105	4,644	5,225	5,806	6,386
	Death	3,287	3,741	4,232	4,761	5,290	5,819
	Disability	3,115	3,545	4,010	4,512	5,013	5,514
1970-1974	Retirement	3,625	4,125	4,667	5,250	5,833	6,417
	Death	3,522	4,008	4,535	5,101	5,668	6,235
	Disability	3,231	3,677	4,159	4,679	5,199	5,719

- AIMEs are approximate and based on the assumption that the worker has had 6% pay raises each year through 2001. AIME calculations for retirement assume that the worker's current earnings stay the same until Normal Retirement Age. Match AIMEs with AIMEs closest to them in Tables 10, 11, and 12 to determine benefits.

TABLE 10—WORKER'S AND SPOUSE'S RETIREMENT BENEFITS*

Average Indexed Monthly Earnings	Worker Age 65 (PIA)	Spouse Age 65	Total Age 65 Benefit	Worker Age 62**	Spouse Age 62	Total Age 62 Benefit	Worker 65 & Spouse 62
6,700	1,905	952	2,857	1,492	698	2,190	2,603
6,675	1,901	950	2,851	1,489	697	2,186	2,598
6,650	1,897	948	2,845	1,485	695	2,180	2,592
6,625	1,893	946	2,839	1,482	694	2,176	2,587
6,600	1,890	945	2,835	1,480	693	2,173	2,583
6,575	1,886	943	2,829	1,477	691	2,168	2,577
6,550	1,882	941	2,823	1,474	690	2,164	2,572
6,525	1,878	939	2,817	1,471	688	2,159	2,566
6,500	1,875	937	2,812	1,468	687	2,155	2,562
6,475	1,871	935	2,806	1,465	686	2,151	2,557
6,450	1,867	933	2,800	1,462	684	2,146	2,551
6,425	1,863	931	2,794	1,459	683	2,142	2,546
6,400	1,860	930	2,790	1,457	682	2,139	2,542
6,375	1,856	928	2,784	1,453	680	2,133	2,536
6,350	1,852	926	2,778	1,450	679	2,129	2,531
6,325	1,848	924	2,772	1,447	677	2,124	2,525
6,300	1,845	922	2,767	1,445	676	2,121	2,521
6,275	1,841	920	2,761	1,442	675	2,117	2,516
6,250	1,837	918	2,755	1,438	673	2,111	2,510
6,225	1,833	916	2,749	1,435	672	2,107	2,505
6,200	1,830	915	2,745	1,433	671	2,104	2,501
6,175	1,826	913	2,739	1,430	669	2,099	2,495
6,150	1,822	911	2,733	1,427	668	2,095	2,490
6,125	1,818	909	2,727	1,424	666	2,090	2,484
6,100	1,815	907	2,722	1,421	665	2,086	2,480
6,075	1,811	905	2,716	1,418	664	2,082	2,475
6,050	1,807	903	2,710	1,415	662	2,077	2,469
6,025	1,803	901	2,704	1,412	661	2,073	2,464
6,000	1,800	900	2,700	1,410	660	2,070	2,460
5,975	1,796	898	2,694	1,406	658	2,064	2,454
5,950	1,792	896	2,688	1,403	657	2,060	2,449
5,925	1,788	894	2,682	1,400	655	2,055	2,443
5,900	1,785	892	2,677	1,398	654	2,052	2,439
5,875	1,781	890	2,671	1,395	653	2,048	2,434
5,850	1,777	888	2,665	1,391	651	2,042	2,428
5,825	1,773	886	2,659	1,388	650	2,038	2,423
5,800	1,770	885	2,655	1,386	649	2,035	2,419
5,775	1,766	883	2,649	1,383	647	2,030	2,413
5,750	1,762	881	2,643	1,380	646	2,026	2,408
5,725	1,758	879	2,637	1,377	644	2,021	2,402

TABLE 10—WORKER'S AND SPOUSE'S RETIREMENT BENEFITS* (Continued)

Average Indexed Monthly Earnings	Worker Age 65 (PIA)	Spouse Age 65	Total Age 65 Benefit	Worker Age 62**	Spouse Age 62	Total Age 62 Benefit	Worker 65 & Spouse 62
5,700	1,755	877	2,632	1,374	643	2,017	2,398
5,675	1,751	875	2,626	1,371	642	2,013	2,393
5,650	1,747	873	2,620	1,368	640	2,008	2,387
5,625	1,743	871	2,614	1,365	639	2,004	2,382
5,600	1,740	870	2,610	1,363	638	2,001	2,378
5,575	1,736	868	2,604	1,359	636	1,995	2,372
5,550	1,732	866	2,598	1,356	635	1,991	2,367
5,525	1,728	864	2,592	1,353	633	1,986	2,361
5,500	1,725	862	2,587	1,351	632	1,983	2,357
5,475	1,721	860	2,581	1,348	631	1,979	2,352
5,450	1,717	858	2,575	1,344	629	1,973	2,346
5,425	1,713	856	2,569	1,341	628	1,969	2,341
5,400	1,710	855	2,565	1,339	627	1,966	2,337
5,375	1,706	853	2,559	1,336	625	1,961	2,331
5,350	1,702	851	2,553	1,333	624	1,957	2,326
5,325	1,698	849	2,547	1,330	622	1,952	2,320
5,300	1,695	847	2,542	1,327	621	1,948	2,316
5,275	1,691	845	2,536	1,324	620	1,944	2,311
5,250	1,687	843	2,530	1,321	618	1,939	2,305
5,225	1,683	841	2,524	1,318	617	1,935	2,300
5,200	1,680	840	2,520	1,316	616	1,932	2,296
5,175	1,676	838	2,514	1,312	614	1,926	2,290
5,150	1,672	836	2,508	1,309	613	1,922	2,285
5,125	1,668	834	2,502	1,306	611	1,917	2,279
5,100	1,665	832	2,497	1,304	610	1,914	2,275
5,075	1,661	830	2,491	1,301	609	1,910	2,270
5,050	1,657	828	2,485	1,297	607	1,904	2,264
5,025	1,653	826	2,479	1,294	606	1,900	2,259
5,000	1,650	825	2,475	1,292	605	1,897	2,255
4,975	1,646	823	2,469	1,289	603	1,892	2,249
4,950	1,642	821	2,463	1,286	602	1,888	2,244
4,925	1,638	819	2,457	1,283	600	1,883	2,238
4,900	1,635	817	2,452	1,280	599	1,879	2,234
4,875	1,631	815	2,446	1,277	598	1,875	2,229
4,850	1,627	813	2,440	1,274	596	1,870	2,223
4,825	1,623	811	2,434	1,271	595	1,866	2,218
4,800	1,620	810	2,430	1,269	594	1,863	2,214
4,775	1,616	808	2,424	1,265	592	1,857	2,208
4,750	1,612	806	2,418	1,262	591	1,853	2,203
4,725	1,608	804	2,412	1,259	589	1,848	2,197

TABLE 10—WORKER'S AND SPOUSE'S RETIREMENT BENEFITS* (Continued)

Average Indexed Monthly Earnings	Worker Age 65 (PIA)	Spouse Age 65	Total Age 65 Benefit	Worker Age 62**	Spouse Age 62	Total Age 62 Benefit	Worker 65 & Spouse 62
4,700	1,605	802	2,407	1,257	588	1,845	2,193
4,675	1,601	800	2,401	1,254	587	1,841	2,188
4,650	1,597	798	2,395	1,250	585	1,835	2,182
4,625	1,593	796	2,389	1,247	584	1,831	2,177
4,600	1,590	795	2,385	1,245	583	1,828	2,173
4,575	1,586	793	2,379	1,242	581	1,823	2,167
4,550	1,582	791	2,373	1,239	580	1,819	2,162
4,525	1,578	789	2,367	1,236	578	1,814	2,156
4,500	1,575	787	2,362	1,233	577	1,810	2,152
4,475	1,571	785	2,356	1,230	576	1,806	2,147
4,450	1,567	783	2,350	1,227	574	1,801	2,141
4,425	1,563	781	2,344	1,224	573	1,797	2,136
4,400	1,560	780	2,340	1,222	572	1,794	2,132
4,375	1,556	778	2,334	1,218	570	1,788	2,126
4,350	1,552	776	2,328	1,215	569	1,784	2,121
4,325	1,548	774	2,322	1,212	567	1,779	2,115
4,300	1,545	772	2,317	1,210	566	1,776	2,111
4,275	1,541	770	2,311	1,207	565	1,772	2,106
4,250	1,537	768	2,305	1,203	563	1,766	2,100
4,225	1,533	766	2,299	1,200	562	1,762	2,095
4,200	1,530	765	2,295	1,198	561	1,759	2,091
4,175	1,526	763	2,289	1,195	559	1,754	2,085
4,150	1,522	761	2,283	1,192	558	1,750	2,080
4,125	1,518	759	2,277	1,189	556	1,745	2,074
4,100	1,515	757	2,272	1,186	555	1,741	2,070
4,075	1,511	755	2,266	1,183	554	1,737	2,065
4,050	1,507	753	2,260	1,180	552	1,732	2,059
4,025	1,503	751	2,254	1,177	551	1,728	2,054
4,000	1,500	750	2,250	1,175	550	1,725	2,050
3,975	1,496	748	2,244	1,171	548	1,719	2,044
3,950	1,492	746	2,238	1,168	547	1,715	2,039
3,925	1,488	744	2,232	1,165	545	1,710	2,033
3,900	1,485	742	2,227	1,163	544	1,707	2,029
3,875	1,481	740	2,221	1,160	543	1,703	2,024
3,850	1,477	738	2,215	1,156	541	1,697	2,018
3,825	1,473	736	2,209	1,153	540	1,693	2,013
3,800	1,470	735	2,205	1,151	539	1,690	2,009
3,775	1,466	733	2,199	1,148	537	1,685	2,003
3,750	1,462	731	2,193	1,145	536	1,681	1,998
3,725	1,458	729	2,187	1,142	534	1,676	1,992
3,700	1,455	727	2,182	1,139	533	1,672	1,988
3,675	1,451	725	2,176	1,136	532	1,668	1,983
3,650	1,447	723	2,170	1,133	530	1,663	1,977
3,625	1,443	721	2,164	1,130	529	1,659	1,972
3,600	1,440	720	2,160	1,128	528	1,656	1,968

TABLE 10—WORKER'S AND SPOUSE'S RETIREMENT BENEFITS* (Continued)

Average Indexed Monthly Earnings	Worker Age 65 (PIA)	Spouse Age 65	Total Age 65 Benefit	Worker Age 62**	Spouse Age 62	Total Age 62 Benefit	Worker 65 & Spouse 62
3,575	1,436	718	2,154	1,124	526	1,650	1,962
3,550	1,432	716	2,148	1,121	525	1,646	1,957
3,525	1,428	714	2,142	1,118	523	1,641	1,951
3,500	1,425	712	2,137	1,116	522	1,638	1,947
3,475	1,421	710	2,131	1,113	521	1,634	1,942
3,450	1,417	708	2,125	1,109	519	1,628	1,936
3,425	1,413	706	2,119	1,106	518	1,624	1,931
3,400	1,410	705	2,115	1,104	517	1,621	1,927
3,375	1,405	702	2,107	1,100	515	1,615	1,920
3,350	1,397	698	2,095	1,094	512	1,606	1,909
3,325	1,389	694	2,083	1,088	509	1,597	1,898
3,300	1,381	690	2,071	1,081	506	1,587	1,887
3,275	1,373	686	2,059	1,075	503	1,578	1,876
3,250	1,365	682	2,047	1,069	500	1,569	1,865
3,225	1,357	678	2,035	1,062	497	1,559	1,854
3,200	1,349	674	2,023	1,056	494	1,550	1,843
3,175	1,341	670	2,011	1,050	491	1,541	1,832
3,150	1,333	666	1,999	1,044	488	1,532	1,821
3,125	1,325	662	1,987	1,037	485	1,522	1,810
3,100	1,317	658	1,975	1,031	482	1,513	1,799
3,075	1,309	654	1,963	1,025	479	1,504	1,788
3,050	1,301	650	1,951	1,019	477	1,496	1,778
3,025	1,293	646	1,939	1,012	474	1,486	1,767
3,000	1,285	642	1,927	1,006	471	1,477	1,756
2,975	1,277	638	1,915	1,000	468	1,468	1,745
2,950	1,269	634	1,903	994	465	1,459	1,734
2,925	1,261	630	1,891	987	462	1,449	1,723
2,900	1,253	626	1,879	981	459	1,440	1,712
2,875	1,245	622	1,867	975	456	1,431	1,701
2,850	1,237	618	1,855	968	453	1,421	1,690
2,825	1,229	614	1,843	962	450	1,412	1,679
2,800	1,221	610	1,831	956	447	1,403	1,668
2,775	1,213	606	1,819	950	444	1,394	1,657
2,750	1,205	602	1,807	943	441	1,384	1,646
2,725	1,197	598	1,795	937	438	1,375	1,635
2,700	1,189	594	1,783	931	435	1,366	1,624
2,675	1,181	590	1,771	925	433	1,358	1,614
2,650	1,173	586	1,759	918	430	1,348	1,603
2,625	1,165	582	1,747	912	427	1,339	1,592
2,600	1,157	578	1,735	906	424	1,330	1,581
2,575	1,149	574	1,723	900	421	1,321	1,570
2,550	1,141	570	1,711	893	418	1,311	1,559
2,525	1,133	566	1,699	887	415	1,302	1,548
2,500	1,125	562	1,687	881	412	1,293	1,537
2,475	1,117	558	1,675	874	409	1,283	1,526

TABLE 10—WORKER'S AND SPOUSE'S RETIREMENT BENEFITS* (Continued)

Average Indexed Monthly Earnings	Worker Age 65 (PIA)	Spouse Age 65	Total Age 65 Benefit	Worker Age 62**	Spouse Age 62	Total Age 62 Benefit	Worker 65 & Spouse 62
2,450	1,109	554	1,663	868	406	1,274	1,515
2,425	1,101	550	1,651	862	403	1,265	1,504
2,400	1,093	546	1,639	856	400	1,256	1,493
2,375	1,085	542	1,627	849	397	1,246	1,482
2,350	1,077	538	1,615	843	394	1,237	1,471
2,325	1,069	534	1,603	837	391	1,228	1,460
2,300	1,061	530	1,591	831	389	1,220	1,450
2,275	1,053	526	1,579	824	386	1,210	1,439
2,250	1,045	522	1,567	818	383	1,201	1,428
2,225	1,037	518	1,555	812	380	1,192	1,417
2,200	1,029	514	1,543	806	377	1,183	1,406
2,175	1,021	510	1,531	799	374	1,173	1,395
2,150	1,013	506	1,519	793	371	1,164	1,384
2,125	1,005	502	1,507	787	368	1,155	1,373
2,100	997	498	1,495	780	365	1,145	1,362
2,075	989	494	1,483	774	362	1,136	1,351
2,050	981	490	1,471	768	359	1,127	1,340
2,025	973	486	1,459	762	356	1,118	1,329
2,000	965	482	1,447	755	353	1,108	1,318
1,975	957	478	1,435	749	350	1,099	1,307
1,950	949	474	1,423	743	347	1,090	1,296
1,925	941	470	1,411	737	345	1,082	1,286
1,900	933	466	1,399	730	342	1,072	1,275
1,875	925	462	1,387	724	339	1,063	1,264
1,850	917	458	1,375	718	336	1,054	1,253
1,825	909	454	1,363	712	333	1,045	1,242
1,800	901	450	1,351	705	330	1,035	1,231
1,775	893	446	1,339	699	327	1,026	1,220
1,750	885	442	1,327	693	324	1,017	1,209
1,725	877	438	1,315	686	321	1,007	1,198
1,700	869	434	1,303	680	318	998	1,187
1,675	861	430	1,291	674	315	989	1,176
1,650	853	426	1,279	668	312	980	1,165
1,625	845	422	1,267	661	309	970	1,154
1,600	837	418	1,255	655	306	961	1,143
1,575	829	414	1,243	649	303	952	1,132
1,550	821	410	1,231	643	301	944	1,122
1,525	813	406	1,219	636	298	934	1,111
1,500	805	402	1,207	630	295	925	1,100
1,475	797	398	1,195	624	292	916	1,089

TABLE 10—WORKER'S AND SPOUSE'S RETIREMENT BENEFITS* (Continued)

Average Indexed Monthly Earnings	Worker Age 65 (PIA)	Spouse Age 65	Total Age 65 Benefit	Worker Age 62**	Spouse Age 62	Total Age 62 Benefit	Worker 65 & Spouse 62
1,450	789	394	1,183	618	289	907	1,078
1,425	781	390	1,171	611	286	897	1,067
1,400	773	386	1,159	605	283	888	1,056
1,375	765	382	1,147	599	280	879	1,045
1,350	757	378	1,135	592	277	869	1,034
1,325	749	374	1,123	586	274	860	1,023
1,300	741	370	1,111	580	271	851	1,012
1,275	733	366	1,099	574	268	842	1,001
1,250	725	362	1,087	567	265	832	990
1,225	717	358	1,075	561	262	823	979
1,200	709	354	1,063	555	259	814	968
1,175	701	350	1,051	549	257	806	958
1,150	693	346	1,039	542	254	796	947
1,125	685	342	1,027	536	251	787	936
1,100	677	338	1,015	530	248	778	925
1,075	669	334	1,003	524	245	769	914
1,050	661	330	991	517	242	759	903
1,025	653	326	979	511	239	750	892
1,000	645	322	967	505	236	741	881
975	637	318	955	498	233	731	870
950	629	314	943	492	230	722	859
925	621	310	931	486	227	713	848
900	613	306	919	480	224	704	837
875	605	302	907	473	221	694	826
850	597	298	895	467	218	685	815
825	589	294	883	461	215	676	804
800	581	290	871	455	213	668	794
775	573	286	859	448	210	658	783
750	565	282	847	442	207	649	772
725	557	278	835	436	204	640	761
700	549	274	823	430	201	631	750
675	541	270	811	423	198	621	739
650	533	266	799	417	195	612	728

* The retirement age when unreduced benefits are available-now 65-will be increased to age 67 in gradual steps starting in the year 2000. If you were born in 1943-1954, your retirement age for full benefits is 66. If you were born in 1955-1959, your retirement age for full benefits is your 66th birthday plus two months for every year you were born after 1954. If you were born in 1960 and after, your retirement age for full benefits is 67.

** Benefits listed are 80% of the corresponding PIA, but age 62 benefits are reduced further if worker is born in 1938 or after. Ex: Benefits is 75% of PIA for workers born in 1943-1954 and 70% of PIA for workers born in 1960 and after.

TABLE 11—SURVIVOR'S BENEFITS

Average Indexed Monthly Earnings	Worker's PIA	Surviving Spouse & 1 Child; or 2 Children	Surviving Spouse & 2 Children; or 3 Children	One Child (No Parent)	Widow or Widower Age 60	Widow or Widower Age 65	Each of Two Parents	Sole Parent	Maximum Family Benefits
6,700	1,905	2,857	3,332	1,428	1,362	1,905	1,428	1,571	3,332
6,675	1,901	2,851	3,325	1,425	1,359	1,901	1,425	1,568	3,325
6,650	1,897	2,845	3,318	1,422	1,356	1,897	1,422	1,565	3,318
6,625	1,893	2,839	3,311	1,419	1,353	1,893	1,419	1,561	3,311
6,600	1,890	2,835	3,306	1,417	1,351	1,890	1,417	1,559	3,306
6,575	1,886	2,829	3,299	1,414	1,348	1,886	1,414	1,555	3,299
6,550	1,882	2,823	3,292	1,411	1,345	1,882	1,411	1,552	3,292
6,525	1,878	2,817	3,285	1,408	1,342	1,878	1,408	1,549	3,285
6,500	1,875	2,812	3,280	1,406	1,340	1,875	1,406	1,546	3,280
6,475	1,871	2,806	3,273	1,403	1,337	1,871	1,403	1,543	3,273
6,450	1,867	2,800	3,266	1,400	1,334	1,867	1,400	1,540	3,266
6,425	1,863	2,794	3,259	1,397	1,332	1,863	1,397	1,536	3,259
6,400	1,860	2,790	3,254	1,395	1,329	1,860	1,395	1,534	3,254
6,375	1,856	2,784	3,247	1,392	1,327	1,856	1,392	1,531	3,247
6,350	1,852	2,778	3,240	1,389	1,324	1,852	1,389	1,527	3,240
6,325	1,848	2,772	3,233	1,386	1,321	1,848	1,386	1,524	3,233
6,300	1,845	2,767	3,227	1,383	1,319	1,845	1,383	1,522	3,227
6,275	1,841	2,761	3,220	1,380	1,316	1,841	1,380	1,518	3,220
6,250	1,837	2,755	3,213	1,377	1,313	1,837	1,377	1,515	3,213
6,225	1,833	2,749	3,206	1,374	1,310	1,833	1,374	1,512	3,206
6,200	1,830	2,745	3,201	1,372	1,308	1,830	1,372	1,509	3,201
6,175	1,826	2,739	3,194	1,369	1,305	1,826	1,369	1,506	3,194
6,150	1,822	2,733	3,187	1,366	1,302	1,822	1,366	1,503	3,187
6,125	1,818	2,727	3,180	1,363	1,299	1,818	1,363	1,499	3,180
6,100	1,815	2,722	3,175	1,361	1,297	1,815	1,361	1,497	3,175
6,075	1,811	2,716	3,168	1,358	1,294	1,811	1,358	1,494	3,168
6,050	1,807	2,710	3,161	1,355	1,292	1,807	1,355	1,490	3,161
6,025	1,803	2,704	3,154	1,352	1,289	1,803	1,352	1,487	3,154
6,000	1,800	2,700	3,149	1,350	1,286	1,800	1,350	1,484	3,149
5,975	1,796	2,694	3,142	1,347	1,284	1,796	1,347	1,481	3,142
5,950	1,792	2,688	3,135	1,344	1,281	1,792	1,344	1,478	3,135
5,925	1,788	2,682	3,128	1,341	1,278	1,788	1,341	1,475	3,128
5,900	1,785	2,677	3,122	1,338	1,276	1,785	1,338	1,472	3,122
5,875	1,781	2,671	3,115	1,335	1,273	1,781	1,335	1,469	3,115
5,850	1,777	2,665	3,108	1,332	1,270	1,777	1,332	1,466	3,108
5,825	1,773	2,659	3,101	1,329	1,267	1,773	1,329	1,462	3,101
5,800	1,770	2,655	3,096	1,327	1,265	1,770	1,327	1,460	3,096
5,775	1,766	2,649	3,089	1,324	1,262	1,766	1,324	1,456	3,089
5,750	1,762	2,643	3,082	1,321	1,259	1,762	1,321	1,453	3,082
5,725	1,758	2,637	3,075	1,318	1,256	1,758	1,318	1,450	3,075
5,700	1,755	2,632	3,070	1,316	1,254	1,755	1,316	1,447	3,070
5,675	1,751	2,626	3,063	1,313	1,251	1,751	1,313	1,444	3,063
5,650	1,747	2,620	3,056	1,310	1,249	1,747	1,310	1,441	3,056
5,625	1,743	2,614	3,049	1,307	1,246	1,743	1,307	1,437	3,049
5,600	1,740	2,610	3,044	1,305	1,244	1,740	1,305	1,435	3,044
5,575	1,736	2,604	3,037	1,302	1,241	1,736	1,302	1,432	3,037
5,550	1,732	2,598	3,030	1,299	1,238	1,732	1,299	1,428	3,030
5,525	1,728	2,592	3,023	1,296	1,235	1,728	1,296	1,425	3,023
5,500	1,725	2,587	3,017	1,293	1,233	1,725	1,293	1,423	3,017
5,475	1,721	2,581	3,010	1,290	1,230	1,721	1,290	1,419	3,010

TABLE 11—SURVIVOR'S BENEFITS (Continued)

Average Indexed Monthly Earnings	Worker's PIA	Surviving Spouse & 1 Child; or 2 Children	Surviving Spouse & 2 Children; or 3 Children	One Child (No Parent)	Widow or Widower Age 60	Widow or Widower Age 65	Each of Two Parents	Sole Parent	Maximum Family Benefits
5,450	1,717	2,575	3,003	1,287	1,227	1,717	1,287	1,416	3,003
5,425	1,713	2,569	2,996	1,284	1,224	1,713	1,284	1,413	2,996
5,400	1,710	2,565	2,991	1,282	1,222	1,710	1,282	1,410	2,991
5,375	1,706	2,559	2,984	1,279	1,219	1,706	1,279	1,407	2,984
5,350	1,702	2,553	2,977	1,276	1,216	1,702	1,276	1,404	2,977
5,325	1,698	2,547	2,970	1,273	1,214	1,698	1,273	1,400	2,970
5,300	1,695	2,542	2,965	1,271	1,211	1,695	1,271	1,398	2,965
5,275	1,691	2,536	2,958	1,268	1,209	1,691	1,268	1,395	2,958
5,250	1,687	2,530	2,951	1,265	1,206	1,687	1,265	1,391	2,951
5,225	1,683	2,524	2,944	1,262	1,203	1,683	1,262	1,388	2,944
5,200	1,680	2,520	2,939	1,260	1,201	1,680	1,260	1,385	2,939
5,175	1,676	2,514	2,932	1,257	1,198	1,676	1,257	1,382	2,932
5,150	1,672	2,508	2,925	1,254	1,195	1,672	1,254	1,379	2,925
5,125	1,668	2,502	2,918	1,251	1,192	1,668	1,251	1,376	2,918
5,100	1,665	2,497	2,912	1,248	1,190	1,665	1,248	1,373	2,912
5,075	1,661	2,491	2,905	1,245	1,187	1,661	1,245	1,370	2,905
5,050	1,657	2,485	2,898	1,242	1,184	1,657	1,242	1,367	2,898
5,025	1,653	2,479	2,891	1,239	1,181	1,653	1,239	1,363	2,891
5,000	1,650	2,475	2,886	1,237	1,179	1,650	1,237	1,361	2,886
4,975	1,646	2,469	2,879	1,234	1,176	1,646	1,234	1,357	2,879
4,950	1,642	2,463	2,872	1,231	1,174	1,642	1,231	1,354	2,872
4,925	1,638	2,457	2,865	1,228	1,171	1,638	1,228	1,351	2,865
4,900	1,635	2,452	2,860	1,226	1,169	1,635	1,226	1,348	2,860
4,875	1,631	2,446	2,853	1,223	1,166	1,631	1,223	1,345	2,853
4,850	1,627	2,440	2,846	1,220	1,163	1,627	1,220	1,342	2,846
4,825	1,623	2,434	2,839	1,217	1,160	1,623	1,217	1,338	2,839
4,800	1,620	2,430	2,834	1,215	1,158	1,620	1,215	1,336	2,834
4,775	1,616	2,424	2,827	1,212	1,155	1,616	1,212	1,333	2,827
4,750	1,612	2,418	2,820	1,209	1,152	1,612	1,209	1,329	2,820
4,725	1,608	2,412	2,813	1,206	1,149	1,608	1,206	1,326	2,813
4,700	1,605	2,407	2,807	1,203	1,147	1,605	1,203	1,324	2,807
4,675	1,601	2,401	2,800	1,200	1,144	1,601	1,200	1,320	2,800
4,650	1,597	2,395	2,793	1,197	1,141	1,597	1,197	1,317	2,793
4,625	1,593	2,389	2,786	1,194	1,138	1,593	1,194	1,314	2,786
4,600	1,590	2,385	2,781	1,192	1,136	1,590	1,192	1,311	2,781
4,575	1,586	2,379	2,774	1,189	1,133	1,586	1,189	1,308	2,774
4,550	1,582	2,373	2,767	1,186	1,131	1,582	1,186	1,305	2,767
4,525	1,578	2,367	2,760	1,183	1,128	1,578	1,183	1,301	2,760
4,500	1,575	2,362	2,755	1,181	1,126	1,575	1,181	1,299	2,755
4,475	1,571	2,356	2,748	1,178	1,123	1,571	1,178	1,296	2,748
4,450	1,567	2,350	2,741	1,175	1,120	1,567	1,175	1,292	2,741
4,425	1,563	2,344	2,734	1,172	1,117	1,563	1,172	1,289	2,734
4,400	1,560	2,340	2,729	1,170	1,115	1,560	1,170	1,286	2,729
4,375	1,556	2,334	2,722	1,167	1,112	1,556	1,167	1,283	2,722
4,350	1,552	2,328	2,715	1,164	1,109	1,552	1,164	1,280	2,715
4,325	1,548	2,322	2,708	1,161	1,106	1,548	1,161	1,277	2,708
4,300	1,545	2,317	2,702	1,158	1,104	1,545	1,158	1,274	2,702
4,275	1,541	2,311	2,695	1,155	1,101	1,541	1,155	1,271	2,695
4,250	1,537	2,305	2,688	1,152	1,098	1,537	1,152	1,268	2,688
4,225	1,533	2,299	2,681	1,149	1,096	1,533	1,149	1,264	2,681

TABLE 11—SURVIVOR'S BENEFITS (Continued)

Average Indexed Monthly Earnings	Worker's PIA	Surviving Spouse & 1 Child; or 2 Children	Surviving Spouse & 2 Children; or 3 Children	One Child (No Parent)	Widow or Widower Age 60	Widow or Widower Age 65	Each of Two Parents	Sole Parent	Maximum Family Benefits
4,200	1,530	2,295	2,676	1,147	1,093	1,530	1,147	1,262	2,676
4,175	1,526	2,289	2,669	1,144	1,091	1,526	1,144	1,258	2,669
4,150	1,522	2,283	2,662	1,141	1,088	1,522	1,141	1,255	2,662
4,125	1,518	2,277	2,655	1,138	1,085	1,518	1,138	1,252	2,655
4,100	1,515	2,272	2,650	1,136	1,083	1,515	1,136	1,249	2,650
4,075	1,511	2,266	2,643	1,133	1,080	1,511	1,133	1,246	2,643
4,050	1,507	2,260	2,636	1,130	1,077	1,507	1,130	1,243	2,636
4,025	1,503	2,254	2,629	1,127	1,074	1,503	1,127	1,239	2,629
4,000	1,500	2,250	2,624	1,125	1,072	1,500	1,125	1,237	2,624
3,975	1,496	2,244	2,617	1,122	1,069	1,496	1,122	1,234	2,617
3,950	1,492	2,238	2,610	1,119	1,066	1,492	1,119	1,230	2,610
3,925	1,488	2,232	2,603	1,116	1,063	1,488	1,116	1,227	2,603
3,900	1,485	2,227	2,597	1,113	1,061	1,485	1,113	1,225	2,597
3,875	1,481	2,221	2,590	1,110	1,058	1,481	1,110	1,221	2,590
3,850	1,477	2,215	2,583	1,107	1,056	1,477	1,107	1,218	2,583
3,825	1,473	2,209	2,576	1,104	1,053	1,473	1,104	1,215	2,576
3,800	1,470	2,205	2,571	1,102	1,051	1,470	1,102	1,212	2,571
3,775	1,466	2,199	2,564	1,099	1,048	1,466	1,099	1,209	2,564
3,750	1,462	2,193	2,557	1,096	1,045	1,462	1,096	1,206	2,557
3,725	1,458	2,187	2,550	1,093	1,042	1,458	1,093	1,202	2,550
3,700	1,455	2,182	2,545	1,091	1,040	1,455	1,091	1,200	2,545
3,675	1,451	2,176	2,538	1,088	1,037	1,451	1,088	1,197	2,538
3,650	1,447	2,170	2,531	1,085	1,034	1,447	1,085	1,193	2,531
3,625	1,443	2,164	2,524	1,082	1,031	1,443	1,082	1,190	2,524
3,600	1,440	2,160	2,519	1,080	1,029	1,440	1,080	1,187	2,519
3,575	1,436	2,154	2,512	1,077	1,026	1,436	1,077	1,184	2,512
3,550	1,432	2,148	2,505	1,074	1,023	1,432	1,074	1,181	2,505
3,525	1,428	2,142	2,498	1,071	1,021	1,428	1,071	1,178	2,498
3,500	1,425	2,137	2,492	1,068	1,018	1,425	1,068	1,175	2,492
3,475	1,421	2,131	2,485	1,065	1,016	1,421	1,065	1,172	2,485
3,450	1,417	2,125	2,478	1,062	1,013	1,417	1,062	1,169	2,478
3,425	1,413	2,119	2,471	1,059	1,010	1,413	1,059	1,165	2,471
3,400	1,410	2,115	2,466	1,057	1,008	1,410	1,057	1,163	2,466
3,375	1,405	2,107	2,457	1,053	1,004	1,405	1,053	1,159	2,457
3,350	1,397	2,095	2,443	1,047	998	1,397	1,047	1,152	2,443
3,325	1,389	2,083	2,429	1,041	993	1,389	1,041	1,145	2,429
3,300	1,381	2,071	2,415	1,035	987	1,381	1,035	1,139	2,415
3,275	1,373	2,059	2,401	1,029	981	1,373	1,029	1,132	2,401
3,250	1,365	2,047	2,387	1,023	975	1,365	1,023	1,126	2,387
3,225	1,357	2,035	2,373	1,017	970	1,357	1,017	1,119	2,373
3,200	1,349	2,023	2,359	1,011	964	1,349	1,011	1,112	2,359
3,175	1,341	2,011	2,349	1,005	958	1,341	1,005	1,106	2,349
3,150	1,333	1,999	2,338	999	953	1,333	999	1,099	2,338
3,125	1,325	1,987	2,327	993	947	1,325	993	1,093	2,327
3,100	1,317	1,975	2,316	987	941	1,317	987	1,086	2,316
3,075	1,309	1,963	2,306	981	935	1,309	981	1,079	2,306
3,050	1,301	1,951	2,295	975	930	1,301	975	1,073	2,295
3,025	1,293	1,939	2,284	969	924	1,293	969	1,066	2,284
3,000	1,285	1,927	2,274	963	918	1,285	963	1,060	2,274
2,975	1,277	1,915	2,263	957	913	1,277	957	1,053	2,263

TABLE 11—SURVIVOR'S BENEFITS (Continued)

Average Indexed Monthly Earnings	Worker's PIA	Surviving Spouse & 1 Child; or 2 Children	Surviving Spouse & 2 Children; or 3 Children	One Child (No Parent)	Widow or Widower Age 60	Widow or Widower Age 65	Each of Two Parents	Sole Parent	Maximum Family Benefits
2,950	1,269	1,903	2,252	951	907	1,269	951	1,046	2,252
2,925	1,261	1,891	2,241	945	901	1,261	945	1,040	2,241
2,900	1,253	1,879	2,231	939	895	1,253	939	1,033	2,231
2,875	1,245	1,867	2,220	933	890	1,245	933	1,027	2,220
2,850	1,237	1,855	2,209	927	884	1,237	927	1,020	2,209
2,825	1,229	1,843	2,199	921	878	1,229	921	1,013	2,199
2,800	1,221	1,831	2,188	915	873	1,221	915	1,007	2,188
2,775	1,213	1,819	2,177	909	867	1,213	909	1,000	2,177
2,750	1,205	1,807	2,166	903	861	1,205	903	994	2,166
2,725	1,197	1,795	2,156	897	855	1,197	897	987	2,156
2,700	1,189	1,783	2,145	891	850	1,189	891	980	2,145
2,675	1,181	1,771	2,134	885	844	1,181	885	974	2,134
2,650	1,173	1,759	2,123	879	838	1,173	879	967	2,123
2,625	1,165	1,747	2,113	873	832	1,165	873	961	2,113
2,600	1,157	1,735	2,102	867	827	1,157	867	954	2,102
2,575	1,149	1,723	2,091	861	821	1,149	861	947	2,091
2,550	1,141	1,711	2,081	855	815	1,141	855	941	2,081
2,525	1,133	1,699	2,070	849	810	1,133	849	934	2,070
2,500	1,125	1,687	2,059	843	804	1,125	843	928	2,059
2,475	1,117	1,675	2,048	837	798	1,117	837	921	2,048
2,450	1,109	1,663	2,038	831	792	1,109	831	914	2,038
2,425	1,101	1,651	2,027	825	787	1,101	825	908	2,027
2,400	1,093	1,639	2,016	819	781	1,093	819	901	2,016
2,375	1,085	1,627	2,006	813	775	1,085	813	895	2,006
2,350	1,077	1,615	1,995	807	770	1,077	807	888	1,995
2,325	1,069	1,603	1,984	801	764	1,069	801	881	1,984
2,300	1,061	1,591	1,973	795	758	1,061	795	875	1,973
2,275	1,053	1,579	1,963	789	752	1,053	789	868	1,963
2,250	1,045	1,567	1,952	783	747	1,045	783	862	1,952
2,225	1,037	1,555	1,941	777	741	1,037	777	855	1,941
2,200	1,029	1,543	1,924	771	735	1,029	771	848	1,924
2,175	1,021	1,531	1,902	765	730	1,021	765	842	1,902
2,150	1,013	1,519	1,880	759	724	1,013	759	835	1,880
2,125	1,005	1,507	1,858	753	718	1,005	753	829	1,858
2,100	997	1,495	1,837	747	712	997	747	822	1,837
2,075	989	1,483	1,815	741	707	989	741	815	1,815
2,050	981	1,471	1,793	735	701	981	735	809	1,793
2,025	973	1,459	1,771	729	695	973	729	802	1,771
2,000	965	1,447	1,750	723	689	965	723	796	1,750
1,975	957	1,435	1,728	717	684	957	717	789	1,728
1,950	949	1,423	1,706	711	678	949	711	782	1,706
1,925	941	1,411	1,684	705	672	941	705	776	1,684
1,900	933	1,399	1,663	699	667	933	699	769	1,663
1,875	925	1,387	1,641	693	661	925	693	763	1,641
1,850	917	1,375	1,619	687	655	917	687	756	1,619
1,825	909	1,363	1,597	681	649	909	681	749	1,597
1,800	901	1,351	1,575	675	644	901	675	743	1,575
1,775	893	1,339	1,554	669	638	893	669	736	1,554
1,750	885	1,327	1,532	663	632	885	663	730	1,532
1,725	877	1,315	1,510	657	627	877	657	723	1,510

TABLE 11—SURVIVOR'S BENEFITS (Continued)

Average Indexed Monthly Earnings	Worker's PIA	Surviving Spouse & 1 Child; or 2 Children	Surviving Spouse & 2 Children; or 3 Children	One Child (No Parent)	Widow or Widower Age 60	Widow or Widower Age 65	Each of Two Parents	Sole Parent	Maximum Family Benefits
1,700	869	1,303	1,488	651	621	869	651	716	1,488
1,675	861	1,291	1,467	645	615	861	645	710	1,467
1,650	853	1,279	1,445	639	609	853	639	703	1,445
1,625	845	1,267	1,423	633	604	845	633	697	1,423
1,600	837	1,255	1,401	627	598	837	627	690	1,401
1,575	829	1,243	1,380	621	592	829	621	683	1,38
1,550	821	1,231	1,358	615	587	821	615	677	1,358
1,525	813	1,219	1,336	609	581	813	609	670	1,336
1,500	805	1,207	1,314	603	575	805	603	664	1,314
1,475	797	1,195	1,293	597	569	797	597	657	1,293
1,450	789	1,183	1,271	591	564	789	591	650	1,271
1,425	781	1,171	1,249	585	558	781	585	644	1,249
1,400	773	1,159	1,227	579	552	773	579	637	1,227
1,375	765	1,147	1,206	573	546	765	573	631	1,206
1,350	757	1,135	1,184	567	541	757	567	624	1,184
1,325	749	1,123	1,162	561	535	749	561	617	1,162
1,300	741	1,111	1,140	555	529	741	555	611	1,140
1,275	733	1,099	1,119	549	524	733	549	604	1,119
1,250	725	1,087	1,097	543	518	725	543	598	1,097
1,225	717	1,075	1,075	537	512	717	537	591	1,075
1,200	709	1,063	1,063	531	506	709	531	584	1,063
1,175	701	1,051	1,051	525	501	701	525	578	1,051
1,150	693	1,039	1,039	519	495	693	519	571	1,039
1,125	685	1,027	1,027	513	489	685	513	565	1,027
1,100	677	1,015	1,015	507	484	677	507	558	1,015
1,075	669	1,003	1,003	501	478	669	501	551	1,003
1,050	661	991	991	495	472	661	495	545	991
1,025	653	979	979	489	466	653	489	538	979
1,000	645	967	967	483	461	645	483	532	967
975	637	955	955	477	455	637	477	525	955
950	629	943	943	471	449	629	471	518	943
925	621	931	931	465	444	621	465	512	931
900	613	919	919	459	438	613	459	505	919
875	605	907	907	453	432	605	453	499	907
850	597	895	895	447	426	597	447	492	895
825	589	883	883	441	421	589	441	485	883
800	581	871	871	435	415	581	435	479	871
775	573	859	859	429	409	573	429	472	859
750	565	847	847	423	403	565	423	466	847
725	557	835	835	417	398	557	417	459	835
700	549	823	823	411	392	549	411	452	823
675	541	811	811	405	386	541	405	446	811
650	533	799	799	399	381	533	399	439	799

317

SOCIAL SECURITY TABLES

TABLE 12—DISABILITY BENEFITS

Average Indexed Monthly Earnings	Disabled Worker	Disabled Worker Spouse and Children	One Child (No Spouse)	Spouse Age 62
6,700	1,905	2,857	952	698
6,675	1,901	2,851	950	697
6,650	1,897	2,845	948	695
6,625	1,893	2,839	946	694
6,600	1,890	2,835	945	693
6,575	1,886	2,829	943	691
6,550	1,882	2,823	941	690
6,525	1,878	2,817	939	688
6,500	1,875	2,812	937	687
6,475	1,871	2,806	935	686
6,450	1,867	2,800	933	684
6,425	1,863	2,794	931	683
6,400	1,860	2,790	930	682
6,375	1,856	2,784	928	680
6,350	1,852	2,778	926	679
6,325	1,848	2,772	924	677
6,300	1,845	2,767	922	676
6,275	1,841	2,761	920	675
6,250	1,837	2,755	918	673
6,225	1,833	2,749	916	672
6,200	1,830	2,745	915	671
6,175	1,826	2,739	913	669
6,150	1,822	2,733	911	668
6,125	1,818	2,727	909	666
6,100	1,815	2,722	907	665
6,075	1,811	2,716	905	664
6,050	1,807	2,710	903	662
6,025	1,803	2,704	901	661
6,000	1,800	2,700	900	660
5,975	1,796	2,694	898	658
5,950	1,792	2,688	896	657
5,925	1,788	2,682	894	655
5,900	1,785	2,677	892	654
5,875	1,781	2,671	890	653
5,850	1,777	2,665	888	651
5,825	1,773	2,659	886	650
5,800	1,770	2,655	885	649
5,775	1,766	2,649	883	647
5,750	1,762	2,643	881	646
5,725	1,758	2,637	879	644
5,700	1,755	2,632	877	643
5,675	1,751	2,626	875	642
5,650	1,747	2,620	873	640
5,625	1,743	2,614	871	639
5,600	1,740	2,610	870	638
5,575	1,736	2,604	868	636
5,550	1,732	2,598	866	635
5,525	1,728	2,592	864	633
5,500	1,725	2,587	862	632
5,475	1,721	2,581	860	631
5,450	1,717	2,575	858	629

319

TABLE 12—DISABILITY BENEFITS

Average Indexed Monthly Earnings	Disabled Worker	Disabled Worker Spouse and Children	One Child (No Spouse)	Spouse Age 62
5,425	1,713	2,569	856	628
5,400	1,710	2,565	855	627
5,375	1,706	2,559	853	625
5,350	1,702	2,553	851	624
5,325	1,698	2,547	849	622
5,300	1,695	2,542	847	621
5,275	1,691	2,536	845	620
5,250	1,687	2,530	843	618
5,225	1,683	2,524	841	617
5,200	1,680	2,520	840	616
5,175	1,676	2,514	838	614
5,150	1,672	2,508	836	613
5,125	1,668	2,502	834	611
5,100	1,665	2,497	832	610
5,075	1,661	2,491	830	609
5,050	1,657	2,485	828	607
5,025	1,653	2,479	826	606
5,000	1,650	2,475	825	605
4,975	1,646	2,469	823	603
4,950	1,642	2,463	821	602
4,925	1,638	2,457	819	600
4,900	1,635	2,452	817	599
4,875	1,631	2,446	815	598
4,850	1,627	2,440	813	596
4,825	1,623	2,434	811	595
4,800	1,620	2,430	810	594
4,775	1,616	2,424	808	592
4,750	1,612	2,418	806	591
4,725	1,608	2,412	804	589
4,700	1,605	2,407	802	588
4,675	1,601	2,401	800	587
4,650	1,597	2,395	798	585
4,625	1,593	2,389	796	584
4,600	1,590	2,385	795	583
4,575	1,586	2,379	793	581
4,550	1,582	2,373	791	580
4,525	1,578	2,367	789	578
4,500	1,575	2,362	787	577
4,475	1,571	2,356	785	576
4,450	1,567	2,350	783	574
4,425	1,563	2,344	781	573
4,400	1,560	2,340	780	572
4,375	1,556	2,334	778	570
4,350	1,552	2,328	776	569
4,325	1,548	2,322	774	567
4,300	1,545	2,317	772	566
4,275	1,541	2,311	770	565
4,250	1,537	2,305	768	563
4,225	1,533	2,299	766	562
4,200	1,530	2,295	765	561
4,175	1,526	2,289	763	559

TABLE 12—DISABILITY BENEFITS

Average Indexed Monthly Earnings	Disabled Worker	Disabled Worker Spouse and Children	One Child (No Spouse)	Spouse Age 62
4,150	1,522	2,283	761	558
4,125	1,518	2,277	759	556
4,100	1,515	2,272	757	555
4,075	1,511	2,266	755	554
4,050	1,507	2,260	753	552
4,025	1,503	2,254	751	551
4,000	1,500	2,250	750	550
3,975	1,496	2,244	748	548
3,950	1,492	2,238	746	547
3,925	1,488	2,232	744	545
3,900	1,485	2,227	742	544
3,875	1,481	2,221	740	543
3,850	1,477	2,215	738	541
3,825	1,473	2,209	736	540
3,800	1,470	2,205	735	539
3,775	1,466	2,199	733	537
3,750	1,462	2,193	731	536
3,725	1,458	2,187	729	534
3,700	1,455	2,182	727	533
3,675	1,451	2,176	725	532
3,650	1,447	2,170	723	530
3,625	1,443	2,164	721	529
3,600	1,440	2,160	720	528
3,575	1,436	2,154	718	526
3,550	1,432	2,148	716	525
3,525	1,428	2,142	714	523
3,500	1,425	2,137	712	522
3,475	1,421	2,131	710	521
3,450	1,417	2,125	708	519
3,425	1,413	2,119	706	518
3,400	1,410	2,115	705	517
3,375	1,405	2,107	702	515
3,350	1,397	2,095	698	512
3,325	1,389	2,083	694	509
3,300	1,381	2,071	690	506
3,275	1,373	2,059	686	503
3,250	1,365	2,047	682	500
3,225	1,357	2,035	678	497
3,200	1,349	2,023	674	494
3,175	1,341	2,011	670	491
3,150	1,333	1,999	666	488
3,125	1,325	1,987	662	485
3,100	1,317	1,975	658	482
3,075	1,309	1,963	654	479
3,050	1,301	1,951	650	477
3,025	1,293	1,939	646	474
3,000	1,285	1,927	642	471
2,975	1,277	1,915	638	468
2,950	1,269	1,903	634	465
2,925	1,261	1,891	630	462

TABLE 12—DISABILITY BENEFITS (Continued)

Average Indexed Monthly Earnings	Disabled Worker	Disabled Worker Spouse and Children	One Child (No Spouse)	Spouse Age 62
2,900	1,253	1,879	626	459
2,875	1,245	1,867	622	456
2,850	1,237	1,855	618	453
2,825	1,229	1,843	614	450
2,800	1,221	1,831	610	447
2,775	1,213	1,819	606	444
2,750	1,205	1,807	602	441
2,725	1,197	1,795	598	438
2,700	1,189	1,783	594	435
2,675	1,181	1,771	590	433
2,650	1,173	1,759	586	430
2,625	1,165	1,747	582	427
2,600	1,157	1,735	578	424
2,575	1,149	1,723	574	421
2,550	1,141	1,711	570	418
2,525	1,133	1,699	566	415
2,500	1,125	1,687	562	412
2,475	1,117	1,675	558	409
2,450	1,109	1,663	554	406
2,425	1,101	1,651	550	403
2,400	1,093	1,639	546	400
2,375	1,085	1,627	542	397
2,350	1,077	1,615	538	394
2,325	1,069	1,603	534	391
2,300	1,061	1,591	530	389
2,275	1,053	1,579	526	386
2,250	1,045	1,567	522	383
2,225	1,037	1,555	518	380
2,200	1,029	1,543	514	377
2,175	1,021	1,531	510	374
2,150	1,013	1,519	506	371
2,125	1,005	1,507	502	368
2,100	997	1,495	498	365
2,075	989	1,483	494	362
2,050	981	1,471	490	359
2,025	973	1,459	486	356
2,000	965	1,447	482	353
1,975	957	1,435	478	350
1,950	949	1,423	474	347
1,925	941	1,411	470	345
1,900	933	1,399	466	342
1,875	925	1,387	462	339
1,850	917	1,375	458	336
1,825	909	1,363	454	333
1,800	901	1,351	450	330
1,775	893	1,339	446	327
1,750	885	1,327	442	324
1,725	877	1,315	438	321
1,700	869	1,303	434	318
1,675	861	1,291	430	315

TABLE 12—DISABILITY BENEFITS (Continued)

Average Indexed Monthly Earnings	Disabled Worker	Disabled Worker Spouse and Children	One Child (No Spouse)	Spouse Age 62
1,650	853	1,279	426	312
1,625	845	1,267	422	309
1,600	837	1,255	418	306
1,575	829	1,243	414	303
1,550	821	1,231	410	301
1,525	813	1,219	406	298
1,500	805	1,207	402	295
1,475	797	1,195	398	292
1,450	789	1,183	394	289
1,425	781	1,171	390	286
1,400	773	1,159	386	283
1,375	765	1,147	382	280
1,350	757	1,135	378	277
1,325	749	1,123	374	274
1,300	741	1,111	370	271
1,275	733	1,099	366	268
1,250	725	1,087	362	265
1,225	717	1,075	358	262
1,200	709	1,063	354	259
1,175	701	1,051	350	257
1,150	693	1,039	346	254
1,125	685	1,027	342	251
1,100	677	1,015	338	248
1,075	669	1,003	334	245
1,050	661	991	330	242
1,025	653	979	326	239
1,000	645	967	322	236
975	637	955	318	233
950	629	943	314	230
925	621	931	310	227
900	613	919	306	224
875	605	907	302	221
850	597	895	298	218
825	589	883	294	215
800	581	871	290	213
775	573	859	286	210
750	565	847	282	207
725	557	835	278	204
700	549	823	274	201
675	541	811	270	198
650	533	799	266	195

TABLE 13 - PIA TABLE FOR PERSONS ELIGIBLE BEFORE 1979*
(Primary Insurance Amount (PIA) and Maximum
Family Benefits Beginning December 2000)

Average monthly wage At least	more than	PIA	Maximum family benefit	Average monthly wage At least	more than	PIA	Maximum family benefit
6,696	6,700	3413.60	5973.80	6,401	6,405	3354.60	5870.50
6,691	6,695	3412.60	5972.00	6,396	6,400	3353.60	5868.80
6,686	6,690	3411.60	5970.30	6,391	6,395	3352.60	5867.00
6,681	6,685	3410.60	5968.50	6,386	6,390	3351.60	5865.30
6,676	6,680	3409.60	5966.80	6,381	6,385	3350.60	5863.50
6,671	6,675	3408.60	5965.00	6,376	6,380	3349.60	5861.80
6,666	6,670	3407.60	5963.30	6,371	6,375	3348.60	5860.00
6,661	6,665	3406.60	5961.50	6,366	6,370	3347.60	5858.30
6,656	6,660	3405.60	5959.80	6,361	6,365	3346.60	5856.50
6,651	6,655	3404.60	5958.00	6,356	6,360	3345.60	5854.80
6,646	6,650	3403.60	5956.30	6,351	6,355	3344.60	5853.00
6,641	6,645	3402.60	5954.50	6,346	6,350	3343.60	5851.30
6,636	6,640	3401.60	5952.80	6,341	6,345	3342.60	5849.60
6,631	6,635	3400.60	5951.00	6,336	6,340	3341.60	5847.70
6,626	6,630	3399.60	5949.30	6,331	6,335	3340.50	5845.90
6,621	6,625	3398.60	5947.50	6,326	6,330	3339.50	5844.10
6,616	6,620	3397.60	5945.80	6,321	6,325	3338.40	5842.30
6,611	6,615	3396.60	5944.00	6,316	6,320	3337.40	5840.50
6,606	6,610	3395.60	5942.30	6,311	6,315	3336.40	5838.70
6,601	6,605	3394.60	5940.50	6,306	6,310	3335.30	5836.80
6,596	6,600	3393.60	5938.80	6,301	6,305	3334.30	5835.10
6,591	6,595	3392.60	5937.00	6,296	6,300	3333.30	5833.20
6,586	6,590	3391.60	5935.30	6,291	6,295	3332.20	5831.50
6,581	6,585	3390.60	5933.50	6,286	6,290	3331.20	5829.60
6,576	6,580	3389.60	5931.80	6,281	6,285	3330.20	5827.80
6,571	6,575	3388.60	5930.00	6,276	6,280	3329.10	5826.00
6,566	6,570	3387.60	5928.30	6,271	6,275	3328.10	5824.20
6,561	6,565	3386.60	5926.50	6,266	6,270	3327.10	5822.30
6,556	6,560	3385.60	5924.80	6,261	6,265	3326.00	5820.60
6,551	6,555	3384.60	5923.00	6,256	6,260	3325.00	5818.70
6,546	6,550	3383.60	5921.30	6,251	6,255	3324.00	5817.00
6,541	6,545	3382.60	5919.50	6,246	6,250	3322.90	5815.10
6,536	6,540	3381.60	5917.80	6,241	6,245	3321.90	5813.30
6,531	6,535	3380.60	5916.00	6,236	6,240	3320.90	5811.50
6,526	6,530	3379.60	5914.30	6,231	6,235	3319.80	5809.70
6,521	6,525	3378.60	5912.50	6,226	6,230	3318.80	5807.90
6,516	6,520	3377.60	5910.80	6,221	6,225	3317.70	5806.10
6,511	6,515	3376.60	5909.00	6,216	6,220	3316.70	5804.20
6,506	6,510	3375.60	5907.30	6,211	6,215	3315.70	5802.50
6,501	6,505	3374.60	5905.50	6,206	6,210	3314.60	5800.60
6,496	6,500	3373.60	5903.80	6,201	6,205	3313.60	5798.80
6,491	6,495	3372.60	5902.00	6,196	6,200	3312.60	5797.00
6,486	6,490	3371.60	5900.30	6,191	6,195	3311.50	5795.20
6,481	6,485	3370.60	5898.50	6,186	6,190	3310.50	5793.40
6,476	6,480	3369.60	5896.80	6,181	6,185	3309.50	5791.60
6,471	6,475	3368.60	5895.00	6,176	6,180	3308.40	5789.70
6,466	6,470	3367.60	5893.30	6,171	6,175	3307.40	5788.00
6,461	6,465	3366.60	5891.50	6,166	6,170	3306.40	5786.10
6,456	6,460	3365.60	5889.80	6,161	6,165	3305.30	5784.40
6,451	6,455	3364.60	5888.00	6,156	6,160	3304.30	5782.50
6,446	6,450	3363.60	5886.30	6,151	6,155	3303.30	5780.70
6,441	6,445	3362.60	5884.50	6,146	6,150	3302.20	5778.90
6,436	6,440	3361.60	5882.80	6,141	6,145	3301.20	5777.10
6,431	6,435	3360.60	5881.00	6,136	6,140	3300.20	5775.30
6,426	6,430	3359.60	5879.30	6,131	6,135	3299.10	5773.50
6,421	6,425	3358.60	5877.50	6,126	6,130	3298.10	5771.60
6,416	6,420	3357.60	5875.80	6,121	6,125	3297.00	5769.90
6,411	6,415	3356.60	5874.00	6,116	6,120	3296.00	5768.00
6,406	6,410	3355.60	5872.30	6,111	6,115	3295.00	5766.20

325

TABLE 13 - PIA TABLE FOR PERSONS ELIGIBLE BEFORE 1979* (continued)
(Primary Insurance Amount (PIA) and Maximum
Family Benefits Beginning December 2000)

Average monthly wage At least	more than	PIA	Maximum family benefit	Average monthly wage At least	more than	PIA	Maximum family benefit
6,106	6,110	3293.90	5764.40	5,811	5,815	3231.60	5655.40
6,101	6,105	3292.90	5762.60	5,806	5,810	3230.60	5653.60
6,096	6,100	3291.90	5760.80	5,801	5,805	3229.60	5651.70
6,091	6,095	3290.80	5759.00	5,796	5,800	3228.50	5649.90
6,086	6,090	3289.80	5757.10	5,791	5,795	3227.40	5648.00
6,081	6,085	3288.80	5755.40	5,786	5,790	3226.40	5646.20
6,076	6,080	3287.70	5753.50	5,781	5,785	3225.30	5644.30
6,071	6,075	3286.70	5751.80	5,776	5,780	3224.30	5642.50
6,066	6,070	3285.70	5749.90	5,771	5,775	3223.10	5640.60
6,061	6,065	3284.60	5748.10	5,766	5,770	3222.10	5638.70
6,056	6,060	3283.60	5746.30	5,761	5,765	3221.10	5636.90
6,051	6,055	3282.60	5744.50	5,756	5,760	3220.00	5635.10
6,046	6,050	3281.50	5742.60	5,751	5,755	3218.90	5633.10
6,041	6,045	3280.40	5740.80	5,746	5,750	3217.90	5631.40
6,036	6,040	3279.30	5738.90	5,741	5,745	3216.80	5629.40
6,031	6,035	3278.30	5737.10	5,736	5,740	3215.80	5627.70
6,026	6,030	3277.30	5735.20	5,731	5,735	3214.70	5625.70
6,021	6,025	3276.10	5733.30	5,726	5,730	3213.60	5623.90
6,016	6,020	3275.10	5731.50	5,721	5,725	3212.60	5622.10
6,011	6,015	3274.10	5729.60	5,716	5,720	3211.60	5620.20
6,006	6,010	3273.00	5727.80	5,711	5,715	3210.50	5618.30
6,001	6,005	3271.90	5725.90	5,706	5,710	3209.40	5616.50
5,996	6,000	3270.90	5724.10	5,701	5,705	3208.30	5614.60
5,991	5,995	3269.80	5722.20	5,696	5,700	3207.30	5612.90
5,986	5,990	3268.80	5720.40	5,691	5,695	3206.30	5610.90
5,981	5,985	3267.70	5718.40	5,686	5,690	3205.10	5609.10
5,976	5,980	3266.60	5716.70	5,681	5,685	3204.00	5607.10
5,971	5,975	3265.60	5714.80	5,676	5,680	3203.00	5605.30
5,966	5,970	3264.50	5712.90	5,671	5,675	3201.90	5603.30
5,961	5,965	3263.50	5711.10	5,666	5,670	3200.80	5601.60
5,956	5,960	3262.40	5709.20	5,661	5,665	3199.80	5599.70
5,951	5,955	3261.30	5707.40	5,656	5,660	3198.70	5597.70
5,946	5,950	3260.30	5705.60	5,651	5,655	3197.70	5595.90
5,941	5,945	3259.30	5703.60	5,646	5,650	3196.50	5594.00
5,936	5,940	3258.10	5701.90	5,641	5,645	3195.40	5592.20
5,931	5,935	3257.10	5699.90	5,636	5,640	3194.40	5590.20
5,926	5,930	3256.10	5698.10	5,631	5,635	3193.30	5588.30
5,921	5,925	3255.00	5696.20	5,626	5,630	3192.20	5586.60
5,916	5,920	3253.90	5694.40	5,621	5,625	3191.20	5584.60
5,911	5,915	3252.90	5692.60	5,616	5,620	3190.10	5582.80
5,906	5,910	3251.80	5690.70	5,611	5,615	3189.10	5580.80
5,901	5,905	3250.80	5688.80	5,606	5,610	3188.00	5579.00
5,896	5,900	3249.60	5687.00	5,601	5,605	3186.80	5577.00
5,891	5,895	3248.60	5685.10	5,596	5,600	3185.80	5575.30
5,886	5,890	3247.60	5683.30	5,591	5,595	3184.70	5573.30
5,881	5,885	3246.50	5681.40	5,586	5,590	3183.60	5571.50
5,876	5,880	3245.40	5679.60	5,581	5,585	3182.60	5569.60
5,871	5,875	3244.40	5677.60	5,576	5,580	3181.50	5567.70
5,866	5,870	3243.30	5675.90	5,571	5,575	3180.50	5565.80
5,861	5,865	3242.30	5673.90	5,566	5,570	3179.30	5563.90
5,856	5,860	3241.20	5672.20	5,561	5,565	3178.20	5562.00
5,851	5,855	3240.10	5670.30	5,556	5,560	3177.20	5560.30
5,846	5,850	3239.10	5668.40	5,551	5,555	3176.20	5558.30
5,841	5,845	3238.10	5666.60	5,546	5,550	3175.10	5556.50
5,836	5,840	3237.00	5664.70	5,541	5,545	3174.00	5554.50
5,831	5,835	3235.90	5662.80	5,536	5,540	3172.90	5552.70
5,826	5,830	3234.80	5661.00	5,531	5,535	3171.90	5550.90
5,821	5,825	3233.80	5659.10	5,526	5,530	3170.80	5548.90
5,816	5,820	3232.80	5657.40	5,521	5,525	3169.60	5547.00

SOCIAL SECURITY TABLES

TABLE 13 - PIA TABLE FOR PERSONS ELIGIBLE BEFORE 1979* (continued)
(Primary Insurance Amount (PIA) and Maximum Family Benefits Beginning December 2000)

Average monthly wage At least	more than	PIA	Maximum family benefit	Average monthly wage At least	more than	PIA	Maximum family benefit
5,516	5,520	3168.60	5545.20	5,221	5,225	3104.10	5432.50
5,511	5,515	3167.60	5543.30	5,216	5,220	3103.00	5430.50
5,506	5,510	3166.50	5541.40	5,211	5,215	3101.90	5428.60
5,501	5,505	3165.40	5539.50	5,206	5,210	3100.90	5426.60
5,496	5,500	3164.40	5537.70	5,201	5,205	3099.70	5424.60
5,491	5,495	3163.30	5535.80	5,196	5,200	3098.50	5422.50
5,486	5,490	3162.20	5534.00	5,191	5,195	3097.50	5420.70
5,481	5,485	3161.00	5531.90	5,186	5,190	3096.40	5418.80
5,476	5,480	3160.00	5530.20	5,181	5,185	3095.00	5416.60
5,471	5,475	3159.00	5528.20	5,176	5,180	3094.00	5414.80
5,466	5,470	3157.90	5526.40	5,171	5,175	3092.90	5412.80
5,461	5,465	3156.80	5524.50	5,166	5,170	3091.80	5410.80
5,456	5,460	3155.80	5522.60	5,161	5,165	3090.70	5408.80
5,451	5,455	3154.70	5520.70	5,156	5,160	3089.50	5406.80
5,446	5,450	3153.60	5518.90	5,151	5,155	3088.40	5404.80
5,441	5,445	3152.40	5516.90	5,146	5,150	3087.30	5403.00
5,436	5,440	3151.30	5514.90	5,141	5,145	3086.10	5400.90
5,431	5,435	3150.30	5513.10	5,136	5,140	3085.10	5398.90
5,426	5,430	3149.20	5511.20	5,131	5,135	3083.80	5397.00
5,421	5,425	3148.10	5509.30	5,126	5,130	3082.80	5395.00
5,416	5,420	3147.00	5507.40	5,121	5,125	3081.70	5393.10
5,411	5,415	3145.80	5505.30	5,116	5,120	3080.60	5391.00
5,406	5,410	3144.80	5503.60	5,111	5,115	3079.30	5389.10
5,401	5,405	3143.70	5501.60	5,106	5,110	3078.20	5387.10
5,396	5,400	3142.60	5499.60	5,101	5,105	3077.10	5385.20
5,391	5,395	3141.50	5497.70	5,096	5,100	3076.00	5383.20
5,386	5,390	3140.50	5495.80	5,091	5,095	3074.80	5381.10
5,381	5,385	3139.30	5493.90	5,086	5,090	3073.70	5379.20
5,376	5,380	3138.30	5492.10	5,081	5,085	3072.60	5377.20
5,371	5,375	3137.10	5490.00	5,076	5,080	3071.30	5374.90
5,366	5,370	3136.00	5488.10	5,071	5,075	3070.20	5373.00
5,361	5,365	3134.90	5486.30	5,066	5,070	3069.10	5370.90
5,356	5,360	3133.80	5484.30	5,061	5,065	3067.80	5369.00
5,351	5,355	3132.80	5482.30	5,056	5,060	3066.80	5366.80
5,346	5,350	3131.70	5480.50	5,051	5,055	3065.60	5364.90
5,341	5,345	3130.50	5478.50	5,046	5,050	3064.40	5362.80
5,336	5,340	3129.40	5476.80	5,041	5,045	3063.10	5360.80
5,331	5,335	3128.30	5474.60	5,036	5,040	3061.90	5358.60
5,326	5,330	3127.30	5472.80	5,031	5,035	3060.90	5356.70
5,321	5,325	3126.10	5470.90	5,026	5,030	3059.60	5354.50
5,316	5,320	3125.00	5469.00	5,021	5,025	3058.40	5352.60
5,311	5,315	3124.00	5467.00	5,016	5,020	3057.20	5350.40
5,306	5,310	3123.00	5465.20	5,011	5,015	3056.10	5348.30
5,301	5,305	3121.80	5463.20	5,006	5,010	3054.90	5346.20
5,296	5,300	3120.60	5461.30	5,001	5,005	3053.70	5344.20
5,291	5,295	3119.50	5459.40	4,996	5,000	3052.40	5342.00
5,286	5,290	3118.50	5457.40	4,991	4,995	3051.20	5339.90
5,281	5,285	3117.40	5455.50	4,986	4,990	3050.10	5337.90
5,276	5,280	3116.30	5453.60	4,981	4,985	3049.00	5335.80
5,271	5,275	3115.20	5451.70	4,976	4,980	3047.70	5333.60
5,266	5,270	3114.20	5449.80	4,971	4,975	3046.50	5331.50
5,261	5,265	3112.90	5447.80	4,966	4,970	3045.30	5329.60
5,256	5,260	3111.90	5446.00	4,961	4,965	3044.10	5327.40
5,251	5,255	3110.80	5443.90	4,956	4,960	3043.10	5325.30
5,246	5,250	3109.70	5442.10	4,951	4,955	3041.70	5323.30
5,241	5,245	3108.60	5440.10	4,946	4,950	3040.60	5321.30
5,236	5,240	3107.50	5438.30	4,941	4,945	3039.40	5319.20
5,231	5,235	3106.50	5436.40	4,936	4,940	3038.30	5317.10
5,226	5,230	3105.40	5434.50	4,931	4,935	3036.80	5315.10

327

TABLE 13 - PIA TABLE FOR PERSONS ELIGIBLE BEFORE 1979* (continued)
(Primary Insurance Amount (PIA) and Maximum Family Benefits Beginning December 2000)

At least	more than	PIA	Maximum family benefit	At least	more than	PIA	Maximum family benefit
4,926	4,930	3035.80	5312.90	4,631	4,635	2964.50	5188.40
4,921	4,925	3034.70	5310.90	4,626	4,630	2963.30	5186.00
4,916	4,920	3033.40	5308.70	4,621	4,625	2962.10	5184.10
4,911	4,915	3032.20	5306.70	4,616	4,620	2960.90	5181.90
4,906	4,910	3031.20	5304.50	4,611	4,615	2959.80	5179.70
4,901	4,905	3029.90	5302.60	4,606	4,610	2958.40	5177.40
4,896	4,900	3028.60	5300.30	4,601	4,605	2957.20	5175.30
4,891	4,895	3027.50	5298.40	4,596	4,600	2955.90	5173.30
4,886	4,890	3026.30	5296.10	4,591	4,595	2954.70	5170.80
4,881	4,885	3025.20	5294.30	4,586	4,590	2953.30	5168.70
4,876	4,880	3023.90	5292.00	4,581	4,585	2952.10	5166.40
4,871	4,875	3022.90	5290.00	4,576	4,580	2950.90	5164.40
4,866	4,870	3021.40	5288.00	4,571	4,575	2949.60	5162.00
4,861	4,865	3020.20	5286.00	4,566	4,570	2948.50	5159.90
4,856	4,860	3019.10	5283.70	4,561	4,565	2947.00	5157.60
4,851	4,855	3018.10	5281.80	4,556	4,560	2945.90	5155.60
4,846	4,850	3016.80	5279.60	4,551	4,555	2944.60	5153.00
4,841	4,845	3015.50	5277.60	4,546	4,550	2943.30	5151.10
4,836	4,840	3014.50	5275.30	4,541	4,545	2942.10	5148.70
4,831	4,835	3013.20	5273.40	4,536	4,540	2940.80	5146.90
4,826	4,830	3012.00	5271.20	4,531	4,535	2939.50	5144.20
4,821	4,825	3010.80	5269.20	4,526	4,530	2938.20	5142.50
4,816	4,820	3009.60	5267.10	4,521	4,525	2937.00	5139.90
4,811	4,815	3008.50	5265.00	4,516	4,520	2935.70	5138.10
4,806	4,810	3007.30	5262.90	4,511	4,515	2934.60	5135.50
4,801	4,805	3006.00	5261.00	4,506	4,510	2933.50	5133.60
4,796	4,800	3004.90	5258.70	4,501	4,505	2931.90	5131.40
4,791	4,795	3003.60	5256.70	4,496	4,500	2930.70	5129.20
4,786	4,790	3002.30	5254.30	4,491	4,495	2929.60	5126.90
4,781	4,785	3001.20	5252.50	4,486	4,490	2928.10	5124.60
4,776	4,780	3000.10	5250.00	4,481	4,485	2926.80	5122.60
4,771	4,775	2998.80	5248.10	4,476	4,480	2925.80	5120.30
4,766	4,770	2997.40	5245.80	4,471	4,475	2924.50	5117.90
4,761	4,765	2996.40	5243.90	4,466	4,470	2923.10	5116.00
4,756	4,760	2995.10	5241.50	4,461	4,465	2921.90	5113.70
4,751	4,755	2993.70	5239.60	4,456	4,460	2920.80	5111.50
4,746	4,750	2992.70	5237.40	4,451	4,455	2919.40	5109.10
4,741	4,745	2991.60	5235.40	4,446	4,450	2918.10	5107.20
4,736	4,740	2990.20	5233.00	4,441	4,445	2916.80	5104.70
4,731	4,735	2988.80	5231.00	4,436	4,440	2915.60	5102.50
4,726	4,730	2987.80	5228.80	4,431	4,435	2914.10	5100.20
4,721	4,725	2986.50	5226.70	4,426	4,430	2912.90	5097.80
4,716	4,720	2985.20	5224.40	4,421	4,425	2911.60	5095.80
4,711	4,715	2984.10	5222.50	4,416	4,420	2910.50	5093.40
4,706	4,710	2982.90	5220.40	4,411	4,415	2908.90	5090.90
4,701	4,705	2981.70	5218.10	4,406	4,410	2907.80	5088.90
4,696	4,700	2980.30	5216.00	4,401	4,405	2906.40	5086.40
4,691	4,695	2979.20	5213.90	4,396	4,400	2904.90	5084.50
4,686	4,690	2978.00	5211.80	4,391	4,395	2903.80	5081.90
4,681	4,685	2976.80	5209.60	4,386	4,390	2902.60	5079.90
4,676	4,680	2975.60	5207.40	4,381	4,385	2901.10	5077.30
4,671	4,675	2974.30	5205.40	4,376	4,380	2899.90	5075.30
4,666	4,670	2973.20	5203.20	4,371	4,375	2898.70	5072.80
4,661	4,665	2972.00	5201.00	4,366	4,370	2897.20	5070.80
4,656	4,660	2970.60	5199.00	4,361	4,365	2895.90	5068.10
4,651	4,655	2969.40	5196.90	4,356	4,360	2894.60	5066.10
4,646	4,650	2968.20	5194.70	4,351	4,355	2893.50	5063.70
4,641	4,645	2967.00	5192.50	4,346	4,350	2892.10	5061.50
4,636	4,640	2965.80	5190.40	4,341	4,345	2890.70	5059.00

TABLE 13 - PIA TABLE FOR PERSONS ELIGIBLE BEFORE 1979* (continued)
(Primary Insurance Amount (PIA) and Maximum
Family Benefits Beginning December 2000)

Average monthly wage At least	more than	PIA	Maximum family benefit	Average monthly wage At least	more than	PIA	Maximum family benefit
4,336	4,340	2889.50	5057.10	4,041	4,045	2809.50	4916.70
4,331	4,335	2888.10	5054.60	4,036	4,040	2807.80	4914.10
4,326	4,330	2886.90	5052.50	4,031	4,035	2806.40	4912.00
4,321	4,325	2885.50	5050.00	4,026	4,030	2805.20	4909.40
4,316	4,320	2884.30	5048.00	4,021	4,025	2803.70	4907.20
4,311	4,315	2883.00	5045.50	4,016	4,020	2802.30	4904.50
4,306	4,310	2881.50	5043.40	4,011	4,015	2801.10	4902.20
4,301	4,305	2880.30	5040.80	4,006	4,010	2799.80	4899.60
4,296	4,300	2879.00	5038.80	4,001	4,005	2798.20	4897.60
4,291	4,295	2877.70	5036.20	3,996	4,000	2796.80	4895.00
4,286	4,290	2876.50	5034.20	3,991	3,995	2795.60	4892.50
4,281	4,285	2875.30	5031.80	3,986	3,990	2794.00	4889.80
4,276	4,280	2873.60	5029.60	3,981	3,985	2792.70	4887.50
4,271	4,275	2872.50	5027.20	3,976	3,980	2791.40	4884.80
4,266	4,270	2871.10	5024.70	3,971	3,975	2789.60	4882.70
4,261	4,265	2869.50	5022.50	3,966	3,970	2788.30	4879.90
4,256	4,260	2868.50	5019.70	3,961	3,965	2787.00	4877.50
4,251	4,255	2867.00	5017.80	3,956	3,960	2785.30	4874.80
4,246	4,250	2865.50	5015.10	3,951	3,955	2784.10	4872.10
4,241	4,245	2864.20	5012.80	3,946	3,950	2782.50	4870.00
4,236	4,240	2862.90	5010.40	3,941	3,945	2781.00	4867.50
4,231	4,235	2861.30	5008.10	3,936	3,940	2779.80	4864.90
4,226	4,230	2860.10	5005.70	3,931	3,935	2778.20	4862.50
4,221	4,225	2858.80	5003.30	3,926	3,930	2776.60	4859.70
4,216	4,220	2857.50	5000.90	3,921	3,925	2775.30	4857.40
4,211	4,215	2855.90	4998.40	3,916	3,920	2774.00	4854.80
4,206	4,210	2854.70	4995.90	3,911	3,915	2772.20	4852.40
4,201	4,205	2853.10	4993.40	3,906	3,910	2771.10	4849.90
4,196	4,200	2851.80	4991.20	3,901	3,905	2769.60	4847.20
4,191	4,195	2850.50	4988.70	3,896	3,900	2768.10	4844.90
4,186	4,190	2848.90	4986.40	3,891	3,895	2766.90	4842.30
4,181	4,185	2847.60	4983.90	3,886	3,890	2765.10	4839.70
4,176	4,180	2846.20	4981.50	3,881	3,885	2763.80	4837.10
4,171	4,175	2845.10	4979.00	3,876	3,880	2762.50	4834.60
4,166	4,170	2843.50	4976.60	3,871	3,875	2760.90	4832.30
4,161	4,165	2842.30	4974.40	3,866	3,870	2759.50	4829.50
4,156	4,160	2841.00	4972.10	3,861	3,865	2758.10	4827.40
4,151	4,155	2839.70	4969.50	3,856	3,860	2756.60	4824.60
4,146	4,150	2838.00	4967.20	3,851	3,855	2755.10	4822.00
4,141	4,145	2836.80	4964.80	3,846	3,850	2753.80	4819.50
4,136	4,140	2835.50	4962.30	3,841	3,845	2752.30	4817.00
4,131	4,135	2833.90	4960.00	3,836	3,840	2751.00	4814.40
4,126	4,130	2832.70	4957.50	3,831	3,835	2749.30	4812.10
4,121	4,125	2831.20	4955.30	3,826	3,830	2748.00	4809.60
4,116	4,120	2829.80	4952.50	3,821	3,825	2746.70	4807.20
4,111	4,115	2828.40	4950.50	3,816	3,820	2745.00	4804.30
4,106	4,110	2827.20	4947.90	3,811	3,815	2743.60	4801.70
4,101	4,105	2825.80	4945.50	3,806	3,810	2742.50	4799.60
4,096	4,100	2824.50	4942.80	3,801	3,805	2740.70	4797.00
4,091	4,095	2822.90	4940.70	3,796	3,800	2739.30	4794.40
4,086	4,090	2821.80	4938.10	3,791	3,795	2738.10	4792.00
4,081	4,085	2820.20	4935.70	3,786	3,790	2736.50	4789.30
4,076	4,080	2818.90	4933.50	3,781	3,785	2735.10	4786.70
4,071	4,075	2817.60	4931.00	3,776	3,780	2733.70	4784.30
4,066	4,070	2816.10	4928.70	3,771	3,775	2732.10	4782.00
4,061	4,065	2814.60	4926.20	3,766	3,770	2730.80	4779.20
4,056	4,060	2813.50	4923.90	3,761	3,765	2729.20	4776.80
4,051	4,055	2812.00	4921.40	3,756	3,760	2728.00	4774.30
4,046	4,050	2810.50	4918.90	3,751	3,755	2726.20	4771.80

329

2001 SOCIAL SECURITY MANUAL

TABLE 13 - PIA TABLE FOR PERSONS ELIGIBLE BEFORE 1979* (continued)
(Primary Insurance Amount (PIA) and Maximum
Family Benefits Beginning December 2000)

Average monthly wage At least	more than	PIA	Maximum family benefit	Average monthly wage At least	more than	PIA	Maximum family benefit
3,746	3,750	2725.10	4769.40	3,451	3,455	2633.90	4610.40
3,741	3,745	2723.60	4766.60	3,446	3,450	2632.40	4607.30
3,736	3,740	2721.80	4763.80	3,441	3,445	2630.80	4604.50
3,731	3,735	2720.70	4761.60	3,436	3,440	2629.40	4601.90
3,726	3,730	2719.00	4758.80	3,431	3,435	2627.70	4599.10
3,721	3,725	2717.40	4756.20	3,426	3,430	2626.40	4596.10
3,716	3,720	2716.10	4753.60	3,421	3,425	2624.40	4593.80
3,711	3,715	2714.20	4751.10	3,416	3,420	2622.70	4590.50
3,706	3,710	2713.10	4748.20	3,411	3,415	2621.50	4587.90
3,701	3,705	2711.80	4745.70	3,406	3,410	2619.70	4585.30
3,696	3,700	2710.00	4743.10	3,401	3,405	2618.30	4582.50
3,691	3,695	2708.50	4740.60	3,396	3,400	2616.50	4579.50
3,686	3,690	2707.20	4737.80	3,391	3,395	2615.20	4577.00
3,681	3,685	2705.50	4735.50	3,386	3,390	2613.30	4574.10
3,676	3,680	2704.20	4732.70	3,381	3,385	2611.90	4571.30
3,671	3,675	2702.70	4730.10	3,376	3,380	2610.40	4568.60
3,666	3,670	2701.00	4727.30	3,371	3,375	2608.60	4565.50
3,661	3,665	2699.70	4724.80	3,366	3,370	2607.10	4563.30
3,656	3,660	2697.90	4721.90	3,361	3,365	2605.70	4560.40
3,651	3,655	2696.50	4719.40	3,356	3,360	2603.90	4557.50
3,646	3,650	2695.30	4716.90	3,351	3,355	2602.50	4554.90
3,641	3,645	2693.50	4714.40	3,346	3,350	2600.80	4552.20
3,636	3,640	2691.90	4711.40	3,341	3,345	2599.40	4549.30
3,631	3,635	2690.40	4708.70	3,336	3,340	2597.40	4546.40
3,626	3,630	2688.80	4705.90	3,331	3,335	2596.10	4543.70
3,621	3,625	2687.20	4703.30	3,326	3,330	2594.50	4540.80
3,616	3,620	2685.80	4700.60	3,321	3,325	2592.90	4538.20
3,611	3,615	2684.20	4697.70	3,316	3,320	2591.30	4535.50
3,606	3,610	2682.50	4695.10	3,311	3,315	2589.70	4532.60
3,601	3,605	2681.10	4692.30	3,306	3,310	2588.30	4529.90
3,596	3,600	2679.50	4689.70	3,301	3,305	2586.60	4527.40
3,591	3,595	2678.10	4687.10	3,296	3,300	2585.00	4524.30
3,586	3,590	2676.40	4684.30	3,291	3,295	2583.50	4521.70
3,581	3,585	2674.80	4681.30	3,286	3,290	2581.70	4518.90
3,576	3,580	2673.10	4678.60	3,281	3,285	2580.20	4515.70
3,571	3,575	2671.50	4675.90	3,276	3,280	2578.40	4512.80
3,566	3,570	2670.00	4673.20	3,271	3,275	2577.10	4510.30
3,561	3,565	2668.60	4670.30	3,266	3,270	2575.30	4507.30
3,556	3,560	2666.90	4667.90	3,261	3,265	2573.60	4504.50
3,551	3,555	2665.30	4665.10	3,256	3,260	2571.80	4501.60
3,546	3,550	2663.90	4662.40	3,251	3,255	2570.40	4498.60
3,541	3,545	2662.30	4659.50	3,246	3,250	2568.90	4496.20
3,536	3,540	2660.70	4657.00	3,241	3,245	2566.90	4493.10
3,531	3,535	2659.10	4653.90	3,236	3,240	2565.50	4490.10
3,526	3,530	2657.70	4651.60	3,231	3,235	2563.90	4487.40
3,521	3,525	2655.80	4648.50	3,226	3,230	2562.20	4484.70
3,516	3,520	2654.50	4645.90	3,221	3,225	2560.40	4481.60
3,511	3,515	2653.10	4643.30	3,216	3,220	2558.90	4478.90
3,506	3,510	2651.40	4640.60	3,211	3,215	2557.20	4475.90
3,501	3,505	2649.90	4637.80	3,206	3,210	2555.70	4473.20
3,496	3,500	2648.30	4634.90	3,201	3,205	2554.20	4470.40
3,491	3,495	2646.50	4632.20	3,196	3,200	2552.70	4467.10
3,486	3,490	2645.00	4629.40	3,191	3,195	2550.80	4464.60
3,481	3,485	2643.40	4626.80	3,186	3,190	2549.10	4461.70
3,476	3,480	2641.80	4623.80	3,181	3,185	2547.70	4458.90
3,471	3,475	2640.20	4621.20	3,176	3,180	2545.80	4455.90
3,466	3,470	2638.90	4618.30	3,171	3,175	2544.50	4453.00
3,461	3,465	2637.20	4615.80	3,166	3,170	2542.50	4450.50
3,456	3,460	2635.70	4612.70	3,161	3,165	2541.00	4447.80

330

TABLE 13 - PIA TABLE FOR PERSONS ELIGIBLE BEFORE 1979* (continued)
(Primary Insurance Amount (PIA) and Maximum
Family Benefits Beginning December 2000)

Average monthly wage At least	more than	PIA	Maximum family benefit	Average monthly wage At least	more than	PIA	Maximum family benefit
3,156	3,160	2539.50	4444.60	2,861	2,865	2439.00	4268.60
3,151	3,155	2537.80	4441.50	2,856	2,860	2437.00	4265.90
3,146	3,150	2536.10	4439.20	2,851	2,855	2435.30	4262.60
3,141	3,145	2534.30	4436.30	2,846	2,850	2433.40	4259.50
3,136	3,140	2532.90	4433.20	2,841	2,845	2432.00	4256.50
3,131	3,135	2531.10	4430.30	2,836	2,840	2429.80	4253.60
3,126	3,130	2529.50	4427.50	2,831	2,835	2428.40	4250.50
3,121	3,125	2528.20	4424.40	2,826	2,830	2426.40	4247.30
3,116	3,120	2526.10	4421.50	2,821	2,825	2424.70	4244.40
3,111	3,115	2524.40	4418.60	2,816	2,820	2423.10	4241.30
3,106	3,110	2522.80	4415.50	2,811	2,815	2421.40	4238.10
3,101	3,105	2521.10	4412.70	2,806	2,810	2419.70	4235.20
3,096	3,100	2519.50	4409.60	2,801	2,805	2418.10	4232.30
3,091	3,095	2517.70	4406.70	2,796	2,800	2416.20	4229.20
3,086	3,090	2516.30	4403.70	2,791	2,795	2414.20	4225.80
3,081	3,085	2514.30	4400.70	2,786	2,790	2412.80	4222.90
3,076	3,080	2512.80	4397.80	2,781	2,785	2410.60	4219.90
3,071	3,075	2511.00	4394.80	2,776	2,780	2409.10	4216.70
3,066	3,070	2509.20	4392.10	2,771	2,775	2407.50	4213.80
3,061	3,065	2507.40	4388.80	2,766	2,770	2405.70	4210.50
3,056	3,060	2506.10	4386.20	2,761	2,765	2403.80	4207.80
3,051	3,055	2504.10	4382.60	2,756	2,760	2402.10	4204.60
3,046	3,050	2502.70	4380.50	2,751	2,755	2400.30	4201.60
3,041	3,045	2500.50	4377.40	2,746	2,750	2398.60	4198.50
3,036	3,040	2499.10	4374.20	2,741	2,745	2397.20	4195.40
3,031	3,035	2497.40	4371.30	2,736	2,740	2395.10	4192.20
3,026	3,030	2495.90	4368.20	2,731	2,735	2393.50	4189.40
3,021	3,025	2494.50	4365.40	2,726	2,730	2391.50	4186.40
3,016	3,020	2492.10	4362.60	2,721	2,725	2390.10	4183.30
3,011	3,015	2491.00	4359.50	2,716	2,720	2388.10	4180.00
3,006	3,010	2489.10	4356.50	2,711	2,715	2386.70	4176.90
3,001	3,005	2487.30	4353.90	2,706	2,710	2384.80	4174.10
2,996	3,000	2485.80	4350.70	2,701	2,705	2382.90	4171.20
2,991	2,995	2484.10	4347.50	2,696	2,700	2381.50	4167.90
2,986	2,990	2482.20	4344.80	2,691	2,695	2379.30	4164.80
2,981	2,985	2480.70	4341.60	2,686	2,690	2377.20	4161.70
2,976	2,980	2479.20	4339.10	2,681	2,685	2375.50	4158.30
2,971	2,975	2477.00	4335.90	2,676	2,680	2373.70	4155.20
2,966	2,970	2475.30	4333.00	2,671	2,675	2372.20	4151.70
2,961	2,965	2473.80	4329.90	2,666	2,670	2369.80	4148.40
2,956	2,960	2471.80	4326.60	2,661	2,665	2367.90	4145.20
2,951	2,955	2470.40	4323.80	2,656	2,660	2366.30	4141.60
2,946	2,950	2468.50	4320.80	2,651	2,655	2364.50	4138.70
2,941	2,945	2466.80	4317.70	2,646	2,650	2362.20	4135.20
2,936	2,940	2465.00	4314.60	2,641	2,645	2360.50	4132.20
2,931	2,935	2463.00	4311.30	2,636	2,640	2358.80	4128.40
2,926	2,930	2461.60	4308.10	2,631	2,635	2357.10	4125.90
2,921	2,925	2459.80	4305.80	2,626	2,630	2355.00	4122.30
2,916	2,920	2458.10	4302.30	2,621	2,625	2352.70	4118.90
2,911	2,915	2456.30	4299.10	2,616	2,620	2351.30	4115.50
2,906	2,910	2454.50	4296.30	2,611	2,615	2349.50	4112.70
2,901	2,905	2452.80	4293.00	2,606	2,610	2347.50	4109.10
2,896	2,900	2450.90	4290.00	2,601	2,605	2345.70	4105.80
2,891	2,895	2449.10	4287.20	2,596	2,600	2343.60	4102.30
2,886	2,890	2447.60	4283.80	2,591	2,595	2341.90	4099.50
2,881	2,885	2445.90	4281.10	2,586	2,590	2339.80	4096.00
2,876	2,880	2444.00	4277.70	2,581	2,585	2338.50	4092.80
2,871	2,875	2442.60	4274.50	2,576	2,580	2336.20	4089.30
2,866	2,870	2440.40	4271.80	2,571	2,575	2334.40	4086.20

TABLE 13 - PIA TABLE FOR PERSONS ELIGIBLE BEFORE 1979* (continued)
(Primary Insurance Amount (PIA) and Maximum
Family Benefits Beginning December 2000)

Average monthly wage At least	more than	PIA	Maximum family benefit	Average monthly wage At least	more than	PIA	Maximum family benefit
2,566	2,570	2332.50	4083.00	2,271	2,275	2213.70	3874.30
2,561	2,565	2330.70	4079.30	2,266	2,270	2211.30	3870.90
2,556	2,560	2328.70	4076.20	2,261	2,265	2209.50	3867.50
2,551	2,555	2326.80	4073.30	2,256	2,260	2207.20	3863.80
2,546	2,550	2324.80	4069.70	2,251	2,255	2205.40	3860.30
2,541	2,545	2323.40	4066.60	2,246	2,250	2203.10	3856.40
2,536	2,540	2321.20	4063.00	2,241	2,245	2201.00	3852.80
2,531	2,535	2319.20	4059.80	2,236	2,240	2199.10	3848.80
2,526	2,530	2317.20	4056.60	2,231	2,235	2196.90	3845.60
2,521	2,525	2315.90	4053.30	2,226	2,230	2194.90	3842.30
2,516	2,520	2313.60	4050.00	2,221	2,225	2192.70	3838.50
2,511	2,515	2311.90	4047.00	2,216	2,220	2190.60	3834.60
2,506	2,510	2309.70	4043.30	2,211	2,215	2188.70	3830.90
2,501	2,505	2308.30	4040.20	2,206	2,210	2186.50	3827.50
2,496	2,500	2306.10	4037.20	2,201	2,205	2184.30	3823.90
2,491	2,495	2304.10	4033.70	2,196	2,200	2182.40	3820.10
2,486	2,490	2302.50	4030.10	2,191	2,195	2180.00	3816.30
2,481	2,485	2300.50	4027.00	2,186	2,190	2178.10	3812.80
2,476	2,480	2298.80	4023.90	2,181	2,185	2176.00	3809.30
2,471	2,475	2297.10	4020.70	2,176	2,180	2174.20	3805.40
2,466	2,470	2294.50	4016.90	2,171	2,175	2172.00	3801.90
2,461	2,465	2292.90	4013.20	2,166	2,170	2169.60	3797.90
2,456	2,460	2290.70	4009.50	2,161	2,165	2167.90	3794.60
2,451	2,455	2288.40	4006.20	2,156	2,160	2165.40	3790.60
2,446	2,450	2286.50	4002.60	2,151	2,155	2163.10	3786.50
2,441	2,445	2284.30	3998.80	2,146	2,150	2160.70	3782.50
2,436	2,440	2282.20	3994.90	2,141	2,145	2158.20	3777.90
2,431	2,435	2280.30	3991.50	2,136	2,140	2156.00	3774.40
2,426	2,430	2278.00	3987.60	2,131	2,135	2153.80	3769.60
2,421	2,425	2276.00	3984.10	2,126	2,130	2151.30	3765.90
2,416	2,420	2273.90	3980.00	2,121	2,125	2148.80	3761.30
2,411	2,415	2272.20	3977.00	2,116	2,120	2146.30	3757.30
2,406	2,410	2269.50	3973.20	2,111	2,115	2144.00	3753.20
2,401	2,405	2267.80	3969.30	2,106	2,110	2141.60	3748.90
2,396	2,400	2265.70	3965.60	2,101	2,105	2139.40	3744.50
2,391	2,395	2263.70	3962.30	2,096	2,100	2136.50	3740.60
2,386	2,390	2261.20	3958.40	2,091	2,095	2134.40	3736.30
2,381	2,385	2259.40	3954.70	2,086	2,090	2132.40	3732.60
2,376	2,380	2257.40	3950.90	2,081	2,085	2129.70	3728.10
2,371	2,375	2255.20	3947.60	2,076	2,080	2127.80	3724.00
2,366	2,370	2253.20	3944.10	2,071	2,075	2125.10	3719.60
2,361	2,365	2250.70	3940.40	2,066	2,070	2122.60	3715.60
2,356	2,360	2249.10	3936.80	2,061	2,065	2120.00	3711.00
2,351	2,355	2246.80	3933.10	2,056	2,060	2118.10	3707.30
2,346	2,350	2244.90	3929.20	2,051	2,055	2115.80	3703.20
2,341	2,345	2242.50	3925.90	2,046	2,050	2113.20	3699.00
2,336	2,340	2240.70	3922.00	2,041	2,045	2110.60	3694.60
2,331	2,335	2238.40	3918.60	2,036	2,040	2108.60	3690.40
2,326	2,330	2236.30	3914.80	2,031	2,035	2106.00	3686.20
2,321	2,325	2234.70	3911.20	2,026	2,030	2103.70	3682.50
2,316	2,320	2232.10	3907.30	2,021	2,025	2101.20	3678.10
2,311	2,315	2230.30	3903.80	2,016	2,020	2099.00	3673.80
2,306	2,310	2227.90	3900.20	2,011	2,015	2096.40	3669.90
2,301	2,305	2225.90	3896.60	2,006	2,010	2094.30	3665.60
2,296	2,300	2224.00	3892.60	2,001	2,005	2091.70	3661.60
2,291	2,295	2222.20	3889.00	1,996	2,000	2089.50	3657.40
2,286	2,290	2219.70	3885.20	1,991	1,995	2086.70	3652.90
2,281	2,285	2217.70	3881.90	1,986	1,990	2084.80	3649.00
2,276	2,280	2215.30	3878.30	1,981	1,985	2082.60	3644.90

SOCIAL SECURITY TABLES

TABLE 13 - PIA TABLE FOR PERSONS ELIGIBLE BEFORE 1979* (continued)
(Primary Insurance Amount (PIA) and Maximum
Family Benefits Beginning December 2000)

Average monthly wage At least	more than	PIA	Maximum family benefit	Average monthly wage At least	more than	PIA	Maximum family benefit
1,976	1,980	2079.90	3640.50	1,681	1,685	1928.80	3376.00
1,971	1,975	2077.50	3636.30	1,676	1,680	1926.40	3371.60
1,966	1,970	2075.20	3632.50	1,671	1,675	1923.60	3367.10
1,961	1,965	2072.50	3627.90	1,666	1,670	1921.10	3362.40
1,956	1,960	2070.30	3624.30	1,661	1,665	1918.30	3357.80
1,951	1,955	2068.00	3619.80	1,656	1,660	1916.00	3353.20
1,946	1,950	2066.00	3615.70	1,651	1,655	1913.30	3348.90
1,941	1,945	2062.90	3611.60	1,646	1,650	1910.80	3344.10
1,936	1,940	2060.90	3607.40	1,641	1,645	1908.30	3339.40
1,931	1,935	2058.60	3603.10	1,636	1,640	1904.90	3334.60
1,926	1,930	2055.80	3599.10	1,631	1,635	1902.70	3330.70
1,921	1,925	2053.90	3594.70	1,626	1,630	1900.10	3325.70
1,916	1,920	2051.10	3590.70	1,621	1,625	1897.30	3321.30
1,911	1,915	2049.00	3586.30	1,616	1,620	1894.80	3316.50
1,906	1,910	2046.20	3582.10	1,611	1,615	1892.00	3312.20
1,901	1,905	2043.90	3577.90	1,606	1,610	1889.20	3307.20
1,896	1,900	2041.40	3573.20	1,601	1,605	1887.10	3302.80
1,891	1,895	2038.60	3568.70	1,596	1,600	1884.10	3298.40
1,886	1,890	2036.00	3563.80	1,591	1,595	1881.50	3293.80
1,881	1,885	2033.30	3559.60	1,586	1,590	1879.20	3288.90
1,876	1,880	2030.80	3554.60	1,581	1,585	1876.20	3284.70
1,871	1,875	2028.20	3550.20	1,576	1,580	1873.80	3280.10
1,866	1,870	2025.30	3545.30	1,571	1,575	1871.20	3275.20
1,861	1,865	2023.40	3541.00	1,566	1,570	1868.40	3270.40
1,856	1,860	2020.30	3536.20	1,561	1,565	1865.80	3266.20
1,851	1,855	2017.70	3531.70	1,556	1,560	1863.30	3261.30
1,846	1,850	2014.70	3527.00	1,551	1,555	1861.10	3257.10
1,841	1,845	2012.60	3522.90	1,546	1,550	1858.20	3252.30
1,836	1,840	2009.90	3518.10	1,541	1,545	1855.50	3248.00
1,831	1,835	2007.10	3513.70	1,536	1,540	1853.10	3243.20
1,826	1,830	2005.00	3508.70	1,531	1,535	1850.30	3238.50
1,821	1,825	2001.70	3504.70	1,526	1,530	1847.40	3233.80
1,816	1,820	1999.40	3499.80	1,521	1,525	1845.00	3229.90
1,811	1,815	1996.80	3495.20	1,516	1,520	1842.40	3225.00
1,806	1,810	1994.20	3490.50	1,511	1,515	1840.10	3220.60
1,801	1,805	1991.40	3486.30	1,506	1,510	1837.30	3215.60
1,796	1,800	1988.80	3481.50	1,501	1,505	1834.60	3211.60
1,791	1,795	1986.30	3476.60	1,496	1,500	1831.70	3206.90
1,786	1,790	1983.80	3472.10	1,491	1,495	1829.60	3202.10
1,781	1,785	1980.90	3468.10	1,486	1,490	1826.50	3197.40
1,776	1,780	1978.50	3463.50	1,481	1,485	1824.30	3193.20
1,771	1,775	1975.60	3458.40	1,476	1,480	1821.20	3188.20
1,766	1,770	1973.00	3453.70	1,471	1,475	1818.80	3183.70
1,761	1,765	1970.70	3449.80	1,466	1,470	1815.80	3179.00
1,756	1,760	1968.10	3444.60	1,461	1,465	1813.20	3174.20
1,751	1,755	1965.20	3440.30	1,456	1,460	1810.30	3169.10
1,746	1,750	1962.70	3435.40	1,451	1,455	1807.70	3164.30
1,741	1,745	1960.10	3431.00	1,446	1,450	1804.90	3159.60
1,736	1,740	1957.70	3426.10	1,441	1,445	1802.10	3154.00
1,731	1,735	1954.70	3421.50	1,436	1,440	1799.40	3149.50
1,726	1,730	1952.20	3416.90	1,431	1,435	1796.60	3144.50
1,721	1,725	1949.80	3412.80	1,426	1,430	1793.80	3140.00
1,716	1,720	1946.80	3408.00	1,421	1,425	1790.80	3135.10
1,711	1,715	1944.70	3404.00	1,416	1,420	1787.70	3130.20
1,706	1,710	1941.80	3398.90	1,411	1,415	1785.50	3125.20
1,701	1,705	1939.10	3394.80	1,406	1,410	1782.20	3120.20
1,696	1,700	1936.20	3390.00	1,401	1,405	1779.70	3115.30
1,691	1,695	1934.50	3385.20	1,396	1,400	1776.90	3110.50
1,686	1,690	1931.70	3380.50	1,391	1,395	1774.10	3105.80

TABLE 13 - PIA TABLE FOR PERSONS ELIGIBLE BEFORE 1979* (continued)
(Primary Insurance Amount (PIA) and Maximum
Family Benefits Beginning December 2000)

Average monthly wage At least	more than	PIA	Maximum family benefit	Average monthly wage At least	more than	PIA	Maximum family benefit
1,386	1,390	1771.60	3101.00	1,091	1,095	1586.90	2777.40
1,381	1,385	1768.80	3095.60	1,086	1,090	1583.20	2771.30
1,376	1,380	1766.40	3090.90	1,081	1,085	1580.40	2765.30
1,371	1,375	1763.20	3085.90	1,076	1,080	1576.60	2759.50
1,366	1,370	1760.00	3080.90	1,071	1,075	1573.20	2753.90
1,361	1,365	1757.20	3075.20	1,066	1,070	1570.00	2747.70
1,356	1,360	1754.40	3070.40	1,061	1,065	1566.60	2741.80
1,351	1,355	1751.50	3065.20	1,056	1,060	1562.50	2736.30
1,346	1,350	1748.30	3059.90	1,051	1,055	1559.70	2729.10
1,341	1,345	1745.40	3055.10	1,046	1,050	1556.60	2724.00
1,336	1,340	1742.50	3049.90	1,041	1,045	1552.70	2718.20
1,331	1,335	1739.40	3044.70	1,036	1,040	1549.40	2712.20
1,326	1,330	1736.80	3039.70	1,031	1,035	1546.30	2706.30
1,321	1,325	1733.70	3034.30	1,026	1,030	1542.30	2700.60
1,316	1,320	1730.80	3029.20	1,021	1,025	1539.40	2694.10
1,311	1,315	1727.90	3023.70	1,016	1,020	1536.40	2688.80
1,306	1,310	1724.50	3018.80	1,011	1,015	1532.60	2682.20
1,301	1,305	1721.30	3013.70	1,006	1,010	1528.50	2676.80
1,296	1,300	1718.90	3008.20	1,001	1,005	1526.20	2670.10
1,291	1,295	1715.90	3003.20	996	1,000	1522.70	2664.70
1,286	1,290	1712.90	2997.80	991	995	1518.80	2658.20
1,281	1,285	1709.90	2992.90	986	990	1515.00	2651.60
1,276	1,280	1707.00	2988.30	981	985	1511.70	2644.90
1,271	1,275	1703.90	2982.20	976	980	1507.20	2638.50
1,266	1,270	1700.90	2977.20	971	975	1503.50	2632.30
1,261	1,265	1697.80	2971.50	966	970	1499.60	2625.70
1,256	1,260	1694.60	2966.20	961	965	1496.80	2618.50
1,251	1,255	1691.50	2960.50	956	960	1492.90	2612.20
1,246	1,250	1688.60	2955.10	951	955	1488.90	2606.00
1,241	1,245	1685.30	2949.60	946	950	1484.80	2598.60
1,236	1,240	1681.70	2944.20	941	945	1481.00	2592.50
1,231	1,235	1678.80	2938.20	936	940	1477.20	2585.60
1,226	1,230	1676.00	2933.20	931	935	1473.40	2579.40
1,221	1,225	1672.50	2927.10	926	930	1469.50	2572.40
1,216	1,220	1669.30	2922.00	921	925	1466.20	2566.30
1,211	1,215	1666.50	2916.50	916	920	1463.10	2559.20
1,206	1,210	1663.00	2911.40	911	915	1458.80	2553.20
1,201	1,205	1660.20	2905.20	906	910	1455.30	2546.40
1,196	1,200	1657.10	2900.10	901	905	1451.40	2539.80
1,191	1,195	1653.70	2894.70	896	900	1447.30	2532.90
1,186	1,190	1650.50	2888.70	891	895	1442.90	2527.30
1,181	1,185	1647.30	2883.80	886	890	1439.70	2519.60
1,176	1,180	1644.60	2878.20	881	885	1436.10	2513.40
1,171	1,175	1641.50	2872.60	876	880	1432.20	2506.80
1,166	1,170	1637.50	2866.70	871	875	1428.40	2499.90
1,161	1,165	1634.70	2860.40	866	870	1425.10	2493.50
1,156	1,160	1631.10	2854.30	861	865	1421.00	2487.00
1,151	1,155	1627.20	2848.00	856	860	1417.10	2480.30
1,146	1,150	1624.40	2842.60	851	855	1413.40	2473.90
1,141	1,145	1621.00	2837.00	846	850	1409.40	2466.80
1,136	1,140	1617.30	2831.20	841	845	1405.80	2461.30
1,131	1,135	1613.70	2824.50	836	840	1402.20	2453.80
1,126	1,130	1610.60	2818.90	831	835	1398.30	2447.80
1,121	1,125	1607.40	2813.00	826	830	1394.50	2440.50
1,116	1,120	1603.90	2807.10	821	825	1390.70	2434.00
1,111	1,115	1600.60	2800.80	816	820	1387.20	2427.70
1,106	1,110	1596.90	2795.50	811	815	1383.00	2421.30
1,101	1,105	1593.40	2789.10	806	810	1379.50	2414.20
1,096	1,100	1590.30	2784.00	801	805	1375.80	2407.90

SOCIAL SECURITY TABLES

TABLE 13 - PIA TABLE FOR PERSONS ELIGIBLE BEFORE 1979* (continued)
(Primary Insurance Amount (PIA) and Maximum
Family Benefits Beginning December 2000)

Average monthly wage At least	more than	PIA	Maximum family benefit	Average monthly wage At least	more than	PIA	Maximum family benefit
796	800	1372.20	2401.30	544	548	1078.90	1956.30
791	795	1367.90	2394.60	539	543	1072.50	1946.30
786	790	1364.10	2387.80	535	538	1066.10	1936.00
781	785	1361.10	2381.70	530	534	1060.50	1928.10
776	780	1356.80	2374.90	525	529	1052.50	1918.30
771	775	1353.40	2368.40	521	524	1047.00	1908.40
766	770	1349.20	2361.90	516	520	1040.80	1901.00
761	765	1345.90	2355.20	511	515	1033.60	1890.50
756	760	1341.80	2348.40	507	510	1026.90	1880.20
751	755	1338.40	2342.40	502	506	1021.00	1872.00
746	750	1333.70	2334.80	497	501	1015.20	1862.20
741	745	1329.80	2328.00	493	496	1008.00	1853.10
736	740	1325.80	2319.20	488	492	1001.80	1845.00
731	735	1320.90	2311.70	483	487	995.10	1835.00
726	730	1316.50	2303.50	479	482	988.30	1825.10
721	725	1311.70	2295.50	474	478	982.10	1816.90
716	720	1307.40	2288.00	469	473	977.10	1806.60
711	715	1303.00	2279.70	465	468	968.90	1797.00
706	710	1297.90	2272.40	460	464	962.80	1788.40
701	705	1293.40	2264.00	455	459	956.40	1778.60
696	700	1288.60	2256.00	451	454	950.30	1768.90
691	695	1284.30	2248.90	446	450	943.50	1761.30
686	690	1280.80	2240.00	441	445	936.90	1751.90
681	685	1275.70	2232.40	437	440	931.30	1741.10
676	680	1271.10	2224.40	432	436	923.90	1733.60
671	675	1266.70	2216.60	427	431	917.90	1713.80
666	670	1261.90	2209.40	422	426	911.60	1693.50
661	665	1257.60	2201.50	418	421	904.10	1673.40
657	660	1253.20	2193.00	413	417	898.10	1657.60
653	656	1249.70	2187.10	408	412	891.60	1638.50
649	652	1245.80	2180.90	404	407	885.60	1618.10
645	648	1240.60	2171.30	399	403	878.40	1602.20
642	644	1234.60	2160.70	394	398	871.90	1582.70
638	641	1229.30	2151.30	390	393	864.10	1562.20
635	637	1223.40	2140.80	385	389	857.40	1546.70
631	634	1217.40	2130.80	380	384	851.20	1527.00
628	630	1211.90	2120.60	376	379	843.70	1507.10
624	627	1205.90	2113.20	371	375	837.10	1490.20
621	623	1200.40	2104.80	366	370	829.50	1471.20
617	620	1194.70	2099.20	362	365	822.90	1451.40
613	616	1188.90	2091.30	357	361	817.00	1435.40
610	612	1183.20	2083.30	352	356	809.00	1415.30
606	609	1177.20	2076.80	348	351	802.80	1395.60
603	605	1171.70	2069.30	343	347	795.20	1379.50
599	602	1166.50	2063.50	338	342	787.70	1359.60
596	598	1160.60	2054.70	334	337	782.40	1340.30
592	595	1154.80	2049.50	329	333	774.10	1323.90
589	591	1149.10	2041.50	324	328	768.00	1303.90
585	588	1142.20	2035.60	320	323	760.70	1284.10
582	584	1137.20	2027.80	315	319	753.60	1268.50
578	581	1131.70	2021.30	310	314	747.80	1248.00
575	577	1126.20	2014.00	306	309	740.00	1228.70
571	574	1120.50	2007.70	301	305	733.60	1212.80
568	570	1115.30	1999.50	296	300	726.90	1192.50
564	567	1108.80	1994.10	292	295	719.10	1172.80
561	563	1103.20	1986.10	287	291	713.30	1157.40
557	560	1097.20	1980.10	282	286	705.70	1137.00
554	556	1092.00	1971.90	278	281	698.80	1117.40
549	553	1085.90	1965.90	273	277	692.30	1100.90

335

TABLE 13 - PIA TABLE FOR PERSONS ELIGIBLE BEFORE 1979* (continued)
(Primary Insurance Amount (PIA) and Maximum
Family Benefits Beginning December 2000)

Average monthly wage At least	more than	PIA	Maximum family benefit	Average monthly wage At least	more than	PIA	Maximum family benefit
268	272	684.70	1082.00	137	141	491.20	737.60
264	267	678.60	1061.80	133	136	484.20	727.60
259	263	670.20	1045.50	128	132	478.20	717.50
254	258	664.30	1026.00	123	127	471.10	707.20
250	253	658.10	1006.40	119	122	463.80	696.10
245	249	649.90	990.20	114	118	456.80	685.80
240	244	643.50	970.10	110	113	450.50	676.10
236	239	637.60	957.20	108	109	443.60	665.60
231	235	630.00	946.00	107	107	436.60	655.90
226	230	623.20	935.60	105	106	429.80	645.70
222	225	615.90	924.40	103	104	421.40	633.30
217	221	608.60	913.90	102	102	415.10	623.20
212	216	601.10	902.30	100	101	409.40	614.40
208	211	595.60	894.10	98	99	401.40	602.80
203	207	588.90	883.80	97	97	394.90	592.90
198	202	581.00	872.70	95	96	387.80	583.00
194	197	574.50	862.50	93	94	381.60	572.90
189	193	567.60	852.50	91	92	375.30	564.10
184	188	560.10	840.80	90	90	368.80	554.50
179	183	554.00	831.20	88	89	361.80	543.30
175	178	546.30	820.20	86	87	356.70	535.50
170	174	539.80	810.40	84	85	349.50	525.50
165	169	532.50	799.50	82	83	342.30	514.40
161	164	525.90	789.70	81	81	336.40	505.50
156	160	519.20	779.50	79	80	330.80	496.40
151	155	511.70	768.10	77	78	323.10	484.80
147	150	505.70	759.00	0	76	318.00	477.50
142	146	498.60	748.20				

FEDERAL EMPLOYEE TABLES

TABLE 1—GENERAL PAY SCHEDULE FOR FEDERAL GOVERNMENT WORKERS EFFECTIVE IN JANUARY 2001

Step	1	2	3	4	5	6	7	8	9	10
GS-1	$14,244	$14,719	$15,193	$15,664	$16,139	$16,418	$16,884	$17,356	$17,375	$17,819
2	16,015	16,395	16,926	17,375	17,571	18,088	18,605	19,122	19,639	20,156
3	17,474	18,056	18,638	19,220	19,802	20,384	20,966	21,548	22,130	22,712
4	19,616	20,270	20,924	21,578	22,232	22,886	23,540	24,194	24,848	25,502
5	21,947	22,679	23,411	24,143	24,875	25,607	26,339	27,071	27,803	28,535
6	24,463	25,278	26,093	26,908	27,723	28,538	29,353	30,168	30,983	31,798
7	27,185	28,091	28,997	29,903	30,809	31,715	32,621	33,527	34,433	35,339
8	30,107	31,111	32,115	33,119	34,123	35,127	36,131	37,135	38,139	39,143
9	33,254	34,362	35,470	36,578	37,686	38,794	39,902	41,010	42,118	43,226
10	36,621	37,842	39,063	40,284	41,505	42,726	43,947	45,168	46,389	47,610
11	40,236	41,577	42,918	44,259	45,600	46,941	48,282	49,623	50,964	52,305
12	48,223	49,830	51,437	53,044	54,651	56,258	57,865	59,472	61,079	62,686
13	57,345	59,257	61,169	63,081	64,993	66,905	68,817	70,729	72,641	74,553
14	67,765	70,024	72,283	74,542	76,801	79,060	81,319	83,578	85,837	88,096
15	79,710	82,367	85,024	87,681	90,338	92,995	95,652	98,309	100,966	103,623

INCORPORATING A 2.70% GENERAL INCREASE LOCALITY PAY ADJUSTMENTS 2001

Combined national and locality pay adjustments for 32 locations in 2001 are listed below.

Atlanta	8.66%	Miami	11.09%
Boston	12.13%	Milwaukee	8.91%
Chicago	13.00%	Minneapolis	10.30%
Cincinnati	10.76%	New York	13.62%
Cleveland	9.17%	Orlando	7.71%
Columbus	9.61%	Philadelphia	10.80%
Dallas	9.71%	Pittsburgh	8.54%
Dayton	8.60%	Portland (OR)	10.32%
Denver	11.90%	Richmond (VA)	8.60%
Detroit	13.14%	Sacramento	10.73%
Hartford	12.65%	St. Louis	8.00%
Houston	16.66%	San Diego	11.31%
Huntsville	8.12%	San Francisco	16.98%
Indianapolis	7.89%	Seattle	10.45%
Kansas City	8.32%	Washington D.C.	10.23%
Los Angeles	14.37%	Rest of United States	7.68%

FEDERAL EMPLOYEE TABLES

TABLE 2—BASIC MONTHLY RETIREMENT ANNUITY FOR
CSRS EMPLOYEES

High-3 Annual Salary	5	10	15	Years of Service 20	25	30	35	40
$15,000	$ 94	$ 203	$ 328	$ 453	$ 578	$ 703	$ 828	$ 953
16,000	100	217	350	483	617	750	883	1,017
17,000	106	230	372	514	655	797	939	1,080
18,000	113	244	394	544	694	844	994	1,144
19,000	119	257	415	574	732	891	1,049	1,207
20,000	125	270	438	604	771	938	1,104	1,271
21,000	131	284	459	634	809	984	1,159	1,334
22,000	138	298	481	665	848	1,031	1,215	1,398
23,000	144	311	503	695	886	1,078	1,270	1,461
24,000	150	325	525	725	925	1,125	1,325	1,525
25,000	156	339	547	755	964	1,172	1,380	1,589
26,000	163	352	574	785	1,002	1,219	1,435	1,652
27,000	169	366	591	816	1,041	1,266	1,491	1,716
28,000	175	379	613	846	1,079	1,313	1,546	1,779
29,000	181	393	634	876	1,118	1,359	1,601	1,843
30,000	188	406	656	906	1,156	1,406	1,656	1,906
31,000	194	420	678	936	1,195	1,453	1,711	1,970
32,000	200	433	700	967	1,233	1,500	1,767	2,033
33,000	206	447	722	997	1,272	1,547	1,822	2,097
34,000	213	460	744	1,027	1,310	1,594	1,877	2,160
35,000	219	474	766	1,057	1,349	1,641	1,932	2,224
36,000	225	488	788	1,088	1,388	1,688	1,988	2,288
37,000	231	501	809	1,118	1,426	1,734	2,043	2,351
38,000	238	515	831	1,148	1,465	1,781	2,098	2,415
39,000	244	528	853	1,178	1,503	1,828	2,153	2,478
40,000	250	542	875	1,208	1,542	1,875	2,208	2,542
41,000	256	555	897	1,239	1,580	1,922	2,264	2,605
42,000	263	569	919	1,269	1,619	1,969	2,319	2,669
43,000	269	582	941	1,299	1,657	2,016	2,374	2,732
44,000	275	596	963	1,329	1,699	2,063	2,429	2,796
45,000	281	609	984	1,359	1,734	2,109	2,484	2,859
46,000	288	623	1,006	1,390	1,773	2,156	2,540	2,923
47,000	294	636	1,028	1,420	1,811	2,203	2,595	2,986
48,000	300	650	1,050	1,450	1,850	2,250	2,650	3,050
49,000	306	663	1,071	1,479	1,888	2,296	2,704	3,113
50,000	312	676	1,092	1,509	1,926	2,342	2,759	3,163
51,000	318	689	1,114	1,539	1,964	2,389	2,814	3,239
52,000	325	704	1,137	1,570	2,004	2,437	2,870	3,304
53,000	331	717	1,158	1,600	2,042	2,483	2,925	3,367
54,000	337	730	1,180	1,630	2,080	2,530	2,980	3,430
55,000	343	744	1,202	1,660	2,119	2,577	3,035	3,494
56,000	350	758	1,224	1,691	2,158	2,624	3,091	3,558
57,000	356	771	1,246	1,721	2,196	2,671	3,146	3,621
58,000	362	784	1,267	1,750	2,234	2,717	3,200	3,684
59,000	368	798	1,289	1,781	2,273	2,764	3,256	3,748
60,000	375	812	1,312	1,812	2,312	2,812	3,312	3,812
61,000	381	825	1,333	1,841	2,350	2,858	3,366	3,875
62,000	387	839	1,355	1,872	2,389	2,905	3,422	3,939

339

TABLE 2—BASIC MONTHLY RETIREMENT ANNUITY FOR
CSRS EMPLOYEES (continued)

High-3 Annual Salary	5	10	15	Years of Service 20	25	30	35	40
63,000	393	852	1,377	1,902	2,427	2,952	3,477	4,002
64,000	400	866	1,399	1,932	2,441	2,999	3,532	4,066
65,000	406	880	1,422	1,964	2,505	3,047	3,589	4,130
66,000	413	894	1,444	1,994	2,544	3,094	3,644	4,194
68,000	425	921	1,488	2,054	2,621	3,188	3,754	4,321
70,000	438	948	1,531	2,115	2,698	3,281	3,865	4,448
72,000	450	975	1,575	2,175	2,775	3,375	3,975	4,575
74,000	463	1,002	1,619	2,235	2,852	3,469	4,085	4,702
76,000	475	1,029	1,663	2,296	2,929	3,563	4,196	4,829
80,000	500	1,083	1,750	2,417	3,083	3,750	4,417	5,083
83,000	519	1,124	1,816	2,507	3,199	3,891	4,582	5,274
86,000	538	1,165	1,881	2,598	3,315	4,031	4,748	5,465
90,000	563	1,219	1,969	2,719	3,469	4,219	4,969	5,719
93,000	581	1,259	2,034	2,809	3,584	4,359	5,134	5,909
96,000	600	1,300	2,100	2,900	3,700	4,500	5,300	6,100
100,000	625	1,354	2,188	3,021	3,854	4,688	5,521	6,354
110,000	688	1,490	2,406	3,323	4,240	5,156	6,073	6,990

TABLE 3—BASIC MONTHLY RETIREMENT ANNUITY
FOR FERS EMPLOYEES

High-3 Annual Salary	5	10	15	20	25	30	35	40
				Years of Service				
$15,000	$ 63	$ 125	$ 188	$ 250	$ 313	$ 375	$ 438	$ 500
16,000	67	133	200	267	333	400	467	533
17,000	71	142	213	283	354	425	496	567
18,000	75	150	225	300	375	450	525	600
19,000	79	158	238	317	396	475	554	633
20,000	83	167	250	333	417	500	583	667
22,000	92	183	275	367	458	550	642	733
24,000	100	200	300	400	500	600	700	800
26,000	108	217	325	433	542	650	758	867
28,000	117	233	350	467	583	700	817	933
30,000	125	250	375	500	625	750	875	1,000
32,000	133	267	400	533	667	800	933	1,067
34,000	142	283	425	567	708	850	992	1,133
36,000	150	300	450	600	750	900	1,050	1,200
38,000	158	317	475	633	792	950	1,108	1,267
40,000	167	333	500	667	833	1,000	1,167	1,333
42,000	175	350	525	700	875	1,050	1,225	1,400
44,000	183	367	550	733	917	1,100	1,283	1,467
46,000	192	383	575	767	958	1,150	1,342	1,533
48,000	200	400	600	800	1,000	1,200	1,400	1,600
50,000	208	417	625	833	1,042	1,250	1,458	1,667
53,000	221	442	663	883	1,104	1,325	1,546	1,767
55,000	229	458	688	917	1,146	1,375	1,604	1,833
57,000	238	475	713	950	1,188	1,425	1,663	1,900
60,000	250	500	750	1,000	1,250	1,500	1,750	2,000
65,000	271	542	813	1,083	1,354	1,625	1,896	2,167
66,000	275	550	825	1,100	1,375	1,650	1,925	2,200
68,000	283	567	850	1,133	1,417	1,700	1,983	2,267
70,000	292	583	875	1,167	1,458	1,750	2,042	2,333
72,000	300	600	900	1,200	1,500	1,800	2,100	2,400
74,000	308	617	925	1,233	1,542	1,850	2,158	2,467
76,000	317	633	950	1,267	1,369	1,643	1,916	2,190
80,000	333	667	1,000	1,333	1,667	2,000	2,333	2,667
83,000	346	692	1,038	1,383	1,729	2,075	2,421	2,767
86,000	358	717	1,075	1,433	1,792	2,150	2,508	2,867
90,000	375	750	1,125	1,500	1,875	2,250	2,625	3,000
93,000	388	775	1,163	1,550	1,938	2,325	2,713	3,100
96,000	400	800	1,200	1,600	2,000	2,400	2,800	3,200
100,000	417	833	1,250	1,667	2,083	2,500	2,917	3,333
110,000	458	917	1,375	1,833	2,292	2,750	3,208	3,667

341

TABLE 4
AMOUNT OF INSURANCE PROTECTION UNDER THE FEDERAL
EMPLOYEES GROUP LIFE INSURANCE ACT
OF 1980 (P.L. 96-427)
EFFECTIVE OCTOBER 1, 1981*

Annual Pay			Amount of Group Life Insurance				
Greater than —	But not greater than —	Basic Insurance Amount	Age 35 and Under	Age 36 (1.9)	Age 37 (1.8)	Age 38 (1.7)	Age 39 (1.6)
$ 0	$ 8,000	$10,000	$20,000	$19,000	$ 18,000	$17,000	$16,000
8,000	9,000	11,000	22,000	20,900	19,800	18,700	17,600
9,000	10,000	12,000	24,000	22,800	21,600	20,400	19,200
10,000	11,000	13,000	26,000	24,700	23,400	22,100	20,800
11,000	12,000	14,000	28,000	26,600	25,200	23,800	22,400
12,000	13,000	15,000	30,000	28,500	27,000	25,500	24,000
13,000	14,000	16,000	32,000	30,400	28,800	27,200	25,600
14,000	15,000	17,000	34,000	32,300	30,600	28,900	27,200
15,000	16,000	18,000	36,000	34,200	32,400	30,600	28,800
16,000	17,000	19,000	38,000	36,100	34,200	32,300	30,400
17,000	18,000	20,000	40,000	38,000	36,000	34,000	32,000
18,000	19,000	21,000	42,000	39,900	37,800	35,700	33,600
19,000	20,000	22,000	44,000	41,800	39,600	37,400	35,200
20,000	21,000	23,000	46,000	43,700	41,400	39,100	36,800
21,000	22,000	24,000	48,000	45,600	43,200	40,800	38,400
22,000	23,000	25,000	50,000	47,500	45,000	42,500	40,000
23,000	24,000	26,000	52,000	49,400	46,800	44,200	41,600
24,000	25,000	27,000	54,000	51,300	48,600	45,900	43,200
25,000	26,000	28,000	56,000	53,200	50,400	47,600	44,800
26,000	27,000	29,000	58,000	55,100	52,200	49,300	46,400
27,000	28,000	30,000	60,000	57,000	54,000	51,000	48,000
28,000	29,000	31,000	62,000	58,900	55,800	52,700	49,600
29,000	30,000	32,000	64,000	60,800	57,600	54,400	51,200
30,000	31,000	33,000	66,000	62,700	59,400	56,100	52,800
31,000	32,000	34,000	68,000	64,600	61,200	57,800	54,400
32,000	33,000	35,000	70,000	66,500	63,000	59,500	56,000
33,000	34,000	36,000	72,000	68,400	64,800	61,200	57,600
34,000	35,000	37,000	74,000	70,300	66,600	62,900	59,200
35,000	36,000	38,000	76,000	72,200	68,400	64,600	60,800
36,000	37,000	39,000	78,000	74,100	70,200	63,300	62,400
37,000	38,000	40,000	80,000	76,000	72,000	68,000	64,000
38,000	39,000	41,000	82,000	77,900	73,800	69,700	65,600
39,000	40,000	42,000	84,000	79,800	75,600	71,400	67,200
40,000	41,000	43,000	86,000	81,700	77,400	73,100	68,800
41,000	42,000	44,000	88,000	83,600	79,200	74,800	70,400
42,000	43,000	45,000	90,000	85,500	81,000	76,500	72,000
43,000	44,000	46,000	92,000	87,400	82,800	78,200	73,600
44,000	45,000	47,000	94,000	89,300	84,600	79,900	75,200
45,000	46,000	48,000	96,000	91,200	86,400	81,600	76,800
46,000	47,000	49,000	98,000	93,100	88,200	83,300	78,400
47,000	48,000	50,000	100,000	95,000	90,000	85,000	80,000
48,000	49,000	51,000	102,000	96,900	91,800	86,700	81,600
49,000	50,000	52,000	104,000	98,800	93,600	88,400	83,200
50,000	51,000	53,000	106,000	100,700	95,400	90,100	84,800

AMOUNT OF INSURANCE PROTECTION UNDER THE FEDERAL EMPLOYEES GROUP LIFE INSURANCE ACT OF 1980 (P.L. 96-427) EFFECTIVE OCTOBER 1, 1981*

Amount of Group Life Insurance						Amount of Group Accidental Death and Dismemberment Insurance
Age 40 (1.5)	Age 41 (1.4)	Age 42 (1.3)	Age 43 (1.2)	Age 44 (1.1)	45 and Over (1.0)	
$15,000	$14,000	$13,000	$12,000	$11,000	$10,000	$10,000
16,500	15,400	14,300	13,200	12,100	11,000	11,000
18,000	16,800	15,600	14,400	13,200	12,000	12,000
19,500	18,200	16,900	15,600	14,300	13,000	13,000
21,000	19,600	18,200	16,800	15,400	14,000	14,000
22,500	21,000	19,500	18,000	16,500	15,000	15,000
24,000	22,400	20,800	19,200	17,600	16,000	16,000
25,500	23,800	22,100	20,400	18,700	17,000	17,000
27,000	25,200	23,400	21,600	19,800	18,000	18,000
28,500	26,600	24,700	22,800	20,900	19,000	19,000
30,000	28,000	26,000	24,000	22,000	20,000	20,000
31,500	29,400	27,300	25,200	23,100	21,000	21,000
33,000	30,800	28,600	26,400	24,200	22,000	22,000
34,500	32,200	29,900	27,600	25,300	23,000	23,000
36,000	33,600	31,200	28,800	26,400	24,000	24,000
37,500	35,000	32,500	30,000	27,500	25,000	25,000
39,000	36,400	33,800	31,200	28,600	26,000	26,000
40,500	37,800	35,100	32,400	29,700	27,000	27,000
42,000	39,200	36,400	33,600	30,800	28,000	28,000
43,500	40,600	37,700	34,800	31,900	29,000	29,000
45,000	42,000	39,000	36,000	33,000	30,000	30,000
46,500	43,400	40,300	37,200	34,100	31,000	31,000
48,000	44,800	41,600	38,400	35,200	32,000	32,000
49,500	46,200	42,900	39,600	36,300	33,000	33,000
51,000	47,600	44,200	40,800	37,400	34,000	34,000
52,500	49,000	45,500	42,000	38,500	35,000	35,000
54,000	50,400	46,800	43,200	39,600	36,000	36,000
55,500	51,800	48,100	44,400	40,700	37,000	37,000
57,000	53,200	49,400	45,600	41,800	38,000	38,000
58,500	54,600	50,700	46,800	42,900	39,000	39,000
60,000	56,000	52,000	48,000	44,000	40,000	40,000
61,500	57,400	53,300	49,200	45,100	41,000	41,000
63,000	58,800	54,600	50,400	46,200	42,000	42,000
64,500	60,200	55,900	51,600	47,300	43,000	43,000
66,000	61,600	57,200	52,800	48,400	44,000	44,000
67,500	63,000	58,500	54,000	49,500	45,000	45,000
69,000	64,400	59,800	55,200	50,600	46,000	46,000
70,500	65,800	61,100	56,400	51,700	47,000	47,000
72,000	67,200	62,400	57,600	52,800	48,000	48,000
73,500	68,600	63,700	58,800	53,900	49,000	49,000
75,000	70,000	65,000	60,000	55,000	50,000	50,000
76,500	71,400	66,300	61,200	56,100	51,000	51,000
78,000	72,800	67,600	62,400	57,200	52,000	52,000
79,500	74,200	68,900	63,600	58,300	53,000	53,000

343

TABLE 4
AMOUNT OF INSURANCE PROTECTION UNDER THE FEDERAL
EMPLOYEES GROUP LIFE INSURANCE ACT
OF 1980 (P.L. 96-427)
EFFECTIVE OCTOBER 1, 1981*

Annual Pay			Amount of Group Life Insurance				
Greater than —	But not greater than —	Basic Insurance Amount	Age 35 and Under	Age 36 (1.9)	Age 37 (1.8)	Age 38 (1.7)	Age 39 (1.6)
51,000	52,000	54,000	108,000	102,600	97,200	91,800	86,400
52,000	53,000	55,000	110,000	104,500	99,000	93,500	88,000
53,000	54,000	56,000	112,000	106,400	100,800	95,200	89,600
54,000	55,000	57,000	114,000	108,300	102,600	96,900	91,200
55,000	56,000	58,000	116,000	110,200	104,400	98,600	92,800
56,000	57,000	59,000	118,000	112,100	106,200	100,300	94,400
57,000	58,000	60,000	120,000	114,000	108,000	102,000	96,000
58,000	59,000	61,000	122,000	115,900	109,800	103,700	97,600
59,000	60,000	62,000	124,000	117,800	111,600	105,400	99,200
60,000	61,000	63,000	126,000	119,700	113,400	107,100	100,800
61,000	62,000	64,000	128,000	121,600	115,200	108,800	102,400
62,000	63,000	65,000	130,000	123,500	117,000	110,500	104,000
63,000	64,000	66,000	132,000	125,400	118,800	112,200	105,600
64,000	65,000	67,000	134,000	127,300	120,600	113,900	107,200
65,000	66,000	68,000	136,000	129,200	122,400	115,600	108,800
66,000	67,000	69,000	138,000	131,100	124,200	117,300	110,400
67,000	68,000	70,000	140,000	133,000	126,000	119,000	112,000
68,000	69,000	71,000	142,000	134,900	127,800	120,700	113,600
69,000	70,000	72,000	144,000	136,800	129,600	122,400	115,200
70,000	71,000	73,000	146,000	138,700	131,400	124,100	116,800
71,000	72,000	74,000	148,000	140,600	133,200	125,800	118,400
72,000	73,000	75,000	150,000	142,500	135,000	127,500	120,000
73,000	74,000	76,000	152,000	144,400	136,800	129,200	121,600
74,000	75,000	77,000	154,000	146,300	138,600	130,900	123,200
75,000	76,000	78,000	156,000	148,200	140,400	132,600	124,800
76,000	77,000	79,000	158,000	150,100	142,200	134,300	126,400
77,000	78,000	80,000	160,000	152,000	144,000	136,000	128,000
78,000	79,000	81,000	162,000	153,900	145,800	137,700	129,600
79,000	80,000	82,000	164,000	155,800	147,600	139,400	131,200
80,000	81,000	83,000	166,000	157,700	149,400	141,100	132,800
81,000	82,000	84,000	168,000	159,600	151,200	142,800	134,400
82,000	83,000	85,000	170,000	161,500	153,000	144,500	136,000
83,000	84,000	86,000	172,000	163,400	154,800	146,200	137,600
84,000	85,000	87,000	174,000	165,300	156,600	147,900	139,200
85,000	86,000	88,000	176,000	167,200	158,400	149,600	140,800
86,000	87,000	89,000	178,000	169,100	160,200	151,300	142,400
87,000	88,000	90,000	180,000	171,000	162,000	153,000	144,000
88,000	89,000	91,000	182,000	172,900	163,800	154,700	145,600
89,000	90,000	92,000	184,000	174,800	165,600	156,400	147,200
90,000	91,000	93,000	186,000	176,700	167,400	158,100	148,800

AMOUNT OF INSURANCE PROTECTION UNDER THE FEDERAL EMPLOYEES GROUP LIFE INSURANCE ACT OF 1980 (P.L. 96-427) EFFECTIVE OCTOBER 1, 1981*

Amount of Group Life Insurance						Amount of Group Accidental Death and Dismemberment Insurance
Age 40 (1.5)	Age 41 (1.4)	Age 42 (1.3)	Age 43 (1.2)	Age 44 (1.1)	45 and Over (1.0)	
81,000	75,600	70,200	64,800	59,400	54,000	54,000
82,500	77,000	71,500	66,000	60,500	55,000	55,000
84,000	78,400	72,800	67,200	61,600	56,000	56,000
85,500	79,800	74,100	68,400	62,700	57,000	57,000
87,000	81,200	75,400	69,600	63,800	58,000	58,000
88,500	82,600	76,700	70,800	64,900	59,000	59,000
90,000	84,000	78,000	72,000	66,000	60,000	60,000
91,500	85,400	79,300	73,200	67,100	61,000	61,000
93,000	86,800	80,600	74,400	68,200	62,000	62,000
94,500	88,200	81,900	75,600	69,300	63,000	63,000
96,000	89,600	83,200	76,800	70,400	64,000	64,000
97,500	91,000	84,500	78,000	71,500	65,000	65,000
99,000	92,400	85,800	79,200	72,600	66,000	66,000
100,500	93,800	87,100	80,400	73,700	67,000	67,000
102,000	95,200	88,400	81,600	74,800	68,000	68,000
103,500	96,600	89,700	82,800	75,900	69,000	69,000
105,000	98,000	91,000	84,000	77,000	70,000	70,000
106,500	99,400	92,300	85,200	78,100	71,000	71,000
108,000	100,800	93,600	86,400	79,200	72,000	72,000
109,500	102,200	94,900	87,600	80,300	73,000	73,000
111,000	103,600	96,200	88,800	81,400	74,000	74,000
112,500	105,000	97,500	90,000	82,500	75,000	75,000
114,000	106400	98,800	91,200	83,600	76,000	76,000
115,500	107,800	100,100	92,400	84,700	77,000	77,000
117,000	109,200	101,400	93,600	85,800	78,000	78,000
118,500	110,600	102,700	94,800	86,900	79,000	79,000
120,000	112,000	104,000	96,000	88,000	80,000	80,000
121,500	113,400	105,300	97,200	89,100	81,000	81,000
123,000	114,800	106,600	98,400	90,200	82,000	82,000
124,500	116,200	107,900	99,600	91,300	83,000	83,000
126,000	117,600	109,200	100,800	92,400	84,000	84,000
127,500	119,000	110,500	102,000	93,500	85,000	85,000
129,000	120,400	111,800	103,200	94,600	86,000	86,000
130,500	121,800	113,100	104,400	95,700	87,000	87,000
132,000	123,200	114,400	105,600	96,800	88,000	88,000
133,500	124,600	115,700	106,800	97,900	89,000	89,000
135,000	126,000	117,000	108,000	99,000	90,000	90,000
136,500	127,400	118,300	109,200	100,100	91,000	91,000
138,000	128,800	119,600	110,400	101,200	92,000	92,000
139,500	130,200	120,900	111,600	102,300	93,000	93,000

345

TABLE 4
AMOUNT OF INSURANCE PROTECTION UNDER THE FEDERAL
EMPLOYEES GROUP LIFE INSURANCE ACT
OF 1980 (P.L. 96-427)
EFFECTIVE OCTOBER 1, 1981*

Annual Pay			Amount of Group Life Insurance				
Greater than —	But not greater than —	Basic Insurance Amount	Age 35 and Under	Age 36 (1.9)	Age 37 (1.8)	Age 38 (1.7)	Age 39 (1.6)
91,000	92,000	94,000	188,000	178,600	169,200	159,800	150,400
92,000	93,000	95,000	190,000	180,500	171,000	161,500	152,000
93,000	94,000	96,000	192,000	182,400	172,800	163,200	153,600
94,000	95,000	97,000	194,000	184,300	174,600	164,900	155,200
95,000	96,000	98,000	196,000	186,200	176,400	166,600	156,800
96,000		99,000	198,000	188,100	178,200	168,300	158,400

AMOUNT OF INSURANCE PROTECTION UNDER THE FEDERAL EMPLOYEES GROUP LIFE INSURANCE ACT OF 1980 (P.L. 96-427) EFFECTIVE OCTOBER 1, 1981*

Amount of Group Life Insurance						Amount of Group Accidental Death and Dismemberment Insurance
Age 40 (1.5)	Age 41 (1.4)	Age 42 (1.3)	Age 43 (1.2)	Age 44 (1.1)	45 and Over (1.0)	
141,000	131,600	122,200	112,800	103,400	94,000	94,000
142,500	133,000	123,500	114,000	104,500	95,000	95,000
144,000	134,400	124,800	115,200	105,600	96,000	96,000
145,500	135,800	126,100	116,400	106,700	97,000	97,000
147,000	137,200	127,400	117,600	107,800	98,000	98,000
148,500	138,600	128,700	118,800	108,900	99,000	99,000

* P.L. 96-427 revised the group term life insurance coverage available to civil service employees. The amounts of group term life shown in this table became effective October 1, 1981.

SERVICEMEMBERS AND VETERANS TABLES

TABLE 1—COMPARATIVE RANKS

Comparative Officer Ranks

GRADE	ARMY	AIR FORCE	MARINE CORPS	NAVY
COMMISSIONED OFFICERS				
O-10	General	General	General	Fleet Admiral
O-9	Lieutenant General	Lieutenant General	Lieutenant General	Vice Admiral
O-8	Major General	Major General	Major General	Rear Admiral (Upper Half)
O-7	Brigadier General	Brigadier General	Brigadier General	Rear Admiral (Lower Half) Commodore
O-6	Colonel	Colonel	Colonel	Captain
O-5	Lieutenant Colonel	Lieutenant Colonel	Lieutenant Colonel	Commander
O-4	Major	Major	Major	Lieutenant Commander
O-3	Captain	Captain	Captain	Lieutenant
O-2	First Lieutenant	First Lieutenant	First Lieutenant	Lieutenant Junior Grade
O-1	Second Lieutenant	Second Lieutenant	Second Lieutenant	Ensign

GRADE	ARMY	AIR FORCE	MARINE CORPS
WARRANT OFFICERS			
W-4	Chief Warrant	Chief Warrant	Com. Warrant over 20 years' service
W-3	Chief Warrant	Chief Warrant	Com. Warrant over 10 years' service
W-2	Chief Warrant	Chief Warrant	Com. Warrant less than 10 years' service
W-1	Warrant Officer, Jr. Grade	Warrant Officer, Jr. Grade	Warrant Officer

Comparative Ranks — Enlisted Personnel

GRADE	ARMY	AIR FORCE	MARINE CORPS	NAVY
E-9	Sergeant Major	Chief Master Sergeant	Sgt. Major & M/Gy. Sgt.	Master Chief Petty Officer
E-8	Master Sergeant	Senior Master Sergeant	1st Sgt. & Master Sgt.	Senior Chief Petty Officer
E-7	Sergeant First Class	Master Sergeant	Gunnery Sergeant	Chief Petty Officer
E-6	Staff Sergeant	Technical Sergeant	Staff Sergeant	Petty Officer, First Class
E-5	Sergeant	Staff Sergeant	Sergeant	Petty Officer, Second Class
E-4	Corporal	Airman, First Class	Corporal	Petty Officer, Third Class
E-3	Private First Class	Airman, Second Class	Lance Corporal	Seaman
E-2	Private	Airman, Third Class	Private, First Class	Seaman Apprentice
E-1	Private (Recruit)	Airman, Basic	Private	Seaman Recruit

TABLE 2—BASIC MONTHLY PAY RATES‡
(eff. January 1, 2001)
2 or Less Years through Over 10 Years

Pay Grade	2 or Less	Over 2	Over 3	Over 4	Over 6	Over 8	Over 10
COMMISSIONED OFFICERS							
O-10	$8,518.80	$8,818.50	$8,818.50	$8,818.50	$8,818.50	$9,156.90	$9,156.90
O-9	7,550.10	7,747.80	7,912.80	7,912.80	7,912.80	8,114.10	8,114.10
O-8	6,838.20	7,062.30	7,210.50	7,252.20	7,437.30	7,747.80	7,819.80
O-7	5,682.30	6,068.40	6,068.40	6,112.50	6,340.80	6,514.50	6,715.50
O-6	4,211.40	4,626.60	4,930.20	4,930.20	4,949.10	5,160.90	5,189.10
O-5	3,368.70	3,954.90	4,228.80	4,280.40	4,450.50	4,450.50	4,584.30
O-4	2,839.20	3,457.20	3,687.90	3,739.50	3,953.40	4,127.70	4,409.70
O-3	2,638.20	2,991.00	3,228.00	3,489.30	3,656.40	3,839.70	3,992.70
O-2	2,301.00	2,620.80	3,018.60	3,120.30	3,184.80	3,184.80	3,184.80
O-1	1,997.70	2,079.00	2,512.80	2,512.80	2,512.80	2,512.80	2,512.80

COMMISSIONED OFFICERS (with over 4 years active duty service as an enlisted member or warrant officer)

Pay Grade	2 or Less	Over 2	Over 3	Over 4	Over 6	Over 8	Over 10
O-3E	—	—	—	$3,489.30	$3,656.40	$3,839.70	$3,992.70
O-2E	—	—	—	3,120.30	3,184.80	3,285.90	3,457.20
O-1E	—	—	—	2,512.80	2,684.10	2,783.10	2,884.20

WARRANT OFFICERS

Pay Grade	2 or Less	Over 2	Over 3	Over 4	Over 6	Over 8	Over 10
W-5	—	—	—	—	—	—	—
W-4	$2,688.00	$2,891.70	$2,974.80	$3,056.70	$3,197.40	$3,336.30	$3,477.00
W-3	2,443.20	2,649.90	2,649.90	2,684.10	2,793.90	2,919.00	3,084.30
W-2	2,139.60	2,315.10	2,315.10	2,391.00	2,512.80	2,649.90	2,750.70
W-1	1,782.60	2,043.90	2,043.90	2,214.60	2,315.10	2,419.20	2,523.30

ENLISTED MEMBERS

Pay Grade	2 or Less	Over 2	Over 3	Over 4	Over 6	Over 8	Over 10
E-9	—	—	—	—	—	—	$3,126.90
E-8	—	—	—	—	—	$2,622.00	2,697.90
E-7	$1,831.20	$1,999.20	$2,075.10	$2,149.80	$2,227.20	2,303.10	2,379.00
E-6	1,575.00	1,740.30	1,817.40	1,891.80	1,969.50	2,046.00	2,122.80
E-5	1,381.80	1,549.20	1,623.90	1,701.00	1,777.80	1,855.80	1,930.50
E-4	1,288.80	1,423.80	1,500.60	1,576.20	1,653.00	1,653.00	1,653.00
E-3	1,214.70	1,307.10	1,383.60	1,385.40	1,385.40	1,385.40	1,385.40
E-2	1,169.10	1,169.10	1,169.10	1,169.10	1,169.10	1,169.10	1,169.10
E-1*	1,042.80	1,042.80	1,042.80	1,042.80	1,042.80	1,042.80	1,042.80
E-1**	964.80	—	—	—	—	—	—

TABLE 2—BASIC MONTHLY PAY RATES‡ (continued)
(eff. January 1, 2001)
Over 12 Years through Over 26 Years

Pay Grade	Over 12	Over 14	Over 16	Over 18	Over 20	Over 22	Over 24	Over 26
COMMISSIONED OFFICERS								
O-10	$9,664.20	$9,664.20	$10,356.00	$10,356.00	$11,049.30	$11,103.90	$11,334.60	$11,737.20
O-9	8,451.60	8,451.60	9,156.90	9,156.90	9,664.20	9,803.40	10,004.70	10,356.00
O-8	8,114.10	8,198.70	8,451.60	8,818.50	9,156.90	9,382.80	9,382.80	9,382.80
O-7	6,915.90	7,116.90	7,747.80	8,280.90	8,280.90	8,280.90	8,280.90	8,322.60
O-6	5,189.10	5,360.70	6,005.40	6,311.40	6,617.40	6,791.40	6,967.80	7,309.80
O-5	4,831.80	5,155.80	5,481.60	5,637.00	5,790.30	5,964.60	5,964.60	5,964.60
O-4	4,629.30	4,781.70	4,935.00	4,986.60	4,986.60	4,986.60	4,986.60	4,986.60
O-3	4,189.80	4,292.10	4,292.10	4,292.10	4,292.10	4,292.10	4,292.10	4,292.10
O-2	3,184.80	3,184.80	3,184.80	3,184.80	3,184.80	3,184.80	3,184.80	3,184.80
O-1	2,512.80	2,512.80	2,512.80	2,512.80	2,512.80	2,512.80	2,512.80	2,512.80

COMMISSIONED OFFICERS (with over 4 years active duty service as an enlisted member or warrant officer)

Pay Grade	Over 12	Over 14	Over 16	Over 18	Over 20	Over 22	Over 24	Over 26
O-3E	$4,189.80	$4,355.70	$4,450.50	$4,580.40	$4,580.40	$4,580.40	$4,580.40	$4,580.40
O-2E	3,589.50	3,687.90	3,687.90	3,687.90	3,687.90	3,687.90	3,687.90	3,687.90
O-1E	2,984.10	3,120.30	3,120.30	3,120.30	3,120.30	3,120.30	3,120.30	3,120.30

WARRANT OFFICERS

Pay Grade	Over 12	Over 14	Over 16	Over 18	Over 20	Over 22	Over 24	Over 26
W-5	—	—	—	—	$4,640.70	$4,800.00	$4,959.90	$5,120.10
W-4	$3,614.10	$3,756.30	$3,892.50	$4,032.00	4,168.20	4,309.50	4,448.40	4,590.90
W-3	3,184.80	3,294.60	3,420.30	3,545.10	3,669.90	3,794.70	3,919.80	4,045.20
W-2	2,851.50	2,949.60	3,058.20	3,169.50	3,280.80	3,391.80	3,503.40	3,503.40
W-1	2,626.80	2,731.50	2,835.90	2,940.00	3,018.60	3,018.60	3,018.60	3,018.60

ENLISTED MEMBERS

Pay Grade	Over 12	Over 14	Over 16	Over 18	Over 20	Over 22	Over 24	Over 26
E-9	$3,197.40	$3,287.10	$3,392.40	$3,498.00	$3,601.80	$3,742.80	$3,882.60	$4,060.80
E-8	2,768.40	2,853.30	2,945.10	3,041.10	3,138.00	3,278.10	3,417.30	3,612.60
E-7	2,454.90	2,529.60	2,607.00	2,683.80	2,758.80	2,890.80	3,034.50	3,250.50
E-6	2,196.90	2,272.50	2,327.70	2,367.90	2,367.90	2,370.30	2,370.30	2,370.30
E-5	2,007.90	2,007.90	2,007.90	2,007.90	2,007.90	2,007.90	2,007.90	2,007.90
E-4	1,653.00	1,653.00	1,653.00	1,653.00	1,653.00	1,653.00	1,653.00	1,653.00
E-3	1,385.40	1,385.40	1,385.40	1,385.40	1,385.40	1,385.40	1,385.40	1,385.40
E-2	1,169.10	1,169.10	1,169.10	1,169.10	1,169.10	1,169.10	1,169.10	1,169.10
E-1*	1,042.80	1,042.80	1,042.80	1,042.80	1,042.80	1,042.80	1,042.80	1,042.80
E-1**	—	—	—	—	—	—	—	—

‡ See Table 1 for rank corresponding with pay rate. Rates are rounded to nearest dollar.
* Basic pay is limited to the rate of basic pay for level V.
** Applies to personnel who have served 4 months or more on active duty.

TABLE 3—CSRS MILITARY MONTHLY RETIREMENT PAY*
Effective January 1, 2001

RETIREES WHO ENTERED SERVICE BEFORE
SEPTEMBER 8, 1980

Pay Grade** Over:	50.00% 20 Yrs	52.50% 21 Yrs	55.00% 22 Yrs	57.50% 23 Yrs	60.00% 24 Yrs	62.50% 25 Yrs	65.00% 26 Yrs	67.50% 27 Yrs	70.00% 28 Yrs	72.50% 29 Yrs	75.00% 30 Yrs
O-10	$5,525	$5,801	$6,107	$6,385	$6,801	$7,084	$7,629	$7,923	$8,216	$8,509	$8,803
O-9	$4,832	$5,074	$5,392	$5,637	$6,003	$6,253	$6,731	$6,990	$7,249	$7,508	$7,767
O-8	$4,578	$4,807	$5,161	$5,395	$5,630	$5,864	$6,099	$6,333	$6,568	$6,803	$7,037
O-7	$4,140	$4,347	$4,554	$4,762	$4,969	$5,176	$5,410	$5,618	$5,826	$6,034	$6,242
O-6	$3,309	$3,474	$3,735	$3,905	$4,181	$4,355	$4,751	$4,934	$5,117	$5,300	$5,482
O-5	$2,895	$3,040	$3,281	$3,430	$3,579	$3,728	$3,877	$4,026	$4,175	$4,324	$4,473
O-4	$2,493	$2,618	$2,743	$2,867	$2,992	$3,117	$3,241	$3,366	$3,491	$3,615	$3,740
O-3	$2,146	$2,253	$2,361	$2,468	$2,575	$2,683	$2,790	$2,897	$3,004	$3,112	$3,219
O-2	$1,592	$1,672	$1,752	$1,831	$1,911	$1,991	$2,070	$2,150	$2,229	$2,309	$2,389
O-1	$1,256	$1,319	$1,382	$1,445	$1,508	$1,571	$1,633	$1,696	$1,759	$1,822	$1,885
W-5	$2,320	$2,436	$2,640	$2,760	$2,976	$3,100	$3,328	$3,456	$3,584	$3,712	$3,840
W-4	$2,084	$2,188	$2,370	$2,478	$2,669	$2,780	$2,984	$3,099	$3,214	$3,328	$3,443
W-3	$1,835	$1,927	$2,087	$2,182	$2,352	$2,450	$2,629	$2,731	$2,832	$2,933	$3,034
W-2	$1,640	$1,722	$1,865	$1,950	$2,102	$2,190	$2,277	$2,365	$2,452	$2,540	$2,628
W-1	$1,509	$1,585	$1,660	$1,736	$1,811	$1,887	$1,962	$2,038	$2,113	$2,188	$2,264
E-9	$1,801	$1,891	$2,059	$2,152	$2,330	$2,427	$2,640	$2,741	$2,843	$2,944	$3,046
E-8	$1,569	$1,647	$1,803	$1,885	$2,050	$2,136	$2,348	$2,439	$2,529	$2,619	$2,709
E-7	$1,379	$1,448	$1,590	$1,662	$1,821	$1,897	$2,113	$2,194	$2,275	$2,357	$2,438
E-6	$1,184	$1,243	$1,304	$1,363	$1,422	$1,481	$1,541	$1,600	$1,659	$1,718	$1,778
E-5	$1,004	$1,054	$1,104	$1,155	$1,205	$1,255	$1,305	$1,355	$1,406	$1,456	$1,506

*   Does not apply to reservists; rounded out to nearest dollar. Participation in the Survivor Benefit Plan reduces these amounts.
**   See Table 1 for rank corresponding with pay grade.

TABLE 4 — RATES OF DEPENDENCY AND INDEMNITY COMPENSATION—SURVIVING SPOUSE AND CHILDREN OF VETERAN WHO DIED BEFORE JANUARY 1, 1993*
38 USC §1311
Effective December 1, 2000

Pay Grade*	Surviving Spouse** Only	Surviving Spouse** and 1 Child	Surviving Spouse** and 2 Children	Extra Per Child
COMMISSIONED OFFICERS				
O-10	1,943***	2,172	2,401	229
O-9	1,771	2,000	2,229	229
O-8	1,653	1,882	2,111	229
O-7	1,509	1,738	1,967	229
O-6	1,396	1,625	1,854	229
O-5	1,239	1,468	1,697	229
O-4	1,125	1,354	1,583	229
O 3	1,063	1,292	1,521	229
O-2	995	1,224	1,453	229
O-1	962	1,191	1,420	229
WARRANT OFFICERS				
W-4	1,090	1,319	1,548	229
W-3	1,031	1,260	1,489	229
W-2	1,001	1,230	1,459	229
W-1	962	1,191	1,420	229
ENLISTED PERSONNEL				
E-9	1,038****	1,267	1,496	229
E-8	995	1,224	1,453	229
E-7	942	1,171	1,400	229

* See Table 1, for rank corresponding to pay grade. Surviving spouses of veterans who die after January 1, 1994, receive a basic monthly DIC rate of $911. Each child is entitled to $229 a month in 2001. Surviving spouses of veterans who die before January 1, 1993, are entitled to the benefits listed above or the new formula, whichever provides the greater benefits.

** Monthly rate for the surviving spouse is increased by $229 if he or she is a patient in a nursing home or is virtually helpless or blind.

*** If the veteran served as Chairman or Vice-Chairman of the Joint Chiefs of Staff or Chief of Staff to one of the services, the surviving spouse's rate shall be $2,083.

**** The payment to a surviving spouse alone if the veteran was Sergeant Major of the Army, Senior Enlisted Advisor of the Navy, Chief Master Sergeant of the Air Force, or Sergeant Major of the Marine Corps, or Master Chief Petty Officer of the Coast Guard is $1,119.

355

SERVICEMEMBERS AND VETERANS TABLES

TABLE 5 — RATES OF DEPENDENCY AND
INDEMNITY COMPENSATION — PARENTS
Effective December 1, 2000

Annual Income Amount	1 Parent Only (1)	Each of 2 Parents Not Living Together (1)	Each of 2 Parents Living Together or Remarried Parent Living with Spouse (2)
$ 800	$445	$320	$300
900	437	314	300
1000	429	307	300
1100	421	300	297
1200	413	292	294
1300	405	284	291
1400	397	276	288
1500	389	268	285
1600	381	260	281
1700	373	252	277
1800	365	244	273
1900	357	236	269
2000	349	228	264
2100	341	220	259
2200	333	212	254
2300	325	204	249
2400	317	196	244
2500	309	188	238
2600	301	180	232
2700	293	172	226
2800	285	164	220
2900	277	156	214
3000	269	148	207
3100	261	140	200
3200	253	132	193
3300	245	124	185
3400	237	116	177
3500	229	108	169
3600	221	100	161
3700	213	92	153
3800	205	84	145
3900	197	76	137
4000	189	68	129
4100	181	60	121
4200	173	52	113
4300	165	44	105
4400	157	36	97
4500	149	28	89
4600	141	20	81
4700	133	12	73
4800	125	5	65
4900	117	5	57
5000	109	5	49
5100	101	5	41
5200	93	5	33
5300	85	5	25
5400	77	5	17
5500	69	5	9
5600	61	5	5
5700	53	5	5
5800	45	5	5
5900	37	5	5
6000	29	5	5
6100	21	5	5
6200	13	5	5
6300-10584	5	5	5
10584-14228	0	0	5
over 14228	0	0	0

(1) Payment based on total annual income.
(2) Payment based on total combined annual income.

357

INDEX

C

G

H

T

Call **1-800-543-0874** to order and ask for operator BB or fax your order to **1-800-874-1916**.

The
**NATIONAL
UNDERWRITER**
Company

The National Underwriter Co. • Orders Dept #2-BB
P.O. Box 14448 • Cincinnati, OH 45250-9786

2-BB

_____ Copies of *2001 Social Security Manual*
  ❑ Print (#286) $17.99 ❑ CD-ROM (#661) $49.00 ❑ Internet (#187) $49.00
_____ Copies of *Social Security Manual* CE Exam & Grading Service
  ❑ Print (#28661) $25.00 ❑ Online (#28667) $25.00 *(CE Credit not available for software)*
_____ Copies of *2001 All About Medicare*
  ❑ Print (#146) $12.75 ❑ CD-ROM (#156) $29.00 ❑ Internet (#157) $29.00
_____ Copies of *All About Medicare* CE Exam & Grading Service
  ❑ Print (#14661) ❑ Online (#14667)

❑ Check enclosed* ❑ Charge my VISA/MC/AmEx (circle one) ❑ Bill Me

*Make check payable to The National Underwriter Company.
Please include the appropriate shipping & handling charges and any applicable sales tax. (see charts above)

Card # _____ Exp. Date _____
Signature _____
Name _____ Title _____
Company _____
Street Address _____
City _____ State _____ Zip _____
Business Phone (_____) _____ Fax (_____) _____
Email _____

**Visit our website at www.nuco.com/ce, or call 1-800-543-0874 for state availability. CE exams are non-refundable once package is opened or online exam is started. Proof of purchase of current edition is required.

The
**NATIONAL
UNDERWRITER**
Company

The National Underwriter Co. • Orders Dept #2-BB
P.O. Box 14448 • Cincinnati, OH 45250-9786

2-BB

_____ Copies of *2001 Social Security Manual*
  ❑ Print (#286) $17.99 ❑ CD-ROM (#661) $49.00 ❑ Internet (#187) $49.00
_____ Copies of *Social Security Manual* CE Exam & Grading Service
  ❑ Print (#28661) $25.00 ❑ Online (#28667) $25.00 *(CE Credit not available for software)*
_____ Copies of *2001 All About Medicare*
  ❑ Print (#146) $12.75 ❑ CD-ROM (#156) $29.00 ❑ Internet (#157) $29.00
_____ Copies of *All About Medicare* CE Exam & Grading Service
  ❑ Print (#14661) ❑ Online (#14667)

❑ Check enclosed* ❑ Charge my VISA/MC/AmEx (circle one) ❑ Bill Me

*Make check payable to The National Underwriter Company.
Please include the appropriate shipping & handling charges and any applicable sales tax. (see charts above)

Card # _____ Exp. Date _____
Signature _____
Name _____ Title _____
Company _____
Street Address _____
City _____ State _____ Zip _____
Business Phone (_____) _____ Fax (_____) _____
Email _____

**Visit our website at www.nuco.com/ce, or call 1-800-543-0874 for state availability. CE exams are non-refundable once package is opened or online exam is started. Proof of purchase of current edition is required.

NO POSTAGE
NECESSARY
IF MAILED
IN THE
UNITED STATES

BUSINESS REPLY MAIL

FIRST CLASS MAIL   PERMIT NO 68   CINCINNATI, OH

POSTAGE WILL BE PAID BY ADDRESSEE

The National Underwriter Co.
Orders Department #2-BB
P.O. Box 14448
Cincinnati, OH 45250-9786

NO POSTAGE
NECESSARY
IF MAILED
IN THE
UNITED STATES

BUSINESS REPLY MAIL

FIRST CLASS MAIL   PERMIT NO 68   CINCINNATI, OH

POSTAGE WILL BE PAID BY ADDRESSEE

The National Underwriter Co.
Orders Department #2-BB
P.O. Box 14448
Cincinnati, OH 45250-9786